Church of England Record Society

Volume 24

THE HOUSEHOLD ACCOUNTS OF WILLIAM LAUD, ARCHBISHOP OF CANTERBURY, 1635–1642

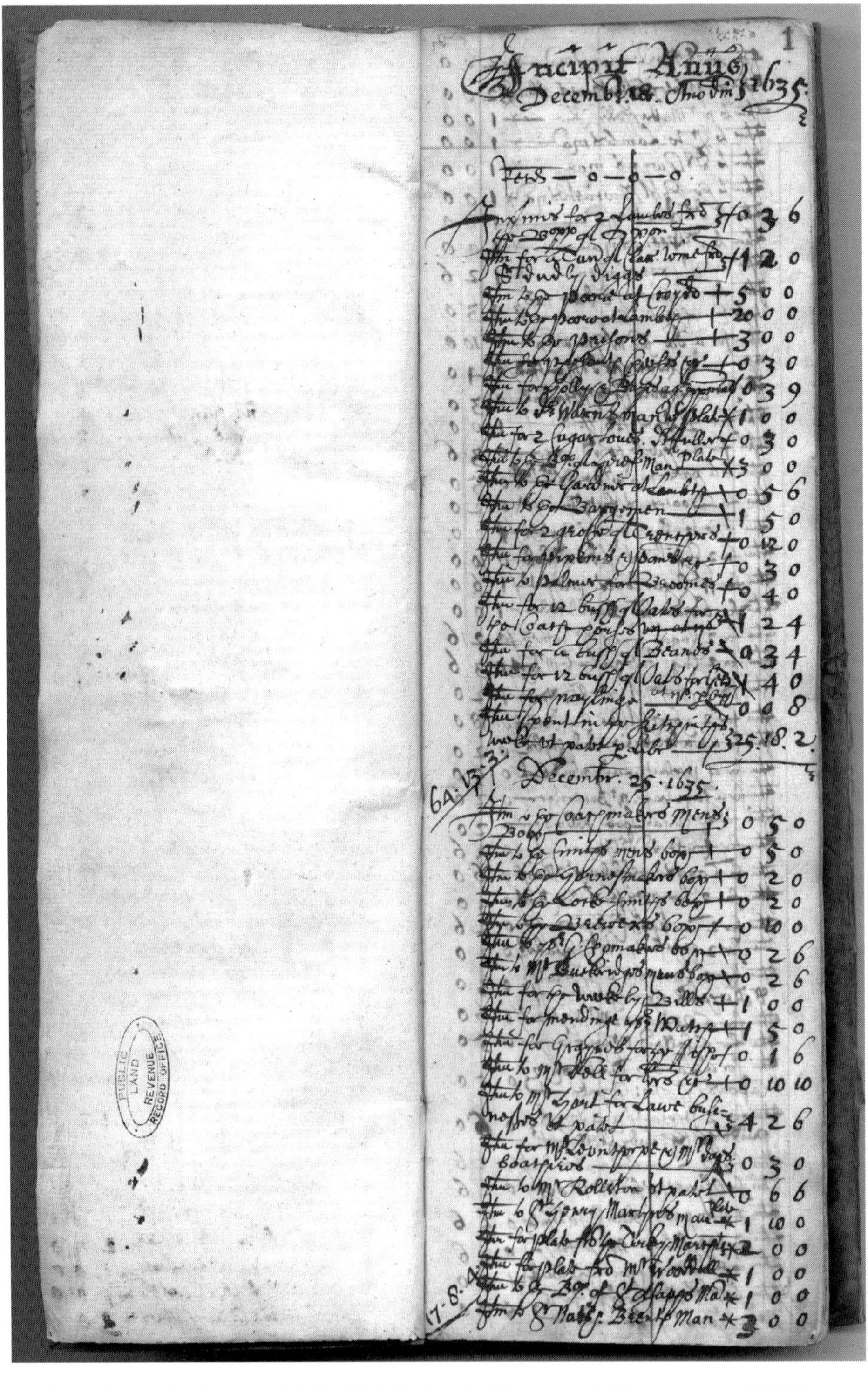

The National Archives, ref. E101/547/5, fo. 1r, The household accounts of William Laud, archbishop of Canterbury, 1635–1642

THE HOUSEHOLD ACCOUNTS OF WILLIAM LAUD, ARCHBISHOP OF CANTERBURY, 1635–1642

EDITED BY

Leonie James

THE BOYDELL PRESS

CHURCH OF ENGLAND RECORD SOCIETY

First published 2019

A Church of England Record Society publication
Published by The Boydell Press
an imprint of Boydell & Brewer Ltd
PO Box 9, Woodbridge, Suffolk IP12 3DF, UK
and of Boydell & Brewer Inc.
668 Mt Hope Avenue, Rochester, NY 14620–2731, USA
website: www.boydellandbrewer.com

ISBN 978-1-78327-386-7

ISSN 1351-3087

Series information is printed at the back of this volume

A catalogue record for this book is available
from the British Library

This publication is printed on acid-free paper

Printed and bound in Great Britain by TJ International Ltd, Padstow, Cornwall

FSC
www.fsc.org
MIX
Paper from
responsible sources
FSC® C013056

For my parents:
Gillian and Peter James

Contents

Acknowledgments

Scholarly editions of manuscripts are not to be undertaken lightly – they command levels of rigour and close inspection that transcend most other academic pursuits; they require a personal commitment and tenacity that is perhaps not reflected in the finished product; and they cannot be done quickly. As William Laud might have put it – and as any scholar who has embarked on a project of this nature will appreciate – they are indeed 'a work of time'. This edition, which conforms to all of the above caveats, but particularly the latter, started life just over twenty years ago. In December 1997, as a final year undergraduate, I first visited The National Archives (then The Public Record Office) in search of Archbishop Laud's household account book and it has been on my mind, on and off, ever since.

Although it has, at times, been an isolated and self-absorbing enterprise, many people have helped me to bring the edition to completion, including Grant Tapsell and Stephen Taylor at COERS; the editorial team at Boydell; Paul Johnson, Euan Roger, Sonja Schwoll and Ruth Selman at The National Archives, Kew; Rachel Cosgrave, Giles Mandelbrote and Andrew Nunn at Lambeth Palace; Christopher Hunswick and Isabel Keating at Alnwick Castle; and Suzanne Foster at Winchester College. Academic colleagues, both beyond and within Kent, have been quick to provide context and have also helped to me to identify some of the more obscure people who appear in the accounts. In this respect, Chris Page and Fiona Pogson deserve particular thanks. Felicity Heal was extremely generous with her time in sending me comments on the draft introduction. My longstanding mentor Ken Fincham also cast his eagle eye over the draft, as well as poring over my very long list of names, to see if I had missed anyone. I want to thank him for this and for drawing my attention to the manuscript in the first place. He should also be acknowledged (finally) for the one and only palaeography lesson that I've ever had, which took place in his kitchen two decades ago!

Other friends, both academic and personal, have also provided advice, support and company throughout, and the most important ones are acknowledged here: Ambrogio Caiani, Andy Cohen, Kathryn Forsyth, Helen Garnett, Esther Gilson, Katie Machin Miles and Sara Wolfson.

Finally, these acknowledgments would be incomplete without reference to my children, Hamish, Freya and Lois, whose vital presence serves as a constant reminder that hanging out with dead people is not very healthy and that the future is more important than the past. They are my *raison d'être* and without them, everything would be meaningless. However, it is to their grandparents – my parents – that the closing tribute belongs. Over the years, they have done countless things to help me and they have stood by me, no matter what I have done. I am, therefore, dedicating this edition to them for their endless encouragement, steadfast support and unconditional love.

Abbreviations

Alumni cantabrigienses	*Alumni cantabrigienses: a biographical list of all known students, graduates and holders of office at the University of Cambridge from the earliest times to 1900*, ed. John Venn and John A. Venn (4 vols., Cambridge, 1922–7)
Alumni oxonienses	*Alumni oxonienses: the members of the University of Oxford 1500–1714: their parentage, birthplace, and year of birth, with a record of their degrees*, ed. Joseph Foster (4 vols., London, 1891)
APC	*Acts of the Privy Council of England*, ed. A. Lyle, R. Monger *et al.* (2 vols., London, 1932–58).
Biographical register of SJC	*A biographical register of St John's College, Oxford, 1555–1660*, ed. Andrew Hegarty (Woodbridge, 2011)
CJ	*Journals of the House of Commons*
Clarendon, *History*	Edward Hyde, *The history of the rebellion and civil wars in England* (2 vols., Oxford, 1849–88)
Complete baronetage	*The complete baronetage*, ed. George Cockayne (2 vols., Exeter, 1900–9)
CSPD	*Calendar of State Papers Domestic*
CSPI	*Calendar of State Papers Ireland*
EHR	*English Historical Review*
Extinct and dormant baronetcies	*A geneaological and heraldic history of the extinct and dormant baronetcies of England*, ed. John Burke and John Burke (London, 1838)
Fasti	*Fasti ecclesiae anglicanae: or a calendar of the principal ecclesiastical dignitaries in England and Wales, and of the chief officers in the ... from the earliest time to year M.DCC.XV*, ed. John Le Neve and T. Duffus Hardy (2 vols., Oxford, 1854)
HJ	*Historical Journal*
HR	*Historical Research*

Knights of England	*The knights of England: a complete record from the earliest times to the present day*, ed. William Shaw (2 vols., London, 1906)
LJ	*Journals of the House of Lords*
LPL	Lambeth Palace Library
ODNB	*Oxford Dictionary of National Biography* (Oxford, 2004); online edition, Jan. 2008.
Str. P.	Strafford Papers, Wentworth Woodhouse Muniments, Sheffield City Archives
TNA	The National Archives, Kew
WWL	*The works of William Laud, sometime lord archbishop of Canterbury*, ed. James Bliss and William Scott (7 vols., Oxford, 1847–60)

Introduction

Sitting in his rooms in the Tower of London on 23 September 1641, William Laud, the imprisoned archbishop of Canterbury, reached for his diary and began writing an account of an event which had taken place that day. Unlike many personal memoirs, which reveal much about the writer's innermost feelings, the archbishop's diary is, on the whole, almost entirely devoid of sentimentality. On this occasion, however, the event which Laud recorded had deep personal and emotional connotations for him: it was the death of his household steward, Adam Torless. Torless – described by the archbishop as 'my ancient, loving and faithful servant' – had ministered to him 'full forty-two years' and his demise came as a source of 'great loss and grief'.[1] As steward to the archiepiscopal household, one of Torless's primary duties during his sustained and loyal service had been to maintain the accounts for both Lambeth and Croydon Palaces, which are edited and interrogated here in full for the first time.[2]

Spanning the period from 18 December 1635 to 14 January 1642, this is the only extant record of the archiepiscopal household for Laud's tenure in office and only one of a handful of similar early modern, ecclesiastical accounts; and yet, it has almost entirely escaped the attention of modern scholars.[3] This neglect is unfortunate, not only because it is the historian's duty to make use of all relevant sources, but also because this document supplements and enhances existing interpretations of Laud and the context in which he was operating. Furthermore, quite apart from its value as a social and economic source, this manuscript – which begins just two years into his archiepiscopate and ceases a year after his impeachment and incarceration – offers a unique prism through which to view the highs and the lows of the archbishop's career. While his diary and correspondence have been edited, published and plundered extensively by scholars for almost two centuries, the archbishop's account book has not – notwithstanding the fact that it provides many new details about his

1 Torless was probably also an *alumnus* of St John's College, Oxford. *Alumni oxonienses*, IV, 1497; *Biographical register of SJC*, p. 457; *WWL*, III, 242.

2 Technically, although we now refer to Lambeth and Croydon as archiepiscopal 'palaces', in the 1630s, the only 'palace' belonging to the archbishops of Canterbury was within the precincts of Canterbury cathedral. Lambeth and Croydon, as well as Bekesbourne and Ford, in Kent, were all manors. For the purposes of this edition, however, the term 'palace' will be adopted to describe the archiepiscopal residences at Lambeth and Croydon.

3 Neither of Laud's twentieth-century biographers – Hugh Trevor-Roper and Charles Carlton – consulted the archbishop's household accounts. Hugh Trevor-Roper, *Archbishop Laud* (Oxford, 1940); Charles Carlton, *Archbishop William Laud* (Basingstoke, 1987). Passing references to the document, however, are to be found in the following works: Kenneth Fincham, 'William Laud and the exercise of Caroline ecclesiastical patronage', *Journal of Ecclesiastical History*, 51, 1 (2000), 79–80, 83 n. 62, 88 n. 89; *The further correspondence of William Laud*, ed. Kenneth Fincham (Church of England Records Society, XXIII, 2018), p. xlv n. 169, p. 186 n. 10; Kenneth Fincham and Nicholas Tyacke, *Altars restored: the changing face of English religious worship 1547 – c. 1700* (Oxford, 2007), p. 259 n. 171; Felicity Heal, *The power of gifts: gift exchange in early modern England* (Oxford, 2015), pp. 37–8; Leonie James, *'This Great Firebrand': William Laud and Scotland 1617–1645* (Woodbridge, 2017), p. 37.

rôle, life and habits that are not evident in other sources. Although fascinating for their own sake, the intrinsic value of such minutiae lies in what they suggest about the archiepiscopal remit and Laud's influence, as well as his associations with fellow courtiers and privy councillors and, of course, the king and members of the royal household. Indeed, it is remarkable that a document of this importance relating to a figure of such unquestionable historical significance should not have been made the focus of detailed inquiry to date.

This scholarly oversight is partly accounted for by the manuscript's unusual provenance, which may in turn explain its fortunate survival. Currently held among the records of the exchequer at The National Archives, Kew,[4] the document's natural home is, of course, Lambeth Palace Library, where most other extant papers pertaining to the archbishops and the Palace are to be found, including an account book for the household under Laud's archiepiscopal predecessor, George Abbot.[5] Mystery surrounds the whereabouts of the document between 1642 – when the final entry in the account book was signed off – and 1912 – the year in which it makes its appearance in a published list of 'various accounts and documents' relating to the exchequer, held at the time in the Public Record Office in Chancery Lane.[6] It is likely that the account book fell into the hands of Laud's enemies in May 1643, when parliament ordered the seizure of goods and books from Lambeth Palace, and William Prynne, Laud's nemesis, burst into his lodgings in the Tower, taking twenty-one bundles of papers, including his diary, in preparation for his trial in 1644.[7] Quite how Laud's accounts came to be deposited – undisturbed and largely unnoticed – among the miscellaneous papers of the King's Remembrancer, an exchequer appointment, remains unclear.[8] The document was certainly not to be found among the exchequer papers when The Public Record Office was established in 1838.[9]

The workings of early modern households have attracted the attention of growing numbers of scholars in recent decades.[10] Certainly, academic editions of household accounts, inventories and probate records – including those of non-élite actors[11] – continue to reach the press, but the focus now is less on the households' heads

---

4 TNA, E101/547/5.

5 LPL, MS 1730.

6 *List of various accounts and documents connected therewith formerly preserved in the exchequer and now in the Public Record Office* (London, 1963 reprint of 1912 edition), p. 322.

7 *WWL*, III, 252, IV, 21.

8 This collection does include one other archiepiscopal household account book from 1521 to 1523 – that of William Warham, archbishop of Canterbury (1503–32); TNA, E101/518/33.

9 *The antient kalendars and manuscripts of his Majesty's exchequer*, ed. Francis Palgrave (3 vols., London, 1836).

10 An excellent summary of the historiography of the household can be found in Antony Buxton, *Domestic culture in early modern England* (Woodbridge, 2015), pp. 1–18.

11 Recent publications of such documents include *The business and household accounts of Joyce Jeffreys, spinster of Hereford, 1638–1648*, ed. Judith Spicksley (Oxford, 2012); *The household account book of Sir Thomas Puckering of Warwick 1620: living in London and the Midlands*, ed. Mark Merry and Catherine Richardson (Oxford, 2012); *Devon household accounts, 1627–59: Henry, fifth earl of Bath, and Rachel, countess of Bath, of Tawstock and London (1637–1655)*, ed. Todd Gray (2 vols., Devon and Cornwall Record Society, 1996); *Household accounts and disbursement books of Robert Dudley, earl of Leicester, 1558–1561, 1584–1586*, ed. Simon Adams (Camden Fifth Series, VI, Cambridge, 1995); *Early Stuart household accounts*, ed. Lionel Munby (Hertfordshire Record Society, II, 1986).

than on the household as a domestic, social, religious and material entity.[12] Moving away from the concerns of earlier interpretations, the work of archaeologists, anthropologists and social, economic and cultural historians is now permitting us to pay closer attention to domestic culture and everyday life from the perspective of the non-élite. Interdisciplinary approaches have further enhanced our understanding of the (now widely recognized) relationship between the material environment, the individual and the wider context. In particular, the rise of material culture as an area of inquiry has contributed to a transformation in how we conceive of the early modern lived experience.

Whilst taking into account this very welcome flourishing of concern for the early modern household as a complex, multifaceted phenomenon, the present volume complements existing scholarship by exposing an élite domestic setting to a selection of perspectives and approaches – by using the text of the accounts to recreate the physical appearance of the household and its head; by demonstrating how the household responded to its immediate social environment and the wider political context; by interrogating the gifts and their givers to identify networks of people in social, political and religious terms; and, more generally, by teasing out the relationship between material objects and political power. Thus – and notwithstanding Laud's humble beginnings – although there is no escaping the fact that the head of the household belonged to the ecclesiastical élite, the intention of this edition is to illustrate the elasticity of an early modern household account book in projecting shards of new light in a number of directions, which themselves intersect with a variety of scholarly themes.

The document

Since no standard format existed for household accounts in the early seventeenth century, a brief description of the document is necessary at this stage. While there was an expectation that income and expenditure for each household department should be accounted for, in reality, monies coming in and out of a household were not always recorded and, certainly, not necessarily recorded in the same place or in the same manner.[13] Some élite households in early modern England kept separate departmental accounts, which monitored cashflow on a smaller scale – in the kitchen, wardrobe, stables or cellars, for instance – while others maintained general records for the household as a whole.[14] In addition, modern conceptions of recording receipts

12 Among the most significant publications to emerge from this recent flourishing of scholarship are *Early modern things: objects and their histories, 1500–1800*, ed. Paula Findlen (London, 2013); Tara Hamling, *Decorating the godly household – religious art in post-Reformation Britain* (New Haven, 2010); Keith Wrightson, *Earthly necessities: economic lives in early modern Britain, 1470–1750* (New Haven, 2000); Lorna Weatherill, *Consumer behaviour and material culture in Britain 1660–1760* (London, 1996).

13 A discussion of late medieval and early modern accounting practices can be found in Kate Mertes, *The English noble household 1250–1600* (Oxford, 1988), pp. 78–86. See also Christopher Woolgar, *The great household in late medieval England* (New Haven, 1999), pp. 44, 65, 87, 180.

14 *Ibid.*, p. 79.

and expenses in order to arrive at a balance did not apply to this period. While some 'auditing' did take place, household accounts were kept less as a record of income and expenditure and more as a demonstration of the head of the household's honesty.[15] Furthermore, the person responsible for maintaining financial records – often, but not always, the steward or treasurer – was not, of course, professionally trained or especially numerate. While this may render such accounts less reliable in fiscal terms, they nevertheless have great value as an historical source. Not only do they bring to light a wealth of information about the composition, membership and activities of the household to which they refer – material which is of considerable wider interest – but, unlike political narratives and personal correspondence, such records contain no obvious bias. Derived from the domestic domain, household accounts are also very distinct – and unique – pieces of evidence.[16]

The document presented here is a very well-preserved example of a handmade paper 'textblock' written in iron gall ink and bound in parchment.[17] It is almost entirely concerned with household expenditure, rather than income. Each of the document's 162 folios feature two columns: the left-hand column giving a brief description of each item of expenditure and the right-hand column detailing the amount of expenditure incurred by the relevant entry (see Frontispiece). Itemized expenditure was recorded on a weekly basis, concluding with a summary of kitchen expenditure for the week in question. At the end of every fortnight, household expenditure was sub-totalled. At the end of every quarter – in mid-March, mid-June, mid-September and mid-December – total household expenditure, including payment of wages, was listed, calculated and recorded. This 'quarter roll' recording of amounts due to servants was standard procedure in many élite homes.[18] Although many households took Michaelmas to be the starting point and end of the financial year, the arrangements in place for Lambeth and Croydon Palaces were slightly different – although not unique – insofar as mid-December, the end of the Michaelmas term, marked the transition from one accounting year to the next. It is not clear whether the account book was presented regularly for audit and, if so, by whom such audit would have been carried out, but the neatness and organization of the script throughout suggests that it may well have been a formal or 'official' copy of a more casual record of daily expenditure jotted down on an ongoing basis. This was a common procedure in a large household.[19] Only on two occasions – in October 1641 – is there any evidence of the accounts having been reviewed by a third party; in both instances, Laud himself signed them off, possibly because a new steward – Walter Dobson – had recently been appointed to replace Torless and it was deemed in order to cast an eye over his first few weeks' work.[20] There is nothing within the accounts themselves to suggest that Laud did this

15 *Ibid.*, p. 77.
16 Buxton, *Domestic culture in early modern England*, p. 9.
17 Thanks to Sonja Schwoll at The National Archives, Kew, for these details.
18 Mertes, *The English noble household*, p. 86.
19 *Ibid.*, p. 77.
20 TNA, E101/5475, fos. 157r, 158r. All subsequent footnote references to the manuscript will cite the folio number only, except where this would lead to confusion, in which case the MS reference *and* the folio number are given.

on a regular basis, but 'auditing' by the master of the household was not unusual in this period.[21]

Although generally in very good condition, the account book presents some minor technical difficulties. A fraction of the manuscript's folios is difficult to decipher. This is especially true of the first thirteen, which have entries recorded both recto and verso, leading to bleeding of ink from one side to another. Torless himself may have found this problematic, because – beginning in October 1636 – he continued transcribing entries recto only.[22] Both household stewards wrote in standard secretary hand – although Dobson's script is perhaps clearer and more 'modern' than that of his predecessor – and this makes the document relatively accessible to the twenty-first-century reader.

The contents of the book were no doubt shaped by its narrow width. Measuring less than 20 cm across, the book left very little space for either steward to record much detail for each entry. This, in turn, brings about a methodological challenge: since the stewards were forced to be succinct, certain entries may appear ambiguous to the untrained eye. For instance, routine items, such as small household equipment, animal fodder, food and linen, are clearly recorded and recognized as legitimate household expenses. However, entries relating to gifts received – which comprise at least half of the total entries in the manuscript and of which there are several hundred – are more confusing, since these receipts are also noted in the accounts as expenditure. For instance, an entry which lists 'a doe from the Lo[rd] Privy Seale' against expenditure of 12s 6d, clearly relates to a gift from Sir Henry Montagu, 1st earl of Manchester.[23] An entry which reads 'for a doe Sir Charles Harbord'[24] with a cost of 8s 0d, however, may lend itself to some ambiguity, for the simple reason that the steward had no space to indicate beyond doubt that the item in question was a gift *from* Harbord, rather than something to be sent *to* him. However, both context and content are important here. There are two main reasons why gifts were recorded as expenditure in the account books of élite households in this period. The first has to do with the fact that it was customary to reward the messenger bringing the gift with a small 'tip' or gratuity for his trouble.[25] Thus, we see many entries for very small sums of money paid to the 'man' delivering a range of items to Lambeth Palace. Indeed, a comparison with the accounts for the household under George Abbot – which is a much larger manuscript than that of his successor, thus enabling the steward to include more detail against each entry – makes it clear that tipping the carrier was common practice.[26] The second – and perhaps more important – reason is that the vast majority of gifts exchanged in this period, whether to senior political figures, like Laud, or among other individuals, families and organizations, consisted of foodstuffs. Food was 'overwhelmingly the most popular choice for gifting' in the

21 Mertes, *The English noble household*, p. 93.
22 Fo. 14r.
23 Fo. 23r.
24 Fo. 114r.
25 Heal, *The power of gifts*, p. 36.
26 LPL, MS 1730; fos. 21v–25r, for instance, list numerous gifts for which the person delivering the item was obviously paid a small tip.

early seventeenth century.[27] As a result, anything consumable was deemed to have a monetary value for the household and everything which was incorporated into the household economy must be noted down, to prevent fraud and waste. While not all households monetized gifts, it was nevertheless very common to value presents in this way and, as we shall see, Archbishop Laud's accounts bear abundant witness to this custom.[28]

In addition to the gifts, which will be discussed further below, the manuscript itself contains all the regular items of household expenditure that one might expect from a source of this nature – food, beverages, kitchen equipment, linen, small furniture, clothing, wages, medical bills, payments to bargemen on the Thames, animal fodder, charitable donations and ship money contributions. However, not every expense associated with the archiepiscopal household under Laud's jurisdiction features in the account book. Some *lacunae* are the result of the fact that the document dates from December 1635. There are no extant accounts for the archbishop's first two years in office, a period which saw the transition from one primate to another and, as a result, some significant refurbishment of Lambeth Palace.[29] These renovations included the purchase of a new altar table and rail for the chapel, improvements to the pews and pulpit, new locks and padlocks for several doors and cabinets in the Palace and some clasps for 'the King's Pictureframe'.[30] In May 1635, further changes were made in the chapel, when some of the windows were repaired and the 'great windowe' was fitted with stained glass featuring 'the King's armes and my Lord Grace's'.[31] Towards the end of the same year, in November 1635, new bellows, keys and 'a wind trunk' were purchased for the organ and further work was done on the stained glass.[32] While some later expenditure on the chapel and its paraphernalia does appear in the account book, the larger, more significant items which were purchased in the period before the inception of the accounts, and which have direct relevance to Laud's controversial ecclesiastical policies, are not to be found here. Other omissions are less easily explained. In June 1636, for example, the 'glass painter' was paid £62 7s 6d for re-glazing Lambeth Palace chapel's windows, but – surprisingly – the account book contains no entry for this significant sum.[33] More trivial omissions of gifts which are known to have been sent, but which did not make their way into the accounts are also puzzling. We can only speculate as to where, if anywhere, such expenditure was recorded, but these oversights or gaps, whether minor or significant, demonstrate that, despite its richness, this document does not represent a complete record of all household expenditure for Lambeth and Croydon for the period concerned.

27 Paul Lloyd, *Food and identity in England 1540–1640: eating to impress* (London, 2015), p. 142.
28 Heal, *The power of gifts*, p. 27.
29 *CSPD 1633–4*, p. 221.
30 TNA, SP 16/246, fo. 169.
31 TNA, SP 16/288, fo. 64.
32 TNA, SP 16 16/301, fo. 154, SP 16/302, fo. 21.
33 Fos. 8v, 161r.

Editorial conventions

In order to retain the integrity of the document, a 'semi-diplomatic transcription' of the manuscript has been adopted in the main text of this edition. This means that while certain steps have been taken to regularize capitalization, contractions and punctuation, the intention has been to produce an edited version which resembles as closely as possible the manuscript, whilst also ensuring clarity for the reader. Original spelling has, however, been retained, even when the same word is spelt differently in quick succession. For instance, on 25 December 1635, an entry for 'shoeinge the 6 coach horses' is shortly followed by another for 'new shoeing' the same animals;[34] similarly, a week later, a payment was made for 'alteringe the harpe', while a consecutive entry records expenditure 'for altering the case',[35] and so on. The rationale for retaining early modern spelling is that modernization would deviate too far from the original script and the edition might, then, fail to convey the true character of the manuscript. The one exception to this rule concerns occurrences of 'ye', which have been modernized to 'the' throughout. All nouns are capitalized in the manuscript, in accordance with contemporary custom, but capitals have been removed in the edition. Thus, an original entry for 'a new Cart & Ropes' appears as 'a new cart & ropes'.[36] Only given names, place names and titles are capitalized in the edition. The exception to this rule concerns titles for household servants, which appear capitalized in the manuscript (eg 'Laundress', 'Sadler', etc.) but which are shown here in lower case.

Throughout the manuscript, numerous words have been contracted. In the edition, such abbreviations are given in full, with the missing letters included in square brackets. For example, 'hogsh[ead]' is routinely abbreviated to 'hogsh' in the original, but has been expanded in the edition, reading 'hogsh[ead]' or 'hogsh[eads]'. Similarly, 'bushel' is almost always recorded as 'bush', but appears as 'bush[el]' or 'bush[els]' when expanded. When inserting missing letters, the early modern spelling, rather than a modern rendering of a word, is adopted, if found elsewhere in full in the manuscript. The word 'paid', which appears as 'p', 'pd' and 'payd', is expanded to 'p[ay]d Dr Turner' or 'p[ayd] Mr Rollston', for example.[37] If a contracted word is spelt variously several times in full in the original, the word is expanded with the most commonly used missing letters. Where the manuscript contained a range of abbreviations for a frequently used word, the expanded version has been standardized – e.g. 'q', 'qrt', 'qurt' or 'qurter' are recurrent contracted variations of 'quarter', which appears expanded, with square brackets denoting missing letters. Contracted titles have been transcribed in full in the edition, again with square brackets around the omitted letters. For instance, 'Lo:' appears as 'Lo[rd]'; 'La:' appears as 'La[dy]', etc. All instances of 'Mr' appear as per the original. Raised contractions, such as

34 Fos. 2r, 2v.
35 Fo. 2r.
36 Fo. 75r.
37 Fos. 85r, 88r.

'M^{trs}' for 'Mistress' have been lowered and expanded, again with square brackets, as appropriate.

Archaic and obsolete words are marked with a crucifix (†) every time they occur and definitions are provided in a 'glossary of words' which is appended to the edition. Where, despite considerable etymological research, it is not possible to identify a word or even to hazard a reasonable guess as to its meaning, a series of ellipses are included within square brackets after the section of the word which *is* identifiable (e.g. '[...]'). Inconsistent and limited punctuation was standard practice in the early modern period, particularly relating to the use of the apostrophe, and this is reflected in the manuscript, which includes such punctuation erratically. In the edition, for the purposes of clarity and consistency, occurrences of the possessive apostrophe have been removed.

The names of approximately 440 different people appear in the accounts, either as gift-givers, visitors to Lambeth and Croydon or household staff and servants. An attempt has been made to identify each and every one of them, from the high profile to the obscure, and from the most frequently cited to those who are only mentioned once. All names for which an identity has been established appear marked with an asterisk (*) throughout the edition. This denotes their inclusion in the 'glossary of names'. This appendix is a crucial reading aid. To keep cross-referencing to a minimum – and to reduce the need for voluminous and excessive referencing – this glossary also includes a brief biographical summary of each person identified, outlining the most significant formal offices and titles held in the period broadly synchronous with the accounts, as well as any known or obvious association with Laud. The compilation of a comprehensive names glossary means that references to people in the edition's footnotes are intended to provide specific context, rather than any factual information pertaining to the person concerned. Despite extensive and rigorous research, however, it still proved impossible conclusively to identify some ninety men and women. All such cases are indicated in the footnotes.

Finally, all dates from 1 January to 24 March, which are written in the accounts in old style, have been adjusted to new style.

The significance of the document

In casting new light on the career of the most controversial and significant man in Charles I's government, a critical interrogation of Laud's account book contributes to a better understanding of ecclesiastical power and politics in seventeenth-century Britain. It enhances current thinking on a range of subjects, including his relationships at court; early modern networks; and the nature of the metropolitical *rôle*, as well as yielding new insights into the wider context in which Laud was operating, all of which will be considered in the paragraphs below. While our primary concern here is to explore the document's value as a political source, the account book, naturally, also has much to tell us about life in an élite household. It is appropriate, therefore, to begin by offering a few examples of such socio-economic insights, before moving to a discussion of politics.

At the most basic level, the document allows us to view the archbishop in a slightly more human light than that in which he has been cast hitherto. The famous portrait of Laud – by Sir Anthony Van Dyck, the completion of which in 1636 is recorded in the accounts and which now hangs in the Fitzwilliam Museum, Cambridge – presents him as an austere figure in plain, ecclesiastical dress. This image, compounded by his reputation for severity and personal coldness, has conditioned us to visualize the archbishop in a rather two-dimensional light.[38] Even so, while reinforcing certain aspects of his life and behaviour, his household accounts also make a subtler appraisal possible.[39] His physical appearance, for one thing, can now be reimagined. Although, naturally, he often wore the clerical 'rotchet' made of 'cambricke cotton' with which we have become so familiar, the archbishop also wore more elaborate clothing when occasion required.[40] In March 1636, for instance, he acquired a gown of 'Turkey grogram', a coarse silken fabric, and for the royal visit to Oxford in August of that year, he was kitted out in a gown of taffeta and velvet, which was designed to make – and must have made – a visual impact.[41] When he presided over the consecrations of fellow bishops – seven of which can be seen in the accounts – he donned an elaborate robe and velvet cap.[42] The archbishop wore gloves and stockings throughout the year and, during winter, he swapped his ordinary shoes for boots and donned a 'beaver hatt' and 'martyn skyns' to keep warm.[43] Taking pride in his appearance extended beyond the 'apprell' which his personal 'taylor' provided on a regular basis.[44] Quarterly payments to 'your Graces barber' attest to his methodical ablutions.[45] He also had access to the best possible medical care, since Sir Simon Baskerville, the king's physician, was paid an annual stipend of £5, as well as further *ad hoc* payments, when his services were required.[46] For a workaholic like Laud, timekeeping was an essential way of keeping on top of a demanding remit which required him to be at court and in council on an almost daily basis. Hence, his watch was regularly sent to the horologist for repair.[47] Although he frequently bemoaned his heavy workload in letters to Wentworth, very rare glimpses emerge from the accounts of a man who was not entirely averse to leisurely pursuits. The existence of a bowling green at Lambeth suggests that this may have been one of his pastimes; in September 1637, when events in England and Scotland were beginning to place him

38 Fos. 7r, 25r.

39 One such theme of Laud's life and career, which is reinforced in the accounts, relates to his passion for collecting ancient – particularly Arabic – manuscripts. For example, see fos. 61r, 86r, 88r, 93r, 99r, 140r.

40 Fos. 7v, 8r, 127r.

41 Fos. 5r, 11v.

42 Fos. 4r, 23r, 44r, 60r, 76r, 94r, 124r, 125r.

43 Fos. 4v, 7r, 94r, 98r, 128r.

44 Fos. 17r, 28r, 34r, 55r, 97r, 110r, 117r, 137r, 143r, 148r, 153r, 157r.

45 Fos. 5r, 12v, 21r, 31r, 39r, 46r, 56r, 66r, 73r, 82r, 90r, 97r, 103r, 110r, 116r, 124r, 130r, 136r, 142r, 148r, 153r.

46 Fos. 2r, 6r, 9r, 12r, 23r, 41r, 63r, 99r, 119r.

47 Fos. 1r, 22r, 33r, 39r, 48r, 60r, 87r, 91r, 98r, 108r, 112r, 120r, 156r.

under considerable pressure, Laud still found the time to indulge in a wager on the outcome of a game.[48]

When he emerged from the sanctuary of his Palace, the archbishop was not only dressed to impress, but he also moved around in style. The location of Lambeth across the river from Westminster and Whitehall meant that water travel was the archbishop's predominant mode of transport and the barge that was kept moored at Lambeth was well maintained and decorated in a suitably opulent fashion.[49] It was adorned with fringe canvas, painted in bright colours, with lanterns on the roof and reeds on the floor. A new 'hulke' was built in September 1639, new oars were acquired and maintenance of the vessel continued after Laud's imprisonment.[50] Similarly, the archiepiscopal coach, drawn by several coach horses and used for the summer remove to Croydon and visits to the royal palaces of Oatlands, Theobalds and Hampton Court, was regularly refitted with lights, handles and other fixtures.[51] This attests to the archbishop's awareness that ostentatious display went hand-in-hand with the exercise of power.

Although his portfolio as archbishop was extensive – requiring his presence at court throughout the period synchronous with the accounts – Laud nevertheless took seriously his responsibilities as the head of a household.[52] Staff employed at Lambeth and Croydon were well looked after. As we have seen, wages were paid quarterly or half-yearly in arrears, in December, March, June and September each year.[53] Other payments for specific tasks and services were made on an ongoing basis. Both the lump-sum and *ad hoc* payments varied considerably, according to the task involved and who was doing it. This is one of the reasons why it is difficult to establish whether Laud's household servants were paid 'the going rate' or whether their wages were subject to the rising inflation which affected all aspects of the monetary system, including the domestic labour market, during the seventeenth century.[54] Although the quarterly wage of £4 10s 0d paid to the 'laundresse' remained static across the six-year period covered by the accounts, other wages were too inconsistent for us to interpret in a meaningful way.[55] For instance, payments to William Duckett, one of the archbishop's most trusted servants, varied dramatically. In June 1636, he received £30 12s 0d 'for howsehuld stuffe bought since December last'. A year later,

---

48 For the game of bowls, see fo. 45r. Laud was not the only bishop to enjoy bowls; see Julian Davies, *The Caroline captivity of the church: Charles I and the remoulding of anglicanism* (Oxford, 1992), p. 203.

49 Fos. 8r, 43r, 62r, 91r.

50 Fos. 110r, 145r, 152r.

51 Fos. 10r, 12r, 12v, 16r, 41r, 45r, 79r.

52 The 'bargemen' on the Thames were paid for their services on 198 occasions between Dec. 1635 and Jan. 1642.

53 Fos. 5v, 8v, 12r, 18r, 26r, 29r, 37r, 46r, 49r, 56r, 66r, 74r, 82r, 89r, 97r, 103r, 110r, 116r, 124r, 130r, 142r, 148r–150r, 153r, 158r–161r.

54 For a discussion, see Roger Richardson, *Household servants in early modern England* (Manchester, 2010), pp. 80–4.

55 Fos. 5r, 8v, 12r, 37r, 66r, 124r, 130r, 136r, 142r, 157r, 160r. The exception is the final payment of £2s 10s 0d, paid in Dec. 1641, just before the accounts come to an end. This lower amount undoubtedly reflects the laundresse's diminished duties and the 'winding down' of the household, following Laud's imprisonment.

his quarterly wage was a mere £6 8s 11d; at the same time, the accounts also record a further thirty-eight one-off payments to Duckett, for boathire and fetching and carrying, as well as the reimbursement of monies he had already paid out to external suppliers of household goods.[56] In this way, remuneration of servants reflected the variety of tasks for which they were employed.

All sixty-nine of Laud's male household servants wore livery, with cloaks of taffeta and 'tawney cloth', the cost of which was covered by the archiepiscopal household and which was replaced every two years in June or July.[57] If, by the late eighteenth century, livery was considered out-of-date and overly flamboyant, in the 1630s, it remained an essential method of displaying the importance of the employer.[58] Equally, it also enabled male servants to wear clothing made of luxury fabrics which they would not, under normal circumstances, have been able to afford.[59] While some early modern households only required the most visible of servants to be dressed in uniform, all of the men in Laud's household were required to wear livery, from the steward and treasurer, down to the slaughterman, the chimney sweep and the clerks of the kitchen.[60] Twelve of the liveried servants with equestrian responsibilities, including the stable grooms, postilions and coachmen, would have sat on ornate 'livery saddles' when mounted, and these were also replaced every few years.[61] Apart from their livery, highly trusted servants, including John Cobb, the organist, and Richard Cobb were also furnished with other clothing, such as suits, cloaks, hats socks and shoes.[62] A range of footwear was provided across the household, with 'great bootes', 'oyld bootes' or 'water bootes' being supplied for staff with outdoor duties.[63] Laud's care for his servants extended beyond the provision of clothing, however. He also ensured that they had access to appropriate medical care, when necessary. For instance, an 'appoticary' was paid annually to treat the whole household, and when either the archbishop or certain servants had particular illnesses, this man attended to them with 'physicke' or 'purging ale'.[64]

While male servants were clothed and cured, there is nothing in the accounts to suggest that the four women known to have been attached to the household were given dress or medical treatment. This was not unusual and the dress issue alone reflected the fact that female household servants were less visible than their male counterparts. Furthermore, the accounts yield far fewer clues about the duties of the female servants who, unlike their male colleagues, were unlikely to have been resident in the household.[65] Although we know that the slaughterhouse was managed by 'Mistress' or 'Widdow' Whaly and that household linen was washed and handled

---

56 Fos. 6v, 29r, 37r, 88r, 143r, 154r.

57 Fo. 6v.

58 Richardson, *Household servants*, pp. 107–8.

59 *Ibid.*, p. 108.

60 LPL, TG1, fo. 33r, supplements the information contained in the accounts, being a check roll of liveried servants, listed by title and showing the amount of fabric allocated for each household *rôle*.

61 Fos. 8v, 74r, 131r.

62 Fos. 16r, 18r, 56r, 88r, 143r.

63 Fos. 13v, 94r, 77r, 107r, 94r.

64 Fos. 2r, 39r, 75r, 113r, 129r, 143r.

65 Woolgar, *The great household*, p. 34.

by the anonymous 'laundresse', the specific tasks assigned to the other women in the household – Elizabeth Hoult, a relative of Laud and a longstanding servant; and Mistress Page, who was taken on in June 1639 – are unclear.[66]

A feature of domestic service in seventeenth-century England, in general, and London, in particular, was that demand outstripped supply, leading to problems of high staff turnover in many élite households.[67] In the household at Lambeth Palace, however, turnover was fairly low, with a number of the servants named in the accounts having served under Laud's predecessors. Given their favourable working conditions, this is unsurprising. Although the accounts for the initial period of Laud's tenure in office are not extant, when a change of regime took place and a new archbishop took over, it looks as though there was considerable continuity in the make-up of the household, as most servants seem to have been appointed for life. The most longstanding employee was Francis Loveday, the gardener to Whitgift, Bancroft and Abbot. [68] Edward Lenthrop, one of several servants with a range of sundry duties, can be found in George Abbot's accounts for 1617.[69] Similarly, Ralph Watts, the housekeeper at Croydon, had served under at least one earlier archbishop and George Hodges, Benjamin Holford, Walter Morris, Edward Nutt and James Southes were certainly in post at Lambeth before 1633.[70]

Continuity of staff from one archbishop to the next was not inconsistent with fluidity of appointment between one archiepiscopal palace and another. An appointment at Croydon Palace did not militate against a member of the household being transferred to Lambeth, if occasion saw fit, and *vice versa*. This is unsurprising, given that the household decamped to Croydon every summer and, although a 'skeleton' staff was retained at Croydon for some of the year, it was inevitable that Lambeth servants would be employed across both palaces. These tended to be the staff with outdoor responsibilities, whose job it was to ensure that the grounds were kept under control, even when Laud was not in residence.[71] Different arrangements were in place for the manors at Ford and Bekesbourne in Kent, which were also attached to the archbishopric, but which had their own staff.[72] As far as we know, Laud never set foot in either house and yet the household's links with both palaces – as well as the agrarian community around Canterbury – can be seen through the accounts. For instance, there was an exchange of livestock between Lambeth and Ford, with horses, sheep, cows and deer being transported from Kent to London

66 Whaly, Hoult and Page were paid quarterly. See fos. 5v, 8v, 12r, 18r, 26r, 29r, 37r, 46r, 49r, 56r, 66r, 74r, 82r, 89r, 97r, 103r, 110r, 116r, 124r, 130r, 142r, 148r–150r, 153r, 160r.

67 Richardson, *Household servants*, p. 81.

68 LPL, TK57, fo. 34r

69 LPL, MS1730, fo. 68r.

70 LPL, TG1, fo. 28r.

71 For instance, fos. 5r, 37r, 53r, 91r include references to Lambeth-based staff also being employed at Croydon.

72 The palace at Ford, no longer extant, was located near the north Kent coast, around six miles from Canterbury, close to Reculver. Bekesbourne Palace survives and is now in private hands; Timothy Tatton-Brown, *A history of the archbishops of Canterbury and their houses* (London, 2000), pp. 73–4.

on a steady, if not frequent, basis.[73] Sir Roger Harflett, the keeper of Bekesbourne manor, often sent parcels of sugarloaves, fish and pheasants to Laud and was among the handful of stalwarts whose gifts continued beyond the archbishop's downfall.[74] Further Kentish links are illustrated in the accounts, which show that the household received wheat, malt and barley from 'yeoman retayners' based in the villages around Canterbury, such as John Denn of Littlebourne, Adam Sprackling of Fordwich and Ambrose Rose of Chislet.[75]

Despite having been provided with bulk orders of grain from the Kentish countryside, Lambeth and Croydon were semi-self-sufficient. The existence of a slaughterhouse in the grounds of Lambeth speaks to the presence of cattle and sheep in pasture in the meadows around both residences, which would have been slaughtered on-site for consumption within the household.[76] Cows were replaced when sent to slaughter and on two occasions, William Piers, bishop of Bath and Wells, donated two 'redd cowes' to the archiepiscopal herd.[77] There seems to have been little bovine exchange between Lambeth and Croydon, but a considerable amount of ovine movement. Sheep were regularly transported in large quantities – in flocks ranging from 57 to 100 – from Lambeth to Croydon and vice versa, as well as being brought 'out of Kent'.[78] This reminds us that, despite its proximity to Whitehall, Lambeth Palace was still a semi-agrarian household.

Sheep and cattle were not, however, the only animals to play a central *rôle* in Lambeth's domestic economy: with England remaining a 'largely horse-drawn society' in this period, horses naturally occupied a pivotal position.[79] Horses were always regarded as symbols of affluence and power by the ruling élite and they were looked after accordingly.[80] Moreover, the household was still semi-itinerant and when it vacated Lambeth every summer, a caravan of carts, drawn by horses, would carry linen, kitchen equipment and other household materials to Croydon. Not only were horses bought, sold and donated to the archbishop, but they were also meticulously cared for, reflecting their importance in economic, social and cultural terms.[81] We have no record of exactly how many horses were kept at Lambeth under Laud, but during Abbot's archiepiscopate, there were thirty-one and there is no reason to suspect any reduction under his successor.[82] We do know, however, that Laud's stables housed several different types of horse – nags, mares, bays, geldings and the much-valued coach horses, responsible for conveying the archbishop as he

---

73 Fos. 7r, 21r, 50r, 73r, 102r, 131r.
74 Fos. 5r, 17r, 27r, 64r, 86r, 98r, 115r, 123r, 149r, 159r.
75 All three of these men had been attached to the household since at least the time of Abbot; Canterbury Cathedral Archives, DCb/j/j/56/194; LPL, TG1, fos. 23v, 28v, TB1, fo. 60r.
76 Fos. 104r and 124r refer to 'cow pasture'/'cowe pasture'. See also fos. 8r, 47r, 78r, 81r, 92r, 107r. Occasionally, cows were taken to Smithfield market and sold.
77 Fos. 53r, 131r.
78 Fos. 13v, 33r, 102r, 130r, 151r, 158r.
79 Peter Edwards, *Horse and man in early modern England* (London, 2007), p. 1. See also Woolgar, *The great household*, pp. 181–96.
80 Edwards, *Horse and man in early modern England*, p. 27.
81 *Ibid.*, p. 7.
82 LPL, MS 1730, fo. 1r.

carried out the primatial *rôle* – and that all of them were well fed, regularly cleaned, bled and treated for ailments, when necessary. Although Lambeth employed its own blacksmith, when Laud was en route to Croydon or one of the outlying royal palaces, a farrier at Shepperton ensured that the horses were well shod.[83] The archbishop's most highly prized equine possession, however, was the great 'Barbary' horse, given to him by William Cavendish, earl of Newcastle, in November 1639.[84] Ownership of one of these thoroughbred, Arabian animals – exclusive to the ruling classes – enhanced the possibilities for overt displays of wealth and influence. In this respect at least, the evidence emerging from the account book demonstrates that Laud was no different to any of his aristocratic peers.[85]

The social spaces around the archiepiscopal palaces are also well served in the account book, which shows that the grounds at Lambeth and Croydon were regularly maintained and the gardens were kept in meticulous order.[86] Hedges were trimmed, lawns were mowed, walkways were cut back and the moats were cleared.[87] A mole catcher was employed at both palaces to prevent the destruction of the grassed areas.[88] Their surroundings, moreover, were clearly decorated in a style which was in keeping with the ornate parks surrounding other élite residences, including Whitehall and Hampton Court, where Laud spent considerable amounts of time.[89] His own gardens were decorated with ponds, arbours, sundials and hedged pathways.[90] New trees, including cypresses, were planted during the autumn.[91] The bowling green at Lambeth was rolled and kept neat.[92] John Tradescant, keeper of the royal gardens at Oatlands from 1630, may well have been consulted over garden layout and design, since he lived near Lambeth Palace and is known to have visited Laud.[93] This concern for aesthetics should come as no surprise, given the archbishop's taste for the 'beauty of holiness', but that it was given expression in a non-spiritual context indicates that he may not, after all, have been indifferent to works of art in a secular setting.[94] Perhaps more pertinently, it also corroborates the view that we should

83 Fos. 9r, 9v, 12r, 12v, 13v, 44r, 46r, 134r.

84 Fo. 114r.

85 Edwards, *Horse and man in early modern England*, p. 27.

86 In 1637, for instance, gardening expenditure was £74 17s 10d (fos. 20r–50r), while in 1639 this figure reached £78 0s 2d (fos. 91r–117r). These costs included gardeners' wages, as well as tools and seeds.

87 For hedges, see fos. 47r, 86r, 104, 117r, 142r, 148r; for lawns, see fos. 108r, 115r, 130r; for walkways, see fos. 10r, 38r, 75r, 107, 130r, 136r; and for moats, see fos. 4v, 6v, 8v, 9v, 75r, 84r, 111r, 137r, 139r.

88 The same person, whose identity is unclear, seems to have worked at both palaces, fos. 5r, 8v, 12r, 18r, 29r, 37r, 46r, 56r, 66r, 74r, 82r, 89r, 97r, 103r, 123r, 130r, 136r, 142r, 148r.

89 These two royal palaces had particularly sumptuous gardens.

90 A sundial was purchased in Mar. 1636 (fo. 4r), it was repaired and painted in Mar. 1639 (fo. 98r) and new poles for the arbours were bought in Jan. 1640 (fo. 121r).

91 Fos. 15r, 18r, 86r, 88r, 93r.

92 Fos. 130r, 136r. The bowling green was still present in the late eighteenth century; Tatton-Brown, *A history of the archbishops of Canterbury and their houses*, p. 72.

93 Fo. 33r. Tradescant was also gardener to George Villiers, duke of Buckingham, the royal favourite, until the latter's assassination in 1628 and was probably known to Laud, who had been Villiers's household chaplain in the 1620s. Roger Lockyer, *Buckingham* (London, 1984), p. 411.

94 David Howarth, *Images of rule – art and politics in the English Renaissance, 1485–1649* (London, 1997), p. 56.

conceive of Lambeth Palace, its people and its environs in the same way as we might consider any other élite household in the period. Tellingly, the upkeep of the grounds continued beyond the archbishop's imprisonment in February 1641, signifying not only his concern to maintain order, but also his hope that he might yet return home to Lambeth.

With some imagination, this mental picture of the Palace exterior can be supplemented with a 'virtual' image of a colourful and musical household interior. Redecorating the chapel, as we have seen, was one of Laud's priorities after he became archbishop in September 1633, when the stained glass was replaced, renovated and the organ was repaired. In June 1638, the chapel also acquired new 'foldinge chayres', 'a stoole of velvett' and 'cushins', and a 'newe organ' was installed and gilded in November 1639.[95] Very little evidence emerges from the accounts about the religious life of the household, but shortly after Laud's imprisonment, an inventory of the chapel shows that, in addition to the ornaments described, it featured a wooden, railed-in altar table, with an altar cloth of crimson and violet damask and taffeta. This is entirely in keeping with Laud's drive for the railing in of altar tables during the 1630s. In front of the altar was a Turkish carpet and its backdrop was a tapestry, telling the biblical story of Abraham and Melchisedek. The chapel's central location in the Palace meant that the sound of the organ would have travelled throughout the household, but secular music may also have been heard at Lambeth. Furthermore, musicians came by boat to the Palace several times a year and there were at least two harps in the household – one of which was given as a gift – while Laud's own harpsichord had pride of place in his drawing room.[96]

Music, then, played a part in the life of the household beyond the chapel, which creates the impression that Lambeth Palace was an agreeable place to live and work. A further embodiment of the household's conviviality – and one which speaks to the archbishop's own ecclesiology – came in the form of the annual celebration of the feast of St Clement. Traditionally celebrated on 23 November, the feast evoked the memory of Pope Clement I, claimed as the patron saint of blacksmiths. Thus, St Clement's festivities often revolved around fire, with the local smith orchestrating a minor explosion around the anvil. In the early modern period, where the festival was still celebrated, this ceremony was often either replaced with or supplemented by beer drinking, songs and bonfires. Special cakes, made with oranges and lemons, were baked for the occasion. There is no way of knowing whether Mr Morris, the Lambeth blacksmith, orchestrated a St Clement's ceremony around his own anvil, but a Lambeth baker was paid 'for St Clements' every November for the duration of the accounts, a custom which continued unchanged even after Laud's imprisonment.[97] Although this sheds fascinating light on an important aspect of domestic social life at the Palace, it is also of some relevance when placed in the context of Laud's

---

95 Fos. 75r, 66r, 114r; TNA, SP16/499, fo. 82. The chairs may well have been the 'folding chaires of leather' recorded in a 1643 inventory of Lambeth Palace chapel, taken when the Palace was ransacked.

96 For musicians, see fos. 45r, 53r, 55r, 61r, 70r, 76r, 87r, 95, 96r, 131r; for the harp, see fos. 2r, 68r; for the harpsichord, see fo. 66r; *WWL*, IV, 447.

97 Fos. 16r, 54r, 88r, 115r, 141r, 159r.

own theological position. The celebration of religious festivals in post-Reformation England was contentious. Indeed, in the mid-sixteenth century, the Elizabethan Book of Common Prayer established a 'national devotional framework' which reduced the number of 'legitimate' religious festival days from 125 to 27. Zealous Protestants, however, saw the continued observation of such calendrical customs as idolatrous and popish.[98] Laud himself was at the forefront of attempts to ensure conformity with the prayer book during the 1630s. Interestingly, St Clement's Day was not among the 'authorized' celebratory days in the Protestant calendar, as defined under the Elizabethan Settlement.[99] This is not to suggest that in permitting his staff to celebrate an 'unauthorized' festival, Laud was the papist that many of his contemporaries considered him to be. Rather, it speaks to the possibility that he was generous as a domestic patriarch in allowing his servants to partake in a festival and privately tolerant of practices that he was not prepared to countenance on a wider, public scale.

If he treated his own servants well, Laud was equally conscientious when it came to rewarding staff at court, a gesture that all senior officers were expected to make in recognition of the royal household's contribution to making the lives of courtiers and councillors easier. Indeed, every December, the archbishop recognized 'the househould at court' for its assistance during the preceding year, even after he had been placed under house arrest.[100] The sums involved were not excessive – Laud's annual donations hovered between £30 and £31, an amount comparable with the donations of other courtiers– but this formal gift, which might also be construed as a fee, differed from the more impromptu, lesser amounts handed to household servants throughout the year, which also feature in the accounts.[101] These seem to have been given as tips directly to individuals – and were often doled out by one of the archbishop's own staff, such as William Duckett or William Dell – whereas the yearly donation was recorded as a 'lump sum'.[102] Although recorded as a 'lump sum', however, it was shared out between a range of royal household staff.[103] In 1639, for instance, gentlemen of the chapel, choristers, bellringers and trumpeters benefited from Laud's generosity, together with pastry cooks, buttery servants, the closet keeper and the sweep.[104]

Generosity towards the indigent was a further manifestation of what might be construed as the archbishop's more benevolent side, with both regular and impromptu charitable donations being made throughout the period.[105] Every Christmas, a

---

98 David Cressy, 'The Protestant calendar and the vocabulary of celebration in early modern England', *Journal of British Studies*, 29, 1 (1990), 31–52.

99 *Ibid.*, 34

100 Fos. 2r, 21r, 58r, 92r, 118r, 144r.

101 Sir Francis Windebank, one of the king's secretaries of state, for instance, gave the royal household £33 4s 6d in Jan. 1637; TNA, SP16/343, fo. 2.

102 Fos. 62r, 70r, 102r 128r, 131r, for instance, record tips to the grooms, porters and butler at star chamber and the cooks at court.

103 Heal, *The power of gifts*, p. 142.

104 TNA, SP/16/441, fo. 1r.

105 Felicity Heal has argued that giving to the poor was an integral and expected component of episcopal 'hospitality', which in itself was derived from the scriptures, in Felicity Heal, 'The archbishops of Canterbury and the practice of hospitality', *Journal of Ecclesiastical History*, 33, 4 (1982), 544–63.

substantial £20 was given to the 'poor of Lambeth', while their Croydon counterparts received £5.[106] Prisoners at the gaols in Ludgate, the Savoy and Southwark were also the recipients of Laud's munificence every Christmas and Easter, while spur-of-the-moment donations were handed out regularly, when the archbishop was travelling to and from court or Croydon Palace.[107] Over and above this, numerous one-off payments – whether 'a poore woman at Epsom', 'a poor maultese', 'a poore dumbe man' or 'to a poore Scottishman' – attest to the willingness of Laud and his entourage to give spontaneously while going about their daily business.[108] Paupers arriving at the gates of Lambeth were treated equally charitably, as were the young children who loitered around the entrances to Whitehall, in the hope of a few shillings as councillors and courtiers came and went.[109] The practice of donating to the poor and the prisons continued beyond Laud's imprisonment.[110] Public criticism of Laud's lack of generosity in comparison with his archiepiscopal predecessors might have been tempered, had his critics been aware of the archbishop's charity towards the poor.[111] Indeed, when compared with Abbot's donations to the poor during his tenure in office, Laud is certainly not found wanting.[112]

Diligence in relieving poverty was matched with equal assiduity when it came to responding to major crown initiatives, such as ship money, the contributions for which were paid in the spring of every year. While appeals flooded in to the privy council from disgruntled subjects complaining about assessment for the levy, the archbishop had no such qualms, making regular, if varied, contributions for every annual levy. A 'fixed sum' of £9 for Lambeth was paid in 1636; in 1637, an additional contribution of £4 was paid for Croydon.[113] The following year, the annual levy for Lambeth remained unchanged, but that for Croydon increased to £5 and a further payment of £4 13s 9d was also made 'for the shipp money for the court'.[114] The amounts given for 1639 went down to £3 for Lambeth and a mere £1 16s for Croydon. However, by March 1640, when the final payments were made, the Lambeth and Croydon contributions had risen back to £9 and £5 respectively.[115]

Far from pertaining to domestic matters only, the expenses of Laud's household are also illustrative of the broader political context in which the archbishop operated. Lambeth may have been separated from Westminster and Whitehall by the Thames, but the household became the focus of public attention at key points in

106 Fos. 1r, 20r, 57r, 91r, 118r, 144r, 161r.
107 Fos. 1r, 5v, 6v, 13r, 20r, 30r, 57r, 67r, 68r, 91r, 100r.
108 Fos. 12r, 106r, 112r, 129r.
109 Fos. 61r, 68r, 112r.
110 Fos. 150r, 161r.
111 Felicity Heal, *Hospitality in early modern England* (Oxford, 1990), p. 277; Peter Heylyn, *Cyprianus anglicus* (London, 1668), p. 244.
112 LPL, MS 1730, 170 folios. See fos. 20v, 24r, 24v, 145v, 146v for 'one-off' charitable donations by Abbot.
113 Fos. 2v, 27r.
114 Fos. 64r, 69r.
115 Fos. 95, 123r.

the period. The household's reaction to the assault on 'Lambeth House' by several hundred London apprentices on 11 May 1640 can be traced through the accounts, for example. In the aftermath of the dissolution of the Short Parliament on 5 May, the continuation of clerical Convocation – customarily dissolved at the same time as parliament – was a contentious move. Not only was it considered 'illegal', but the new ecclesiastical canons, which were under discussion at the session after parliament was dissolved, were highly controversial.[116] In particular, the vagueness of the infamous *et cetera* oath in canon 6 seemed to bind all clergy who swore it to the king's – and Laud's – interpretation of religious orthodoxy.[117] Laud was blamed for the decision. Forewarned of the attack, he managed to escape to his lodgings at Whitehall before the trouble broke out, but the apprentices were unaware of this when they stormed the Palace in the early hours of 11 May, to hunt down 'the fox'.[118] The accounts bear witness to the flurry of activity – and expense – which arose from the attack. Two 'munitioning peeces', 'shott' and gunpowder were sent over from the Tower; 'musketeers' were fetched by boat; and '13 skeanes of match' were acquired to be placed in 'lynstocks' around the Palace. When the crowd had been dispersed, the 'rebells' were carried 'to the gatehouse at Westminster'.[119] There had been signs of trouble even before May 1640, however. In late June 1637, John Bastwick, Henry Burton and William Prynne were sentenced to mutilation by the court of star chamber, following the publication of 'seditious' material against the crown's religious policies. Having presided over the sentencing, the archbishop was widely held responsible for 'persecuting the saints and shedding the blood of the martyrs' and further libels were spread against him.[120] That very same week, it looks as though the Palace acquired six new cases of pistols and repaired the armour for six horsemen, who were to be equipped with swords, this purchase implying that Laud's household may have been privy to the private concerns for his personal safety expressed in his diary and personal correspondence.[121] However, difficulties arise when seeking to interpret the meaning of further instances in which armour was repaired and munitions were purchased, simply because the quantities involved seem excessive for a household this size. It is perfectly plausible, for instance, that six men in the Lambeth household would need access to the armour acquired in June 1637, but less likely that the overhaul of '25 footmans armor' in March 1638 was intended for use in the archiepiscopal household, since Laud only employed two footmen.[122] An alternative – and possibly more plausible – hypothesis is that this latter entry records Laud's contribution to the armaments of the royal household. Certainly, in early 1639, shortly before Charles I departed for his first campaign

116 Esther Cope, 'The Short Parliament of 1640 and Convocation', *Journal of Ecclesiastical History*, 25, 2 (1974), 167–84.

117 For a discussion, see Davies, *Caroline captivity*, pp. 276–81.

118 Fos. 39r, 127r, 139r; *WWL*, III, 235, 284; Heylyn, *Cyprianus anglicus*, p. 425.

119 Fo. 127r.

120 *WWL*, III, 229. Some of the libels against Laud from May 1640, including 'Landless Will of Lambeth strand', can be found in the excellent web resource compiled by Alastair Bellany and Andrew McRae www.earlystuartlibels.net.

121 LPL, TG1, fo. 33r; TNA, E101/547/5, fo. 39r; *WWL*, III, 228, VI, 500.

122 LPL, TG1, fo. 33r; TNA, E101/547/5, fo. 66r.

against the Scots, the king 'invited … all private persons of quality and the Bishops' to supply him with horses. The purchase of armour for nine light horsemen and fourteen additional corslets recorded in the accounts, in May 1639, may well have been Laud's contribution to the king's war effort, since even before the outbreak of Anglo-Scottish hostilities, armour was in pitifully short supply in England.[123] Again, in August 1640, when the armorer at Lambeth paid for further munitions, including '19 carabyns', this purchase is just as easily understood in the context of the second Bishops' War – which was ongoing – as the archiepiscopal palace.[124] Although clerical armaments were by no means unheard of in this period – the clergy within the diocese of Canterbury alone possessed 24 horses, 106 muskets and 100 corslets in 1635, for example – pending further research, we cannot be entirely certain whether Laud was expanding his own arsenal from mid-1637 onwards, or whether he was contributing to the royal armoury.[125] Either interpretation, though, lends credence to the archiepiscopal household's responsiveness to events which had political significance.

Similarly – and paradoxically – the absence of certain routine entries from the accounts can be just as contextually illustrative as the presence of others. The lack of any weekly payments to bargemen or carriers between 22 July 1636 and 13 January 1637, for example, corresponds to the time period in which a major plague epidemic swept through London, killing at least 10,400 people.[126] Apart from a brief couple of days at Lambeth around 12 July, the archbishop was away from his main seat of residence for seven months, having left for Croydon in late June.[127] During this time, outside of the period spent at Oxford for the royal visit in August, Laud relocated the archiepiscopal household to Croydon Palace and most of the court relocated to Hampton Court, with a reduced presence at Oatlands or Windsor. The king also spent time at Royston, one of his royal hunting lodges.[128] When the court returned to Whitehall in the New Year, twelve carts carried the archiepiscopal household back to Lambeth in the week of 13 January.[129] It is well known that the élite vacated the capital during the summer months when the risk of plague was greater, but we can infer from the accounts, not only how the household reacted to an epidemic of plague, but also the detrimental impact that this must have had on the livelihoods of ordinary people, like the bargemen, who had no choice but to remain in the city. In this respect, the document serves as an indicator of the wider social context, as well as the political narrative.

This latter point leads to another area of interest: the impact of Laud's downfall

123 TNA, SP16/396, fo. 60, E101/547/5, fo. 101r. See also Mark Fissel, *The bishops' wars: Charles I's campaigns against Scotland, 1638–1640* (Cambridge, 1994), p. 154.

124 Fo. 135r.

125 In 1635, William Dell, Laud's secretary, compiled an inventory of clergy-owned armaments in Canterbury diocese; TNA, SP/16/306, fo. 161.

126 Stephen Porter, *The great plague* (London, 2009), p. 26.

127 Fo. 10r for the July payment to the bargemen; fo. 23r for the Jan. 1637 payment. This can be cross-referenced to Laud's correspondence, which shows that after 12 July 1636, no further letters were written from Lambeth until 17 Jan. 1637; *WWL*, V, 138, VII, 307.

128 *WWL*, VII, 288.

129 Fo. 23r.

on the household. From his arrest on 18 December 1640 until the cessation of the accounts on 13 January 1642, the household was winding down incrementally. By September 1641, at least two household servants – John Cobb, the organist and his brother, Richard – had been taken on in other noble households, and it is likely that other staff were seeking employment elsewhere.[130] However, the most obvious and immediate effect of the archbishop's absence was the reduction in expenditure for meals and hospitality. For the period from December 1635, when the accounts begin, to December 1640, when Laud was charged in the House of Commons, the cost recorded for weekly kitchen expenses – including food, but excluding wages for servants – ranged from £21 5s 1d to £39 3s 7d, this latter amount being recorded in September 1637, the point at which Laud's career was, arguably, reaching its zenith.[131] When Laud was placed under house arrest, kitchen costs fell instantly to £19 1s 10d and continued gradually to dwindle thereafter, the final entry in January 1642 being for a mere £5 10s 2d.[132] While a select few servants continued to be paid, the household seems to have been downsizing almost as soon as Laud was placed under house arrest in Charing Cross. From February 1641, when he was moved to the Tower, many of the entries recorded relate to expenses incurred as a result of his imprisonment, reflecting the fact that prisoners were expected to contribute towards the cost of their own incarceration. Such expenses ranged from the more obvious charges for 'removing stuffe from Mr Maxwells' and for 'wharfage' to one-off tips and gratuities to the 'workmen of the White Tower', the 'plummer', 'carpenter' and 'souldiers'.[133] Laud also funded repairs to the windows in his chambers, paid for his own food and bought padlocks and keys.[134] While the physical conditions of his imprisonment cannot be discerned, he was, on one occasion, permitted to 'see the park', suggesting that he had some freedom of movement around the Tower precincts.[135] In this respect, the account book acts as a barometer of Laud's own personal fortunes, since through it we can trace his career at both its highest and lowest points.

The account book also goes a long way towards rectifying the common misperception that Laud drew on little support besides that of the king. Just like the king's, Laud's power, too, was relational – much more so than has hitherto been appreciated. Through an analysis of the several hundred names which occur in the account book – either as gift-givers, visitors to Lambeth or people with whom Laud dealt on a professional level – we can see that he was surrounded by a web of social relationships, which were not restricted to the nobility, bishops, clergy and judges, but also comprised

130 John Cobb was taken on by Rachel, countess of Bath in Sept. 1641 and his brother Richard also found employment within the household. *Devon household accounts*, ed. Gray, II, pp. 24, 136. Thanks to Professor Chris Page for drawing my attention to the Cobbs' fortunes after 1641.

131 Fos. 11v, 45r.

132 Fos. 143r, 160r.

133 Fos. 147r, 149r, 150r, 152r, 149r.

134 Fo. 152r.

135 Fo. 150r.

civil lawyers, MPs, gentry and merchants. Appointed to the privy council in April 1627, by the time of the accounts' start date of December 1635, the archbishop was a familiar face at court, attending on a very regular basis. Naturally, therefore, much of his contact with many of the people who appear in the accounts was face-to-face, but the constant stream of gifts he received for the duration of the accounts add a further dimension to our understanding of his perceived influence, his networks and his standing within the body politic. Thus, the account book provides a new prism through which to explore connexions and associations between Laud and the people who were at the centre of British political life.

The majority of the names which feature in the accounts appear in the context of gift-giving. Before moving to an analysis of the gifts and gift-givers, however, we need to establish what gifts meant in this period. As Felicity Heal has shown, for monarchs, the New Year held a central place in the process of gift exchange. Originating from the early days after the Norman conquest, the New Year ritual of courtly giving was a manifestation of fealty and service, in which the crown received gifts from its 'tenants-in-chief' – the higher nobility, barons and bishops – in return for a gift from the king, usually in the form of plate or gilt.[136] While practice had varied across the centuries, by the late Elizabethan period, the monarch presided over a lavish ceremony of gift exchange. In its early seventeenth-century guise, gifting endured as a means by which the king's chief subjects showed that they were incorporated into royal service. What had changed was that, while there was still some reciprocity involved, donors did not always receive a corresponding gift from the crown.[137] In the early days of James I's reign, the 'going rate' for a gift to the king by an earl or a bishop was £20, in exchange for which a small amount of plate or gilt was given.[138] As Charles I's chief ecclesiastical advisor, Laud's regular New Year's gift of £40 to the monarch is predictable, if generous.[139] The archbishop continued sending his gift to the king after his imprisonment in the Tower, the final instance being recorded in December 1641.[140] There is no record of any reciprocal seasonal gift from the king to Laud, although during the hunting season every year, Charles sent either a 'stagg' in June or July, or a 'hynd' or 'bucke' in October or November. The last gift entered in the accounts from the king to Laud was received in July 1640, with a further gift from a royal hunt being recorded in September of that year.[141]

Since ministers, nobles and courtiers 'mimicked' the gifting ceremony, it comes as no surprise to learn that archbishop Laud was the recipient of a vast array of gifts each New Year, the flow of goods beginning in mid-December and continuing into January. Since gift-giving was an important aspect of the 'rhetoric of service' which implied a 'mutual political relationship' between giver and receiver, the following

136 Heal, *The power of gifts*, p. 93.
137 *Ibid.*, p. 94.
138 *Ibid.*, p. 129.
139 Fos. 2r, 21r, 58r, 92r, 118r, 144r, 161r.
140 Fo. 161r.
141 Although nine gifts of deer were recorded as definitely 'from the Kinge', an additional five were sent from 'Theobalds', the royal hunting lodge; fos. 9r, 13r, 39r, 52r, 72r, 77r, 116r, 129r, 133r (from Charles I); fos. 11v, 81r, 106r, 107r, 135r (from Theobalds).

overview of gifts suggests that Laud was considered to be a significant potential power-broker.[142] The relationships between the gift-giver and the recipient are of central interest here, but it is worth briefly examining the nature of some of the gifts, before moving to a discussion of who gave them.

Predictably – and in keeping with customary norms – food was the most commonly received commodity at Lambeth Palace.[143] As a gift, food differed from other goods, because it had an obvious purpose within the household – it could be consumed and enjoyed, either during a feast or banquet or privately by the household and its head. The result was that less gratitude was expected on the receipt of a consumable gift, than for inedible items, because it had an inherent use by the recipient.[144] Although Laud was criticized for his lack of hospitality, this did not prevent people from gifting food to him.[145] Indeed, there is no evidence of Bacchanalian feasting in his household accounts, but they are littered with mundane and luxury edible presents.[146] A survey of the account book reveals that Laud's gift roll included at least 57 lamprey pies, 59 sugar loaves, 122 cheeses, 58 pheasants, 62 cakes and 7 Westphalia gammons, plus countless varieties of wine (such as sack, canary and claret), numerous parcels of lamb, beef, fish (particularly during Lent), apricots, melons, apples and oranges. Nutmeg, cloves, mace, pepper, sugar, other spices and more wine were also donated by the mercantile companies.[147] Far and away the most popular gift, however, came from the deer parks of the king, the nobility and higher gentry – a staggering 223 deer were delivered to the gates of Lambeth Palace between December 1635 and December 1640, and a further smattering of such gifts came after Laud's imprisonment. This conforms to the contemporary *more* that venison was the gift of choice for the most prestigious givers.[148]

Edible goods may have been routinely and regularly given, but luxury items also feature and those with religious connotations are particularly noteworthy. Eight communion cups and covers were donated between December 1637 and January 1640; and eighteen gifts of 'plate'; two basins; and five gifts of candlesticks were received.[149] The givers of the communion cups – Sir Henry Guildford, Sir John Bankes and Edmund Woodhall – may have been among a constituency of people supportive of Laud's religious policies. Certainly, Bankes is known to have been an admirer of the work of Lancelot Andrewes, Laud's 'Arminian' mentor.[150] Both he and Woodhall had professional dealings with the archbishop in their official capacities as the king's attorney general and registrar of the prerogative court of Canterbury respectively, but little is known of Guildford, a Kentish gentleman. As with any gift – and particularly when the only evidence of its existence is to be found in an account

142 Heal, *The power of gifts*, p. 1.
143 *Ibid.*, p. 35.
144 *Ibid.*, p. 36.
145 Heylyn, *Cyprianus anglicus*, p. 505; Heal, 'The archbishops of Canterbury and the practice of hospitality', 259.
146 Heal, *Hospitality in early modern England*, p. 282.
147 Fos. 58r, 59r, 92r, 116r.
148 Heal, *The power of gifts*, pp. 40–2.
149 Fos. 1r, 3r, 21r, 22r, 58r, 59r, 92r, 93r, 114r, 115r, 119r.
150 Conrad Russell, *The causes of the English civil war* (Oxford, 1990) pp. 101–2.

book – determining the exact motivation for giving is very difficult but, certainly, a gift of this nature, which deviates from the standard gift of food, is unlikely to have been given by someone who was unaware of its significance.

Precious gifts were not only inanimate, however. As we have seen, horses were an integral part of Laud's life and they were, without doubt, the most valuable gift given to the archbishop in the period 1635 to 1641. He received at least thirteen horses between May 1636 and March 1640, five of which were given by the well-known equestrian enthusiast, William Cavendish, earl of Newcastle.[151] Other horse-donors included John Bridgeman, bishop of Chester; Robert Bertie, 1st earl of Lindsey; Edward Cecil, Viscount Wimbledon; Philip Herbert, 4th earl of Pembroke; Sir William Jones; Sir John Lambe; and Sir George Willmott, a Berkshire landowner knighted by Charles I in 1628.[152] Equine gifts, therefore, came from a bishop, three earls, a judge of the king's bench and a senior civil lawyer, as well as an upwardly mobile member of the higher gentry.[153] Of course, with only the household accounts as a guide, we cannot be absolutely sure whether these beasts were 'pure gifts', as opposed to household purchases, since we know that gifts and purchases were monetized in the same way in the document. However, letters of thanks for some of the horses received go some considerable way towards settling this issue.[154]

A brief survey of the people who – and organizations which – sent gifts to the archbishop gives an indication of his perceived influence. As we shall see, these gifts confirm existing associations, show the cessation of others and also reveal new ones. Unsurprisingly, over forty Church of England clergymen – many of them fellow *alumni* of St John's College, Oxford – and approximately half of the English bishops participated in gifting.[155] As a proportion of the overall clerical and episcopal total, this is nowhere near the maximum number possible, but Laud's brethren on the English episcopal bench regularly made offerings to the archbishop, both at New Year and at other times. The occasional gift can be construed as gratitude for an ecclesiastical appointment, such as the one and only gift received from Theophilus Field, which arrived at Lambeth just one week after Field's promotion to the bishopric of Hereford in December 1635.[156] Many more of them, however, are indicative of longer-standing affiliations. Gifts from the likes of John Bancroft, bishop of Oxford; John Bridgeman, bishop of Chester; Richard Mountague, bishop of Chichester; Robert Skinner, bishop of Bristol; and Richard Neile, archbishop of York – all of whom are known to have been Laud's allies and acolytes – clearly fall into this latter category.[157] Other episcopal donors – including John Owen, bishop of St Asaph; Thomas Morton, bishop of Durham; and Godfrey Goodman, bishop of

---

151 Fos. 35r, 70r, 82r, 114r.

152 *Knights of England*, II, 195.

153 Fos. 7r, 33r, 34r, 38r, 73r, 112r, 123r.

154 Stafford Record Office, D1287/18/2 (P/399/145); *WWL*, VII, 418.

155 There were twenty-four bishops and two archbishops on the English mainland, plus Sodor and Man. For a list, see Davies, *Caroline captivity*, p. 319.

156 Fo. 1r.

157 For Laud's *rôle* in ecclesiastical patronage, see Fincham, 'William Laud and the exercise of Caroline ecclesiastical patronage', 69–93.

Gloucester – remained on the margins of Laud's favour.[158] Goodman, for one, spent much of the later 1630s under a cloud, after the 1635 metropolitical visitation found him lax in enforcing a range of policies. Goodman, in fact, was the only bishop in Convocation who refused to subscribe the 1640 canons, telling Laud that he would rather be 'torn with wild horses' than do so.[159] A spell in Westminster Gatehouse eventually convinced Goodman of the error of his ways.[160] Consequently, his gifts to Laud, several of which came after the archbishop's imprisonment in the Tower, are perplexing. If they were Goodman's attempt at ingratiating himself with Laud, they came a bit too late and, in any case, it is unlikely that a few lamprey pies and the occasional cheese would have been sufficient to win Laud's approval.[161] Perhaps the example of Goodman simply serves as a reminder of the difficulties involved in trying to ascertain the individual motives behind gift-giving.

In this connexion, episcopal absences or infrequent appearances are also worth noting, since some bishops who were closely associated with Laud and his policies scarcely feature. Although the lack of gifts from John Williams, bishop of Lincoln – a thorn in Laud's side for much of the 1630s – is entirely to be expected, other cases are more perplexing. Matthew Wren, bishop of Ely, was supposed to have been preferred to his first bishopric by Laud in 1634 and was probably the most energetic of all the bishops in enforcing certain aspects of Caroline ecclesiastical policy, such as altar policy and the book of sports.[162] Thus, one might expect to find regular gifts from – or references to – Wren in Laud's accounts. With the exception of the book that Wren sent to the archbishop just before being translated to the bishopric of Ely in March 1638, there were no other gifts.[163] The accounts do reveal, however, that Laud baptized Wren's son in July 1639, a small piece of evidence that is not shown in any other source.[164] Equally, William Juxon, Laud's 'protégé' and successor as bishop of London – and lord treasurer from March 1636 – makes relatively few appearances, although the rather endearing gift of a 'catt' in late May 1640 may have been a way of cheering up his archiepiscopal colleague during the controversy in Convocation over the new ecclesiastical canons.[165] What should we make of these cases? No doubt scholars wishing to downplay Laud's ecclesiastical prominence could use these examples – and that of Juxon in particular – as evidence of the archbishop's unimportance, but the fact that the pair saw each other almost daily, at court and on the privy council, probably meant that Juxon did not feel the need

158 For Laud and Owen, see *ibid.*, p. 80.

159 *WWL*, III, 287.

160 For a discussion, see Davies, *Caroline captivity*, pp. 270–1.

161 Fos. 25r, 31r, 147r.

162 Fo. 64r. Wren meted out 'extensive censures' to clergy who refused to read the book of sports during divine service and implemented Laud's metropolitical directives relating to the receiving of communion and the communion table with 'unparalleled vigour'. Davies, *Caroline captivity*, pp. 188, 219. For Laud's *rôle* in Wren's appointment to Hereford in 1634, see Fincham, 'William Laud and the exercise of Caroline ecclesiastical patronage', 79.

163 Fo. 64r.

164 Fo. 106r. The child, William, was Wren's fourth son. He was Laud's godson and, as such, received a bequest of £100 from the archbishop on his death; *WWL*, IV, 448.

165 Fos. 6v, 10r, 40r, 64r, 129r.

regularly to ingratiate himself with his ecclesiastical superior.[166] As for Wren, his vigour in carrying out royal and archiepiscopal instructions may have reduced the need for him to make any further effort to seek approval or advancement.

It is now well-established that, despite having no formal authority outside England, Laud's reach extended beyond the English borders. This is borne out by the occasional gifts he received from Scottish and Irish prelates – Patrick Lindsay, archbishop of Glasgow; Walter Whitford, bishop of Brechin; and John Bramhall, bishop of Derry.[167] The isolated gifts from Whitford and Lindsay, sent in March 1636 and January 1637 respectively, were received at a time when two flagship Scottish ecclesiastical policies in which Laud played a significant *rôle* were being finalized: the 1636 canons and the 1637 prayer book.[168] If their one-off gifts bear witness to a specific working relationship at a given time, Bramhall's offerings, which are scarcely more frequent, were given in the context of a much more established and well-documented ongoing professional collaboration. Bramhall's correspondence with Laud and Thomas Wentworth, the lord deputy of Ireland, bears witness to the fact that all three of them worked tirelessly from the mid-1630s onwards to reform the Irish church.[169] Gift-giving as a form of politics was complex and is, therefore, open to ambivalent interpretations.

Laud's clerical connexions are perhaps less remarkable, and certainly less interesting, than his associations with the laity, and it is to this group of characters – namely, MPs, diplomats, courtiers, privy councillors, members of the royal household and the gentry – that we shall now turn, with a view to teasing out the unexpectedly broad range of Laud's reach. Again, gifts are of central importance in plotting the lay networks in which Laud was enmeshed, but other entries – particularly those which record visits to and from the laity – are equally telling. Although he received criticism from contemporaries for his 'uncourtly' attitude towards his neighbours, especially within the community of Kent, gifts were received from at least fifteen members of the Kentish gentry and nobility, including Sir Thomas Boswell, Sir Edward Boys, Sir Thomas Colepeper and Sir Matthew Mennes.[170] It is worth stressing, however, that these were occasional donations and none of these men participated in the annual New Year gifting process. At least forty former and future MPs also gave regular gifts, which may seem surprising, given Laud's known anti-parliamentary stance during the 1630s. While reasons of space prevent us from giving due attention to even a fraction of these men, a brief survey shows that they represented constituencies in the counties of Cambridgeshire, Gloucester, Hampshire,

166 Laud's patronage of Juxon has been disputed; see Brian Quintrell, 'The church triumphant?: the emergence of a spiritual lord treasurer 1635–1636', in *The political world of Thomas Wentworth, earl of Strafford*, ed. Julia Merritt (Cambridge, 1996), pp. 81–108.

167 Fos. 5v, 23r, 87r, 102r, 133r.

168 For Laud's *rôle* in the Scottish canons, see James, *Firebrand*, pp. 80–110, and in the prayer book, see *ibid.*, 92–7. Cf. John Morrill, 'A British patriarchy? Ecclesiastical imperialism under the early Stuarts', in *Religion, Culture and Society in early modern Britain*, ed. Anthony Fletcher and Peter Roberts (Cambridge, 1994), pp. 209–37.

169 The definitive analysis remains John McCafferty's *The reconstruction of the Church of Ireland: Bishop Bramhall and the Laudian reforms 1633–1641* (Cambridge, 2007).

170 Fos. 57r, 61r, 79r, 87r, 112r; Heylyn, *Cyprianus anglicus*, p. 505.

Hertfordshire, Huntingdonshire, Kent, Oxfordshire, Suffolk, Surrey and Sussex, as well as those further afield in Cornwall, Wales and northern England. Many of them served on local peace commissions too. They were, therefore, men of parts. Eight diplomats also make an appearance, including Sir Thomas Edmondes, Sir Robert Honywood, Sir Thomas Roe and Sir Henry Wotton.[171] Roe, for one, was a friend of Laud, but the others' associations with the archbishop are not evident elsewhere.[172] Reasons of space also prevent an in-depth analysis of each and every member of the privy council and court whose name crops up in the accounts, but some notable entries invite reflexion. It is perhaps unremarkable to find that Laud received a host of regular gifts from his colleagues on the English privy council – Edward Barrett, Lord Newburgh; Sir William Becher; Lord Goring, Sir Edward Cecil; Thomas Howard, earl of Arundel, Sir Thomas Jermyn; and Laurence Whittaker, for instance – and two of their Scottish counterparts – Sir John Stewart, 1st earl of Traquair; and Robert Douglas, Viscount Belhaven. Equally unsurprising is the absence of any gift from Sir Francis Windebank, the English secretary of state with whom Laud fell out in late 1635, although the '4 pheasants Lady Windebank' sent in December of that year may have been an attempt at a peace offering.[173]

Other entries confirm or enhance what we know about Laud's relationship with specific councillors. Gifts from – and visits to – Algernon Percy, 10th earl of Northumberland, are closely related to Northumberland's career progression, for example. In April 1636, shortly after his appointment as admiral of the ship money fleet, the archbishop received a gift from the earl.[174] The following year, when this commission was renewed, Northumberland sent further presents.[175] In May 1638, shortly after the earl was appointed to the prestigious post of lord high admiral of England, the first such appointment since Buckingham's assassination in 1628, a flurry of activity is recorded in the accounts, as the earl was 'gravely ill' and not expected to survive. Laud either visited him, or sent an emissary to Northumberland, on more than ten occasions in May.[176] When he had recovered, the earl sent venison to Lambeth.[177] While it is known that both Laud and Wentworth lobbied the king to promote Northumberland in 1638, the accounts suggest that he may have had a hand in the earl's earlier office as well. Neither is it clear, from other sources, that the archbishop went to such lengths to ensure that his efforts would not be in vain. Thus, Laud's accounts reinforce working associations and confirm the cessation of longstanding political partnerships, but they also reveal new dimensions to others.

More exceptional are the gifts Laud received from courtiers and councillors with

171 Fos. 4v, 6r, 9r, 15r, 25r, 31r, 33r, 34r, 44r, 46r, 47r, 52r, 61r, 89r, 102r, 120r, 129r, 141r, 144r. Diplomats also acted as couriers, bringing books and manuscripts from the continent back to Laud's library at Lambeth; fos. 96r, 97r, 99r.

172 Thanks to Laud's efforts, Roe's wife, Lady Eleanor, was eventually able to join him on his embassy in Hamburg. For her gifts to the archbishop, both before and after her departure, see fos. 68r, 81r, 129r.

173 Fo. 1v.

174 Fo. 6v.

175 Fos. 27r, 31r, 32r.

176 Fos. 71r, 72r.

177 Fo. 84r.

whom he shared no obvious friendship or political alliance, many of which were donated outside the New Year period. As such, they are perhaps better understood in the context of a search for affinity, than as a mere gesture. Sir Francis Cottington, chancellor of the exchequer, is a pertinent example here. Laud's personal antipathy towards Cottington, which was mutual, is widely known: in the archbishop's correspondence with Wentworth, for instance, he frequently disparaged Cottington as 'Lady Mora's waiting maid', pouring scorn on the chancellor's close partnership with Sir Richard Weston, the lord treasurer. And yet, from December 1638, Cottington sent Laud venison on six occasions.[178] In January 1640, Laud even paid him a visit.[179] If such donations were purely customary, one might expect them to have been recorded throughout the period of the accounts, but they were not. A possible explanation is that there was a suspension of hostilities towards the end of 1638, when Cottington and Laud were forced together in the interests of helping the king resolve the Scottish crisis.[180] Another example of a gift-giver whose relationship with Laud has been construed in negative terms is Sir Robert Heath, attorney general to Charles I until 1634, when he was removed from office.[181] It has been claimed that Laud 'engineered' Heath's downfall, ostensibly for his moderation in sentencing those accused in star chamber, but possibly also for his suspected 'puritanism', although this view has been challenged.[182] It seems doubtful that Heath's gifts demonstrate support for Laud's ecclesiastical policies, given that he was 'a strong anti-Arminian Calvinist', but what he did share with the archbishop was a commitment to royal authority.[183] Rare occurrences of gifts also yield tantalizing clues about Laud's political standing, while also highlighting, once again, the difficulties of ascribing certain motivations to a gift. In March 1638, for instance, a gift of '3 lamprey pies' arrived at Lambeth Palace from the godly peer, William Fiennes, Viscount Saye and Sele.[184] At the time, Saye – increasingly identified as an opponent of the crown's ecclesiastical policies during the 1630s and a leading member of the Providence Island Company, which has been described as a coalition of 'religio-political initiatives' operating in 'direct defiance' of the archbishop – had announced his intention to emigrate to one of his plantations in New Hampshire.[185] In the event, he did not go, but one wonders whether the pies were intended as an ironic parting gift to the archbishop whose religious worldview Saye so despised. It is impossible to know, but these examples also raise the possibility that pragmatism could override principle when it came to politics, as

178 Fos. 92r, 103r, 115r, 131r, 134r, 140r.

179 Fo. 120r.

180 James, *Firebrand*, p. 143.

181 Fos. 1v, 22r, 60r, 119r.

182 For example, at the trial of Sherfield in 1633. Trevor-Roper, *Archbishop Laud*, p. 111. For the debate on Laud's *rôle* in Heath's fall, see Thomas Barnes 'Cropping the Heath: the fall of a chief justice, 1634', *HR*, 64 (1991), 338–42.

183 Lawrence Reeve, 'Sir Robert Heath's advice for Charles I in 1629', *Bulletin of the Institute of Historical Research*, 59 (1986), 215–24, at 217. Both Heath and Laud were, however, committed to the rehabilitation of royal authority during Charles I's personal rule.

184 Fo. 65r.

185 Robert Brenner, *Merchants and revolution – commercial change, political conflict and London's overseas traders 1550–1653* (Cambridge, 1993) p. 275; David Smith, 'Fiennes, William, first Viscount Saye and Sele (1582–1662)', *ODNB*.

the donors may have recognized (albeit grudgingly) that Laud was a political force that one could not afford to ignore.

This may well explain the presence in Laud's accounts of gifts from merchants, mercantile organizations and livery companies. If, by the 1620s, some such companies – disheartened by James I's *largesse* towards his favourites – had begun to think twice about the benefits of customary gifting, this did not dissuade them from giving luxury items to Laud.[186] At first glance, Laud and the merchants seem incongruous bedfellows, given the archbishop's unwelcome interference in the religious activities of the chaplains of the Merchant Adventurers in 1630, for instance, or his attempt to influence the affairs of the soapboilers in 1634.[187] His associations with one such organization, the Merchant Taylors' Company, went back to his days as president of St John's College, Oxford. In 1632, he was appointed as a freeman of the company and in 1634, he helped them select a new headmaster, William Staple. However, in light of his adverse dealings with several of the leading guilds, one could be forgiven for thinking that the interests of Laud and merchants were incompatible.[188] Nevertheless, the list of mercantile companies and trade associations whose gifts appear in the accounts includes the obvious Merchant Taylors, but also the East India Company, the Eastland Company, the Levant Company, the Merchant Adventurers, the Company of Stationers, the Parish Clarks' Company *and* the Company of Soapboilers.[189] Almost without exception, these were sent at New Year, signifying a recognition of Laud's senior status.[190] Of even greater interest are the gifts Laud received from high-profile men associated with the merchant community, such as Sir Morris Abbot, Sir Christopher Clitheroe, Sir William Courten, Sir Nicholas Crisp, Sir Henry Garway, Sir Job Harby, Sir William Leachland, Sir Paul Pindar and Sir William Russell.[191] The notable feature of these gifts is that they were not always sent in December or January. The fact that they were offered by individuals and at irregular times of the year suggests that these particular donors, in going beyond the basic level of customary offering, saw Laud as a potential patron. This kind of gift-giving also speaks to the existence of a link – however tenuous it might have been – between Laud and leading members of the mercantile community, which has not emerged from other sources.[192]

Is there any evidence in the accounts to suggest the presence of a 'network' of

---

186 Heal, *The power of gifts*, p. 134.

187 Carlton, *Archbishop Laud*, pp. 116–17; Conrad Russell, *The fall of the British monarchies 1637–1642* (Oxford, 1995), p. 37; Trevor-Roper, *Archbishop Laud*, p. 221. It should not be forgotten, though, that Laud had some involvement with mercantile affairs, through his membership of the committee established in May 1634 to regulate the activities of the Merchant Adventurers; *CSPD 1634–5*, p. 9.

188 *Biographical register of SJC*, p. 141.

189 Fos. 1v, 21r, 22r, 57r, 85r, 58r, 92r, 93r, 113r, 119r, 120r.

190 Only the Eastland Company deviated from this practice, sending wine in May or June – fos. 71r, 103r, 129r.

191 Fos. 4r, 7v, 59r, 85r, 93r, 113r.

192 Merchants also appear in the accounts as couriers, bringing manuscripts and books from abroad back to the archbishop's library at Lambeth. For instance, George Carteret brought Laud '3 Arrabicke books' back from Morocco in Nov. 1638 and 'Captain Methall' brought manuscripts; fos. 87r, 126r.

lay Laudians? Several names are worth mentioning in this connexion, including Sir Robert Banastre, Sir William Maynard and Sir John Scudamore. All three men gave gifts to Laud during the 1630s.[193] Little is known of Banastre, sheriff of Northamptonshire from 1637, but his restoration of the parish church at Passenham surely attests to his personal preference for the 'beauty of holiness'. William, Lord Maynard – Banastre's son-in-law – is also known for his Arminianism and chapel-building.[194] Similarly, Scudamore – an old friend of Laud – renovated Abbey Dore in Herefordshire in such a way as to imply his inclination towards Laudianism, even if he was careful not openly to commit himself.[195] We have already seen that Sir John Bankes, Edmund Woodhall and Sir Henry Guildford gifted communionware to the archbishop. It is possible, therefore, that these men gave gifts not only in recognition of Laud's standing within the political and ecclesiastical community, but also because they approved of the measures he was taking to enhance the Church of England's ceremonial and sacramental attributes.

Much of the discussion above has suggested that gifts were sent to Laud as a matter of court etiquette; to thank him for his help in ecclesiastical advancement; to demonstrate support for his religious policies; or in recognition of his political significance. It would be misleading, however, to imply that all the gifts he received originated from ambitious careerists or as a political expedient. On the contrary, some gifts were unquestionably indicative of a deeper friendship. For instance, Sir Thomas Wentworth, his 'closest friend', sent him several gifts, and he also received regular presents from figures such as Sir William Cavendish, earl of Newcastle, and Frances Stuart, duchess of Richmond, whom he clearly regarded as his friends and *confidants*.[196] The extended family of John Buckeridge, Laud's earlier tutor and mentor, who lived close to Lambeth Palace, feature in the archbishop's New Year gift list and Laud himself returned the favour with an annual donation of £5.[197] Relatives – such as John Robinson and Edward Moreton also gave gifts, as did a number of Buckingham's former clients.[198] Among the latter were Sir Thomas Aylesbury, Sir William Becher, Sir John Hippesley, Sir Francis Leigh, Sir Robert Pye and Sir Peter Wyche. Their presence in the accounts may not, necessarily, reflect the fact that they shared with Laud a particular attachment to their former patron, but these men foreground an interesting point about how early modern 'networks' might be explained. Although all of these men may have been united by the fact of owing their earlier advancement to the royal favourite, they were also connected in other ways, both to each other and to other groups reflected in the accounts. For example,

193 Fos. 4v, 27r, 38r, 52r, 54r, 58r, 73r, 86r, 105r, 119r, 122r, 130r, 141r.

194 Peter Lake, 'The Laudian style', in *The early Stuart church, 1603–1642*, ed. Kenneth Fincham (Basingstoke, 1992), p. 169. Bannastre had the interior walls of the church decorated with paintings. Particularly noteworthy are those which flanked the altar; John Fielding, 'Arminianism in the localities: Peterborough diocese 1603–1642', in *The early Stuart church*, ed. Fincham, p. 106; Fincham and Tyacke, *Altars restored*, pp. 259–60; Nicholas Tyacke, *Anti-Calvinists – the rise of English Arminianism, c. 1590–1640* (Oxford, 1987), p. 219.

195 Ian Atherton, 'Viscount Scudamore's Laudianism', *HJ*, 34, 3 (1991), 567–96.

196 Fos. 14r, 27r, 35r, 67r, 82r, 87r, 114r, 122r; Carlton, *Archbishop Laud*, p. 146; *WWL*, IV, 443.

197 Fos. 1r, 1v, 4v, 23r, 58r, 92r, 93r, 94r, 118r, 119r, 142r, 145r.

198 Fos. 5v, 28r, 64r, 68r, 112r; Stafford Record Office, D1287/18/2/P/399/153.

Hippesley, Leigh and Pye were MPs; Hippesley was also a client of Laud's purported enemy, Francis Cottington; Pye was also a merchant; Wyche was a diplomat; and Becher was on the privy council. Of course, it is well known that influential men in this period carried out multiple functions and that their actions must be appraised in a range of socio-political contexts, but the point bears retelling if we are to make any sense of Laud's account at all.

A final word on gifts will bring matters to a close. As we have seen, the archbishop was the recipient of a huge range of gifts for the duration of the accounts, when he was at the height of his power, but these gifts ceased instantaneously in mid-December 1640, when he was accused of high treason in the House of Commons.[199] This dramatic change in his personal fortunes came at a time of year when, ordinarily, a steady flow of fruit, cakes, pies, wine, spices, meat and fish from the great and the good would be delivered to the gates of Lambeth Palace and it is immediately reflected in the household's accounts. Usually, the archbishop would receive around fifty gifts across the New Year period, but at the end of 1640, he received a mere six.[200] What is striking about this development is that almost everybody, including the king and the handful of people whom Laud counted among his friends, stopped giving. If we look briefly at the names of the people who did continue to send gifts after his imprisonment, we find an eclectic mix, which includes Edward Barrett, Lord Newburgh; William Merrick, a civil lawyer; Lady Elizabeth Norris; Richard Sterne, one of Laud's household chaplains; and Thomas Turner, a royal chaplain.[201] And, almost without exception, these gifts were 'one-offs', scattered across the year and not to be repeated. If most people declined to send gifts to the archbishop after his downfall, a few continued, but on a reduced scale, such as Walter Curll, bishop of Winchester, whose regular gift of a whole venison during every summer's hunting season was downgraded to 'halfe a buck' in July and August 1641.[202] Since gifts played such a material part in Lambeth Palace's domestic economy, their absence must have been keenly felt. However, quite apart from the effect that it had on the household itself, this stopping of the flow of bounty is indicative of both Laud's precarious personal position and the wider political context. Whether the earlier gifts were given as a customary gesture, a demonstration of open support or as a symbol of friendship, by December 1640, having anything to do with the archbishop – now a disgraced crown servant – was no longer politically expedient.[203]

---

199 James, *Firebrand*, p. 146.

200 For example, over Christmas and New Year 1638, he received fifty-two gifts (fos. 91r–93r); and for the corresponding period in 1639, he received fifty-seven (fos. 120r–123r). For 1640, see fos. 143r–144r.

201 Fos. 143r, 144r 147r, 152r, 156r, 157r.

202 Fos. 10r, 55r, 92r, 93r, 103r, 105r, 130r, 155r, 156r, 159r.

203 Fos. 118r, 119r, 120r, 121r.

Conclusion

The decision to publish this document was shaped by the belief that it has a lot to tell us about the nature of power and politics in seventeenth-century Britain. The object of this exercise has been not only to cast the spotlight on the archbishop himself, but also to consider how this document enhances current thinking on the nature of Laud's *rôle*, his relationships at court and his associations with people who were at the heart of the British polity.

While scholars are familiar with Laud in his capacity as Charles I's senior advisor, by drawing attention to this document we can now visualize the archbishop exercising his authority in an entirely new way – as the head of an élite household. The accounts suggest that he approached his domestic responsibilities with the same vigour, energy and attention to detail that he adopted in the sphere of high politics. And in the pursuit of royal service, although he came from a relatively lowly background, Laud nevertheless adopted many of the trappings of noble life. These insights add nuance to the rather dull and pedantic reputation which he has earned in the centuries since his death.[204]

The value of the document extends far beyond the confines of the household, however. By showing that material objects can tell us a great deal about political power, the archbishop's accounts provide a new prism through which to view his relationships and associations with people. These are of paramount importance because, in the early modern period, when the organs of governmental bureaucracy were in their infancy, politics was personal, rather than institutional. Indeed, members of every conceivable political interest group can be found in the document – episcopal, clerical, parliamentary, diplomatic, conciliar, aristocratic, courtier and mercantile – which conveys the clear impression that the archbishop was part of an extensive and multifaceted human web. Of course, in view of his ecclesiastical status, some of these are to be expected, but others speak to the existence of overlapping networks of interest, whether political, religious, official, informal or personal. Such details remind us that, while Laud's formal jurisdiction was confined to the church, he was nevertheless viewed as a political force to be reckoned with, even for colleagues at court and in council who found him a difficult colleague. Connexions with people are also relevant in the context of Laud's spectacular fall from grace in late 1640: specifically, the claim that one of the reasons for the archbishop's abandonment was that he had failed to spend sufficient time and effort on building alliances and networks. This important document has proven beyond doubt that he was indeed abandoned, both by his royal master, Charles I, and others. What is has also shown us, however, is that while it may well be true that Laud 'did court persons too little', it is absolutely not the case that they failed to 'court' him.[205]

204 Trevor-Roper, *Archbishop Laud*, p. 305.
205 Clarendon, *History*, I, 132.

THE ACCOUNTS

The household accounts of William Laud, archbishop of Canterbury, December 1635 to January 1642

Incipit Anno
Decemb[er] 18 Ano Dm 1635

	l	s	d
[fo. 1r]			
Inprimis for 2 lambes from the Bishop of Oxon*[1]	0	3	6
for a tun of claret wine from Sir Dudley Diggs*	1	2	0
to the poore at Croydon	5	0	0
Item to the poore at Lambeth	20	0	0
Item to the prisons	3	0	0
Item for pheasants and cheeses	0	3	0
Item for holly and bay	0	3	9
Item to Dr Warners* man with plate	1	0	0
Item for 2 sugar loaves Dr Fuller*	0	3	0
Item to the Bishopp of Herefords* man plate[2]	3	0	0
Item to the gardner at Lambeth	0	5	6
Item to the bargemen	1	5	0
Item for 2 grosse of trenchers†	0	12	0
Item for pipkins† and pom[an]dres†	0	3	0
Item to Palmer* for broomes	0	4	0
Item for 12 bush[els]† of oates for the coach horses	1	2	4
Item for a bush[el]† of beanes	0	3	4
Item for 12 bush[els]† of oates for the geldings	1	4	0
Item for naylinge	0	1	8
Item spent in the kitchen this week ut patet p[er] libr[um][3]	25	18	2[4]

Decemb[er] 25 1635

Item for the coachmakers mens box	0	5	0
Item for the smiths mens box	0	5	0
Item to the harnessmakers box	0	2	0
Item to the locksmiths box	0	2	0

---

1 In Sept. 1635, shortly before receiving this gift, Laud had visited John Bancroft* at Cuddesdon, Oxford, where the latter had recently completed the building of a new bishop's palace; *WWL*, III, 224.

2 Theophilus Field*, nominated to the bishopric of Hereford on 7 Dec. 1635. This is the only gift from Field recorded in the accounts.

3 A literal translation of this phrase, which appears throughout the manuscript, is 'as is clear from the book'. A modernized understanding of it would perhaps be 'all paid and accounted for here'.

4 On 14 Dec., Laud received an impromptu visit at Lambeth from Prince Charles Louis, elector palatine of the Rhine and entertained him for dinner, along with 'my Lord of Dover' and William, Lord Craven. The prince, who was Charles I's nephew, had been in England since late November on a mission to secure the king's support for military action to recover the Palatinate. This week's kitchen expenditure may include the costs of entertaining the prince; TNA, C115/108 (N4) 8580; *WWL*, III, 225.

Item to the brewers box	0	12	0
Item to yr Graces shoemakers box	0	2	6
Item to Mr Buckeridges* mens box	0	2	6
Item for the weekly bills	1	0	0
Item for mending yr G[races] watch	1	5	0
Item for graynes for the fishe	0	1	6
Item to Mr Dell* for letters	0	10	10
Item to Mr Hart* for law business ut patet	4	2	6
Item to Mr Levinthrope* viii days boathire	0	3	0
Item to Mr Rollston* ut patet	0	6	6
Item to Sir Henry Martyns* man plate	1	10	0
Item for plate from the Turkey Merchants*	2	0	0
Item for plate from Mr Woodall*	1	0	0
Item to the Bishop of St Asaphs* man	1	0	0
Item to Sir Nathaniel Brents* man	3	0	0

[fo. 1v]

Item to Dr Manwarings* man	2	0	0
Item for plate from the Merchant Advent[urer]s*	2	0	0
Item to Mr Mattersheds* sone	1	0	0
Item to Sir John Lambes* man	1	0	0
Item to Dr Gwyns* man	1	0	0
Item to the Earl of Newcastles* man	1	0	0
Item to Dr Ducks* man	1	0	0
Item to Dr Reeves* man	1	0	0
Item to Mr Cranes* man	1	2	6
Item for a hynd and does from the Earl of Salisbury*[5]	4	3	0
Item for a doe from Mr Parkinson[6]	0	10	0
Item to 2 swans Dr Mountford*	0	4	0
Item for 2 does from Ford	1	0	0
Item for a cheese &c from Dr Googe*	0	3	6
Item to a poore man with verses	0	5	0

---

5 At the time of sending this gift, William Cecil, 2nd earl of Salisbury* was actively engaged in trying to prevent the removal of the earl of Cork's family tomb from the east end of Dublin cathedral. This initiative, which was being pushed by Laud and Thomas Wentworth*, lord deputy of Ireland, was to make way for an 'altarwise' communion table at the east end of the cathedral, where the tomb had formerly stood.

6 A positive identification of 'Mr Parkinson' remains elusive, although his gifts are recorded in the accounts on nine occasions, at different times of the year, until July 1641. It is possible that he was John Parkinson (*c*. 1566–1650), apothecary, herbalist and author of the 1629 publication, *A garden of all sorts of pleasant flowers ... with a kitchen garden ... and an orchard*, dedicated to Henrietta Maria. For this, Parkinson was given the title *botanicus regius primarius* by Charles I. An alternative identity for Parkinson is that he was 'Mr Parkinson of the Roles' to James I in 1613, although it is unlikely that (and not known whether) this latter Parkinson, who may have been the 'John Parkinson' admitted to Lincoln's Inn in 1618, was still alive or active in this office during the 1630s; *CSPD 1613–14*, p. 41, no. 67; *The records of the honourable society of Lincoln's Inn*, ed. William Baildon and William Paley (London, 1896), p. 180; Juanita Burnby, 'Parkinson, John (1566/7–1650)', *ODNB*.

Item for boathire for Mr Snaithe*	0	2	0
Item to the scullery mens box	1	0	0
Item for 2 sugar loaves and a doe Dr Crooke*	0	10	0
Item for 11 sugar loaves Marchants[7]	1	6	0
Item for 6 more from Brentwood	1	0	0
Item for 2 sugar loaves Mr Creswell*	0	2	6
Item for 2 sugar loaves and a lambe Mr Knight[8]	0	3	6
Item for 2 hogsh[eads]† of wine Sir Ro[ber]t Heath*	1	2	0
Item for 2 hogsh[eads]† of claret Earl of Cleveland*	0	18	0
Item for a woodcock pie Lady Styles*	0	2	0
Item for 4 pheasants Lady Windebank*[9]	0	5	0
Item for a sugar loaf Mr Buckeridge*	0	2	6
Item for a sugar loaf Reddinge	0	2	0
Item for fowle from Dr Sterne*	0	3	6
Item for Westfalia tongs† Dr Merricke*	0	6	0
Item for 2 lamprey† pies Sir M[aurice] Bartley*	0	3	0
Item for 2 turkeys Mr Seymour[10]	0	2	6
Item for 2 pheasants Mr Whitaker*	0	2	0
Item for 2 swans and 2 pheasants Sir Rich[ard] Harrison*	0	3	0
Item for a sallmon Mr Secretary*	0	5	0
Item for a lamb, 2 turkeys and capons, Sir Tho[mas] Grymes*	0	5	0
Item for 2 pheasants & 2 doz of puddings &c Lady Shelly[11]	0	6	0
Item for 2 lambs from Windsor	0	2	6
Item for olyves &c from Mr Wragge*	0	2	6
Item for 2 lamprey† pies Sir John Winter*	0	2	6
Item 2 pheasants Mr Morly[12]	0	2	6
Item to the bargemen this week	1	0	0
Item to Mrs Buckeridge* for a New Years gifte	5	0	0

[fo. 2r]

Item for a New Years gift for the Kinge[13]	40	0	0
Item to the househould ut patet[14]	30	4	6
Item for 12 bush[els]† of oates for the coach horses	1	4	0

7 It is not clear from which company this gift originated, since several mercantile organizations sent gifts to Lambeth Palace, including the East India Company*, the Levant Company*, the Eastland Company* and the Merchant Adventurers*.

8 Possibly 'Mr Knight the Registrar' of the court of high commission; *CSPD 1639–40*, p. 95, no. 54.

9 No further gifts from Lady Edith Windebank* appear in the accounts, probably due to the breakdown in relations between her husband – Sir Francis, secretary of state to Charles I – and Laud, in late 1635.

10 This is the first or two entries in the accounts for 'Mr Seymour', whose identity remains elusive.

11 See under Sir John Shelley*.

12 This is the sole entry in the accounts for 'Mr Morly', whose identity remains elusive.

13 Charles I received annual New Year's gifts of £40 from Laud for the duration of the accounts, the final gift being given in the week of 31 Dec. 1641.

14 Laud participated in the custom whereby senior officers of state rewarded the servants of the royal household with a gift, or payment, every New Year, for their services during the preceding year. For a discussion, see 'Introduction', p. xxviii above.

Item for a bush[el]† of beanes	0	3	4
Item for 13 bush[els]† of oates for geldings and colts	1	6	0
Item for shoeinge and naylinge the coach horses	0	3	10
Item for 12 broomes for the stable	0	2	0
Item spent in the kitchen this week ut patet p[er] libr[um]	30	17	1
Some of this fortnight and paid Januar[y] 11 1636	219	0	10

Januar[y] 1 1636

Inprimis for a pipe of canary a tun of claret Farmers Customes*	1	0	0
Item to 3 carriers and porters with it	0	19	6
Item for 4 sugar loaves Mr Turner*[15]	0	5	0
Item to Mr Ellis[16] his man	2	0	0
Item to Knight* for 3 days in lopping willows &c	0	4	1
Item to Pallmer* for broomes	0	4	6
Item to the bargemen[17]	1	7	0
Item for 12 bush[els]† of oates for the coach horses	1	4	0
Item for a bush[el]† of beanes	0	3	4
Item for 13 bush[els]† of oates for geldings and colts	1	6	0
Item spent in the kitchen this week ut patet p[er] libr[um]	28	11	9

Januar[y] 8 1636

Item for fowle from Dr Martyn*	1	0	0
Item a fresh sallmon Mr Secretary*	0	5	0
Item for boathire Mr Snaith*	0	2	0
Item to Mr Pearse[18] of the chappell	0	5	0
Item to your Grace for Dr Baskerfield*[19]	5	0	0
Item to Mr Dell* for his boathire	0	17	6
Item to Mr Browne* for a press for coapes and 3 frames for 3 pictures	0	19	0
Item for a coach Mr Levinthrope*	0	5	0
Item for Mr Squire*	2	10	0
Item for alteringe the harpe	4	0	0
Item for altering the case	0	15	0
Item for 2 pounds of stringes	0	8	0
Item for portages and boathires	0	7	0

15 Christopher Turnor*, lawyer. Not to be confused with Dr Thomas Turner*.
16 Possibly John Ellis, clerk of the chapel at Lambeth; LPL, TG1, fo. 28r.
17 Laud went to court several times over this Christmas and New Year period. On 2 Jan. 1636, for instance, he officiated at the christening of the newborn Princess Elizabeth, second daughter of Charles I and Henrietta Maria, born on 28 Dec. 1635; *WWL*, III, 225.
18 Probably Thomas Pearce, or Pearse* of the chapel royal.
19 In addition to *ad hoc* payments, a stipend of £5 was paid to the royal physician every Jan. for the duration of the accounts.

Item to the appoticary for this whole yeare ut patet	4	7	6

[fo. 2v]

Item for bringing cakes and cheeses &c	0	6	0
Item for boathires	0	1	4
Item to the gardner of Lambeth	0	11	7
Item to the bargemen	1	1	0
Item for 12 bush[els]† of oates for the coach horses	1	4	0
Item for a bush[el]† of beanes	0	3	4
Item for 12 bush[els]† of oates for geldings	1	4	0
Item for new shoeing the 6 coach horses at ii^{s}	0	14	0
Item for cutting the flappes from nayles	0	1	0
Item spent in the kitchen this week up patet p[er] libr[um]	25	18	9
Some of this fortnight paid Januar[y] 22 1636	90	16	2

Januar[y] 15 1636

Inprimis p[ay]d for your Grace taxes toward the shipping at Lambeth[20]	9	0	0
Item to Mr Badger* for binding books ut patet	0	19	10
Item to Mr Snaith* for hardwax glove sticks &c ut patet	0	6	10
Item for sweetmeats &c from the Lady Wake*[21]	0	10	0
Item to Mr Millers[22] ma[n] with a swan	0	5	0
Item for 2 pheasants from Mr Reeves[23]	0	2	6
Item for puddings &c Lady Shelly[24]	0	2	6
Item to the Counsell Chamber Keeper[25]	0	1	6
Item to the bargemen	1	0	0
to the gardner at Lambeth	0	7	6

---

20 This is the first of ten ship money contributions, which were usually paid for both Lambeth and Croydon. The final payments were recorded in Mar. 1640, not long before the opening of the Short Parliament. The levy, which was initially payable only in maritime counties, was extended across the country in 1635 and, thereafter, increasingly condemned as a prerogative tax – indeed, it is worth noting that it is referred to here as a 'your Grace taxes' – was eventually abolished in Aug. 1641; *Constitutional documents of the puritan revolution 1625–1660*, ed. Samuel Gardiner (Oxford, 1889), pp. 189–92.

21 By the time of this gift, Lady Anna Wake* was in considerable debt, some of which had been incurred prior to the death of her husband, Sir Isaac, former English ambassador in Venice, following arrears of expenses due to him. Her precarious financial position led to a star chamber case – of which she was 'keen to be free' in early 1636 – and this may have prompted the gift to Laud, as well as 'a great dish', given to the king around the same time; *CSPD 1635–6*, p. 143, no. 8, p. 249, no. 57.

22 This is one of only two entries in the accounts referring to 'Mr Miller', whose identity remains elusive.

23 This is the first of three entries in the accounts relating to 'Mr Reeves' who is also referred to as 'Mr Jo: Reeve'. A definitive identity remains elusive, but it is possible that he was 'John Reve', vice-principal of Hart Hall, Oxford; *WWL*, V, 193.

24 See under Sir John Shelley*.

25 It was not uncommon for servants at court to be given *ad hoc* payments or tips, either by Laud himself, or – as in this case – by his household servants.

Item to the gardner at Croydon	0	15	2
Item for 12 bush[els]† of oates for the coatch horses at ii^{s} ii^{d}	1	6	0
Item for a bush[el]† of beanes	0	3	4
Item for 13 bush[els]† of oates for geldings and colts	1	8	2
Item spent in the kitchen this week ut patet p[er] libr[um]	27	16	0

Januar[y] 22 1636

Item for bringing 2 box of herring from Yarmouth	0	12	0
Item for 3 pheasants from Mr Goddard[26]	0	2	6
Item for bringing a cake	0	1	0
Item given to John Mills*	1	0	0
Item for 5 pheasants Mr Chamberlyn*[27]	0	3	6
Item for a pipe of canary from the Comp[any] of Vintners*	1	0	0
Item for broomes and mopps	0	4	4

[fo. 3r]

Item to the bargemen	1	3	0
Item to the gardner at Lambeth	0	6	6
Item to the gardner at Croydon	0	9	6
Item for pitch for the graynrye	0	0	6
Item for a brawne Sergeant Hendon*	0	10	0
Item for 2 hares Sir Hen[ry] Mildmay*[28]	0	2	0
Item for boathire and Counsell Chamber Keep[er] Mr Snaith*	0	2	0
Item for 12 bush[els]† of oates for the coach horses at ii^{s} ii^{d}	1	6	0
Item for a bush[el]† of beanes	0	3	4
Item for 12 bush[els]† of oates for geldings	1	6	0
Item for naylinge the coach horses	0	1	0
Item for bleeding and drenching them	0	12	0
Item spent in the kitchen this week ut patet p[er] libr[um]	28	18	4
Some this fortnight payd Februar[y] 8 1636	82	7	10

26 This is the sole entry in the accounts relating to 'Mr Goddard', whose identity remains elusive.

27 There are several possible identities for 'Mr Chamberlyn'. He is unlikely to have been Sir Philip Herbert*, lord chamberlain of the king's household, since he is referred to as 'Lord Chamberlayne' elsewhere in the accounts. He may have been the merchant 'Mr Chamberlain', resident in London in 1636; or, he may have been Richard Chamberlain, clerk to the court of wards. On the other hand, it is possible that he was Robert Bateman, chamberlain of London from 1626 to 1643, who was a member of the committee responsible for collecting money to fund the repair of St Paul's cathedral, of which Laud was head; *CSPD 1633–4*, p. 442, no. 74; *CSPD 1635–6*, p. 226, no. 97; *CSPD Addenda 1625–1649*, p. 496, no. 94; *The correspondence (c. 1626–1659) of Dorothy Percy Sidney, Countess of Leicester*, ed. Michael Brennan, Noel Kinnamon and Margaret Hannay (London, 2010), p. 175; www.historyofparliamentonline.org/volume/1604–1629/member/bateman-robert-1561–1644.

28 At the time of this gift, Mildmay had just been appointed to work on a sub-committee of the treasury commission, of which Laud was the leading member, to regulate the production of gold and silver thread; *CSPD 1635–6*, p. 176, no. 10a.

Januar[y] 29 1636

Inprimis for apparell for yr Grace ut patet	2	14	4
Item for lyning the footmans cloak	0	13	6
Item for the fiermakers box	0	10	0
Item to Mr Dell* for letters	0	10	4
Item to Mr Cobb* for boathire	0	1	0
Item to the gardner at Lambeth	0	3	8
Item to the bargemen	1	11	0
Item for 12 bush[els]† of oates for the coach horses at ii^{s} iiii^{d}	1	8	2
Item for a bush[el]† of pease	0	0	0
Item for 13 bush[els]† of oates for geldings and colts	1	8	2
Item for naylinge coach horses	0	1	0
Item for 7 bits to the great saddles at v^{s} a peace	1	15	0
Item for 3 cabistones†	0	9	0
Item spent in the kitchen this week ut patet p[er] libr[um]	26	8	10

Februar[y] 5 1636

Item for bringing plate	1	0	0
Item for plate Mr Cooke[29]	0	10	0
Item for 2 lamprey† pies Gloucester	0	2	0
Item given at the Star Chamber[30]	0	3	6
Item for boathire Mr Snaith*	0	1	0
Item for a present of capons from Sir Charles Caesar*	0	6	0
Item for sweete meats and pies from the Lord Sherwood*[31]	0	6	0
Item to the bargemen	1	10	0

[fo. 3v]

Item to the gardner at Lambeth	0	2	6
Item for 12 bush[els]† of oates for the coach horses	1	6	0
Item for a bush[el]† of pease	0	0	0
Item for 12 bush[els]† of oates for geldings	1	6	0
Item for naylinge	0	0	10
Item for 19 broomes stable	0	3	2

---

29 This is the first of two gifts, received from 'Mr Cooke', whose identity remains elusive.

30 When he attended meetings of the prerogative court of star chamber – which took place on Wednesday and Friday mornings during law terms throughout the calendar year – the archbishop sometimes made *ad hoc* payments, in the form of a tip or donation, to porters, other household servants or the occasional pauper waiting outside the chamber entrance.

31 William, Lord Sherard* had recently brought a case before star chamber against Sir Henry Mynne (see under Lady Jane Mynne*), claiming that Mynne had slandered both Sherard and his wife, Abigail. In the same week that he sent this gift to Laud, he appeared before a tribunal in Westminster Hall convened by Philip Stanhope, 1st earl of Chesterfield, in an attempt to arbitrate between the two parties; *Cases in the high court of chivalry, 1634–1640*, eds. Richard Cust and Andrew Hopper (London, 2006), p. 257.

Item spent in the kitchen this week ut patet p[er] libr[um]	27	10	0
Some of this fortnight payd Februar[y] 19 1636	71	10	10

Februar[y] 12 1635/6

Inprimis to the gardner at Croydon for 26 bush[els]† of primrose at xii^d p[er] bush[el]† &c ut patet	1	7	5
Item to Pallmer* for broomes	0	3	0
Item to Mr Dell* for letters	0	13	0
Item for to G[eorge] Hodges* for drinkinge glasses and crewetts	0	8	8
Item to the bargemen ut patet	1	9	0
Item to the gardner at Lambeth	0	1	8
Item for 12 bush[els]† of oates for the coach horses at ii^s ii^d	1	6	0
Item for a bush[el]† of pease	0	0	0
Item for 14 bush[els]† of oates for geldings and colts	1	10	4
Item spent in the kitchen this week ut patet p[er] libr[um]	29	14	1

Februar[y] 19 1635/6

Item given Sir Marmaduke Lloyds*[32] man with sugar &c	0	3	6
Item for 2 lampr[ey]† pies Gloucester	0	1	6
Item for 4 more from Somerset	0	2	6
Item to 2 men to cleane wood 2 dayes a peece	0	4	4
Item for bringinge a brawn from Littlebourne	0	6	0
Item for boathire and spectacles	0	5	0
Item to Mr Watts* for cleaninge the moate and garden ut patet	0	19	0
Item for small nets and malt for the fishe	0	17	8
Item for 1750 quicke setts and for settinge them	1	0	6
Item to the bargemen this weeke	1	15	0
Item for 12 bush[els]† of oates for c[oach] horses	1	6	0
Item for a bush[el]† of pease	0	0	0
Item for 13 bush[els]† of oates for geldings	1	8	2
Item for 12 removes for c[oach] horses	0	2	0
Item spent in the kitchen this week ut patet p[er] libr[um]	27	18	5
Some of this fortnight payd Febr[uary] 25 1636	73	12	9

32 The week before this gift arrived, Lloyd had been granted the office of chief justice of Glamorgan, Brecon and Radnor; *CSPD 1635–6*, p. 200, no. 74a.

[fo. 4r]
Februar[y] 26 1636

Receaved for the consecration[33]			
12 bush[els]† of wheat at vi^{s}	6	12	0
For wood and coals	2	10	0
Item for 50 quarters of barly	55	0	0
Item for Mr Rose* at 22^{s}			
Item for 40 quarters from Mr Denn*	44	0	0
Inprimis given for bringing North Down ale	0	2	6
Item for a cake from Dr Layfield*	0	2	0
Item for a paire of galoshes† Mr Snaith*	0	3	0
Item to him for boathire	0	1	6
Item for bringing […]	0	1	6
Item for apples from the Arch B[isho]p of York* to court[34]	0	2	0
Item to the gardner at Croydon	1	3	0
Item for apples from Mr Barnard*	0	2	0
Item for sturgeon from Dr Willson*	0	5	0
Item to the gardner at Lambeth	0	9	2
Item to the bargemen	1	8	0
Item for 12 bush[els]† of oates for the coach horses	1	6	0
Item for a bush[el]† of pease	0	0	0
Item for 14 bush[els]† of oates for the geldings and colts	1	10	4
Item for naylinge	0	1	0
Item spent in the kitchen this week ut patet p[er] libr[um]	31	18	1

March 4 1636

Item to the kitchenman for bringing 52 quart[er]s of wheate ut patet at xiiij^{d} p[er] q[ua]rter from Mr Rose*	3	1	3
Item to the porter for carryinge it into graynary at iij ^{d} per q[ua]rter	0	13	2
Item for bringing herrings and salmon out of Scotland	0	6	0
Item for sturgeon from Captain Crispe*	0	6	0
Item for broomes and mopps	0	4	8
Item for Bunce[35] for all chardges	1	0	2
Item for the appoticarys bill p[ay]d	3	13	0
Item to Mr Browne* for a folding bedstedd	1	15	0
Item to Mr Dell* for boathire & like to Chichester &c ut patet	0	16	2
Item for a sundiall Mr Snaith*	0	3	9

---

33 Laud consecrated Dr Roger Manwaring* as bishop of St David's on 28 Feb. 1636; *WWL*, III, 226.

34 Although appointed to the archbishopric of York in 1632, Richard Neile* was a 'devoted Londoner' who spent much of his time in the capital; Andrew Foster, 'Neile, Richard (1562–1640)', *ODNB*.

35 This is the first of three entries in the accounts for 'Bunce', who was probably retained to provide occasional services at Croydon Palace. Bunce was also employed once to provide services during Laud's early imprisonment in the Tower.

Item for his boathire	0	1	6
Item to the gardner at Lambeth	0	14	2
Item to the bargemen this week	1	5	0
Item to Knight* for 4 dayes work about the slaughterhouse	0	4	8
Item to Rob[er]t George* for 5 dayes work about the house	0	5	10
Item for 2 fleeches of bacon from Mr Ramsey*	0	2	0

[fo. 4v]

Item for bringing lamprey† pies	0	3	6
Item for 12 bush[els]† of oates for the coach horses	1	6	0
Item for a bush[el]† of pease	0	0	0
Item for 13 bush[el]† of oates for geldings	1	8	2
Item for 24 removes	0	4	0
Item spent in the kitchen this week ut patet et p[er] libr[um]	26	14	6
Some of this fortnight payd March 15 1636	83	2	4

March 11 1636

Rec[eave]d for your Graces bill of impost	24	0	0
And for a hogsh[ead]† of claret Dr Goad*	5	0	0

Item given Mr Terringhams* man with Venice glasses	1	0	0
Item for a pie Mr Attorney*	0	2	0
Item for 2 pies Mr Job Harby*	0	5	0
Item for salmon and eels out of Ireland	0	10	0
Item for fishe Sir W[illia]m Curtane*	0	5	0
Item orrenges &c Sir Tho[mas] Roe*[36]	0	3	0
Item for herrings Lord Chamberlyn*	0	12	0
Item to Mr Buckeridge* for a newe beaver hatt and for an old one	4	17	0
Item for a fresh sallmon Mr Harfleet*	0	4	6
Item to Mr Snaith* for peares from the Arch B[isho]pp of York*	0	3	0
Item given for boathire (Temple)	0	2	6
Item to the gardner at Croydon ut patet p[er] bill[37]	2	4	8
Item to the gardner at Lambeth ut patet	1	5	7
Item to the bargemen	1	10	0
Item for herrings and stronge water† out of Scotland	0	12	0
Item for a fresh sallmon Mr Whittaker*	0	5	0

36 At the time of this gift, Roe was actively petitioning the lords of the treasury for several thousand pounds owed to him from the sale and purchase of jewellery on behalf of the king at least four years prior. Laud was one of the treasury lords, acting *in lieu* of a permanent successor to Sir Richard Weston, the previous lord treasurer, who had died in Mar. 1635. A new appointment was imminent, for details of which, see n. 46 below; *CSPD 1635–6*, p. 1, no. 5, p. 202, no. 94.

37 This is an Anglo-Latin phrase which appears frequently in the accounts and is taken to mean ‘all paid according to the bill’.

Item for a brawne &c Sir R[obert] Banister*[38]	0	2	6
Item for 2 barr[els of] oysters Mr Dayd*	0	2	0
Item for 12 bush[els]† of oates for the coach horses	1	6	0
Item spent in the kitchen this week ut patet p[er] libr[um]	24	1	8
For this quarter			
Payd the brewer for 24 hogsh[eads]† of viij^{d} & 7 hogsh[eads]† at vi^{d} beere layd in this q[ua]rter	46	7	0
Item for signing the bill of impost of xij tun at iij^{s} Mr Leachland*	1	17	0
Item for 1 hogsh[ead]† of canary wine i^{l} xviij^{s} ix^{d} for redd & claret to fill the vessells this yeare ut patet	25	0	9
[fo. 5r]			
Item for 3 bush[els]† of oates for swans and poultry this q[ua]rter	0	6	0
Item to the laundresse for soape, starche & ashes and washing besides wages	4	10	0
Item to M[is]tr[es]s Hoult* for this q[ua]rter	4	0	0
Item to Eliz Hoult* for this halfe yeare	2	0	0
Item for old Whaley* q[ua]rters rent	0	12	6
Item for the mole catchers q[ua]rt[e]ridge heare and at Croydon	0	8	6
Item to Morris* the smith for shoeing geldings &c ut patet	2	16	6
Item to the sadler ut patet	5	19	4
Item to the goldsmith for mending plate &c this yeare ut patet	1	1	5
Item for 60 ells† of fine ell† broad Gentish cloth for 6 paire of sheetes at ii^{s} vi^{d} p[er] ell†	7	11	0
Item for makinge & markinge them	0	6	0
Item for trimming a paire of old sheetes	0	6	0
Item for 24 dozen flaxen napkins ut patet	11	15	0
Item for makinge & markinge 12 doz of them at xij^{d}	0	12	0
Item for the other 12 doz at ix^{d}	0	9	0
Item to Tho[mas] Sadler* for a Turkey grogram† gowne for yr Grace ut patet	9	0	0
Some of this weekes laying out paid March 30 1636	105	19	9

Some total of this quarters expenses and laying out cometh to the some of ut patet

dcclxxxvj^{l}
xviij^{s}
vj^{d}

Adam Torlesse*

38 Shortly before sending this gift, Sir Robert Banastre* had been summoned to appear before the privy council for 'default of arms' in Lancashire, following his failure to sign the warrants for the payment of muster-masters in the county; *CSPD 1635*, p. 529, no. 37b; *CSPD 1636–7*, p. 276, no. 45.

The Second quarter beginning March 18 1636

Rec 0–0–0

Inprimis p[ay]d for 2 lamprey† pies from Gloucester	0	2	0
Item for cheeses from Mr Smith[39]	0	2	0
Item for North Devon ale	0	1	0
Item for Mr Holt[40] Mr Cobb* &c for boathire	0	3	6
Item p[ay]d to Mr Dell* ut patet	0	19	6
Item to the gardner for seedes ut patet p[er] bill	1	2	10
Item to the bargemen ut patet	1	12	10
Item for allmond butter	0	3	0

[fo. 5v]

Item for 12 bush[els]† of oates for the coach horses at ii^{s} ii^{d}	1	6	0
Item for a bush[el]† of pease	0	0	0
Item for 13 bush[els]† of oates for the geldings	1	8	2
Item for naylinge coach horses	0	1	0
Item spent in the kitchen this weeke ut patet p[er] libr[um]	32	19	8
Some of this weeke payd March 30 1636	40	6	8

March 25 1636

Inprimis for bringing 2 dry stalls of books by water	1	0	0
Item for herrings and stronge water† from the Bishop of Glascoe*[41]	0	10	0
Item to Mr Rollston* & Mr Cobb* for boathire	0	2	0
Item to Mr Levinthrope* & Mr Holford* for boathires	0	2	0
Item for a p[air] of galoses† at Croydon	0	4	0
Item to Mr Snaythe* for boathires	0	2	0
Item to the gardner at Croydon	1	12	2
Item to the gardner at Lambeth	0	15	0
Item to the bargemen	1	6	0
Item for 12 bush[els]† of oates for the coach horses	1	2	0
Item for a bush[el]† of beanes	0	3	4

---

39 This is the sole entry in the accounts for 'Mr Smith', whose identity remains elusive, given the common nature of the surname. Indeed, there are references to 'Smiths' going by the name of Francis, George, John, Miles, Oliver, Ralph, Richard, Thomas and William in Laud's *Works*. Of these, Thomas Smith can be eliminated, as he was a household servant, having been appointed bailiff of Croydon manor in 1638; LPL, TK57, fo. 3; *WWL*, VII, 701. See also n. 275 below.

40 'Mr Holt', a household servant, appears on two occasions in the account book, but his identity and *rôle* remain elusive. He may well have been related to Elizabeth Holt / Hoult*, another servant.

41 Patrick Lindsay, archbishop of Glasgow*. This gift came shortly after all fourteen of the Scottish bishops had been sent a copy of the newly published Scottish canons, in which Laud had a significant, advisory *rôle*. For more on Laud, the Scottish bishops and the canons, see James, *Firebrand*, pp. 80–111; David Stevenson, 'Lindsay, Patrick (1566–1644)', *ODNB*.

Item for 11 bush[els]† of oates for the geldings and colts	1	3	10
Item for naylinge coach horses	0	1	2
Item spent in the kitchen this weeke ut patet p[er] libr[um]	25	11	6

Aprill 1 1636

Item to Pallmer* for broomes	0	4	0
Item to Mr Levinthrope* for a coach and boathire	0	6	0
Item to the barber and Mr Rollston*	0	3	0
Item for cumyn anys[eed] and hempseedes for pigeons	0	2	2
Item give to 13 prisons against Easter	3	0	0
Item to the D[uchess] of Buckinghams* porter	0	2	0
Item for bringing allmon butter	0	2	0
Item for lamprey† pies Ald[erman] Robinson*	1	12	0
Item to Mr Browne* for a sawe &c	0	6	0
Item to the gardner at Croydon	0	17	10
Item to the bargemen this week	1	11	0
Item to the gardner at Lambeth	0	12	0
Item to Mr Dell* for letters ut patet	0	12	0
Item for 12 bush[els]† of oates for coach horses	1	6	0
Item for a bush[el]† of beanes	0	3	4
Item for 12 bush[els]† of oates for the geldings	1	6	0
Item for naylinge	0	0	10
Item spent in the kitchen this weeke ut patet p[er] libr[um]	28	5	4
Some of this fortnight payd Apr[il] 15 1636	74	10	6

[fo. 6r]

Receaved xl in situ

Inprimis given the Earl of Cleavelands*[42] man with 3 lamprey† pies	0	2	6
Item to Dr Baskerfield* p[ayd] Mr Southes*	1	0	0
Item p[ay]d Mr Badger* for binding manuscripts &c ut patet	4	2	0
Item for sweeping the great chamber chimney	0	0	8
Item for sawing and cutting wood	0	2	0
Item to Knight* for binding bob[b]ins and cutting nettles &c	0	3	6
Item to W[illiam] Duckett* for apprell for John Cobb* ut patet	1	7	10
Item to him for the footman	1	6	6
Item to the gardner at Lambeth	1	0	4
Item to the bargemen this week	0	17	0

42 Around the time of this gift, the family of Thomas Wentworth, earl of Cleveland*, was brought into disrepute by the behaviour of Cleveland's son and heir, Thomas (*c*. 1613–65). The younger Thomas had just fought a duel at court – his second in a year – and for this, as well as some choice words to Philip Herbert*, lord chamberlain of the king's household, he was committed to the Tower briefly over the summer of 1636; *CSPD 1636–7*, p. 8, no. 31.

Item to Dr Baskerfield* & Mr Snaith*	2	0	0
Item to Mr Dell*	1	0	0
Item for a p[air] of cissors Mr Rollston*	0	2	6
Item for 12 bush[els]† of oates for the coach horses	1	6	0
Item for a bush[el]† of beanes	0	3	4
Item for 14 bush[els]† of oates for the geldings and colts	1	10	4
Item for new shoeing the 6 coach horses	0	14	0
Item spent in the kitchen this weeke ut patet p[er] libr[um]	28	11	4

Apr[il] 15 1636

Item for yr Graces offeringe	3	0	0
Item to the porter at Whitehall	0	1	0
Item to yr Grace for Mr Harbord*	13	0	0
Item for Mr Solicitor*	15	0	0
Item to the gardner at Croydon	1	9	4
Item to the gardner at Lambeth	0	10	0
Item to the bargemen	1	6	0
Item for mopps and broomes	0	5	10
Item to Mr Seldens* man and boathire Mr Snaith*	0	4	6
Item to Sir Tho[mas] Edmondes* man Mr Dell*	0	10	0
Item for letters & boathires	0	7	6
Item for 12 bush[els]† of oates for coach horses	1	6	0
Item for a bush[el]† of beanes	0	3	4
Item for 13 bush[els]† of oates for the geldings	1	8	2
Item for a sett of newe harnesses with a postilian saddle &c ut patet	18	5	6
Item for a bitte ut patet	0	16	6
Item for horses at Waddon[43]	0	0	6
Item to the pewterer for a newe pewter vessells & change of old ut patet p[er] bill	8	9	0
Spent in the kitchen this week ut patet p[er] libr[um]	32	18	6
Some total of this fortnight payd May 7 1636	44	11	6

[fo. 6v]

Rec[eave]d of Mr Rose* for 50 quarters of mault	50	0	0
Inprimis to the 2 children of the chappell & boathires	0	7	0
Item for 24 yds of tawney cloath for 16 coates at xi^{s} vi^{d}	13	16	0
Item for 2 ells† of taffety for 12 coates at xiij^{s} p[er] ell†	1	6	0
Item for 44 liverys to be paid in money at xx^{s} a peece	44	0	0
Item for bringing cyder	0	2	4
Item to the gardner at Lambeth	0	13	2

---

43 Waddon was within the manor of Croydon.

Item bringinge 67 Kent weathers† out of Kent ut patet[44]	2	15	6
Item to the bargemen ut patet	1	5	6
Item for 12 bush[els]† of oates for the coach horses	1	6	0
Item for a bush[el]† of beanes	0	3	4
Item for 12 bush[els]† of oates for the geldings and colts	1	6	0
Item for naylinge coach horses	0	1	3
Item spent in the kitchen this week ut patet p[er] libr[um]	34	10	6

Aprill 29 1636

Item given the Lo[rd] Chomlyes* man	0	10	0
Item for peares Lo[rd] Northumberland*[45]	0	4	0
Item to Mr Cobb* for boathires	0	2	0
Item to Mr Dell* for the Lo[rd] Treasurers* coach man &c ut patet[46]	1	2	8
Item spent in 13 journeys into Kent	3	5	6
Item to the gardner at Lambeth	0	11	9
Item to the bargemen this week	1	4	6
Item for Mr Watts* for cleansing the moate and the pitcher ut patet	2	4	0
Item for mendinge fishing netts	0	9	2
Item for a sturgeon Sir Hen[ry] Mildmay*[47]	1	5	0
Item for bringing a cheese La[dy] Venn*	0	2	0
Item for lamprey† pies Mr Dutton*	0	2	6
Item for 2 firkins† of sturgeon	0	10	0
Item to Mr Tompkins* man &c	0	2	0
Item for 12 bush[els]† of oates for c[oach] horses	1	6	0
Item for a bush[el]† of beanes	0	3	4
Item for 7 bush[els]† of oates for geldings	0	5	2
Item for removing and nayling coach horses	0	1	5
Item spent in the kitchen this weeke ut patet p[er] libr[um]	34	16	10
Some of this fortnight payd May 7 1636	150	10	5

---

44 These sheep may have been among the '74 weathers' provided for the King's entertainment at Oxford in August 1636. For a list of other livestock, food, provisions and money donated for the royal visit, see TNA, SP16/348 f.178.

45 In Mar. 1636, shortly before the receipt of this gift, Algernon Percy, 10th earl of Northumberland* had been appointed commander of the ship money fleet, an office to which he was again appointed the following year; *CSPD 1635–6*, p. 310, no. 81b.

46 William Juxon*, bishop of London, was appointed to the office of lord treasurer, on 6 Mar. 1636. The office, which had been left vacant by the death, in Mar. the previous year, of Richard Weston, earl of Portland, had been in commission ever since and Laud had been *de facto* head; *WWL*, III, 223, 226.

47 As master of the king's jewels, Mildmay's path crossed with that of Laud, who sat on the committee for trade, a sub-committee of the privy council. In mid-Mar. 1636, for instance – and not long before this gift arrived at Lambeth – Laud was in attendance at a meeting of the trade committee, at which Mildmay's name came up in connexion with the value of English silver; *CSPD 1635–6*, p. 291, no. 141.

May 6 1636

Inprimis to Mr Snaith* for boathires	0	2	6
Item to the Lo[rd] Privy Seals* porter	0	2	0
Item to the prisons at Ludgate	0	1	0

[fo. 7r]

Item for hearnshawes† from Ford	0	5	0
Item for Arabian books ut patet	12	7	6
Item for apparell for yr Grace ut patet	14	9	0
Item for Mr Squires* q[ua]rt[e]ridge	2	10	0
Item for 20 books for the Kings day & Gunpowder Treason[48]	0	15	0
Item for broomes and moppes p[ayd] Palmer*	0	6	3
Item for boathire Mr Rollston*	0	2	0
Item to the bargemen ut patet	1	10	6
Item to the gardner at Lambeth ut patet	1	2	2
Item for 12 bush[els]† of oates for the coach horses	1	6	0
Item for a bush[el]† of beanes	0	3	4
Item for 12 bush[els]† of oates for the geldings	1	6	0
Item for naylinge	0	0	7
Item spent in the kitchen this week ut patet p[er] libr[um]	29	9	8

May 13 1636

Item for a buck from the Lo[rd] Newburgh*	1	1	0
Item p[ay]d Mr Browne* for a pedestall sent to St Jo[hns] Coll[ege]	0	12	0
Item for casing 2 pictures sent thither	0	3	6
Item to Mr Rollston* for boathires	0	2	0
Item to Mr Badger* for books	0	15	6
Item for halfe a bucke from the Lo[rd] Chamberlayne*	0	7	0
Item for a bucke from the Earl of Thanet*[49]	0	12	0
Item to the gardner at Croydon	1	15	6
Item to the gardner at Lambeth	0	10	4
Item to the bargemen this weeke	1	15	6
Item for bookes, shoes &c for your Grace ut patet	2	0	0
Item to the sadler for a footcloth of vellvett ut patet	18	4	9
Item for 12 bush[els]† of oates for the coach horses	1	4	0
Item for a bush[el]† of beanes for geldings	0	3	4
Item for 24 removes & boathire	0	4	10

48 This is the only reference in the accounts to either of these important markers in the English Protestant calendar. The 'Kings day' was the anniversary of Charles I's accession, on 27 Mar. 1625; and 'Gunpowder Treason', celebrated, of course, on 5 Nov. each year; Cressy, 'The Protestant calendar', pp. 31–52.

49 Shortly before sending this gift, John Tufton*, earl of Thanet, had petitioned the privy council regarding potential damage to the salt marshes around Rye harbour, East Sussex, in which he and a number of other local gentry had a commercial interest; *CSPD 1635–6*, p. 396, no. 93.

Item for sending the geldings unto Ford	0	17	6
Item spent in the kitchen this week ut patet p[er] libr[um]	28	16	7
Some total of this fortnight payd May 23 1636	126	8	10

May 20 1636

Inprimis p[ay]d Mr Dell* ut patet p[er] bill	0	19	4
Item for a buck Sir Ma[urice] Bartley*	1	1	0
Item for gloves and a brushe for yr Grace Mr Southes*	0	6	9
Item to Mr Bridgemans* man with an horse[50]	3	0	0

[fo. 7v]

Item for broomes and mopps	0	3	9
Item to the bargemen	1	0	6
Item given at the Star Chamber[51]	0	4	6
Item for sugar and pepper from Mr Wooddall*	0	6	0
Item for a sallmon from Captain Crispe*	0	6	0
Item for 2 basketts for the kitchen	0	2	8
Item for a sacke of beanes kitchen	0	2	8
Item for haye for 12 horses at Kingstone one night	0	10	0
Item for p[ro]vinder† & ashes &c	0	11	10
Item for 12 bush[els]† of oates for the coach horses	1	4	0
Item for a bush[el]† of beanes	0	3	4
Item for 13 bush[els]† of oates for geldings	1	6	0
Item for naylinge	0	2	10
Item spent in the kitchen this weeke ut patet p[er] libr[um]	27	2	6

May 27 1636

Item to Sir N[icholas] Caryes* man with birds[52]	0	2	0
Item to Mr Snaith* for boathire	0	7	10
Item for a pheasant from Mr Holloway*	0	2	6
Item for an Amberly trout† Mr Barnard*	0	5	0
Item to Mr Vandikes* man p[ayd] Mr Dell*[53]	3	0	0

---

50 This gift was delivered by Orlando Bridgeman*, on behalf of his father, John Bridgeman*, bishop of Chester. The archbishop conveyed his thanks to Bridgeman for the beast in early July, writing that 'It is more then tyme to give you thankes for the Nagge you sent me, and to pray you hartily to excuse me, that I did it not by your Sonne when he brought me the Horse'; Staffordshire Record Office, D1287/18/2 (P/399/145).

51 See n. 30 above.

52 This is the first of four gifts from Nicholas Carew*, sent between May and Sept. 1636. At the time, Carew – a JP for Surrey – was in contact with William Dell*, Laud's secretary, over the illegal 'grubbing'† of land around Lambeth. Carew asked Dell to bring the matter to Laud's attention and to report back; *CSPD 1635–6*, p. 279, no. 75.

53 This payment to van Dyck's servant suggests Laud may have been still sitting for the portrait in May 1636, although it is not clear whether this was the first sitting; Michael Jaffe, 'Van Dyck studies I: the portrait of archbishop Laud', *Burlington Magazine*, 124 (1982), 598–607.

Item for 2 basketts for the pantler†	0	4	8
Item for bringing cheeses Geo[rge] Hodges*	0	5	0
Item for bookes, shoes, spurres &c ut patet for yr Grace Mr Snaith*	1	11	0
Item to Mr Dell* ut patet p[er] bill	0	13	0
Item for boathire Mr Southes* & Joyner*	0	2	0
Item for a beaver hatt for your Grace	4	10	0
Item to the gardner at Lambeth	0	10	10
Item to the bargemen this weeke	0	15	0
Item for haye for 12 horses at Kingston 1 night at x^{d}	0	10	0
Item for p[ro]vinder† ut patet	0	11	10
Item for 6 removes & naylinge	0	1	6
Item for 12 bush[els]† of oates for the coach horses at xxii^{d}	1	2	0
Item for a bush[el]† of beanes	0	3	4
Item for 12 bush[els]† of oates for the geldings	1	2	0
Item spent in the kitchen this weeke ut patet p[er] libr[um]	33	8	8
Item paid Tho[ma]s Sadler* for apparell for your Grace ut patet	24	8	10
Item for apparell for Jo[hn] Cobb*	6	15	0
Item for apparell for the footman	2	19	6
Item for 101 ells† of diapp† tablinge ut patet p[er] bill	25	3	6
Item for 307 yards of diapp† for 1 doz of napkins and 14 towells	27	17	3
Item for 44 yards of lockra[m]† for 28 ordinary towels at xxiij^{d}	3	7	0
Item for 2 peeces of cambricke† at viii^{s} p[er] ell† for 2 rotchetts	4	16	0
[fo. 8r]			
Item for 30 ells† of Holland† at iij^{s} viij^{d} p[er] ell†	5	12	9
Item for makinge 21 table cloths and cupboards at xiij^{d} a peece	0	7	0
Item for makinge and markinge 18 dozen of napkins of flax	0	18	0
Item for makinge 4 towells at iiij^{d}	0	1	4
Item for 18 lockra[m]† towells	0	1	6
Item for makinge 2 rotchetts	0	6	0
Item for 4 paire of gloves	0	4	0
Item for lace and tape for them	0	1	6
Item for markinge 12 handkerch[er]s	0	2	0
Item for makinge 12 p[aires] of socks, 6 capps and 2 p[aires] of boothoses	0	3	6
Item for makinge and markinge 12 pillowsleeves	0	2	6
Item for 30 ells† of cloth at xiiij^{d} for xij dresser cloths kitchen and for makinge them	1	16	6
Item for 24 ells† of cloth at xiij^{d} for 24 towells for the kitchen	0	17	6
Some totall of this fortnight payd June 8 1636	194	10	10

June 3 1636

Inprimis given to George[54] for his wages	5	0	0
Item for yr G[races] offeringe at Whitsontyde	3	0	0
Item to Mr Snaith* for bringinge wine glasses and boathire	0	4	6
Item to the gardner at Croydon	0	14	0
Item to the gardner at Lamb[eth]	0	19	10
Item for broomes	0	2	9
Item for bringinge cheeses	0	11	0
Item for 12 bush[els]† of oates for the coach horses at xxij^{d}	1	2	0
Item for a bush[el]† of beanes	0	3	4
Item for 11 bush[els]† of oates for the geldings	1	0	2
Item for nayling	0	1	3
Item spent in the kitchen this weeke ut patet x libr	30	4	1

June 10 1636

Item p[ay]d to Mr Dell* ut patet p[er] bill	0	17	6
Item to Mr Browne* for a frame for the K[ing] & Q[ueens] pitchures &c[55]	2	10	6
Item to Mr Snaith* for bookes, boathire, &c ut patet	0	18	8
Item to the gardner at Croydon	0	11	4
Item to the gardner at Lamb[eth]	0	16	5
Item for reed for the barge	0	1	0
Item for bringinge Mr Mustards* purristt mare Mr Dobson*	0	5	0
Item for 12 cartes for remove to Croydon at v^{d} and labourers	3	5	6
Item for hay for 11 horses at Kingston one nyght	0	11	0
Item for p[ro]vinder† for them	0	13	2

[fo. 8v]

Item for bleeding and drenching the coach horses	0	12	0
Item for new shoeinge them	0	14	0
Item for dressing a lambes foote	0	2	6
Item for 12 bush[els]† of oates for them	1	2	0
Item for a bush[el]† of beanes	0	3	4
Item for 12 bush[els]† of oates for geldings	1	2	0
Item spent in the kitchen this weeke ut patet p[er] libr[um]	31	17	5

For this quarter

Payd the brewer for x hogheads of viij^{s} & 71 hogsh[eads]† of vj^{s} beare layd in this q[ua]rter ut patet	37	19	0
Item to the wine coop for rackinge and hoopinge wine &c ut patet	7	14	7
Item for bottles & corkes for court	0	11	4

54 Either Robert George* or George Hodges*, both household servants.
55 For the gilding of the picture frames, see n. 101 below.

Item for a pewter salt spoons trenchers† & pipkins† ut pate	1	9	2
Item to M[is]tr[es]s Hoult* for this q[ua]rter	4	0	0
Item to Mr Squire* for this q[ua]rter	2	10	0
Item to the rent of the slaughterhouse	0	12	6
Item to the mole catcher for this q[ua]rter	0	8	6
Item to the laundresse for ashes soape & washing beside wages	4	10	0
Item to her for hoopinge tubbes flasketts† payles & washing bowles	0	18	6
Item to William Duckett* for howsehuld stuffe bought since December last ut patet	30	12	0
Item payd by him for Jo[hn] Cobb*	1	15	0
Item for the footman ut patet	0	19	10
Item to the sadler for x livery sadles with furniture & cloathe	8	16	0
Item to him for sadles bridles & other necessaryes ut patet	6	16	10
Item to Morris* the smith for shoeing bleedinge & drenching geldings ut patet	3	3	0
Item for 700 of deales† at 4^{l} 15^{s} j^{d} hundred of poles at iij^{l} xv^{s} joists xx^{s} 5 longe deales† x^{s} & for loading iiij^{s} in toto	40	19	0
Item for 6 cases of knives at xj^{s} the case	3	6	0
Item to Mr Watts* for clensinge the moat &c this q[ua]rter ut patet	2	7	0
Item for a newe nett and mendinge the old	0	11	2
Item for seedes & potts &c for the pigeons	0	2	6
Item to Jo[hn] Newton* for driving cowes, shoeing horses & washinge sheepe &c ut patet	0	16	8

[fo. 9r]

Item to Mr Watts* for broomes, mopps &c for this yeare	0	12	0
Some of this fortnights laying out p[ay]d June 27	245	16	10

Some total of this quarters expenses & layings out cometh to the some of
ix^{c}
lxxx^{l}
vj^{s}
vij^{d}
All even Ada[m] Torlesse*

The third quarter beginning June 17 1636

Rec[eave]d 100^{l} of Mr Barton*

Inprimis for a buck from Richmond	0	15	0
Item for 100 of carpes from Mr Evelyn*	1	5	0
Item to Sir Jo[hn] Shellys* man with 2 Amberly trowts†	0	5	0
Item to Mr Dell* ut patet	0	8	6
Item to the gardner at Croydon	0	5	6
Item for 12 bush[els]† of oates for the coach horses	1	2	0
Item for a bush[el]† of beanes	0	3	6

Item for 15 bush[els]† of oates for geldings	1	7	6
Item spent in the kitchen this weeke ut patet p[er] libr[um]	29	0	11
Item for a stagg from the Kinge	1	5	0
Item for a bucke Sir Jo[hn] Epslye*	0	12	6
Item to Sir Tho[mas] Roes* footman cherrys	0	2	0
Item to Mr Southes* &c for boathires	0	1	0
Item given away at Sir Tho[mas] Roes*[56]	2	8	6
Item for broomes & mopps	0	1	6
Item to yr Gr[ace] for Dr Baskerfield*	5	0	0
Item to the hieman for bringing 50 q[ua]rters of wheate from Mr Rose*	2	17	6
Item for carrying it into the graynary	0	13	6
Item to the gardner at Lambeth	0	7	6
Item to the gardner at Croydon	0	3	8
Item to Mr Badger* for paper & a manuscript	0	5	0
Item for a sallmon from Dr Hackett*	0	5	0
Item for bringing bacon & cheeses	0	3	0
Item for a bayl for 11 horses at Kingston on Friday	0	8	10
Item for hay for xj at Chersey 1 night	0	11	0
Item for p[rov]inder† & oslers†	0	11	10
Item for farriage at Sheppton	0	2	6
Item for 12 bush[els]† of oates for coach horses	1	2	0
Item for a bush[el]† of beanes	0	3	6
Item for 14 bush[els]† of oates for geldings	1	5	8
Item for naylinge coach horses	0	1	3
Item spent in the kitchen this weeke ut patet p[er] libr[um]	25	18	8
Some total of this fortnight p[ay]d July 7 1636	79	3	0

[fo. 9v]
July 1 1636

Rec[eave]d 0–0–0			
Inprimis given in the buttery at court by Mr Rollston*	0	12	6
Item for truches† from Mr Dade*	0	12	6
Item to the gardner at Croydon	0	9	4
Item to Constable* for 5 dayes work about the moate &c	0	5	0
Item for 11 horses haye at Chersey one night	0	11	0
Item for p[rov]inder† & oslers† &c	0	13	6
Item for farriage at Sheppton	0	4	0

56 Roe was keen to cultivate Laud's friendship and also invited him to stay at his house in Cranford, Middlesex, the following month, *en route* to Oxford for the royal visit. Laud agreed to stay on condition that Roe and his wife did not go to any trouble and on the understanding that the archbishop would 'be gone betimes in the morning, without eating'. If the Roes agreed to these terms, Laud promised to be 'more free … at my return'; *WWL*, VII, 265–6.

Item for 12 bush[els]† of oates for the coach horses	1	2	0
Item for a bush[el]† of beanes	0	3	6
Item for 13 bush[els]† of oates for geldings	1	3	10
Item for naylinge coach horses	0	0	9
Item for 6 broomes for the stable	0	1	0
Item spent in the kitchen this weeke ut patet p[er] libr[um]	24	1	10

July 8 1636

Item to the bargemen Friday	0	7	6
Item for a bucke Earl of Cleveland*	0	13	6
Item to the gardner at Croydon	0	9	0
Item to the gardner at Lambeth	0	9	0
Item for a p[air] of new bootes for the moate	1	4	6
Item to Mr Dell* ut patet p[er] bill	0	11	0
Item for bringing fruite	0	3	6
Item to the bargemen Thursday	0	7	6
Item to the hieman for bringing 40 q[ua]rters of wheate from Mr Denn*	2	9	0
Item for the carridge of it to Croydon by carts	1	15	10
Item for 12 horses haye at Chersey one night	0	12	0
Item for p[rov]inder† & oslers†	0	13	6
Item for farriage at Sheppton & Oatlands[57]	0	5	0
Item for 12 bush[els]† of oates for the coach horses	1	2	0
Item for a bush[el]† of beanes	0	3	6
Item for 14 bush[els]† of oates for the geldings	1	5	8
Item for removing coach horses	0	4	4
Item p[ay]d for a drumme for the stable	0	16	6
Item spent in the kitchen this weeke ut patet p[er] libr[um]	23	11	10
Some total of this fortnight payd July 20 1636	67	6	3

[fo. 10r]
Lambeth

Inprimis for mowing & making 47 acres of meadowe at vj^{s} p[er] acre	14	2	0
Item for the carridge of 77 loads of haye at xx^{d} p[er] load	6	8	4
Item for labourers to layet it into the barnes & raking after the carts &c ut patet p[er] libr[um]	3	12	6

Croydon

Item for mowing 64 acres at xx^{d} p[er] acre	5	7	6

57 Laud spent a few days at Oatlands Palace in early July. He travelled there from Croydon, where he had been since at least 23 June and returned to Lambeth around 12 July for three days. When a serious outbreak of the plague hit London, continuing into the autumn, the archbishop did not go back to Lambeth again until Jan. 1637; Staffordshire Record Office, D1287/18/2 (P/399/145); *WWL*, V, 144, 147, VII, 259, 307.

Item for making the 64 acres & laying the haye into the barnes ut patet p[er] libr[um]	8	4	6
Item to the carridge of 61 loads of haye into the barnes ut patet p[er] libr[um]	4	7	6
Item for plowinge 43 acres at vj[d] p[er] acre	13	1	0
Item p[ay]d for 4 bush[els]† of pease & for harrowing &c ut patet	1	11	10
Item for threshinge oates pease tares† & wheate ut patet	4	9	5
Item for bindinge strawe sould	0	6	6
Some total for haymakinge & plowinge &c p[ay]d July 20	61	11	1

July 15 1636

Rec[eave]d for 30 q[ua]rters of wheate from Mr Spratlinge* declare	62	13	6
Inprimis to Robin[58] for letters, a box and goinge to the Lo[rd] Treasurer*	0	6	0
Item for cheeses from Sir N[icholas] Carye*	0	1	0
Item for a bucke Lo[rd] Wimbledon*	0	15	0
Item to the gardner at Croydon	0	6	9
Item to the gardner at Lambeth	0	3	10
Item for a bucke D[uchess] of Richmond*	1	0	0
Item to the shoemaker for shoes	0	0	6
Item for 11 horses hay at Winsore one night	1	2	0
Item for p[rov]inder† & oslers† &c	0	19	9
Item for a light for the coach[59]	0	0	6
Item for 12 clawths† for the coach	0	2	2
Item for nayles for them	0	1	0
Item for naylinge coach horses &c	0	1	7
Item for broomes for stable	0	1	0
Item for 12 bush[els]† of oates for the coach horses at home	1	2	0
Item for a bush[el]† of beanes	0	3	6
Item for 13 bush[els]† of oates for geldings	1	4	10
Item spent in the kitchen this weeke ut patet p[er] libr[um]	24	12	10

July 22 1636

Item for cheeses from Sir Nich[olas] Carye*	0	1	0
Item for yr G[races] offeringe	3	0	0
Item to the bargemen	0	7	6
Item for 2 bucks from the B[isho]p of Winton*	1	5	0

58 This is the sole entry in the accounts for 'Robin', who was either a household servant or messenger.

59 Laud was already *in situ* at Croydon Palace by 15 July, where he stayed until 20 Aug., before moving to Oxford for the royal visit. When he entered Oxford, he travelled 'in his Coach wth sixe horses', so he may well have travelled in similar style en route to Croydon. Arnold Taylor, 'The royal visit to Oxford in 1636: a contemporary narrative', *Oxoniensia*, 1 (1936), 151–8.

Item for another from Mr Packenham[60]	0	12	6
Item to the gardner at Croydon	0	8	6
Item for horses meale & the expenses in the journey to Oxford	2	1	4
Item for bringing plumbs	0	1	0
Item for a graye nagg†	6	1	0
Item for 12 bush[els]† of oates for the coach horses	1	2	0
Item for a bush[el]† of beanes	0	3	6
Item for 14 bush[els]† of oates for geldings	1	5	8
Item for shoeinge & naylinge	0	1	5
Item spent in the kitchen this weeke ut patet p[er] libr[um]	26	12	8
Some total of this fortnight payd Aug[ust] 4 1636	75	5	6

July 29 1636

Rec[eave]d for wood sould att Norwood 99^{l} 9^{s} 10^{d}

Inprimis p[ay]d Mr Hart* for searches about the vicinityes ut patet	1	11	6
Item for a bucke from Richmond	0	15	0
Item for another from Sir Humfry Styles*			
Item for 2 trowts &c Mr Barnard*	0	5	6
Item to Pallmer* for broomes	0	4	2
Item to the gardner at Croydon	0	6	2
Item to the gardner at Lambeth	0	8	10
Item for a coate for the postilian	1	15	0
Item for a p[air] of bootes for him	0	12	0
Item to the smith for tooles	0	11	4
Item for shoeing geldings heare	1	2	11
Item for 12 bush[els]† of oates for coach horses	0	0	0
Item for a bush[el]† of beanes	0	3	6
Item for 11 bush[els]† of oates for geldings & 6 for Mr Secretaryes*	1	7	6
Item for naylinge coach horses	0	1	3
Item spent in the kitchen this weeke ut patet p[er] libr[um]	26	2	10

August 5 1636

Item to Dr Turners* man with cheeses	0	2	6
Item for 2 bucks from Farnham	1	5	0
Item for 20 partridges from Dr Howell*	0	5	0
Item to Sir Jo[hn] Tunstalls* ma[n]	0	1	0
Item to Mr Dell* ut patet	0	8	6

60 This is the sole entry in the accounts for ‘Mr Packenham’, whose identity remains elusive. A further entry refers to ‘Mrs Packenham’.

Item to the Lady Garden[er]s[61] man with muskmelons†	0	3	6
Item to the gardner at Lambeth	0	13	11

[fo. 11r]

Item to the gardner at Croydon	0	8	6
Item to Holland* for 5 dayes work about clay gravell beds &c	0	5	0
Item for a gelding bought Thomas Bright[62]	7	0	0
Item for 12 bush[els]† of oates for coach horses	0	0	0
Item for a bush[el]† of beanes	0	3	6
Item for 12 bush[els]† of oates for geldings	0	0	0
Item for a seeve & naylinge	0	1	3
Item spent in the kitchen this weeke ut patet p[er] libr[um]	27	14	4

For Oxford[63]

Item for 24 yards of ginger lynen cloth at xj[s] vj[d] p[er] yrd for 5 suits & cloakes ut patet	13	16	0
Item for 52 oz ½ of lace at ij[s] iiij[d] p[er] oz for them	6	2	6
Item for 7 yrds of velvett at xix[s] p[er] yrd for 2 jacketts	6	13	0
Item for bayes taffaty & lyninges & bringing them ut patet	20	2	6
Item for Jo[hn] Cobb* ut patet	1	18	6
Item for taffaty bayes & making a velvet gowne for yr Grace ut patet	7	10	0
Item for 4 shirts & 4 bands for Jo[hn] Cobb* & footman	1	15	4
Some total of this fortnights payd Aug[ust] 20 1636	132	12	4

August 12 1636

Inprimis to Rob[ert] George* for letters and comminge to Croydon[64]	0	4	6
Item for his boathires with letters 9 weekes	0	6	0
Item for Sir Henry Burtons* man with 2 swans	0	3	6
Item to the gardner at Lambeth	0	7	7
Item to the gardner at Croydon	0	7	1
Item to Mr Watts* for packthread† &c and for making a new nett ut patet	2	14	9

61 This is the sole entry in the accounts relating to 'Lady Gardener', whose identity remains elusive. A possible candidate is Rebecca, the wife of Sir Thomas Gardiner (1591–1652), lawyer and politician, who was recorder of London in 1636. Gardiner, who emerged as a staunch supporter of episcopacy in the Long Parliament, was specifically requested by Laud to act as counsel during his impeachment, a request which was turned down twice by the Commons. What renders this identity questionable is that Gardiner, the husband of the possible donor, was not knighted until 1641, some five years after receipt of this gift. An alternative identity is that she was the wife of Sir William Gardener of Peckham, knighted by Charles I at Hampton Court in 1626; *Knights of England*, II, 191; *LJ*, IV, 176; Alan Orr, 'Gardiner, Sir Thomas (1591–1652), *ODNB*.

62 This is the sole entry in the accounts for 'Thomas Bright', whose identity remains elusive.

63 The royal visit to Oxford to open formally the new Canterbury quadrangle at St John's College began on 29 Aug. The queen, king and his nephews – Princes Charles Louis and Rupert – attended until 1 Sept. Laud 'came privately' into Oxford with a retinue of 'forty or fifty horse', separate from the royal party, which travelled from nearby Woodstock Palace; *WWL*, V, 155.

64 Laud left Croydon Palace for Oxford on 20 Aug. and returned on 3 Sept.; *WWL*, V, 155; VI, 277.

Item for a bayl at Puttney for xj horses	0	4	8
Item for 12 bush[els]† of oates for the coach horses	0	0	0
Item for a bush[el]† of beanes	0	3	6
Item for 12 bush[els]† of oates for geldings	0	0	0
Item for a newe shoeinge 6 coach horses	0	14	0
Item for shoeing & bleedinge the trottinge geldings	0	2	6
Item spent in the kitchen this week ut patet p[er] libr[um]	30	11	6

[fo. 11v]
August 19 1636

Item to Mr Doylyes* man with 2 coach geldings	1	0	0
Item to Mr Dell* ut patet p[er] bill	0	13	0
Item for 2 buckes from Sir Fr[ancis] Lee*	0	13	6
Item for 12 bush[els]† of oates for the coach horses	0	0	0
Item for a bush[el]† of beanes	0	3	6
Item for 18 bush[els]† of oates for the geldings to Oxford	0	0	0
Item spent in the kitchen this week ut patet p[er] libr[um]	21	5	1

August 26

Item spent in the kitchen this week ut patet p Libr	8	8	4

September 2 1636[65]

Item for a pike from Mr Chune[66]	0	4	0
Item to Pallmer* for broomes	0	4	6
Item to the gardner at Lambeth for 3 weeks	1	3	7
Item to the gardner at Croydon for 2 weeks	2	2	2
Item for 12 bush[els]† of oates for the coach horses	0	0	0
Item for a bush[el]† of beanes	0	3	6
Item for 12 bush[els]† of oates for geldings	0	0	0
Item for 6 broomes for the stable	0	1	0
Item for removing & naylinge	0	2	2
Item for 3 loads of strawe laid in at x^{s} p[er] load	1	10	0
Item given Morris* the smith	1	0	0
Item spent in the kitchen this weeke ut patet p[er] libr[um]	25	12	4
Some total of these 4 weekes payd Septemb[er] 14 1636	100	6	3

65 On 1 Sept., Laud left Oxford after dinner and spent the night at the house of John Bancroft*, bishop of Oxford, at Cuddesden. His steward, Adam Torless*, and 'some few of my servants' stayed behind with Bancroft, while Laud continued on his journey to Croydon. At the 'earnest invitation' of Sir William Jones*, Laud slept at the judge's house in Henley-on-Thames on the night of 2 Sept., reaching Croydon Palace the following day; *WWL*, V, 155.

66 This is the sole entry in the accounts for 'Mr Chune', whose identity remains elusive.

Septemb[er] 9 1636

Inprimis given the B[isho]p of Oxford* 2 men with cra[y]fishe[67]	1	10	0
Item for a stagg from Theobalds	1	10	0
Item for a bucke from Sir Nich[olas] Carye*	0	15	0
Item for another from Sir Humpf[rey] Styles*	0	13	6
Item for a doe Earl of Cleveland*	0	10	0
Item for 2 lambes & fruite	0	5	0
Item for haye for 11 horses at Chersey 2 nights	0	14	8
Item for 6 bush[els]† of oates & 2 pecks† of beanes	0	18	4
Item for oslers† chamberlynes and coach	0	2	6

[fo. 12r]

Item for the gardner at Lambeth	0	7	9
Item for the gardner at Croydon	0	8	4
Item for farriage at Sheppton	0	4	0
Item for naylinge	0	1	0
Item for 12 bush[els]† of oates for the coach horses at home	0	0	0
Item for a bush[el]† of beanes	0	0	0
Item for 14 bush[els]† of oates for geldings	0	0	0
Item for 14 bush[els]† of oates for the waggoners	0	0	0
Item spent in the kitchen this weeke ut patet p[er] libr[um]	28	16	5

For this quarter

Payd the brewer for 24 hogsh[eads]† of viij^{s} 6 hogsh[eads]† of x^{s} & 120 hogsh[eads]† of vj^{s} beare this q[ua]rter	72	18	0
Item for M[is]tr[es]s Hoult* for this q[ua]rter	4	0	0
Item for Eliz[abeth] Hoult* for this q[ua]rter	2	0	0
Item to Mr Squire* for this q[ua]rter	2	10	0
Item to the mole catcher for this q[ua]rter	0	8	6
Item for the rent of the ground by the slaughterhouse this q[ua]rter	0	12	6
Item to the laundresse for ashes, soape, starch & besides wages for this q[ua]rter	4	10	0
Item for 170 doz of candles exchanged for 147 done & 2 l of tallowe at ij^{s} the doz for the exchange p[ai]d over in money[68]	2	15	6
Some of this weekes laying out payd Septemb[er] 28	126	11	0

67 This gift, received less than a week after Laud had stayed with Bancroft, arrived while the archbishop was settling back into Croydon Palace after his 'weary, expenseful business at Oxford'. Writing from Croydon on 12 Sept., Laud confided to Wentworth that 'the sickness increases, so as that we are like to have no Michaelmas Term'; *WWL*, VII, 285.

68 Used or 'done' candles and tallow were exchanged for new candles, the expenditure entered in the account book amounting to the difference between the value of those being received (170 doz.) and those received (147 doz.). Laud's household appears to have produced its own tallow, which is worthy of note, as it has been claimed that this aspect of the 'cottage industry' was neglected by archiepiscopal and other noble households in the early modern period. See Mertes, *The English noble household*, pp. 100–1.

Some total of this quarters expenses & laying out in howsekeeping &c cometh to the some of	642	15	5
All even Ada^m Torlesse*			

The Fourth quarter beginning September 16 1636

Rec[eave]d 0–0–0

Inprimis given Sir Symo[n] Baskerfields* man[69]	0	10	0
Item to Mr Bostock*	1	0	0
Item for a glister† &c for Jo[hn] Cobb*	0	5	0
Item for Mr Holford* for a poore woman at Epsom water†	0	4	6
Item to Mr Dell* ut patet	0	3	0
Item to the gardner at Croydon	0	6	8
Item for a stagg Sir Arth[ur] Manwaringe*	1	5	0

[fo. 12v]

Item for partridges pheasants from the Clerk of the Check[70]	0	5	0
Item for 11 horses haye at Sheppton 2 nights	0	14	8
Item for 6 bush[els]† of oates & 2 pecks† of beanes for them	0	18	4
Item to the oslers† and chamberlynes	0	2	0
Item for farriage at Sheppton	0	4	6
Item for light for the coach	0	0	6
Item for landing of horses at Waybridge[71]	0	3	6
Item for plate & washers for the coach	0	3	0
Item for removing 4 coach horses	0	3	0
Item for cuttinge a colt	0	3	0
Item for 12 bush[els]† of oates for the coach horses at home	0	0	0
Item for a bush[el]† of beanes	0	0	0
Item for 12 bush[els]† of oates for geldings	0	0	0
Item spent in the kitchen this weeke ut patet p[er] librum[um]	25	19	9
Some of this weeke payd Septemb[er] 28 1636	532	10	9

69 This payment, which suggests that Laud was visited by the royal physician, may well have related to an accident which befell him on 19 Aug., just before he left Croydon Palace for Oxford. Without providing details, the archbishop recorded in his diary that he was 'in great danger of breaking my right leg'. It may also simply be the case that Baskerville, who was knighted by Charles I at Oxford on 30 Aug., called upon Laud while he was in the locality; *Knights of England*, II, 204; *WWL*, III, 227.

70 There were several administrative posts within government and the royal household which held the title 'Clerk of the Check' (or Cheque). These included the clerk of the check responsible for keeping lists of household staff; a similarly entitled officer responsible for representing naval officers in the shipyards at Chatham, Deptford and Portsmouth; and a clerk of the check in the chapel royal. It is not clear which 'Clerk' sent this gift to Laud and it is the only such entry recorded in the accounts, but the latter seems most likely. In Sept. 1636, the clerk of the check to the chapel royal was one Thomas Day, who had been appointed to the post in May, on the death of the previous incumbent, John Stephens; Edward Rimbault, *The old cheque book or book of remembrance of the chapel royal from 1561 to 1744* (London, 1872), pp. 12, 48.

71 Oatlands Palace was in Weybridge, so this entry suggests that Laud was on his way to attend the king at the relocated court.

Septemb[er] 23 1636

Receaved 0–0–0

Inprimis for Epsom water† for Jo[hn] Cobb* and footman	0	4	0
Item to yr G[races] barber for 2 q[ua]rters	1	0	0
Item to the gardner at Lambeth	0	7	2
Item to the gardner at Croydon	1	5	2
Item to the sadler for the last q[ua]rter ut patet	2	10	0
Item to Morris* the smith for shoeing the last q[ua]rter ut patet	2	16	0
Item for haye for 13 horses at Winsore 2 nights[72]	1	1	8
Item for 9 bush[els]† of oates & a bush[el]† of beanes	1	9	6
Item for oslers† chamberlyns & coach	0	3	6
Item for 12 bush[els]† of oates for coach horses at home	0	0	0
Item for a bush[el]† of beanes	0	3	6
Item for 13 bush[els]† of oates for geldings at home	0	0	0
Item for removing 2 coach horses	0	1	4
Item spent in the kitchen this weeke ut patet p[er] libr[um]	35	19	8

[fo. 13r]
Septemb[er] ult 1636

Item to Dr Willsons* man with a great trout	0	10	0
Item to W[illiam] Duckett* for apprell for Jo[hn] Cobb*	2	0	0
Item for the footman ut patet	1	4	4
Item for bringing the weekly bills & letters from Lambeth[73]	0	3	0
Item to the gardner at Croydon	0	8	0
Item for 13 horses haye at Winsore 2 nights	0	19	6
Item for 9 bush[els]† of oates and a bush[el]† of beanes for them	1	12	0
Item for oslers,† chamberlynes & coach	0	2	6
Item for 12 bush[els]† of oates at home for coach horses	0	0	0
Item for a bush[el]† of beanes	0	3	6
Item for 13 bush[els]† of oates for geldings	0	0	0
Item for removing & naylinge coach horses & roapes	0	3	4
Item to Morris & Martyn for Leicester-Shire gold[74]	1	0	0
Item spent in the kitchen this weeke ut patet p Libra	31	19	5
Some of this fortnight payd Octob[er] 14 1636	87	7	1

72 This – and other similar entries below – indicates that Laud had lodgings at Windsor, during the court's temporary relocation to the castle during the serious outbreak of plague.

73 The administration of the archiepiscopal household continued during Laud's extended absence from Lambeth, with the delivery to Croydon of letters and other paperwork.

74 As Morris was a blacksmith and farrier, and Martyn was responsible for other equestrian-related duties, this was possibly gold which could be smelted to be used for spurs or other horse paraphernalia.

October 7 1636

Rec[eave]d 0–0–0

Inprimis given Mr Payes[75] man with sweetemeates	0	2	6
Item to younge Wright* of St Johns	1	0	0
Item to the prisons at Kingston	0	1	6
Item for an hynd from the Kinge	1	5	0
Item for x partridges from Mr Dade*	0	2	6
Item to the butler for hooping 4 sacks	0	2	0
Item for 4 coale basketts	0	2	0
Item for broomes & mopps	0	4	2
Item to the gardner at Lambeth	0	18	8
Item to the gardner at Croydon	0	9	6
Item for 15 horses haye at Winsore 2 nights	1	2	6
Item for 10 bush[els]† of oates & a bush[el]† of beanes	1	15	0
Item for oslers† chamberlynes & coach	0	2	6
Item for broomes for the stable	0	1	0
Item for naylinge	0	0	10
Item for 12 bush[els]† of oates for coach horses at home	0	0	0
Item for a bush[el]† of beanes	0	3	6
Item for 12 bush[els]† of oates for geldings	0	0	0
Item for 12 bush[els]† B[isho]p of Oxon*	0	0	0

[fo. 13v]

Item spent in the kitchen this weeke ut patet p[er] libr[um]	36	12	10

October 14 1636

Item to Nutt* the slaughterman for bringing 61 Kent sheepe out of Kent ut patet p[er] bill	2	14	6
Item for sending pewter to London	0	3	0
Item to Holland* for 7 dayes worke and a halfe about durt &c	0	7	6
Item for bringing the weekly bills this fortnight	0	1	0
Item for a doe from the Lo[rd] Newburgh*	0	10	0
Item for another Sir Humfrey Styles*	0	10	0
Item for looking to the cattell in the stubbs 3 weeks	0	10	6
Item to Jo[hn] Newton* for a p[air] of tankard to carry milke in	0	10	6
Item to him for hedging in the stubbs and parke &c ut patet	0	11	0
Item for moving the walkes that was grubb[e]d†	0	2	8
Item to the gardner of Croydon this weeke ut patet	0	14	8
Item for a p[air] of great bootes	1	5	6
Item for a bush[el]† of tares† pigeon	0	3	8

75 This is the sole entry in the accounts for 'Mr Paye', whose identity remains elusive.

Item for 12 bush[els]† of oates for the coach horses at ij^{s}	1	4	0
Item for a bush[el]† of beanes	0	3	6
Item for 12 bush[els]† of oates for geldings	1	4	0
Item for new shoeing the coach horses	0	14	4
Item for bringing x quarters of oates from Lambeth	0	9	2
Item for bleedinge coach horses	0	3	0
Item for farriage at Sheppton	0	4	2
Item spent in the kitchen this weeke ut patet p[er] libr[um]	31	15	5
Some of this fortnight payd Octob[er] 26 1636	88	6	2

[fo. 14r]
October 21 1636

Receaved for 5 quarters of the park wheate	10	4	0
Inprimis given for 6 cheeses from Dr Smith* and chardges at the Inn	0	7	6
Item p[ai]d for a cart goinge twice to Lambeth for wine and apples	0	15	0
Item to John Newton* for firing the harvest ut patet[76]	6	18	6
Item for mowing making and carrying of 5 loads of later month haye ut patet	2	8	10
Item for 10 bush[els]† of wheate for seed and for plowing the beane field ut patet	4	4	6
Item for lyninge and trimminge a hat for your Grace	0	7	0
Item to the shoemaker for 5 p[aires] of shoes and a p[aire] of galoshes†	1	7	0
Item to the gardner at Croydon	0	8	4
Item to the gardner at Lambeth	0	0	0
Item for 12 bush[els]† of oates for the coach horses	1	4	0
Item for a bush[el]† of beanes	0	3	6
Item for 17 bush[els]† of oates for geldings and colts at ij^{s}	1	14	0
Item for 2 bush[els]† for Sir Tho[mas] Roes* and Sir John Lambes* horses	0	4	0
Item for a lanterne for the stable	0	1	6
Item spent in the kitchen this weeke ut patet p[er] libr[um]	25	13	5

October 28 1636

Item for a doe from Sir Thomas Alsbury*	0	10	0
Item for another Sir Nicholas Carey*	0	10	0
Item for martlemas beefe† Lord Deputy*[77]	0	5	0

76 'Firing the harvest' was the act of burning the stubble, following the harvesting of crops.

77 In a letter to Wentworth dated 26 Sept., Laud anticipated the arrival of 'the excellent hung beef you have provided for me' and expressed disappointment that he could not share it with the lord deputy. Laud advised Wentworth, who had been at court in June and July, that if he should return to Ireland 'by the South', he should avoid staying in London because of the plague and proposed instead to accommodate him at Croydon Palace; *WWL*, VII, 289.

Item for the footman the last q[ua]rter	0	2	6
Item for 2 mens charges and hire horses to and from Ford	2	9	6
Item to Dr Turner* for 4 poore mens gownes	6	10	10
Item to Mr Dell* ut patet	0	5	0
Item to the gardner at Croydon ut patet	0	15	2
Item to Francis for a bayle for x horses at Puttney Satturday	0	6	8
Item for haye and p[rov]inder† for 14 horses at Hampton Court[78]	0	13	0
Item for mending coach harness	0	13	0
Item for 12 bush[els]† of oates for coach horses	1	4	0
Item for a bush[el]† of beanes	0	3	6

[fo. 15r]

Item for 17 bush[els]† of oates for geldings & colts at ij^{s}	1	14	0
Item for naylinge	0	1	3
Item spent in the kitchen this week ut patet x Libr	25	0	11
Some of the fortnight payd Novemb[er] 10 1636	86	10	5

Novemb[er] 4 1636

Inprimis to the sadler for 4 clothes for the 4 colts at vii^{s}	1	8	0
Item for 4 lether collars at xviij^{d} and 2 chasing halters	0	9	4
Item to the gardner at Croydon	0	4	4
Item to the gardner at Lambeth	0	18	7
Item to the bargeman ut patet	0	9	8
Item for broomes p[ayd] Palmer*	0	4	0
Item for a coale baskett for the hall	0	1	2
Item for 13 horses hay at viij for 3 nights	1	6	0
Item for 12 bush[els]† of oates 1 bush[el]† of beanes and others &c	2	1	0
Item for 12 bush[els]† of oates for the coach horses	1	4	0
Item for a bush[el]† of beanes	0	3	6
Item for 17 bush[els]† of oates for geldings	1	14	0
Item for removing and nayling	0	1	10
Item spent in the kitchen this week ut patet p[er] libr[um]	24	3	6

Novemb[e]r 11 1636

Item given to the 2 butteryes and seller at the court	0	15	0

78 In an 'unprecedented' move for an archbishop of Canterbury, Laud had secured permanent lodgings at Hampton Court by late 1633. In early 1637, he moved within the palace, occupying rooms which had been assigned previously to Lucy Hay, countess of Carlisle*. The countess 'was very willing' to hand them over to Laud, since she was rarely resident there herself; Str. P. 13/151; *WWL*, III, 224, VII, 329.

Item to Mr Snaithes* for galoshes†, l[et]t[e]rs and licorishe[79]	0	7	9
Item for a doe from Sir Tho[ma]s Edmondes*	0	10	0
Item to the gardner at Croydon for 12 trees ut patet	1	5	2
Item to the gardner at Lambeth	0	13	10
Item for the weekly bills 4 tymes	0	2	0
Item to Mr Dell* for Mr Badger*	0	10	0
Item for 13 horses haye at Winsor 2 nyghts	0	17	4
Item for 9 bush[els]† of oates and 3 pecke† of beanes for them &c	1	10	8
Item for 12 bush[els]† of oates for the coach horses at home	1	4	0
Item for a bush[el]† of beanes	0	3	6

[fo. 16r]

Item for 17 bush[els]† of oates for the geldings	1	14	0
Item for 2 shoes and 9 removes	0	2	8
Item for 4 lynchpins for the coach	0	1	0
Item spent in the kitchen this week ut patet	26	17	11
Some of this fortnight payd Novemb[er] 24	70	19	11

Novemb[er] 18 1636

Inprimis to Mr Herberts* man with deare shott	0	2	0
Item for St Clements night to the baker[80]	0	10	0
Item to the gardner at Lambeth	0	12	4
Item to the gardner at Croydon	0	6	9
Item for bringing sheep from Lambeth to Croydon	0	3	0
Item for a p[air] of boots for Francis[81] & for a hatt for his man	1	3	0
Item for 14 bush[els]† of oates for the coach horses at xxi^{d} p[er] bush[el]†	1	4	6
Item for a bush[el]† of beanes	0	3	6
Item for 15 bush[els]† of oates for geldings	1	6	3
Item for nailing coach horses	0	1	3
Item for 9 broomes	0	1	6
Item for strawe by Jo[hn] Newton*	1	8	10
Item for a coach geldinge bought of Sir Jo[hn] Tunstall*	16	5	0
Item spent in the kitchen this week ut patet p[er] libr[um]	26	4	4

---

79 In the early modern period, liquorice was used in both cooking and drinks, but was also chewed, like tobacco, as a way of staving off hunger. Joan Thirsk, *Food in early modern England – phases, fads, fashions 1500–1760* (London, 2006), pp. 35, 65.

80 Traditionally, the feast of St Clements was celebrated on 23 Nov. and a pudding of oranges and lemons was eaten. The archiepiscopal household celebrated this festival every year until Nov. 1641, by which point Laud was already in the Tower. For a discussion, see 'Introduction', p. 00 <xi> above.

81 Francis Loveday*, the gardener.

Novemb[er] 25 1636

Item given the B[isho]p of Oxons* 2 men	0	10	0
Item for bringing letters from Lambeth	0	1	6
Item for bringing a hogsh[ead]† of claret	0	2	0
Item for cleaving wood	0	1	0
Item to the gardner at Croydon	0	19	2
Item to the gardner at Lambeth	0	15	10
Item for a fee to Mr Solicitor*	5	0	0
Item for gloves for yr Grace	1	2	0
Item to the prisons and boathire p[ayd] Mr Dell*	0	2	6
Item for haye 13 horses att Winsor 3 nights	1	6	0
Item for 12 bush[els]† of oates a bush[el]† of beanes &c for them	2	1	8
Item for bleeding, drenching and shoeing Tonstall	0	5	4
Item for removing and naylinge the other coach horses	0	3	8
Item for a p[rov]inder† tubb for colts	0	3	9
[fo. 17r]			
Item for a p[air] of bootes	0	12	0
Item for 14 bush[els]† of oates for the coach horses at home	1	4	6
Item for a bush[el]† of beanes	0	3	6
Item for 16 bush[els]† of oates for geldings and colts	1	8	0
Item spent in the kitchen this week ut patet p[er] librum]	23	1	6
Some of this fortnight payd Decemb[er] 8 1636	89	3	2

December 2 1636

Inprimis to the prisoners at Kingston	0	0	6
Item for pheasants & letters Winsor[82]	0	2	0
Item to the Lady D[uchess] of Richmonds* keeper with a doe &c	1	10	0
Item for 13 horses hay at Winsor 2 nights	0	17	4
Item for 9 bush[els]† of oates & 3 peck† of beanes for them &c	1	12	4
Item for rough nayling them	0	1	6
Item for 14 bush[els]† of oates for coach horses at home	1	4	6
Item for a bush[el]† of beanes	0	3	6
Item for 17 bush[els]† of oates for geldings and colts	1	11	2
Item for removing and naylinge coach horses	0	4	4
Item spent in the kitchen this week ut patet p[er] libr[um]	27	10	7

[82] During the extended outbreak of plague in London in 1636, Laud had split his time between Croydon and whichever royal palace the king was occupying. On 3 Dec., while at Windsor, he received letters from Wentworth, which are probably those referred to here, to which Laud replied, from Croydon, two days later. He informed the lord deputy that he hoped that that the freezing weather would 'kill the infection at the root'; *WWL*, VII, 300.

Decemb[er] 9 1636

Item for 2 does from Ford	0	15	0
Item for a brawne Mr Geeves[83]	0	10	0
Item to Capt[ain] Crispe* his men Mr Dell*	2	10	6
Item for Mr Harbart* fee	3	0	0
Item to a blind minister	0	2	6
Item for a baskett for the silver plate	0	4	6
Item for a baskett for chickens	0	1	10
Item for sugar loaves Mr Harfleet*	0	5	0
Item for pheasants & mallards from Sir Jo[hn] Shelly*	0	5	0
Item for a hynd Earl of Salisbury*	1	5	0
Item for broomes & moppes	0	4	6
Item to the gardner at Lambeth	0	12	8
Item to the gardner at Croydon	0	14	2
Item for apprell for your Grace ut patet p[er] bill	7	11	0
Item for a suite & cloake &c for John Cobb*	6	8	2
Item for the footman ut patet	4	1	0

[fo. 18r]

Item for the 4 groomes coates ut patet	9	10	0
Item for the postilians coate &c	1	7	3
Item for haye for 13 horses at Kingston 2 nights	0	17	4
Item for 8 bush[els]† of oates & 3 pecke† of beanes &c for them	1	10	2
Item for 14 bush[els]† of oates for coach horses at home	1	4	6
Item for a bush[el]† of beanes	0	3	6
Item for 16 bush[els]† of oates for geldings and colts	1	8	0
Item for removing and naylinge	0	1	9
Item for oylinge the postilians leather coate	0	1	6
Item spent in the kitchen this weeke ut patet p[er] libr[um]	27	12	3

For this quarter

Payd the brewer for 6 hogsh[eads]† of x^{s} beere, 12 hogsh[eads]† of $viij^{s}$ & 73 hogsh[ead]† of vj^{s} beere layd in at Croydon this q[ua]rter	44	11	0
Item for a dozen of candles taken in at $iiij^{s}$ $viij^{d}$ p[er] doz	18	13	4
Item to John Newton* for 18 bush[els]† of oates for the poultry	1	11	6
Item for 3 bush[els]† of tares† for the pigeons there	0	11	0
Item for 11 bush[els]† of oates for swans	0	19	3
Item for 4 bush[els]† of light barley for the wild pigeons	0	10	0
Item for graynes for fish	0	3	6
Item for pease strawe matte for dryinge the fish at Lambeth	0	18	0
Item to Mrs Hoult* for this q[ua]rter	4	0	0

83 This is the first entry – of two – recording a gift of 'brawne' from 'Mr Geeves', whose identity remains elusive.

Item to Mr Squire* for this q[ua]rter	2	10	0
Item for the rent of the ground by the slaughterhouse	0	12	6
Item for the mole catchers q[ua]rt[e]ridge	0	8	6
Item to the laundress for ashes, soape, starche and besides wages	4	10	0
Item for hooping tubbs mending bringing and for ashe cloth strayners &c	1	9	6
Item for 2 doz of towells & 3 cottons for the kitchen and scullery	1	2	0
Item for a cyprus tree Mr Watts*	0	3	0
Item for plowing the walkes in the parke	0	8	8
Item for harnesses and collars for the cart horses	0	8	10
Item to the smith for shoeing since August	6	0	5
Item for worke in the kitchen and garden &c ut patet	0	19	8
Item for 6 loads of straw from Will Gouldwell[84] at x^{s} p[er] load	3	0	0
Item for 5 gross of trenchers† bought since Midsomer	1	15	0
Some of this fortnight payd Decemb[er] 22 1636	202	10	6

Some total of this quarters expenses and laying out cometh to ut patet — vj^{c} lvij^{l} viij^{s} o^{d}

All payd A[dam] T[orless]*

Some total of this years expenses and laying out cometh to ut patet p[er] libr[um] — iij^{m} lxvij^{l} xi^{s} vj

All even Decemb[er] 22 1636
Adam Torlesse*

[fo. 20r]
Incipit Anno
Decemb[e]r 16 1636

Inprimis given to the poore of Lambeth against xxmas	20	0	0
Item to the poore of Croydon	5	0	0
Item to the prisons in London	3	0	0
Item for 2 lambs from Mr Dale*	0	5	0
Item to Dr Paskes* 2 men	0	15	0
Item to Mr Dell* ut patet	1	1	6
Item for the weekly bills 4 tymes	0	2	0
Item to the gardner at Lambeth	0	7	0
Item to the gardner at Croydon	1	9	11
Item for bringing wine &c from Lambeth	0	7	0
Item for haye for 13 horses at Kingston 2 nights	0	17	4
Item for 8 bush[els]† of oates & 3 pecks† of beanes	1	9	8
Item for 14 bush[els]† of oates for coach horses at home	1	4	6
Item for a bush[el]† of beanes	0	3	6

84 This is the sole entry in the accounts for 'Will Gouldwell' whose identity remains elusive. A further entry relates to 'Mrs Goldwell' and another to 'Mr Goldwell'.

Item for 17 bush[els]† of oates for geldings & colts	1	9	9
Item for 16 new shoes for 4 coach horses	0	9	4
Item for nailing the other 3	0	0	9
Item for a cutting knife for hay	0	2	6
Item spent in the kitchen this week ut patet p[er] libr[um]	25	1	3

Decemb[e]r 23 1636[85]

Item given Dr Crooks* man with fowle	1	0	0
Item to the Lady Cades[86] man with turkey	0	2	6
Item for your Grace's offering	3	0	0
Item to the brewers mens box	0	5	0
Item to the smiths men	0	2	0
Item to Rob[ert] George* for letters into London and Cant[erbury] &c	0	5	0
Item for cleaving wood	0	1	6
Item to Mr Newdigates* man with Westfalia tongue†	0	5	0
Item for 2 lambs Dr Higgs*	0	5	0
Item for turkeys &c Mr Parkinson[87]	0	2	6

[fo. 21r]

Item for 2 does from Ford	0	18	0
Item for Westfalia tongue† from Dr Merricke*	0	2	6
Item for partridges W. Thomas[88]	0	2	0
Item for 2 brace of pheasants from Dr Burton*	0	5	0
Item for a lamb & 2 turkeys from Sir Tho[mas] Grymes*	0	5	0
Item for a doe from Mr Hugh May*	0	12	6
Item for another Mr Parkinsons[89] man	0	10	0
Item for a lambe and 2 pheasants from Mr Knight[90]	0	5	0
Item for fowle from Dr Sterne*	0	10	0
Item for a doe &c Sir Jo[hn] Shelly*	0	10	0
Item for 2 pheasants Mr Munkton[91]	0	2	6
Item to the scullery box	0	10	0
Item to your Graces barber p Mr Snaith*	0	10	0
Item more him ut patet	0	8	0
Item for broomes	0	4	6

85 Laud spent a low-key Christmas at Hampton Court, from where he reported to Wentworth that there was no news and that everything was 'still'; *WWL*, VII, 306.

86 Probably Lady Cade, the wife of Sir William Cade, who pursued an alimony case against her husband in the court of high commission in 1634 and 1635; *CSPD 1634–5*, p. 108, no. 3, p. 258, no. 1, p. 532, no. 1; *CSPD 1635*, p. 178, no. 3.

87 See n. 6 above.

88 This is the sole entry in the accounts for 'W. Thomas', whose identity remains elusive.

89 See n. 6 above.

90 See n. 8 above.

91 This is the first of two entries in the accounts relating to 'Mr Munkton', whose identity remains elusive.

Item for 14 bush[el]† of oates for coach horses at xxi[d]	1	4	6
Item for a bush[el]† of beanes	0	3	6
Item for 16 bush[el]† of oates for geldings & colts	1	8	0
Item for broomes & nailing	0	2	4
Item spent in the kitchen this weeke ut patet p[er] libr[um]	26	19	11
Some of this fortnight payd Januar[y] 10 1636	104	7	3

December 30 1636

Inprimis given Mr Solicitors* gent	1	0	0
Item to the Lady Mynces* 2 men with a cushin	2	10	0
Item to Mr Attorneys* gent with a gilt bowle	2	10	0
Item for your G[race]s New Year's gift to the Kinge	40	0	0
Item to the househould ut patet[92]	31	5	6
Item for plate from the Marchant Adventurers*	1	0	0
Item for 2 sugar loaves Mr Creswell*	0	2	6
Item for gold from Mr Pearse*	0	10	0
Item given Pitcher	2	0	0
Item to Pitcher for a fowling peece	1	0	0

[fo. 22r]

Item to Loveday* the gardner	1	0	0
Item to Mr Watts* 2 mayds	0	12	0
Item to the smith for shoeing	0	17	10
Item for 2 hogsh[eads]† of claret from the Marchant Taylors*	1	5	0
Item to Mr Daniel Harbyes* man with sattyn	1	0	0
Item for a cake M[is]tr[es]s Brigham[93]	0	5	0
Item for 2 candlesticks Turkey Marchants*	2	0	0
Item for 2 hogsh[eads]† of claret Sir Robert Heath*	1	0	0
Item for 2 hogsh[eads]† of claret Mr Jo[hn] Reeve[94]	0	10	0
Item for a gilt bowl Mr Wooddall*	1	0	0
Item 6 shirts 12 handkerchers Mr Henshawe*	1	5	0
Item given more by Mr Dell*	0	3	6
Item to the brewers of Putney's mens box	0	7	0
Item given to the needles	0	10	0
Item for bringing the hogsh[eads]† of sack from the Station[er]s*	0	10	0
Item for 15 horses haye at Kingston 2 nights	1	0	0
Item for 9 bush[el]† of oates & 3 pecks† of beanes for them	1	12	10

---

92 This payment, Laud's annual donation to the royal household's servants, was the highest such amount recorded in the accounts. See n. 14 above.

93 Probably Emilia Brigham, the widow of Richard Brigham of Lambeth, who had died in early 1636. Adam Torless*, Laud's steward, acted as registrar for the inventory of Brigham's goods, taken in June 1636 and certified in 1637; *CSPD 1635–6*, p. 547, no. 82.

94 See n. 23 above.

Item for 14 bush[el]† of oates	1	4	6
Item for a bush[el]† of beanes	0	3	6
Item for 17 bush[el]† of oates for geldings & colts at xxi^d p bush[el]†	1	9	9
Item for 12 shoes and 12 removes for coach horses	0	9	0
Item for a mopp for the coach	0	0	6
Item spent in the kitchen this weeke ut patet p[er] libr[um]	24	15	11
Some of this weeke payd Januar[y] 10	124	19	4

Januar[y] 6 1637

Receaved for meate and coals at the Consecration	vij		
Inprimis for 2 lambes and fowle from Mr Oliver*	0	5	0
Item for 12 partridges from Sir Henry Snellgrave*	0	5	0
Item for 2 lambs from Dr Higgs*	0	5	0
Item to Ald[erman] Garrowayes* man & letters Mr Snaith*	0	11	0
Item for mending your Graces watch	0	12	0

[fo. 23r]

Item for a tun of claret from Mr Job Harby*	1	0	0
Item to Mr Hores* man with gloves	0	1	0
Item to Mr Dell* ut patet	0	14	0
Item to Mr Mabb* for letters broomes and clearing the house[95]	1	5	8
Item for 4 fleetches of bacon from Dr Stanley*	0	2	6
Item for a doe from the Lo[rd] Privy Seale*	0	12	6
Item for cheeses from the Lady Mynce*	0	3	0
Item for pheasants Mr Whittaker*	0	5	0
Item for a brawne Mr Dade*	0	5	0
Item for turkeys, capons &c from the Bishop of Brichain*[96]	0	6	0
Item for 6 dozen of corks for bottles from the court &c	0	3	0
Item for the hire of 12 carts for the remove from Croydon	3	7	0
Item for 12 bush[el]† of oates for coach horses at xxi^d	1	4	6
Item for a bush[el]† of beanes	0	3	6
Item for 17 bush[el]† of oates for geldings & colts	1	9	9
Item for nayling coach horses	0	1	4
Item for a shovel for the stable	0	1	8
Item spent in the kitchen this weeke ut patet p[er] libr[um]	29	15	8

95 The 'house' (Croydon Palace) was being cleaned in readiness for the removal of the household back to Lambeth, which took place during the same week.

96 Walter Whitford*, bishop of Brechin, was among a handful of Scottish bishops supportive of crown policy in Scotland under Charles I and was particularly in favour of the new prayer book for Scotland, which, at the time of this gift, was still in press and would eventually be published in the late spring of 1637.

Januar[y] 13 1637

Item for your Graces offering at the consecration[97]	3	0	0
Item to your Grace for Sir Simon Baskerfield's* stipend	5	0	0
Item to your Grace for M[is]tr[es]s Batty[98]	3	0	0
Item to M[is]tr[es]s Buckeridge* for a new years gift	0	3	0
Item for partridges &c from Dr Warren[99]	0	3	0
Item to the gardner at Croydon	0	15	7
Item to the gardner at Lambeth	0	7	9
Item for all money of your Graces first fruits and fees	0	18	6
Item for bringing the weekly bills this year	1	0	0
Item to the bargeman ut patet	0	6	20
Item for a book M[is]tr[es]s Lucas[100]	0	5	0
Item to Mr Dell* ut patet	0	14	0
Item for light gold	0	5	0
Item to Mr Babb* for gilding the frames of the K[ing] & Q[ueens] pictures[101]	5	0	0

[fo. 24r]

Item to Mr Pallmer* for broomes & mopps	0	7	4
Item to the heathman for bringing 52 quarters of wheat from Mr Rose*	2	12	6
Item to the porters for carrying it into the granary	0	13	0
Item for 14 horses haye at Kingston one night	0	9	4
Item for 5 bush[el]† of oates & 2 pecks† of beanes for them &c	0	19	4
Item for 14 bush[el]† of oates for coach horses at home	1	4	6
Item for a bush[el]† of beanes	0	3	6
Item for 17 bush[els]† of oates for geldings & colts at xxi[d]	1	9	9
Item for nayling coach horses	0	1	0
Item spent in the kitchen this weeke ut patet p[er] libr[um]	26	1	1
Some of this fortnight paid Januar[y] 24	109	9	5

Januar[y] 20 1637

Rec[eave]d for fast money	12	0	0

---

97 Robert Skinner* was consecrated bishop of Bristol on 15 Jan. 1637. It has been suggested that this promotion was the result of Skinner's generosity in donating funds for the restoration of St Paul's cathedral; Davies, *Caroline captivity*, p. 77; Vivienne Larminie, 'Skinner, Robert (1591–1670)', *ODNB*.

98 This is the sole entry in the accounts relating to 'Mistress Batty', whose identity remains elusive.

99 Possibly Robert Warren*, Church of England clergyman.

100 This is the sole entry in the accounts relating to a gift from 'Mistress Lucas', whose identity remains elusive. Lucas has the distinction of being the only female recorded as having given the archbishop a book.

101 Babb, the carpenter and painter, had been employed at both Lambeth and Croydon prior to this. In Nov. 1635, for instance, he gilded 'his grace's arms with the see richly gilded over the chapel door' at Lambeth, and at Croydon, he painted 'the benches in the orchard, by the brook side, and in the bowling green'; *CSPD 1635*, p. 487, no. 9.

& of Mr Barton*	22	12	6
Inprimis to Dr Woods* man with sugar	0	2	6
Item to your Grace about money given to charitable uses	2	0	0
Item for a salmon Mr Creswell*	0	2	6
Item for pheasants &c Mr Doyly*	0	6	6
Item for a sugar loafe Mr Turner*	0	5	0
Item to the gardner at Lambeth	0	14	8
Item to the bargeman	0	5	0
Item to Rob[ert] George* for l[et]t[e]rs and work about the house	0	8	0
Item for 14 horses hay at Kingston 2 nights	0	18	8
Item for 7 bush[els]† of oates & pecks† of beanes &c	1	6	10
Item for 14 bush[els]† of oates for coach horses at home	1	4	6
Item for a bush[el]† of beanes	0	3	6
Item for 16 bush[els]† of oates for geldings & colts	1	8	0
Item for nayling coach horses	0	1	0
Item for 12 broomes for the stable	0	2	0
Item spent in the kitchen this week ut patet	29	14	0

[fo. 25r]

Item p[ay]d Mr Dell* ut patet	0	15	0
Item to Dr Lewes* man with pies &c	0	2	6
Item for boathire Mr Day[102] ut patet	0	1	0
Item for 2 lamprey† pies from Glouc[e]s[ter]	0	5	0
Item to S[i]r Tho[mas] Roes* man	0	2	6
Item to the gardner at Lambeth	0	6	4
Item to the gardner at Croydon	1	6	0
Item to the bargemen this week	1	5	0
Item for apples from Fulham[103]	0	1	0
Item to Mr Bemboe*	6	0	0
Item to the fire maker	0	10	0
Item for oysters from Dr Aylett*	0	2	6
Item for 2 cheeses Judge Jones*	0	2	0
Item for 14 bush[els]† of oates for the coach horses at xxi[d]	1	4	6
Item for a bush[el]† of beanes	0	3	6
Item for 17 bush[els]† of oates for geldings & colts	1	9	9
Item for bleeding and drenching the coach horses	1	1	0
Item for removing and nayling them	0	1	6
Item spent in the kitchen this weeke ut patet p[er] libr[um]	24	5	0
Some total of this fortnight payd Febr[uary] 10 1637	78	6	9

102 This is the first of two entries for payments to 'Mr Day' for boathire. Day seems not to have been attached to the archiepiscopal household, so was probably a hired waterman.

103 This may have been a gift from William Juxon*, bishop of London, whose episcopal palace was in Fulham.

Februar[y] 3 1637

Inprimis to Mr Wooddalls* man with sugar and pepper	0	6	0
Item to Mr Cobb* for boathire	0	3	6
Item to Sir Ant[hony] Vandykes* man p[ayd] Mr Snaith*[104]	1	0	0
Item to your Graces shoemakers men	0	2	6
Item to him for boathires	0	1	6
Item to the bargemen	1	5	0
Item to the gardner at Lambeth	0	12	7
Item for puddings &c D[uchess] of Richmond*	0	14	0
Item to Sir Tho[mas] Roes* man	0	2	0
Item for herrings from Yarmouth	0	11	0
Item for 14 bush[els]† of oates for the coach horses at xxi^{d}	1	4	6
Item for a bush[el]† of beanes	0	3	6
Item for 16 bush[els]† of oates for the geldings	1	8	0
Item for removing and nayling coach horses	0	1	6
Item spent in the kitchen this week ut patet p[er] libr[um]	28	7	8

[fo. 26r]
Februar[y] 10 1637

Item to Judge Jones* man with a fresh salmon	0	3	6
Item to the porters for carrying in 20 chald[ers] of sea coals at xxj^{d} p[er] chalder	1	7	0
Item for lyteridge at viijd p[er] chald[e]r	0	13	6
Item given unto Collyns[105] for his payment in sowing the w'land	0	10	0
Item for 100 dozen of candles taken in at iiij^{s} viij^{d} p[er] doz	23	6	8
Item to Sir H[enry] Williams* man[106]	2	0	0
Item for manuscripts Sir Jo[hn] Burroughs*	2	5	0
Item for the chappell & wages	2	10	0
Item to Dr Lewes* man &c	0	12	0
Item for sack & claret Company of Vintners*	1	10	0
Item to Mr Dell* ut patet	1	1	4
Item to the gardner at Croydon ut patet	2	0	0
Item to the gardner at Lambeth	1	0	9
Item to the bargemen	1	10	0
Item for a […] dictionary	0	10	0

104 This is the second of two payments to Sir Anthony van Dyck's man, an earlier payment of £3 having been made in May 1636. It is possible that this final payment was made on completion of the portrait. See n. 53 above.

105 This is the sole entry for a payment to 'Collyns', whose function within the household or community around Lambeth remains unclear. On this occasion, the payment relates to 'sowing' the fields, so he may have been a groundsman or other manual labourer.

106 This is the sole entry in the accounts relating to 'Sir H Williams' and probably refers to the recently deceased Sir Henry Williams*.

Item given away at the Star Chamber[107]	0	5	6
Item for making a paire of sleaves and for strings	0	1	6
Item for checkerd cheeses from Mr Hutchinson[108]	0	2	6
Item given a blind mynister &c	0	4	0
Item for 14 bush[els]† of oates for the coach horses	1	4	6
Item for a bush[el]† of beanes	0	3	6
Item for 17 bush[els]† of oates for geldings & colts at xxj[d]	1	9	9
Item for shoeing coach horses	0	1	5
Item spent in the kitchen this week ut patet p[er] libr[um]	27	19	8
Some total of this fortnight payd Februar[y] 21 1637	108	15	4

Februar[y] 17 1637

Receaved

Inprimis to Mr Solicitors* man with lamprey† pies	0	10	0
Item to him againe with 12 pheasants	0	12	6
Item to Mr Subdeane* p[ayd] Mr Holt[109]	2	0	0
Item given to Eliz[abeth] Hoult*	5	0	0
Item to the porters at the garden stayres	0	12	6
Item to the bargemen this weeke	1	5	0
Item to the gardner at Lambeth	2	14	3
Item to Palmer* for broomes	0	5	0
Item for 14 bush[els]† of oates for the coach horses	1	4	6

[fo. 27r]

Item for a bush[el]† of beanes	0	3	6
Item for 16 bush[els]† of oates for geldings	1	8	0
Item for nayling coach horses	0	1	0
Item spent in the kitchen this week ut patet p[er] libr[um]	28	14	7

Februar[y] 24 1637

Item for 12 cheeses from Sir Philip Manwaringe*	0	7	0
Item for 2 lamprey† pies Mr Subdean*	0	2	0
Item p[ay]d for shipping money for Croydon[110]	4	0	0
Item p[ay]d for shipping money for Lambeth[111]	9	0	0
Item for bringing a crozier staff from the Lo[rd] Marshall*	0	5	0
Item for 4 cheeses Lady Savage*	0	6	0

107 See n. 30 above.
108 Probably William Hutchinson*, Church of England clergyman.
109 See n. 40 above.
110 See n. 20 above.
111 See n. 20 above.

Item to a messenger from court	0	2	6
Item for pheasants and partridges from Dr Mountford*	0	3	6
Item to Mr Dell* for herrings &c ut patet	1	15	0
Item for oyle from Mr Job Harby*	0	13	0
Item to the gardner at Croydon	1	0	10
Item to the gardner at Lambeth	1	13	0
Item to the bargemen	1	9	0
Item for a fresh salmon Mr Harfleet*	0	6	0
Item 2 cheeses Lord Harbert*	0	5	0
Item for fish Lord Deputy*[112]	0	6	0
Item to the waterman for Scottish herrings	0	2	6
Item for 14 bush[els]† of oates for coach horses at xxi^{d}	1	4	6
Item for a bush[el]† of beanes	0	3	6
Item for 17 bush[els]† of oates for geldings & colts	1	9	9
Item for 16 shoes & 12 removes for coach horses	0	11	4
Item spent in the kitchen this week ut patet p[er] libr[um]	27	19	2
Some total of this fortnight payd March 7 1637	97	15	5

March 3 1637

Inprimis given to the Earl of Northumberlands* gent	0	10	0
Item to Stephen[113] for combes &c	0	10	0
Item given a schollar for Gresham Colledge	2	0	0
Item to Mr Pearse* for wine from Lord Scudamore*	1	0	0
Item for a cake from Mr Powell[114]	0	2	6
Item for a veal Mr Farrant[115]	0	10	0
Item for fish out of Ireland[116]	0	12	6

---

112 Writing to Wentworth on 5 Apr., Laud thanked the lord deputy for 'the fish you sent … [which] proved very good'; *WWL*, VII, 331.

113 This is the first entry in the accounts for 'Stephen', who was paid on six occasions between Mar. 1636 and Mar. 1641 for sundry duties, including boathire and fetching and carrying things to and from Lambeth.

114 Probably Edward Powell*, or his father John, of Southwark.

115 Since there were no other known associates of Laud named 'Mr Farrant', this could possibly refer to Daniel Farrant (d. 1651), instrument maker, court musician to James I and member of the 'Corporation of Musick' in Westminster from 1635. Farrant, who served at court until 1642, would have seen Laud on a regular basis and may have had some links with musicians in the archbishop's household; Andrew Ashbee, 'Farrant, Daniel (d. 1651)', *ODNB*; *CSPD 1603–10*, p. 383, no. 95.

116 This gift was probably the 'fat salt eels' sent by Thomas Wentworth*, lord deputy of Ireland; and the 'eels and salmon' sent by John Bramhall, bishop of Derry*, for which the archbishop asked Wentworth to 'thank his Lordship heartily' on 5 Apr. The fish clearly made an impression on Laud, who was still mentioning the 'fattest and the fairest [eels] that ever I saw' in his correspondence to Wentworth four months later, in Aug. 1637. Wentworth also sent Laud a heavily perfumed cap, which the archbishop was not sure whether he should wear 'by day or by night'. There is no record of the cap in the accounts; *WWL*, VI, 499, VII, 331.

[fo. 28r]

Item to the bargemen	1	0	0
Item to the gardner at Croydon	2	2	10
Item to the gardner at Lambeth	1	5	2
Item to Mr Cobb* for boathire	0	1	0
Item for mendinge the fishing netts	0	6	6
Item for 14 bush[els]† of oates for the coach horses at xxi[d]	1	4	6
Item for a bush[el]† of beanes	0	4	1
Item for 16 bush[els]† of oates for geldings & colts	1	8	0
Item spent in the kitchen this week ut patet p[er] libr[um]	26	18	0

March 10 1637

Item to Mr Whitlocks* man with a present of fish	0	10	0
Item for 2 lamprey† pies from Sir William Sands*	0	2	0
Item for a cake & cheeses Mr Morris*	0	2	6
Item for 4 cheeses B[isho]p of Glouc[e]s[ter]*	0	5	0
Item for a frame for a picture	1	2	0
Item to Mr Seargeant Walthews* man with citterne peeles†	0	2	6
Item to Mr Snaith* for Sir William Beechers* man	0	2	6
Item for a chard pie Mr Attorney*	0	2	0
Item for 2 cheeses Dr Morton*	0	2	0
Item for allmon butter	0	3	0
Item p[ay]d John Robinson* for a peece of grogram† ut patet	10	3	6
Item to Tho[mas] Sadler* for apprell for your Grace ut patet	8	3	0
Item to the bargemen this week	1	0	0
Item to the gardner at Lambeth	0	13	5
Item for boathire Mr Day[117]	0	2	0
Item to the gardner	1	0	0
Item to Mr Dell* ut patet p[er] bill	0	15	2
Item to a messenger from court[118]	0	2	6
Item for 14 bush[els]† of oates for the coach horses at xxj[d]	1	4	6
Item for a bush[el]† of beanes	0	4	1
Item for 17 bush[els]† of oates for geldings & colts	1	9	9
Item for 4 newe shoes & nayling the coach horses	0	3	0
Item for cuttinge the colt	0	3	0
Itme for 6 loads of straw at Lambeth & x[s] at Croydon	3	13	0
Item spent in the kitchen this weeke ut patet p[er] libr[um]	26	16	8
Some total of this fortnight payd March 25 1637	98	2	2

---

117 See n. 102 above.

118 The messenger may have brought news of the birth of Princess Ann, the seventh child and third daughter of Charles I and Henrietta Maria, who was born on 17 Mar. 1637, but died before reaching her fourth birthday. Laud christened the child on 30 Mar.; *WWL*, III, 228.

[fo. 29r]

For this quarter

Payd the brewer of Putney for 32 hogsh[eads]† of viij^{d} & 146 hogsh[eads]† & 1 kinderkin† of vj beere	85	1	0
Item to M[is]tr[es]s Hoult* for this q[ua]rter	4	0	0
Item to Mr Squire* for this q[ua]rter	2	10	0
Item to M[ist]r[es]s Whaley* for the slaughterhouse	0	12	6
Item to the mole catcher for this q[ua]rter	0	8	6
Item to the laundress for ashes, soape, starch &c besides wages	4	10	0
Item for hooping tubbs	0	7	0
Item to Morris* the smith for shoeing & drenching the geldings	5	14	1
Item to Abbot* the sadler for newe horse cloathes, bridles &c for coach horses & geldings ut patet	10	16	6
Item for payles and shovells for the stable	0	10	8
Item to the harnessmaker ut patet	1	6	10
Item to Mr Brigham[119] the coachmaker for 2 sets of wheels & repaynting both coaches	26	17	10
Item to William Duckett* ut patet	4	4	3
Item to him for John Cobb* ut patet	3	9	8
Item to the footman ut patet	1	8	7
Item for signing the bill of impost of xiij tun at Mr Leachlands*	1	19	0
Item for 2 hogsh[eads]† of canary at xxiij for redd and claret iiij^{l} xxi^{d} and for other chardges ut patet p[er] bill	29	3	6
Item for 8 dozen and 1 napkin at xi^{s} p[er] doz	4	8	11
Item for 18 dozen at vi^{s} vij^{s} & viij^{s} p[er] doz ut patet p[er] bill	6	9	4
Item for making and marking the 26 doz at xvi^{d} per doz	1	6	0
Item for 88 ells† of whited canvas at xvij^{d} p[er] ell†	6	6	0
Item for makinge and marking them at vj^{d} a peece	0	4	8
Item for 53 ells† of lockeram† at xviij^{d} p[er] ell† for 30 towells	3	19	6
Item for making them at j^{d} a peece	0	2	6
Item for 300 lings at viij^{l} vj^{s} viij^{d} for 500 gabberdines† at iij^{l} v^{s} with iij^{l} ix^{s} ix^{d} for the fraight	43	14	9
Item for matts and drying the old fish	1	5	0
Item to Mr Crowes[120] for 100 deales† and 60 poles sent to Oxford ut patet	14	10	0
Item for 12 chamberpotts sent hither	1	10	0
Some total for this quarter payd March 25 1637	266	16	7

119 Possibly Mr Brigham who lived 'in Westminster, by the Palace Gate'; *WWL*, VII, 605.

120 This is the sole entry in the accounts for 'Mr Crowe', whose identity remains elusive, although this entry suggests that he worked with wood.

[fo. 30r]
The Second quarter beginning March 17 1637

Rec[eave]d 0–0–0			
Inprimis given for bringing 6 fleeches of bacon Dr Worrall*	0	6	0
Item for Mr Cobb* for boathire	0	1	0
Item for a salmon from Cl[erk] of Checke[121]	0	2	6
Item for oysters & eringoe roots†	0	5	0
Item for herrings and sallmon out of Scotland	0	3	6
Item for lamprey† pies Glouc[ester]	0	3	0
Item for oysters Mr Dade*	0	2	0
Item to the gardner at Lambeth	1	3	4
Item to the bargeman	1	0	0
Item for 14 bush[els]† of oates for coach horses	1	8	0
Item for a bush[el]† of beanes	0	4	1
Item for 16 bush[els]† of oates for geldings & colts	1	12	0
Item for nayling coach horses	0	0	11
Item for broomes for the stable	0	5	0
Item spent in the kitchen this week ut patet p[er] libr[um]	27	8	5

March 24 1637

Item for 2 tearses† of claret wine from Mr Gatch[122]	0	7	0
Item for herrings Lord Belhaven*	0	5	0
Item for oysters Dr Aylett* & Colchester	0	4	0
Item to Mr Attorneys* man	0	2	0
Item a salmon Mr Denn*	0	3	0
Item given to the prisons against Easter	3	0	0
Item to Pallmer* for broomes, mopps, &c	0	8	6
Item to the gardner at Croydon ut patet p[er] bill	3	2	0
Item to the bargemen	1	10	0
Item to the gardner at Lambeth	0	17	5
Item to Mr Snaith* for 3 p[aires] of shoes & boathire	0	13	6
Item 14 bush[els]† of oates for coach horses	1	8	0
Item for a bush[el]† of beanes	0	4	1
Item for 16 bush[els]† of oates for geldings & colts	1	12	0
Item for 4 new shoes & nayling	0	3	0
Item spent in the kitchen this week ut patet p[er] libr[um]	28	12	4
Some total of this fortnight payd Apr[il] 6 1637	76	16	7

121 See n. 70 above.
122 This is the sole entry in the accounts for 'Mr Gatch', whose identity remains elusive.

[fo. 31r]
March ult 1637

Rec[eave]d 0–0–0

Inprimis for 2 lamprey† pies from the B[isho]p of Glouc[e]s[ter]*	0	2	6
Item for a tun of claret from the Master of the Rolls*	1	0	0
Item for 1 hogsh[ead]† from Mr Price[123]	0	5	0
Item for 2 lamprey† pies Alderman Rob[inson] of Glouc[e]s[ter]*	0	1	6
Item for a salmon pie Dr Parry*	0	2	6
Item p[ay]d Mr Badger* for books sent to the Q[ueen] of Bohemia*[124]	6	17	6
Item to him for manuscripts ut patet	7	12	6
Item to Mr Dell* ut patet	0	13	4
Item to the gardner at Lambeth	0	15	5
Item to the gardner at Croydon	2	1	1
Item for a lamprey† pie Sir Th[omas] Roe*	0	2	0
Item for a cake Mr Gryme[125]	0	2	6
Item for 14 bush[els]† of oates for the geldings & colts	1	10	0
Item spent in the kitchen this week ut patet p[er] libr[um]	33	19	8

Aprill 7 1637

Item p[ay]d Mr Snaith* for yr G[races] barbers q[ua]rt[e]ridge	0	10	0
Item for a glass case & furniture	0	10	0
Item for the footman this halfe yeare	0	6	0
Item to the E[arl] of Northumberlands* ma[n] and boathire[126]	0	4	0
Item for 2 barr[el]s of herring Mr Bray*	0	5	0
Item for 6 trouts Mr Mustard*	0	2	6
Item to the gardner at Lambeth	1	6	11
Item to the bargemen this week	1	10	0
Item to Mr Dell* ut patet	1	5	6

---

123 This is the sole entry in the accounts for 'Mr Price', whose identity remains elusive. It is possible that he was the 'Mr Price', listed as one of the 'gentleman retayners' at Croydon Palace in 1631 and 1632; LPL, TG1, fos. 23v, 28v.

124 Laud had written to Elizabeth of Bohemia, Charles I's sister, on 28 Feb., informing her that her 'books are ready and stay only for the brass cuts for your arms' and they were sent shortly afterwards. Although it is not possible to identify which books they were, Elizabeth replied to the archbishop on 13 Apr., reporting that the 'books are come, but they are not yet out of the ship' and thanking him for his 'token of love'; *CSPD 1636–7*, p. 566, no. 66; *WWL*, VII, 323.

125 This is the sole entry in the accounts relating to 'Mr Gryme', whose identity remains elusive.

126 It is likely that Algernon Percy, 10th earl of Northumberland* called upon Laud this week, or vice versa, since the earl commented in a letter to Sir Thomas Roe* of 6 Apr., that 'so soone as this tyme of vacation from businesse is past, I intend to visit' the archbishop. The purpose of the visit was to discuss one 'Mr Doughtie', who was about to take up two clerical livings, and of whom Northumberland commented that he would be happy to appoint as his own household chaplain, if he did not have one already. He was probably referring to John Doughty, a moderate Calvinist clergyman. There is some doubt as to whether Doughty may, after all, have ever become Northumberland's chaplain; *Alumni oxonienses*, I, 417; *CSPD 1636–7*, p. 557, no. 36; John Morgan, 'Doughtie, John (1598?–1672), *ODNB*; *WWL*, III, 214.

Item for 14 bush[els]† of oates for the coach horses at ij^{s}	1	8	0
Item for a bush[el]† of beanes	0	4	1
Item for 16 bush[els]† of oates for geldings & colts	1	12	0
Item for removing and nayling	0	1	11
Item spent in the kitchen this week ut patet p[er] libr[um]	28	8	2
Some total of this fortnight payd Apr[il] 15 1637	95	12	8

[fo. 32r]
Aprill 14 1637

Rec[eave]d of Mr Barton* for wood	100	0	0
Mr Denn* for barly	60	0	0
Item give[n] yr Gr[ace] by Mr Holford*	5	0	0
Item for a key at the court	0	2	6
Item for his boathire to the D[uchess] of R[ichmond]*	0	1	0
Item to the bargemen	0	10	0
Item for 14 bush[els]† of oates for the coach horses at ij^{s}	1	8	0
Item for a bush[el]† of beanes	0	4	1
Item for 15 bush[els]† for geldings & colts at ij^{s}	1	10	0
Item for nayling coach horses	0	2	0
Item spent in the kitchen this week ut patet p[er] libr[um]	33	14	11

Apr[il] 21 1637

Item for sweetmeats from the Duchess of Richmond* Mr Cobb*	0	10	0
Item for bringing a clocke p[ayd] Mr Snaith*	1	0	0
Item for b[…] from the E[arl] of Northumberland*	0	10	0
Item for a p[aire] of bookes for yr G[race] & boathire p[ayd] Mr Snaith*	0	13	0
Item for bringing bacon cheeses &c from Sir H[enry] Spiller* & Mr Ramsey*	0	6	0
Item for puddings &c from the Duchess of Richmond*	0	10	0
Item to Tho[mas] Sadler* & Mr Rollston*	0	7	6
Item to the gardner at Croydon ut patet	1	18	6
Item to the bargemen ut patet	1	5	0
Item to the gardner at Lambeth	1	9	6
Item spent in the journey into Kent[127]	3	10	0
Item for the slaughtermans chardges in bringing 87 Kent sheepe	3	5	8
Item for 14 bush[els]† of oates for the coach horses at ij^{s}	1	8	0
Item for a bush[el]† of beanes	0	4	1
Item for 12 bush[els]† of oates for geldings & colts	1	4	0

127 These costs were incurred by the household staff responsible for driving livestock from Kent to Lambeth, to which the following entry relates.

Item for 16 removes for coach horses	0	2	8
Item spent in the kitchen this week ut patet p[er] libr[um]	32	11	10
Some total of this fortnight payd May 4 1637	96	15	3

[fo. 33r]
Aprill 28 1637

Inprimis given Sir George Willmotts* man for bringing an horse[128]	2	0	0
Item to Mr Dell* for boathires, letters &c ut patet	0	8	4
Item to Mr Watts* for a newe nett & mending for old one	1	5	6
Item to him for pigeones meale	0	8	6
Item to the bargemen this week	1	10	0
Item to the gardner at Lambeth	0	9	2
Item for 13 bush[els]† of oates for the coach horses at ij^{s}	1	6	0
Item for nayling coach horses	0	2	3
Item spent in the kitchen this weeke ut patet p[er] libr[um]	29	4	2

Maye 5 1637

Item to the D[uke] of Buckinghams* gardner[129]	0	2	0
Item to the watchmaker	0	2	0
Item to the poore at the Star Chamber[130]	0	1	0
Item for gylding myters at Oxford	1	10	0
Item for a warrant for the preacher	0	2	6
Item for a dozen of drinking glasses	0	19	0
Item for 2 doz of double bottles	0	12	0
Item for a doz of q[ua]rt and 2 doz of pint bottles	0	9	0
Item for a doz of corkes & for boathire & partridge	0	4	6
Item to the gardner at Croydon	3	10	2
Item to the gardner at Lambeth	0	13	5
Itme to the bargemen	1	5	0
Item for wine &c Sir Rob[er]t Honeywood*	0	2	0
Item for bringing cherryes	0	2	6
Item to Rob[er]t George* for going to the carryier 3 tymes	0	2	0
Item for his going to Croydon	0	2	6
Item for a panel and furniture to carry p[ro]vision to Croydon	0	5	0
Item for 13 bush[els]† of oates for the coach horses at ij^{s}	1	6	0
Item for a bush[el]† of beanes	0	4	1
Item for 11 bush[els]† of oates for geldings & colts	1	2	0

128 This horse was either named Great Willmott, or Little Willmott, as subsequent entries show horses with both names.
129 John Tradescant*, who had acted as gardener to Buckingham from 1623 to 1628.
130 See n. 30 above.

& for shoeing	0	1	4
Item spent in the kitchen this week ut patet p[er] libr[um]	28	7	1
Some total of this fortnight payd May 15 1637	79	9	1

[fo. 34r]

Rec[eave]d for 50 quarters of barly xxv

Inprimis for bringing 2 cakes & a cheese	0	3	0
Item to Sir Tho[mas] Roes* man	0	2	6
Item for a buck Lord Newburgh*	1	0	0
Item to Lo[rd] Finchs* man bacon	0	6	0
Item to Mr Dell* ut patet	0	9	0
Itme to the gardner at Lambeth	0	17	8
Item to the bargemen	1	5	0
Item for 12 bush[els]† of oates for coach horses	1	4	0
Item for a bush[el]† of beanes	0	4	1
Item for 13 bush[els]† of oates for geldings	1	6	0
Item for removing & naylinge	0	1	4
Item for 2 shovells for granary	0	1	6
Item spent in the kitchen this weke ut patet p[er] libr[um]	26	2	0

May 19 1637

Item to Mr Holford* for boathire	0	2	0
Item to Sir Ro[bert] Phillipps* man cheeses	0	2	6
Item to the E[arl] of Lyndsey* gent &c with an horse[131]	4	0	0
Item given at the Star Chamber[132]	0	5	6
Item for boathire Mr Cobb*	0	2	0
Item to Mr Doylys* ma[n] with turkeys &c	0	5	0
Item for a buck Lo[rd] Bellhaven*	0	12	6
Item to the gardner at Lambeth	0	18	0
Item to the gardner at Croydon	1	6	9
Item to the bargemen	1	0	0
Item for mending yr G[races] clocke	0	2	0
Item to Knight* for mowing grass and the yards	0	2	6
Item to Tho[mas] Sadler* for apprell for yr Grace ut patet	3	3	6
Itme for 40 ells† of Holland† for 12 shirts for yr Gr[ace] at iij^{s} x^{d}	7	13	4
Item for making them	0	12	0
Item for apprell for Jo[hn] Cobb* ut patet p[er] bill	6	5	11

131 This was the third equine gift that the archbishop had received since 28 Apr. and was given by Robert Bertie, 1st earl of Lindsey* (1582–1642), the royalist peer. This 'earl of Lyndsey' should not be confused with John Lindsay, 17th earl of Crawford and 1st earl of Lindsay (1596–1678), who emerged as a leading opponent of Caroline policy in Scotland from 1633 onwards; John Young, 'Lindsay, John, seventeenth earl of Crawford and first earl of Lindsay (1596–1678)', *ODNB*.

132 See n. 30 above.

Item for 4 shirts for him & tape	1	0	6
Item for 6 towells & making 6 handkerchers for him	0	8	6
Item for apprell for the footman	4	9	8
Item for 4 shirts for him & tape	1	0	6
Item for Nich[olas]* chardges with colts &c into Kent	1	12	0
Item for Rob[ert] George* with him	0	8	0
Item for a sallmon from Mr Webb*	0	3	0

[fo. 35r]

Item for 2 bucks Sir W[illiam] Kellygree*	1	0	0
Item for 3 firkins† of sturgeon	0	11	0
Item for 12 bush[els]† of oates for coach horses	1	4	0
Item for a bush[el]† of beanes	0	4	1
Item for 13 bush[els]† of oates for geldings	1	6	0
Item for 4 shoes & 8 removes	0	3	8
Item for cuttings the horse &c	0	8	0
Item to Mr Wattson[133] for hooping the butts	0	6	0
Item for bleeding & drenching the coach geldings foote	0	2	0
Item spent in the kitchen this weeke ut patet p[er] libr[um]	26	6	6
Some total of this fortnight payd Jun[e] 1 1637	100	19	0

May 26 1637

Rec[eave]d for Butts	6	13	4
Of Mr Barton*	120	0	0

Inprimis for your G[races] offering	3	0	0
Item for bringing cheeses and strawberryes	0	3	0
Item to Mr Woodalls* ma[n] with sugar & pepp[er]	0	5	0
Item for mending the last case of knives	0	4	0
Item to Mr Cobb* & Mr Snaith* for boathire	0	1	8
Item for an horse from the Earl of Newcastle*[134]	6	0	0
Item to the Lady Wakes* man	0	5	0
Item for letters, boathire &c by Mr Dell* ut patet	0	9	9
Item to Pallmer* for mopps, broomes & stuffe for andirons†	0	13	0
Item to the gardner at Croydon	0	16	4
Item to the gardner at Lambeth	0	13	8
Item to the bargemen	0	13	4
Item for 12 bush[els]† of oates for the coach horses	1	4	0

---

133 This is the first of three entries in the accounts for 'Mr Wattson', who was probably a local tradesman, supplying occasional services to the household.

134 Newcastle, who was the most generous gift-giver, would go on to donate four further horses to the archbishop between Apr. 1638 and Nov. 1639.

Item for a bush[el]† of beanes	0	4	1
Item for 13 bush[els]† of oates for geldings	1	6	0
Item for nayling coach horses	0	1	0
Item spent in the kitchen this week ut patet p[er] libr[um]	28	18	4

June 3 1637

Item for a buck from Sir Maurice Bartley*	1	0	0
Item for a buck Sir Jo[hn] Epsley*	0	16	0
Item for a stagg Earl of Salisbury*	1	5	0

[fo. 36r]

Item for 2 trouts Sir Jo[hn] Shelly*	0	5	0
Item for mutton Sir Jo[hn] Lamb*	0	5	0
Item for bringing cherryes &c Mr Snaith*	0	4	0
Item to the gardner at Lambeth	0	14	0
Item to the bargeman	1	0	0
Item p[ay]d for 2 coach horses	40	16	0
Item spent in the journey xx^{s} give[n] to Mr Wattson[135]	5	2	6
Item for 10 bush[els]† of oates for coach horses	1	0	0
Item for a bush[el]† of beanes	0	4	1
Item for 13 bush[els]† of oates for geldings at ij^{s}	1	6	0
Item for 16 newe shoes for coach horses	0	10	0
Item spent in the kitchen this week ut patet p[er] libr[um]	28	8	9
Some total of this fortnight payd Jun[e] 15 1637	127	14	6

June 9 1637[136]

Rec[eave]d 0–0–0

Inprimis to the hyethman for bringing Mr Roses* 50 quarters of wheate at xiiij^{d} p[er] quart[er]	3	1	2
Item to the porters for carrying it into the granary at iij^{d} p[er] q[ua]rt	0	13	0
Item to Mr Dell* ut patet p[er] libr[um]	0	14	8
Item to the gardner at Croydon	2	4	1
Item to the bargemen	0	10	0
Item to the gardner at Lambeth	0	11	3
Item for 16 bush[els]† of oates for coach horses at ij^{s}	1	12	0
Item for a bush[el]† of beanes	0	4	1

135 See n. 133 above.

136 It was during this week, on 14 June, that Laud gave his speech in star chamber at the censure of William Prynne, Henry Burton and John Bastwick, the puritan ministers. The speech was printed and in circulation by 25 June; *WWL*, III, 228.

Item for 13 bush[els]† of oates for geldings at ij^{s}	1	6	0
Item for bleeding and drenching Little Willmott	0	2	6
Item for naylinge coach horses	0	1	11
Item for a bale for xj horses at Greenwich Sunday	0	4	1
Item for 9 loads of strawe layd in this q[ua]rter	4	11	0
Item spent in the kitchen this week ut patet p[er] libr[um]	28	3	4

[fo. 37r]

For this quarter

Payd the brewer of Putney for 12 hogsh[eads]† of viij^{s} and 61 hogsh[eads]† of vj^{s} beere layd in this q[ua]rter ut patet	34	13	0
To M[is]tr[es]s Hoult* for this q[ua]rter	4	0	0
To Mr Squire* for this q[ua]rter	2	10	0
To the Widd[ow] Whaly* for this q[ua]rter for the slaughterhouse	0	12	6
To the mole catcher for this q[ua]rter	0	8	6
To the laundresse for ashes, soape, starche &c besides wages	4	10	0
Item for lynes payles piggins† and ashe cloth	0	13	11
Item for 30 ells† of cloth for 12 dresser clothes at xiiij^{d}	1	15	0
Item for making them	0	2	0
Item for lace for kerchetts & marking 12 handkerchers	0	2	6
Payd W[illiam] Duckett* for this q[ua]rter ut patet p[er] bill	6	18	1
Item to him for John Cobb*	0	17	6
Item to him for the footman ut patet	8	17	6
Item for carrying 2 loads of wine to Croydon	0	10	0
Item to Morris* the smith for drenching and shoeing geldings &c this q[ua]rter ut patet	4	12	0
Item to Martyn[137] for rowelling† 2 geldings at Croydon	0	8	0
Item for 2 bush[els]† of oates for poultry & a bush of tares† for pigeones	0	7	0
Item to the lyterman† for 20 chald[er] of coales at viij^{d} & porters at xxj^{d} p[er] chald &c	2	5	6
Some total of this weeke &c payd June 27 1637	121	8	1

Some total of this Quarters expenses and laying out cometh to the some of

vj^{c} lxxxxvij^{l} viij^{s} ij^{d}

137 See n. 74 above.

[fo. 38r]
The Third quarter beginning June 17 1637

Receaved 0–0–0			
Inprimis p[ay]d Mr Badger* for binding manuscripts ut patet[138]	4	8	9
Item for a cake & cheeses from Mr Powell*	0	5	0
Item for a buck Lo[rd] Maynard*	1	0	0
Item for a sallmon pie Sir Jo[hn] Lambe*	0	2	0
Item for 3 Fordish trouts Lo[rd] Finch*	0	6	0
Item for a buck with appartments Lo[rd] Chamberlayne*	1	2	0
Item to the gardner at Lambeth	0	13	4
Item to the bargemen	0	15	0
Item for 16 bush[els]† of oates for the coach horses	1	12	0
Item for a bush[el]† of beanes	0	4	1
Item for 11 bush[els]† of oates for the geldings at ij^{s}	1	2	0
Item for a bayl at Greenwich for 10 horses on Sunday	0	4	0
Item for a bayl for 8 horses on Tuesday	0	3	0
Item for nayling coach horses	0	1	2
Item spent in the kitchen this weeke ut patet p[er] libr[um]	28	14	0
Item for mowing making and bringinge hay at Lambeth this yeare ut patet p[er] libr[um]	21	19	6
Item for mowing making and bringinge hay at Croydon this yeare ut finite patet	17	0	2
Some total of this weeke payd June 27 1637	79	12	0

June 23 1637[139]

Rec[eave]d of Mr Barton* for wood	80	0	0
& for a mortuary for the Bishop of Bangor*[140]	10	0	0
Inprimis given the Bishop of Chesters* man with cheeses	0	7	0

---

138 This could well refer to Laud's 'book of the Records in the Tower', to which he referred in his diary, since it was delivered to him on 10 June. According to the archbishop, the book 'concerned the clergy' and was 'collected and written in vellum'; *WWL*, III, 228.

139 This was an important week in terms of privy council business. At the meeting held on 28 June, which Laud attended, the decision was taken to proceed against William Fiennes*, Viscount Saye and Sele in star chamber, for several offences relating to the use of his lands in Lincolnshire. Fiennes, a godly peer and opponent of extra-parliamentary government, was keen to face justice, in order to use the opportunity to highlight the illegality of ship money. In the end, no action was taken against Fiennes and the defendant in the ensuing high-profile ship money 'test case' was John Hampden, not Fiennes; Smith, 'Fiennes', *ODNB*.

140 Edmund Griffith*, bishop of Bangor, died on 26 May 1637; Gwynfor Jones, 'Griffith, Edmund (1570–1637)', *ODNB*.

Item for a nagg† from Judge Jones*[141]	2	0	0
Item for a mare Lo[rd] Wimbleton*[142]	3	0	0
Item for 4 Westfalia gammons Mr Laurence Halsey[143]	0	2	6
Item for a cake M[is]tr[es]s Morgan[144]	0	2	0
Item for cheeses La[dy] Mynne* Dr Smith*, &c			

[fo. 39r]

Item for bringing strawberryes severall tymes	0	2	6
Item for broomes p[ayd] Pallmer*	0	3	6
Item to yr G[races] barber for the last q[ua]rter	0	10	0
Item for the footeman	0	3	0
Item for trowts Lo[rd] Finch*	0	2	6
Item for a buck D[uchess] of Richmond*	1	0	0
Item for a stagg the Kinge	1	10	0
Item to the gardner at Lambeth	1	10	2
Item to the gardner at Croydon	1	10	0
Item to the bargemen	0	15	0
Item for 16 bush[els]† of oates for coach horses at ij^{s}	1	12	0
Item for a bush[el]† of beanes	0	4	1
Item for a bush[el]† of beanes for geldings at ij^{s}	1	4	0
Item for bleedinge and drenchinge Little Willmott	0	3	0
Item for cutting 2 colts	0	10	0
Item for bleedinge and drenchinge them	0	5	0
Item for 9 newe shoes & nayling	0	6	3
Item to the harnessmaker for worke this q[ua]rt[e]r ut patet	1	9	10
Item for a sett of newe harnesses for 6 horses ut patet	12	0	0
Item for 3 setts of head raynes for 6 horses	3	0	0
Item for 16 newe pypes for them to save their sides	2	0	0
Item for 7 newe bitts at ij^{s} vj^{d}	0	17	6
Item spent in the kitchen this weeke ut patet p[er] libr[um]	27	4	1

141 William Jones*, one of the king's bench judges, sat on star chamber with Laud and as a result, may have spent considerable time with him in June and July 1637, when the puritan ministers Burton, Bastwick and Prynne, and John Williams, bishop of Lincoln, were brought before the court. Jones's horse was the fourth such gift received by the archbishop in a period of two months.

142 As a privy councillor, Edward Cecil, Viscount Wimbledon* was entitled to sit on star chamber and in this capacity, may well have had contact with Laud. The archbishop had recently taken steps to prevent Wimbledon from intervening in the appointment of curates at Mortlake and Putney, which were within his lands, but in the gift of the provost of Queen's College, Oxford. This gift, the fifth horse given to the archbishop since late Apr., suggests that there were no hard feelings; *WWL*, VI, 488.

143 This is the sole entry in the accounts for 'Mr Laurence Halsey', whose identity remains elusive.

144 This is the sole entry in the accounts for 'Mistress Morgan', who may have been the wife of 'Mr Morgan' referred to on one other occasion. See n. 453 below.

June 30 1637

Item to the armorer[145] for making 6 horsemens armor serviceable at iij^{l} x^{s} a peece	21	0	0
Item for 6 cases of pistolls with flaskes moulds &c at 35^{s}	10	10	0
Item for fitting 6 swords[146]	1	10	0
Item for 6 newe bitts to them	0	15	0
Item p[ay]d the appoticary for physicke for your G[races] & househould for 3 yeares ut patet	6	2	10
Item for physicke for Jo[hn] Cobb*	1	17	0
Item to the footman with v^{s} given	0	18	0
Item to the watchmaker Mr Snaithe*	0	1	6
Item to Mr Cobb* for boathires	0	1	0
Item to Mr Sutches* for letters	0	1	0
Item given away at the Star Chamber[147]	0	5	6
Item for 2 sugarloaves Mr Downer*[148]	0	2	0
Item to the gardner at Lambeth	0	13	0

[fo. 40r]

Item to the bargemen	1	0	0
Item for muskemelons from Sir Tho[mas] Grymes*	0	5	0
Item for mullets Lo[rd] Treasurer*	0	6	0
Item for 16 bush[els]† of oates for the coach horses at ij^{s}	1	12	0
Item for a bush[el]† of beanes	0	4	1
Item for 12 bush[els]† of oates for geldings	1	4	0
Item for nayling and gyrths† for the postilians sadle	0	2	2
Item for a bayle at Greenwich for x horses Sunday	0	4	0
Item spent in the kitchen this weeke ut patet p[er] libr[um]	27	19	8

Some total of this fortnight paid July 14 1637

July 7 1637

Rec[eave]d of Mr Rose* for 50 quarters of mault at 24^{s}			
Inprimis to Mr Dell* for boathires, letters &c ut patet	0	13	10

145 Probably John Foster*.

146 The atmosphere in London following the public mutilation of Burton, Bastwick and Prynne on 30 June was highly charged and the archbishop was the target of popular animosity, manifested in a range of libels, some of which Laud collected and kept, recording in his diary that he did so as a 'memento for the last of June'. It is possible, therefore, that these armaments were bought to reinforce Lambeth Palace in light of the heightened social and political anxiety; *WWL*, III, 228. For a discussion, see 'Introduction', p. xxx–xxxi above.

147 This payment corresponds broadly to the timeframe in which the cases against Burton, Bastwick and Prynne and Bishop Williams were heard in star chamber. See n. 30 above.

148 Shortly before sending this gift, Thomas Downer* had petitioned Laud and other members of the privy council for their assistance in a tithes dispute with his neighbour, Sir Henry Calthrop; *CSPD 1637*, p. 121, no. 120.

Item to the Seargeant Confect[i]ons* man &c p Mr Snaith*	0	3	10
Item to Mr Badger* for binding manuscripts &c ut patet	3	15	6
Item to Pallmer* for broomes & mopps	0	6	0
Item to the bargemen ut patet	1	1	0
Item to the gardner at Lambeth	0	10	2
Item to the gardner at Croydon	1	8	0
Item for 6 bush[els]† of oates for coach horses at ij^s^	1	12	0
Item for a bush[el]† of beanes	0	4	1
Item for 12 bush[els]† of oates for geldings	1	4	0
Item for 12 shoes & 13 removes for coach horses	0	9	2
Item for bleedinge & drenching Wattson	0	5	0
Item for a bayl at Greenwich for 10 horses	0	4	0
Item spent in the kitchen this week ut patet p[er] libr[um]	28	9	0

July 14 1637

Item p[ay]d for 13 carts for removes to Croydon[149]	3	5	0
Item for the carridge of 3 loads of sea coales thither	0	15	0
Item to Knight* & other to helpe remove stuffe	0	9	0
Item to Mr Cobb* for boathire	0	1	0
Item to Mr Snaith* for boathire	0	1	7

[fo. 41r]

Item for facing your G[races] hatt	0	6	6
Item to the Lady Styles* man &c	0	3	6
Item for Sir Simon Baskerfield*	5	0	0
Item for carpes from Mr Evelyn*	1	5	0
Item for 3 newe forks for the buttery	0	10	0
Item for dressing 3 old ones	0	2	0
Item for spicketts† fossets† &c	0	2	2
Item to the gardner at Lambeth	0	16	2
Item to the gardner at Croydon	0	9	6
Item for 14 horses haye at Chertsey 1 night at viij^d^	0	9	4
Item for 5 bush[els]† of oates & 2 pecks† of beanes &c	0	18	10
Item for farryage at Sheppton	0	5	0
Item for nayling &c	0	1	11
Item for 2 clowts† for the coach	0	3	0
Item for mending postilian saddle and a drawing knife	0	2	6
Item for 16 bush[els]† of oates for coach horses	0	0	0
Item for a bush[el]† of beanes	0	4	1

149 After the archbishop vacated Lambeth on 14 July, his usual summer stay at Croydon Palace was interspersed with regular visits to court and one known return to Lambeth in Croydon on 3 Aug. to marry James, duke of Lennox to Mary Villiers. He was back in residence at Lambeth by 7 Oct., his birthday; *WWL*, VII, 372. See n. 163 below.

Item for 10 bush[els]† of oates for geldings	0	0	0
Item to the cl[erk] of the kitchen[150] for cleaver mincing knives & other necessaryes ut patet	2	14	8
Item spent in the kitchen this week ut patet p[er] libr[um]	28	0	10
Some total of this fortnight payd July 27 1637	86	12	12

July 27 1637

Rec[eave]d for Mr Spratling* barly	78	0	0
For his wheat	54	12	6
For 26 loads of hay	45	10	0
Inprimis to the heathman for bringing Mr Denns* 40 q[ua]rters of Kent wheate	2	13	0
Item to 7 cartes for bringing it to Croydon at v^s	1	15	0
Item to the porters and others chardges	0	8	0
Item to Palmer* for broomes & stuffe andirons†	0	5	2
Item to Mr Dell* for letters boathires &c ut patet	0	10	4
Item to the gardner at Lambeth	0	11	10
Item to the gardner at Croydon	0	10	6
Item for 14 horses haye at Chersey 2 nights at viij^d	0	18	8
Item for 8 bush[els]† of oates & 2 pecks† of beanes for them &c	1	6	10
Item for farriage at Sheppton	0	5	0

[fo. 42r]

Item for 12 newe ropes & naylinge the coach horses	0	6	0
Item for 2 broomes	0	1	0
Item for 16 bush[els]† of oates for the coach horses	0	0	0
Item for a bush[el]† of beanes	0	3	9
Item for 11 bush[els]† of oates for the geldings	0	0	0
Item spent in the kitchen this week ut patet p[er] libr[um]	28	13	3

July 28 1637

Item given yr Grace for Francis Loveday*	2	0	0
Item for 2 bucks from Farnham	1	6	0
Item for sturgeon pheasants &c from Dr Howell*	0	7	0
Item for bringing the weekly bills	0	1	0

150 Thomas Shelton*.

Item to Phillipp for letters[151]	0	1	6
Item to the gardner at Croydon	0	12	0
Item for a p[aire] of shoes for yr G[race][152]	0	4	6
Item for altering stockings &c	0	1	6
Item for hay for 14 horses att Chersey one night	0	9	4
Item for 16 bush[els]† of oates for coach horses of Downe	0	0	0
Item for a bush[el]† of beanes	0	3	9
Item for 12 bush[els]† of oates for geldings	0	0	0
Item for 12 shoes & 6 removes for the coach horses	0	8	0
Item for straw layd in since coming to Croydon	2	0	0
Spent in the kitchen this week ut patet p[er] libr[um]	29	4	4
Some total of this fortnight payd Aug[ust][ust] 10 1637	76	9	7

August 4 1637

Rec[eave]d 0–0–0

Inprimis given to Mr Dayes children[153] p[ayd] Mr Snaith*	0	5	0
Item to the gardner at Lambeth	1	2	4
Item to the gardner at Croydon	0	12	6
Item for haye for 14 horses Chersey 1 night at viij[d]	0	9	4
Item for 5 bush[els]† of oates and a peck† of beanes &c	0	17	4
Item for ferryage at Shepton	0	5	0

[fo. 43r]

Item for 3 newe rollers & 4 lathe raynes for them	0	7	0
Item for 16 bush[els]† of oates for the coach horses at home	0	0	0
Item for a bush[el]† of beanes	0	3	9
Item for 11 bush[els]† for geldings	0	0	0
Item for 8 removes & nayling	0	2	0
Item for 2 buckles and billetts	0	0	6
Item for mending the c[oach] horses sadles &c	0	4	9
Item spent in the kitchen this week ut patet p[er] libr[um]	27	17	0

151 An important letter may well have been among this package delivered by 'Phillipp', the messenger. The letter in question was written by John Stewart, 1st earl of Traquair* around 23 July – during the summer, a letter could take a mere four days to reach London from Scotland – informing Laud that a riot had taken place in St Giles's kirk, Edinburgh, when the new Scottish prayer book was read for the first time during a Sunday service. This event marked the beginning of Charles I's Scottish troubles. For the archbishop's response to Traquair and his reaction to the news, see James, *Firebrand*, p. 115; *WWL*, VI, 491.

152 It is possible that this item was purchased for Laud to wear while officiating at the marriage of James, duke of Lennox, cousin to Charles I, to Mary Villiers, the only daughter of the late royal favourite, Buckingham, which took place in Lambeth Palace chapel on 3 Aug.1637; *WWL*, III, 229.

153 Possibly the same 'Mr Day' who was used for boathire across the Thames. See n. 102 above.

August 11 1637

Item for a present from the Countesse of Dorsett*	0	10	0
Item for yr G[races] offering	3	0	0
Item for 2 bucks from Farnham	1	8	0
Item to Mr Dell* ut patet	0	14	6
Item for a buck Earl of Cleaveland*	0	15	0
Item for another Sir H[umfry] Styles*	0	10	0
Item to the gardner at Lambeth	1	8	0
Item to the gardner at Croydon	0	9	0
Item a buck Mrs Packenham[154]	0	6	0
Item for 16 bush[els]† of oates for the coach horses	0	0	0
Item for a bush[el]† of beanes	0	3	9
Item for 12 bush[els]† for geldings	0	0	0
Item for bleeding 5 coach horses	0	2	6
Item for removing and nayling	0	1	6
Item for 6 broomes	0	1	0
Item for farriage at Sheppton	0	4	8
Item spent in the kitchen this weeke ut patet p[er] libr[um]	26	1	10
Item p[ay]d unto Mr Deane of Salisbury* for your Grace	58	13	6
Some total of this fortnight paid August 24	126	15	9

August 18 1637

Receaved 0–0–0

Inprimis for pheasants from the Lo[rd] Wimbleton*	0	5	0
Item for 2 bucks from Farnham	1	10	0
Item for 2 doz of partridges from Mr Abbot*	0	5	0
Item for 10 pheasants from Dr Paske*	0	10	0
Item for partridges Mr Mills[155]	0	5	0
Item for mendinge yr G[race] barge	8	2	0
Item for broomes p[ayd] Pallmer*	0	2	6

[fo. 44r]

Item to the gardner at Lambeth	0	14	10
Item to the gardner at Croydon	0	14	6
Item for 16 bush[els]† of oates for the coach horses	0	0	0
Item for a bush[el]† of beanes	0	3	9

154 See n. 60 above.

155 This 'Mr Mills', not to be confused with John Mills*, servant to the archiepiscopal household, was possibly John Mills, a Kentish farmer, who lived in Canterbury, but also held lands in the parsonage of Herne, Kent. Subsequent gifts from Mills – of fruit and poultry – suggest that he donated home-grown produce to the household. Mills, along with fifteen other parishioners, appealed to the sheriff of Kent in 1635 against double-ratings for ship money; *CSPD 1635*, p. 601, no. 47.

Item for 12 bush[els]† for geldings	0	0	0
Item for removing and nayling	0	1	2
Item for gyrths† and strapps for sadles	0	2	4
Item spent in the kitchen this weeke ut patet p[er] librum]	28	8	10

Aug[ust] 25 1637

Item to Sir Henry Burtons* man with peares & grapes	0	2	0
Item for nutts from Mr Goldwell[156]	0	1	0
Item for 20 partridges from Sir Henry Snellgrave*	0	5	0
Item to the poore at Kingston	0	1	0
Item to the gardner at Lambeth	0	13	0
Item to the gardner at Croydon	0	12	6
Item for peares from Sir M[atthew] Mynce*	0	5	0
Item for a bucke Sir H[umfrey] Styles*	0	10	0
Item for another from Sir Tho[mas] Edmondes*	0	12	6
Item for haye for 15 horses at Chersey 2 nights at viij[d]	1	0	0
Item for a bush[el]† of oates & 2 pecks† of beanes &c	1	6	10
Item for farriage at Sheppton	0	2	6
Item for 15 horses at Putney	0	8	0
Item for 16 bush[els]† of oates for coach horses at home	0	0	0
Item for a bush[el]† of beanes	0	3	9
Item for 12 bush[els]† of oates for geldings	0	0	0
Item for nayling coach horses	0	1	4
Item for a p[aire] of boots for the postilian	0	12	0
Item spent in the kitchen this weeke ut patet p[er] libr[um]	35	4	6
Some total of this fortnight payd Septemb[er] 7 1637	83	5	10

September 1 1637

Rec[eave]d of Mr Barton* and for wheate and fierr at consecration	5	5	0
Inprimis given to yr Grace for the offeringe at the consecration[157]	3	0	0
Item p[ay]d Alderman Robinson* for lamprey† pies sent in Lent	3	16	0
Item to Mr Dell* for Dr Moortons* broad seale &c ut patet	8	18	8
Item to the ewry man† for bringing mellons and grapes	0	5	6

[fo. 45r]

Item for bringing the weekly bills & letters	0	3	6
Item for 2 bucks from Farnham	1	10	0
Item for 6 turkeys & 2 partridges from Mr Bucknor*	0	5	0

156 See n. 84 above.

157 On 3 Sept. 1637, William Roberts* was consecrated bishop of Bangor at Croydon Palace; *WWL*, VI, 507.

Item for a buck from the Earl of Cleaveland*	0	15	0
Item to the gardner at Lambeth	1	0	4
Item to the gardner at Croydon	0	15	2
Item for 16 bush[els]† of oates for coach horses of Downe	0	0	0
Item for a bush[el]† of beanes	0	3	9
Item for 12 bush[els]† for geldings	0	0	0
Item for 16 newe shoes & 16 removes for coach horses	0	13	0
Item spent in the kitchen this weeke ut patet p[er] libr[um]	32	1	10

Septemb[er] 8 1637

Item for a staff from Sir Arth[ur] Manwaring*	1	5	0
Item given in the winesellers at court	0	5	0
Item in the beareseller there	0	5	0
Item to Mr Mills[158] his man swan	0	2	6
Item to the musitians of Redding	0	10	0
Item for a buck Sir Tho[mas] Alsbury*	0	10	0
Item to Mr Winch[159] for the poore	1	0	0
Item to the bellringers	0	5	0
Item to Mr Pococks* man	0	2	6
Item to yr G[race] at bowles[160]	0	1	0
Item to a young man to beare his chardges home	2	0	0
Item given in Sir Henry Martyns* house	4	10	0
Item to the stables here & abroad	1	7	6
Item to the prison at Kingston	0	0	6
Item for a buck from Nonsuch	0	12	6
Item for another Lo[rd] Wimbleton*	0	15	0
Item to the gardner at Lambeth	0	13	10
Item to the gardner at Croydon	1	8	8
Item for 15 horses hay at Chersey 2 nights at viij^{d}	0	19	4
Item for 8 bush[els]† of oates & 2 pecks† of beanes &c there	1	6	10
Item for farriage at Sheppton	0	2	6
Item for mending the coach &c	0	9	6
Item for 15 bush[els]† of oates for coach horses of Downe	0	0	0
Item for a bush[el]† of beanes	0	3	9
Item for 11 bush[els]† of oates for geldings	0	0	0
Item for drenching G[rea]t Willmott	0	3	0
Item for shootinge	0	0	10
Item spent in the kitchen this weeke ut patet p[er] libr[um]	39	3	7

158 See n. 155 above.
159 This is the sole entry in the accounts for 'Mr Winch', whose identity remains elusive.
160 A gem of an entry, this payment of a shilling probably represents a wager or a bet on the outcome of a game of bowls.

Some of this fortnight payd Oct[ober] 2 1637	109	11	1

[fo. 46r]
Septemb[er] 15 1637

Inprimis for 20 pheasants from the E[arl] of Dorsett*	0	12	0
Item for carpe from Mr Bucknor*	0	3	6
Item for grapes Sir Tho[mas] Roe*	0	5	0
Item for a doe Sir Nic[holas] Carey*	0	15	0
Item to Mr Dell* for the organmaker sent into Scottland &c[161]	5	5	6
Item to Pallmer* for broomes	0	5	0
Item to the gardner at Lambeth	0	7	0
Item to the gardner at Croydon	0	14	3
Item for 14 horses haye at Kingston 2 nights at viij^{d}	0	18	8
Item for 8 bush[els]† of oates & 3 pecks† of beanes &c there	1	9	6
Item for cutting Willowby	0	5	0
Item for 16 bush[els]† of oates for the coach horses at home	0	0	0
Item for a bush[el]† of beanes	0	3	9
Item for 14 bush[els]† of oates for the geldings	0	0	0
Item for 3 stones for the stable	0	2	0
Item for broomes	0	1	0
Item for nayling coach horses	0	1	4
Item spent in the kitchen this week ut patet p[er] libr[um]	28	9	3

For this quarter

Payd the brewer for 5 hogsh[eads]† of x^{s} 17 hogsh[eads]† of viij^{s} & 93 hogsh[eads]† of vj^{s} beare ut patet	55	16	0
Item to Mrs Hoult* for this q[ua]rter	4	0	0
Item to Mr Squire* for this q[ua]rter	2	10	0
Item to Mrs Whaly* for the rent of the slaughterhouse	0	12	6
Item to the mole catcher	0	5	0
Item to the laundress for ashes, soape, starch &c besides wages	4	10	0
Item to yr Graces barber	0	10	0
Item for the footman	0	3	0
Item to Abbot* the sadler for this halfe years bill ut patet	3	17	4
Item to Morris* [the smith] for shoeinge geldings &c ut patet	3	17	10

[fo. 47r]

Item to the laundress for hooping tubbs this q[ua]rter	0	13	10

[161] There is no extant evidence, in Laud's correspondence or elsewhere, to shed further light on this entry, which suggests that someone attached to his household, possibly John Burwood, who installed a new organ in Lambeth Palace in Nov. 1639, may have been sent to Scotland to repair or install a new organ in a chapel there. Hinting at the archbishop's Scottish links, this is intriguing, as Laud is now known to have been far more involved in Scottish policy than previously thought. Pending further research, however, the full background to this entry will remain a mystery.

Item to her for 4 bush[els]† of roses for the lynen	0	4	8
Item to Mr Watts* for graynes for the fish	0	9	8
Item for pigeons meale	0	7	6
Item for broomes & mopps this yeare for the house	0	10	10
Item for bringing mellons and apricocks this sumer	0	7	0
Item to Jo[hn] Newton* for strawe	0	16	0
Item for cutting the braks† in the walks at the park	0	7	0
Item for mending hedges and clensing the river at the stubbs	0	11	8
Item for pigeons meale at the park	0	14	8
Item for drenching a cowe &c	0	3	6
Item to W[illiam] Duckett* for curtayns, canvas, lyinge hangings &c ut patet p[er] bill	11	18	2
Item to him for John Cobb*	1	9	0
Item to him for the footman	0	5	6
Item to Comfort* the smith for shoeing horses from Christmas to Midsomer ut patet	0	19	2
Item for 4 syeths &c deliv'd unto Pitcher this yeare	0	13	11
Item more to him for shoeing geldings &c since Midsomer ut patet p[er] bill	3	9	0
Some of this weeke &c payd Octob[er] 2 1637	140	0	6

Some total of this quarters expenses laying out cometh to the some of viij^{c} xxxiij^{l} ix^{s} j^{d}

[fo. 48r]

The Fourth quarter beginning September 22 1637

Receaved 0–0–0

Inprimis for mendinge yr G[races] watch	0	1	6
Item for cakes & cheeses from the Lady Howland[162]	0	3	0
Item to the gardner at Lambeth	1	3	6
Item to the bargemen	0	7	6
Item to the gardner at Croydon	0	19	3
Item to Sir Jo[hn] Apslyes* man	0	2	6
Item for bringing weekly bills	0	1	0
Item for 16 bush[els]† of oates for the coach horses	0	0	0
Item for a bush[el]† of beanes	0	3	9
Item for 13 bush[els]† of oates for the geldings of Downe	0	0	0
Item for dressing the bald horses shoulder	0	4	0
Item for drenching G[rea]t Willmott and fyling his teeth	0	4	0

162 This is the sole entry in the accounts relating to a gift from 'Lady Howland', whose identity remains elusive. She may, however, have been the wife of 'Sir John Howland of Streatham', who acted as JP for Hertfordshire from at least 1634; *APC*, XXXXVI, 89; *CSPD 1630–1*, p. 89, no. 249.

Item for 2 pecks† of mault for mashes for him	0	2	6
Item for nayling coach horses	0	1	0
Item spent in the kitchen this weeke ut patet p[er] libr[um]	27	13	3

September 29 1637

Item given Mr Warwicks* man & groome with a geldinge	2	10	0
Item given away at Sir Tho[mas] Roes*	2	10	0
Item given unto Fra[ncis] Loveday*	2	0	0
Item to Pitcher for boote	1	0	0
Item to Mr Watts* ma[n] & 2 mayds	1	0	0
Item to John Newton's* man	0	5	0
Item for a newe fishinge nett	2	18	8
Item for 12 carts for a remove to Lambeth	3	12	0
Item to labourers for removing the stuffe at Croydon & Lambeth	0	10	0
Item to Palmer* for broomes	0	3	8
Item to the gardner at Lambeth	0	18	7
Item to him for boathire & letters this summer	0	12	0
Item to the bargemen on Sunday	0	5	0
Item to John Newton* for hedging 4 days at the parks	0	4	8
Item to Knight* for bringing sheepe &c from Croydon	0	3	0

[fo. 49r]

Item for 15 horses haye at Kingston 3 nights at viij^{d}	1	10	0
Item for 12 bush[els]† of oates for them at iij^{d} p[er] bush[el]†	1	16	0
Item for 3 pecks† of beanes	0	7	0
Item for 8 bush[els]† of oates for coach horses our own all spent	0	0	0
Item for 8 bush[els]† more bought at ij^{s} vj^{d} p[er] bush[el]†	1	0	0
Item for a bush[el]† of beanes	0	3	9
Item for 14 bush[els]† of oates for geldings at ij^{s} vj^{d}	1	15	0
Item for removing & nayling	0	1	7
Item for shoeing ag[ains]t 8 removes	0	6	6
Item for strawe at Croydon	0	13	4
Item spent in the kitchen this weeke ut patet p[er] libr[um]	33	11	8
Some total of this fortnight payd Octob[er] 9 1637	91	5	2

October 6 1637[163]

Receaved 0–0–0

Inprimis to yr Grace for Mr Solicitor's* fee	5	0	0

---

163 Laud returned to Lambeth for his birthday on 7 Oct., having been there for almost three months. It was on this date that he first notified Wentworth of the summer's events in Scotland, including the reaction to the Scottish prayer book; *WWL*, VII, 372.

Item for Mr Harberts* fee	3	0	0
Item p[ay]d Dr Turner* for 5 gownes given to 5 poore men in Redding ut patet	7	19	0
Item to John Floodd* for his board wages ut patet	4	3	6
Item for his halfe yeares wages ended at Mich[ael]mas	2	10	0
Item for 2 Cheddar cheeses from Dr Chaffin*	0	2	6
Item for boathire Mr Snaith*	0	1	0
Item for a manuscript from Sir John Burroughs* p[ayd] Mr Dell*	0	12	0
Item for a doe Sir Tho[mas] Alsbury*	0	12	0
Item for letters, boathire &c	0	4	0
Item to the gardner at Lambeth	1	8	8
Item to the bargemen	0	6	0
Item to the gardner at Croydon	1	16	0
Item for 4 sconces†	0	4	0
Item for 8 partr[idges] & 1 pheasant from Sir Ed[ward] Gressom*	0	5	0
Item for 12 partr[idge] Mr Denn*	0	2	6
Item for 4 pheasants Mr Evelyn*	0	5	0
Item for 12 partr[idges] Archd[eacon of] Cant[erbury]*	0	2	6
Item for a doe Sir Tho[mas] Edmunds*	0	10	0
Item for 2 swans Dr Lewes*	0	5	6
Item to Mr Mabb* for letters, broomes, mopps &c this summer ut patet	0	19	3

[fo. 50r]

Item for hay for 14 horses at Kingston 2 nights at viij^{d}	0	18	8
Item for 8 bush[els]† of oates for them	1	4	0
Item for 2 pecks† of beanes &c	0	5	6
Item for 16 bush[els]† of oates for coach horses at ij^{s} vj^{d} at home	2	0	0
Item for a bush[el]† of beanes	0	3	9
Item for 14 bush[els]† of oates for geldings	1	15	0
Item for 16 shoes & 8 removes	0	11	8
Item for drenching the bald horse	0	2	6
Item for 4 loads of straw at xj^{s} layd in by Mrs Goldwell[164]	2	4	0
Item spent in the kitchen this week ut patet p[er] libr[um]	33	8	11

Octob[er] 13 1637

Item to Dr Smith's* man with cheeses	0	2	6
Item p[ay]d Mr Matthewes[165] for 50 of deals† sent to Oxford	45	3	0
Item to Mr Harbys* man with globes	1	0	0
Item to Mr Cobb* for boathire	0	1	0

---

164 This is the sole entry in the accounts relating to 'Mrs Goldwell', whose identity remains elusive, although she was probably the wife of 'Mr Goldwell' and possibly also related to 'Will Gouldwell'. See n. 84 above.

165 This is the sole entry in the accounts for 'Mr Matthewes', whose identity remains elusive.

Item to Mr Sutches* for the D[uchess] porter	0	1	0
Item to the yeoman of the wineseller for bottles & corkes 3 doz	0	13	8
Item to the bargemen	1	0	0
Item to the gardner at Lambeth	1	10	0
Item to the slaughterman for bringing 100 Kent weathers† out of Kent ut patet	3	16	0
Item for 2 cheese Lo[rd] Harbord*	0	3	6
Item to the Lady D[uchess] of Richmonds* man	0	5	0
Item for 12 partridges Dr Warren*	0	2	6
Item for 2 does from Ford	0	15	0
Item for 14 horses hay at Kingston 2 nights at viij^{d}	0	18	8
Item for 8 bush[els]† of oates	1	4	0
Item for 3 pecks† of beanes &c for them	0	7	0
Item for 16 bush[els]† of oates for coach horses at home	2	0	0
Item for a bush[el]† of beanes	0	5	0
Item for 14 bush[els]† of oates for geldings	1	15	0
Item for removing and nayling coach horses	0	0	10
Item spent in the kitchen this weeke ut patet p[er] libr[um]	27	12	3
Some total of this fortnight payd Octob[er] 23 1637	161	18	5

[fo. 51r]
October 20 1637

Rec[eave]d for the B[isho]p of Rochesters* mortuary xl[166]			
Inprimis given Mr Sydney[167] Mr Soliticors* clark p[ayd] Mr Dell*	2	0	0
Item for boathire & letters ut patet	0	7	6
Item for bringing apples	0	1	8
Item to Stephen[168] for a glass and case for your Grace	0	12	0
Item to the bargeman	0	18	6
Item to the gardner at Lambeth	0	15	10
Item to Mr Doylys* man with pheasants &c	0	5	0
Item to the D[uchess] of Richmonds* man	0	2	6
Item for hay for 14 horses at Kingston 2 nights at viij^{d}	0	18	8
Item for 8 bush[els]† of oates there	1	4	0
Item for 3 pecks† of beanes &c	0	7	6
Item for 16 bush[els]† of oates for coach horses at home at ij^{s} vj^{d}	2	0	0
Item for a bush[el]† of beanes	0	5	1
Item for 14 bush[els]† of oates for geldings	1	15	0

166 John Bowle*, bishop of Rochester, died in London on 9 Oct. 1637 and was buried in St Paul's cathedral; Charles Knighton, 'Bowle, John (d. 1637)', *ODNB*.

167 This is the sole entry in the accounts for 'Mr Sydney', who acted as clerk to Sir Edward Littleton*, solicitor-general and about whom little else is known.

168 See n. 113 above.

Item for shoeing coach horses	0	3	6
Item for 18 broomes for the stable	0	3	0
Item for spent in the kitchen this week ut patet p[er] libr[um]	27	18	5

October 27 1637

Item to Pallmer* for 3 lether basketts for charcoales	0	5	8
Item for a shovell and stuffe for the andirons† &c	0	2	2
Item for broomes & mopps	0	4	10
Item for an hynd from the Countesse of Westm[ore]land*	1	5	0
Item to the Lo[rd] of Somsetts* gent	1	0	0
Item to Mr Marks[169] for a p[aire] of shoes &c	0	5	0
Item to the keeper at the garden gate at Whitehall[170]	0	11	0
Item to the gardner at Croydon	1	11	4
Item to the gardner at Lambeth	1	8	10
Item to the bargemen	1	5	0
Item for a doe Lo[rd] Newburgh*	0	10	0
Item for a brawne Mr Quiney[171]	0	5	0
Item for pheasants & partr[idge] Mr Williscot*	0	6	0
Item for a cake & partridge Mr Powell*	0	5	0
Item for oysters Mayor of Colchester*	0	3	6
Item for 15 bush[els]† of oates for the coach horses at ij^{s} vj^{d}	1	17	6
Item for a bush[el]† of beanes	0	5	1
Item for 15 bush[els]† of oates for geldings	1	17	6
Item for 4 shoes & naylinge	0	3	0
Item spent in the kitchen this week ut patet p[er] libr[um]	25	15	0

[fo. 52r]

Item p[ay]d for 300 of linges at vx^{l} xiij^{s} iiij^{d}	29	0	0
Item for 500 of gabbedines† at iiij^{l} viij^{s}	17	0	0
Item for the chardges by sea & lands & laying them in ut patet	2	14	6
Item for dryinge the old fishe	0	16	0
Item for 100 doz of candles at iiij^{s} viij^{d} p[er] dozen layd in	23	6	8
Item for 26 dozen of candles att iiij^{s} vj^{d} p[er] doz	5	17	0

169 This is the sole entry in the accounts for 'Mr Marks', whose identity remains elusive. Given that this entry relates to shoes, Marks may well have been a cobbler.

170 This particular payment of a tip at the gates to Whitehall Palace came at a time when there was much going on for Laud. On 22 Oct., he recorded in his diary that there was 'a great noise' at court about the conversion of Anne Blount, countess of Newport, to Catholicism. Laud's 'free speech' to the king in privy council shortly afterwards, in which he complained of the 'increasing of the Roman party' and 'the freedom at Denmark House', where the Henrietta Maria's chapel held Catholic services, caused a breach in the already cool relationship between the archbishop and the queen. Laud told Wentworth on 1 Nov. that, as a result of the incident, she was 'very angry and took great exception to me'; *WWL*, III, 229–30, VII, 381.

171 This is the sole entry in the accounts for 'Mr Quiney', who may have been Abraham Quiney of Stratford-upon-Avon; *WWL*, III, 403.

Some total of this fortnight payd Novemb[er] 14 1637	157	18	3

Novemb[er] 3 1637

Receaved of Mr Barton*

Inprimis for 2 does from the Lo[rd] Privy Seal*	1	5	0
Item for 4 cheeses & 2 pies from Sir John Peashall*	0	5	0
Item for a sallmon Sir G[eorge] Sands*	0	5	0
Item to Mr Dell* for letters, boathire &c	0	7	0
Item to the porters man at Whitehall p[ayd] Mr Holford*	0	4	6
Item to Mr P[atrick] Younges* man with a book[172]	1	0	0
Item to Mr Millers[173] man with fruit	0	2	0
Item to the clockmaker	0	2	6
Item for a hyne from the Kinge[174]	1	11	0
Item to the gardner at Lambeth	0	11	2
Item to the bargemen	1	10	0
Item for a cake D[eane] of Litchfield*[175]	0	2	6
Item for a doe Lo[rd] Maynard*	0	10	0
Item for 4 pheasants Mr Champneys[176]	0	2	6
Item for 4 pheasants Sir Ro[bert] Honeywood*	0	2	6
Item for 15 bush[els]† of oates for coach horses	1	17	6
Item spent in the kitchen this weeke ut patet p[er] libr[um]	25	2	3

Novemb[er] 10 1637

Item for a doe from Richmond	0	10	0
Item for another Mr Parkinson[177]	0	6	0
Item for pepper & sugar Mr Woodall*	0	5	0
Item for 2 cheeses Sir P[hilip] Manwaring*	0	2	6
Item p[ay]d Tho[mas] Sadler* for a suite & cloake for John Cobb*	7	14	6

172 Patrick Younge*, the royal librarian, appears only once in the accounts and there is no record of which book he gave to Laud on this occasion. It may well have been a volume in Greek. The only known interaction between Laud and Younge occurred in Jan. 1634, when the archbishop had instructed Augustin Lindsell, bishop of Peterborough and Younge, as 'his Majesty's printers', to establish a Greek press so that 'such manuscripts as are in his Majesty's library, or in either of his Universities' might be made accessible to 'his subjects are learned' in Greek; *WWL*, VI, 342–3.

173 See n. 22 above.

174 Laud reported to Wentworth shortly after this that the king 'hath a boil upon his left thigh, which hath put him to a great deal of pain'. Given the nature of this gift to the archbishop, either the king's affliction emerged in the days after this entry, or it was not so bad as to have prevented Charles from hunting; *WWL*, VII, 384.

175 At the time, Samuel Fell*, dean of Lichfield, was actively trying to procure advancement to the bishopric of Rochester, following the death of John Bowle* a month earlier. Fell's moderate Calvinism meant that this promotion eluded him; Andrew Hegarty, 'Fell, Samuel (bap. 1584, d. 1649)', *ODNB*.

176 This is the first of three entries for 'Mr Champneys', whose identity remains elusive. He may have been 'Mr Champneys' of north Kent, who became involved in dispute with the navy office over the provision of goods for the second Bishops' War; *CSPD 1640*, p. 130, no. 77.

177 See n. 6 above.

Item for 4 Cheshire cheeses from the Lady Savage*	0	6	0
Item given towards Keelys funerall[178]	2	0	0

[fo. 53r]

Item to Jo[hn] Newton* for layinge basons into the house at Croydon	0	1	0
Item for marking sheepe and sending horses to Lambeth	0	1	8
Item to Mr Cobb* for boathire	0	3	0
Item to the musitians boathire three tymes	0	5	0
Item to the gardner at Lambeth	0	15	3
Item to the bargemen	1	0	0
Item to the gardner at Croydon	1	11	0
Item for 14 bush[els]† of oates for coach horses	1	15	0
Item for a bush[el]† of beanes	0	5	1
Item for 17 bush[els]† of oates for geldings	2	2	6
Item for bleedinge the coach horses and drenching 3 of them	0	11	0
Item for 4 shoes & 4 removes	0	3	0
Item for Nich[olas]* chardges into Kent and backe with horses	1	13	0
Item for 7 bayles of strawe for litter at Croydon	0	6	4
Item spent in the kitchen this week ut patet p[er] libr[um]	25	14	11
Some of this fortnight payd Novemb[er] 27 1637	84	14	9

Novemb[er] 17 1637

Rec[eave]d xv^{l} v^{s} iij^{d}

Inprimis for a doe from the E[arl] of Winchelsey*	0	10	0
Item for 2 Cheddar cheeses from the B[isho]p of B[ath] & Wells*	0	6	0
Item for bringing 2 redd cowes from him	1	10	0
Item for a doe, partr[idge] pheasants &c from Sir Hen[ry] Wallop*	1	5	0
Item to Mr Badger* for binding manuscripts	1	19	6
Item for 6 pheasants Sir H[enry] Spellar*	0	5	0
Item to the gardner at Lambeth	0	8	6
Item to the bargemen	1	6	0
Item for 14 bush[els]† of oates for coach horses	1	15	0
Item for a bush[el]† of beanes	0	5	1
Item for 17 bush[els]† of oates for geldings	2	2	6
Item spent in the kitchen this week ut patet p[er] libr[um]	25	7	1

178 This deceased 'Keely' may be related to John Keely or Keelie who had been retained at Lambeth Palace as a bargeman since at least 1631; LPL, TG1, fos. 23v, 28v.

[fo. 54r]
Novemb[er] 24 1637

Item for a doe C[ountess] of Carlisle*[179]	0	10	0
Item given at the Star Chamber servants[180]	0	9	0
Item for 2 p[aires] of shoes for yr Grace	0	9	0
Item for a key for linin chest and boathire Mr Snaith*	0	2	4
Item to the baker on St Clement[181] p[ayd] Mr Holford*	0	10	0
Item to Mr Holford* for boathire	0	1	0
Item to Pallmer* for broomes	0	4	0
Item to Mr Harfleets* ma[n] with sugar	0	5	0
Item for an hyne Lo[rd] Lyndsey*	1	1	0
Item to the gardner at Lambeth	0	7	2
Item to the bargemen	1	12	0
Item to the gardner at Croydon	1	2	0
Item to Mr Dell* ut patet	0	13	4
Item for x partridges Mr Denn*	0	2	6
Item for 2 pheasants Mr Whittaker*	0	2	0
Item for 2 swans Dr Lewes*	0	2	6
Item for 14 bush[els]† of oates for coach horses	1	15	0
Item for a bush[el]† of beanes	0	5	1
Item for 18 bush[els]† of oates for geldings	2	5	0
Item for removinge & naylinge coach horses	0	2	0
Item spent in the kitchen this weeke ut patet p[er] libr[um]	23	18	1
Some of this fortnight paid Decemb[er] 7 1637	72	17	8

Decemb[er] 1 1637

Receaved xxij^{l} vij^{s} vij^{d}			
Inprimis for bringing a sugar loafe from Mr Holloway*	0	2	6
Item for pearemaynes† Mr Mills[182]	0	1	0
Item to Mr Rollston* for boathire	0	1	0
Item for 2 does from Ford	0	17	0

179 Although Laud had no direct or close personal relationship with Lucy Hay*, countess of Carlisle, they were connected by their mutual association with Wentworth, through whom the countess was in the process of negotiating the surrender of her share of certain Irish monopolies on the wine imports. This was the only gift recorded in the accounts from the countess to the archbishop and may have reflected her gratitude to him for interceding on her behalf with Wentworth. In addition, the countess herself, who was one of the queen's ladies-in-waiting, may well have interceded on Laud's behalf when he fell out with Henrietta Maria a couple of months before; *CSPI 1633–47*, p. 175, no. 594; *WWL*, III, 230, VI, 513, VII, 398, 408.

180 See n. 30 above.

181 See n. 80 above.

182 See n. 155 above.

Item for a brawne Mr Dandy[183]	0	5	0
Item for 2 collars of brawne from Sir Robert Bannister*[184]	0	2	0
Item to the bargemen this weeke	1	2	0
Item to the gardner at Lambeth	0	4	10
Item for 14 bush[els]† of oates for coach horses	1	15	0
Item for a bush[el]† of beanes	0	5	1

[fo. 55r]

Item for 18 bush[els]† of oates for geldings	2	5	0
Item for 12 shoes 6 removes and naylinge	0	8	6
Item spent in the kitchen this week ut patet p[er] libr[um]	25	8	7

Decemb[er] 8 1637

Item for 2 sugar loaves from the B[isho]pp of Landaffe*	0	5	0
Item for a peacocke Mr Snaith*	0	1	0
Item to the clockmaker	0	2	0
Item for musitians boathire	0	4	0
Item to Dr Paskes* man with Westfalia gamons tongue &c	0	11	0
Item for bringing sugar loaves Mr Southes*	0	12	0
Item to yr Graces taylor for apprell ut patet	14	17	4
Item for 40 yds of freesh† for livery coates xxij^{d} p[er] yrd	4	8	0
Item for 2 ells† of taffaty for the 12 coates	1	4	0
Item to the Earl of Salisburys* gent p[ayd] Mr Dell*	1	0	0
Item to Sir Humprey Fosters* man	2	0	0
Item for letters boathire &c	0	8	6
Item to the gardner at Lambeth	0	2	7
Item to the bargemen	1	10	0
Item for a lanterne	0	2	8
Item for 2 lambes B[isho]p of Oxon*	0	5	0
Item for 2 lambes Dr Higgs*	0	5	0
Item for an hyne Earl of Salisbury*	1	5	0
Item for 2 does B[isho]p of Winton*	1	0	0
Item for a gr[ea]t pie Lo[rd] Sherwood*	0	12	0
Item for 3 pheasants Mr Watts*	0	2	6
Item for a lamprey† pie	0	1	0
Item for a bush[el]† of oates for coach horses	1	15	0
Item for a bush[el]† of beanes	0	5	1
Item for 20 bush[els]† of oates for geldings & colts	2	10	0

183 This is the sole entry in the accounts for 'Mr Dandy', whose identity remains elusive.

184 Earlier in 1637, Sir Robert Banastre* had been appointed sheriff of Northamptonshire, an office which gave him responsibility for collecting the county's collection of ship money contributions; *CSPD 1637*, p. 40, no. 38, p. 53, no. 14.

[fo. 56r]

Item for nayling coach horses	0	1	0
Item for 14 loads of strawe layd in this q[ua]rt[e]r xj^{s} vj^{d}	8	0	0
Item spent in the kitchen this week vt patet p[er] libr[um]	28	13	6
For this quarter			
Payd the brewer for 4 hogsh[eads]† of viij^{s} & 160 hogsh[eads]† of vj^{s} beare layd in since Midsomer ut patet	90	12	0
Item to M[is]tr[es]s Hoult* for this q[ua]rter	4	0	0
Item to Mr Squire*	2	10	0
Item to yr Graces barber	0	10	0
Item for the footman	0	3	0
Item to M[is]tr[es]s Whaly* for the rent in the slaughterhouse	0	12	6
Item to the mole catcher for this q[ua]rter	0	5	0
Item to the laundress for ashes, soape, starch and besides wages	4	10	0
Item for hooping tubbs & a flasket† &c	0	7	10
Item for 3 doz of course towells for the kitchen	1	6	0
Item for 3 cottons for the scullery	0	4	9
Item for a q[ua]rter of oates for the poultry at the park	0	17	4
Item for 13 bush[els]† for swans & poultry at home	1	12	6
Item to Morris* the smith for shoeing geldings &c ut patet	5	15	8
Item to Abbot* the sadler ut patet p[er] bill	6	16	0
Item William Duckett* for household stuff &c ut patet	38	4	11
Item layd out by him for John Cobb* ut patet	2	7	6
Item for the footman ut patet	1	9	6
Item to Tho[mas] Sadler* for a suite & cloake &c for the footman	6	8	9
Some total of this fortnight p[ay]d Decemb[er] 20	273	13	11
Some total of this quarters expenses & laying out ut patet	viij^{c} xlij^{l}	viij^{s}	8^{d}
Some total of this years expenses & laying out cometh to ut patet	3362	18	2

All accompted and even
Ada[m] Torlesse*

[fo. 57r]
Incipit Anno
December 15 1637
First quarter
Rec[eave]d 0–0–0

Imprims for bringing an hogsh[ead]† of sack Station[er]s*	0	10	0
Item given to the prisons against ag[ain]st Xmas	3	0	0
Item given the poore of Lambeth against Xmas	20	0	0
Item to the poore of Croydon	5	0	0

Item to Sir G[eorge] Chytes* ma with a lambe pheas[ant] & partr[idge]	0	5	0
Item for 6 tearses† of claret wine Mr Job Harby*	1	0	0
Item for 2 hogsh[eads]† Marchants[185]	1	0	0
Item for an hogsh[ead]† Mr Mornings[186]	0	5	0
Item for a doe & 3 pheasants	0	12	0
~~*[entry struck through]*~~	~~*0*~~	~~*10*~~	~~*0*~~
Item for a brawne Sir Tho[mas] Culpeper*	0	10	0
Item for a lambe & pheas[ant] Sir Jo[hn] Shelly*	0	5	0
Item for 2 lambes Mr Dale*	0	3	6
Item for 2 does 3 pheas[ants] and a cheese Dutchess of Richmond*	1	5	0
Item for a brawne Mr Geeves[187]	0	6	0
Item to the bargemen	1	0	0
Item to the gardner at Lambeth	0	1	8
Item for 14 bush[els]† of oates for the coach horses a ij^{s} viij^{d}	1	11	6
Item for a bush[el]† of beanes	0	5	1
Item for 19 bush[els]† of oates for geldings at ij^{s} iij^{d}	2	2	9
Item for removing & naylinge	0	1	6
Item spent in the kitchen this week ut patet p[er] libr[um]	28	10	6

Decemb[e]r 22 1637

Item for 2 sugarloaves Dr Collyns*and his Coll[ege]	0	2	0
Item for fowle from Dr Crooke*	1	0	0
Item for 3 tearses† of claret from Dr Pawle*	0	10	0
Item to the butler for 6 doz of corks	0	3	0
Item to Knight* for holly &c	0	2	6
Item to Pallmer* for broomes	0	8	0
Item for yr G[races] offering on xxmas day	3	0	0

[fo. 58r]

Item to the brewers mens box	0	10	0
Item to Morris* the smiths men	0	3	6
Item to Bryans* man	0	2	0
Item to the harnessmakers men	0	2	0
Item to the coachmakers men	0	5	0
Item for a silver salt L[ord] Earl of Dorsett*	1	0	0
Item for a cupp & cover Mr Woodall*	1	0	0
Item for another Mr Bucknor*	1	0	0
Item for 2 stopes† Turkey Merchants*	1	0	0
Item for spices East Ind[ia] Company*	1	0	0

185 This gift of wine was probably sent by the Merchant Taylors' Company, since similar gifts were received from this organization in Dec. 1636 and Dec. 1638.

186 This is the sole entry in the accounts for 'Mr Mornings', whose identity remains elusive.

187 See n. 83 above.

Item to the gardner at Lambeth	0	3	4
Item to the bargemen	0	7	0
Item to the gardner at Croydon	1	4	6
Item to Mr Dell* ut patet	0	5	0
Item for 6 pheasants Mr Dayd*	0	3	0
Item for a turkey Lady Cade[188]	0	2	6
Item for 2 turkeys Mr Buckeridge*	0	5	0
Item for fowle Dr Sterne*	0	9	0
Item for a lamb &c Sir Tho[mas] Grymes*	0	5	0
Item for a doe Earl of Cleveland*	0	12	0
Item for a lamb Mr Bricke[189]	0	2	6
Item for 14 bush[els]† of oates for coach horses at ij^s iij^d	1	11	6
Item for a bush[el]† of beanes	0	5	1
Item for 20 bush[els]† of oates for geldings & colts	2	5	0
Item spent in the kitchen this week ut patet p[er] libr[um]	26	18	4
Some of this fortnight payd Januar[y] 4 1638	115	11	3

December 29 1637

Receaved Mr Newell v^l for wine			
Inprimis for yr Graces newe years gifte to the Kinge	40	0	0
Item given in newe years gifts to the househould ut patet[190]	30	5	6
Item for a new years gift from the B[isho]p of St Asaph*	1	0	0
Item for plate from Sir Nathaniel Brent*	2	0	0
Item to M[is]tr[es]s Buckeridge* for a newe years gifte	5	0	0
Item for 2 sugarloaves Mr Downer*	1	0	0
Item for the Lady Harbys man[191]	1	0	0
Item for plate from Mr Attorney*	2	0	0
Item for plate Lo[rd] Scudamore*	2	0	0
Item for plate Sir Henry Gilford*	1	0	0
Item for plate Merchant Advent[urers]*	2	0	0
[fo. 59r]			
Item to Mr Knights[192] boye	0	5	0
Item for plate &c Sir Henry Martyn*	1	0	0
Item for a tun of claret wine from Mr Warwick*	1	18	0
Item for a bason & ewer† from Capt[ain] Crispe*	2	2	6
Item for 4 candlesticks B[isho]p of St Asaph*	1	0	0

188 See n. 86 above.

189 This is the sole entry in the accounts relating to ‘Mr Bricke’, whose identity remains elusive.

190 See n. 14 above.

191 This is the sole entry in the accounts relating to ‘Lady Harby’, who was possibly Elizabeth, the wife of Sir Job Harby*.

192 See n. 8 above.

Item to the scullery mens box	0	10	0
Item to Dr Tillesleys sone[193] &c	1	1	6
Item to Mr Henshawes* man	1	0	0
Item for a salt Mr Morris Abbot*[194]	1	0	0
Item for a bason Mr Ball[195]	1	0	0
Item to Mr Daniel Harbyes* man	1	0	0
Item to Mr Pearces* man	0	10	0
Item given to the Beare & Oliv[e]	0	5	0
Item to Sir John Lambes* man	1	0	0
Item for a cabinett M[is]tr[es]s Burwood[196]	1	0	0
Item to Mr Cobb* for boathire	0	1	0
Item for 3 lambs Sir And[rew] Jeynor*	0	6	0
Item for an hyne E[arl] of Lyndsey*	0	17	0
Item for 2 swans &c Dr Merrick*	0	5	0
Item for 2 lamprey† pies Sir Morris Bartlett*	0	2	6
Item for Westfal[ia] bacones, tongues and sturgens Dr Merrick*	0	6	0
Item for orranges & lemons Mr Wragg*	0	2	0
Item for spices East Ind[ia] Company*	0	5	0
Item for a cheese Dr Googe*	0	3	6
Item for 6 sugarloaves Mr Tuck[197]	0	2	0
Item for a cake Edgerley the Carrier of Oxford	0	2	0
Item for lambs Mr Homes[198]	0	6	0
Item for partr[idge] & bacon from Mr Doyly*	0	3	6
Item for 4 fleetches of bacon from Dr Stanley*	0	2	0
Item for 14 bush[els]† of oates for the coach horses at ij^{s} iij^{d}	1	11	6
Item for a bush[el]† of beanes	0	5	1
Item for 19 bush[els]† of oates for the geldings	2	2	9
Item for removinge & naylinge	0	1	9
Item for mendings a buckett &c	0	1	2
Item for 18 broomes	0	3	0
Item spent in the kitchen this week ut patet p[er] libr[um]	29	18	7

193 This entry refers to John, son of Richard Tillesley (1582–1624), a Church of England clergyman and *alumnus* of St John's College, Oxford. During his career, Tillesley was on the periphery of Laud's circle, having been collated to his first living by Laud's friend and mentor John Buckeridge. E. Carlyle, 'Tillesley, Richard (1582–1624), Church of England clergyman', *ODNB*.

194 This may be a mis-recording of a gift from Sir Maurice Abbot*, or it may well have been sent by another person with a similar name. Among a number of prominent 'Abbots'active in London during the 1630s was Sir Maurice's son, Edward – a merchant, like his father – and it may well be that Edward, as well as Sir Maurice, gave gifts to Laud; *CSPD 1635*, p. 156, no. 77h; *Knights of England*, II, 188.

195 This is the sole entry in the accounts relating to 'Mr Ball', whose identity remains elusive.

196 It is possible that this cabinet was made by John Burwood*, carpenter, and delivered by his wife, Mistress Burwood.

197 This is the sole entry in the accounts for a gift from 'Mr Tuck', whose identity remains elusive.

198 This is the sole entry in the accounts relating to 'Mr Homes' whose identity remains elusive.

[fo. 60r]

Item for 4 capons 2 turkeys &c from Sir John Lambe*	0	2	0
Item for an hyne &c D[uchess] of Richmond*	0	13	0
Item for 2 sugarloaves Mr Creswell* the porter	0	2	6
Item for the needles on Twelfth Night	0	10	0
Item for 2 sugarloaves Mr Barnard*	0	5	0
Item for 2 pair chickens Dr Turner*	0	2	6
Item for boathire &c to court p[ayd] Ralphe [Watts]*	0	2	8
Item give the prisons Mr Cobb*	0	3	0
Item to the bargemen	0	17	0
Item for 14 bush[els]† of oates for coach horses at ij^{s} iij^{d}	1	11	6
Item for a bush[el]† of beanes	0	5	1
Item for 18 bush[els]† of oates for geldings & colts	2	0	6
Item for 4 shoes & 8 removes	0	3	8
Item spent in the kitchen this week ut patet p[er] libr[um]	26	18	9
Some of this fortnight payd Januar[y] 19 1638	174	2	0

Januar[y] 12 1638

Rec[eave]d meale 20 bush[els]†	5	10	0
ffier at consecr[ation]	2	10	0
& of Mr Barton* for wood	87	14	11
Inprimis given the B[isho]p of Oxfords* man with a cake	0	6	0
Item for another from M[is]tr[es]s Everleigh of Oxford[199]	0	2	0
Item for yr G[races] offeringe at the consecration[200]	3	0	0
Item for making clean yr G[race]s watch	0	1	0
Item for 2 hogsh[eads]† wine from Sir Robert Heath*	1	0	0
Item for 6 chickens cheeses from Mr Huchenson*	0	2	6
Item to Mr Snaith* for gloves for yr Grace	0	6	5
Item to your shoemakers men	0	4	6
Item to Jo[hn] Mills* for boathire about the great horse	0	1	6
Item to Roger* for boathire to & from court	0	3	0
Item to Pallmer* for broomes	0	5	0
Item for 14 bush[els]† of oates for the coach horses at ij^{s} iiij^{d}	1	11	6
Item for a bush[el]† of beanes	0	5	1

[fo. 61r]

Item for 17 bush[els]† of oates for geldings	1	18	3

---

199 Although recorded here as 'Mistress Everleigh of Oxford', the identity of this gift-giver remains elusive. Since her gift was recorded in the accounts immediately after an entry for a gift from John Bancroft*, the bishop, Mistress Everleigh may well have been connected to him and/or his household.

200 John Warner* was consecrated bishop of Rochester at Lambeth Palace in Jan. 1638, following the death of John Bowle*, the previous encumbant, in Oct. 1637; Knighton, 'Bowle, John (d. 1637)', *ODNB*.

Item for a bayl at Sir Henry Martyns*	0	1	6
Item for 12 removes	0	2	0
Item spent in the kitchen this week ut patet p[er] libr[um]	26	6	7

Januar[y] 19 1638

Item for Mr Pococks* pension for 2 q[ua]rters ending at Lady Day next ut patet	20	0	0
Item for 4 pheas[ants] 4 brand geese & puddings from Sir Jo[hn] Shelly*	0	10	0
Item for the musitians boathire	0	1	0
Item for 2 fleeches of bacon from Mr Parkinson[201]	0	4	0
Item for 6 lamprey† pies M[is]tr[es]s Dutton*	0	3	6
Item for 3 sugarloaves Dr Wood*	0	2	6
Item for a broad goose pie pheas[ant] & partr[idge] Sir Humphrey Foster*	0	2	6
Item for 4 pheas[ants] Sir Ed[ward] Boys*	0	5	0
Item to the keep[er] of the garden gate & boy	0	11	0
Item to the prisons Mr Holford*	0	3	6
Item to Sir Tho[ma]s Roes* man &c	0	3	6
Item for a kegg of sturgeon from Mr Losage[202]	0	2	6
Item for 2 barr[els] of herring from Yarmouth	0	11	0
Item for 12 broad goose pies from the B[isho]p of Chichester*	0	5	0
Item for puddings &c Dutchess of Richmond*	0	7	6
Item for 12 lambes Dr Higgs*	0	5	0
Item for pearmaynes† Mr Mills[203]	0	1	0
Item to the gardner at Lambeth	0	5	9
Item to the bargemen	1	5	0
Item to Mr Ramsey* p[ayd] Mr Dell* ut patet	0	11	0
Item to him for letters and boathire	0	11	4
Item for 14 bush[els]† of oates for coach horses	1	11	6
Item for a bush[el]† of beanes	0	5	1
Item for 16 bush[els]† of oates for geldings	1	16	0
Item for drenching G[reat] Willcox	0	3	0
Item spent in the kitchen this weeke ut patet p[er] libr[um]	29	15	11
Some of this fortnight payd Febr[uary] 6 1638	95	19	11

[fo. 62r]

Rec[eave]d of Dr Goad* vj[l] for wine			
Item given Pallmer* the fyer maker	0	10	0
Item for pheas[ants] partr[idges] &c from Sir Capell Beadle*	0	6	0
Item for a p[er]fume & letters &c p[ayd] Mr Snaith*	0	4	6

201 See n. 6 above.
202 This is the sole entry in the accounts relating to 'Mr Losage', whose identity remains elusive.
203 See n. 155 above.

Item for turkey, capons & partr[idge] &c Dr Warren*	0	7	0
Item for puddings &c from the Dutchess of Richmond*	0	5	0
Item to the gardner at Lambeth	0	8	2
Item to the bargemen	1	5	0
Item to Mr Browne* for putting upp the roofe of the barge	0	16	0
Item to the gardner at Croydon	0	19	0
Item for 2 cheeses Sir H[umfry] Foster*	0	1	0
Item for 14 bush[els]† of oates for coach horses	1	11	6
Item for a bush[el]† of beanes	0	5	1
Item for 15 bsh of oates for geldings	1	13	9
Item for 8 shoes & naylings	0	5	8
Item for drenching Little Willmott	0	3	0
Item spent in the kitchen this weeke ut patet p[er] libr[um]	27	5	9

Febr[uary] 2 1638

Item for 2 barr[els] of sallmon & 3 of elles from the B[isho]p of Londonderry*	1	6	0
Item for 4 lamprey† pies Sir Morris Bartlett*	0	5	0
Item for a firkin† of sturgeon Dr Willson*	0	5	0
Item for a broad goose pie Dr Merrick*	0	3	6
Item for a box of sugar Searg[eant] Hendon*	1	8	0
Item for a sallmon pie Dr Parry*	0	5	0
Item to the groome, butler and porter at the Star Chamber[204]	0	6	6
Item to the gardner at Lambeth	0	2	5
Item to the bargemen	1	7	0
Item for 14 bush[els]† of oates for coach horses	1	12	0
Item for a bush[el]† of beanes	0	5	1
Item for 16 bush[els]† of oates for geldings	1	18	0
Item for 4 shoes & removing the coach horses	0	3	4
Item spent in the kitchen this weeke ut patet p[er] libr[um]	32	5	0
Some of this fortnight payd Febr[uary] 15 1638	78	2	1

[fo. 63r]
Rec[eave]d 0–0–0

Inprimis to yr Grace for Sir Symon Baskerfield*	5	0	0
Item to Ald[erman] Garrowayes* ma[n] p[ayd] Mr Dell*	0	10	0
Item for gold E[arl] of Traquare*[205]	0	10	0

---

204 See n. 30 above.

205 For the past four years, John Stewart*, 1st earl of Traquair, had built up a working rapport with Laud, since both crown servants were engaged in implementing a range of royal policies in Scotland and they had to correspond on matters pertaining to church revenue, episcopal appointments and, increasingly, the growing tension arising from the reaction to the 1637 prayer book. References to this gift of 'gold' cannot be found in other sources, but it probably came in the form of plate, rather than coinage.

Item to Mr Dell* for letters & boathire	0	7	0
Item for cakes & boathire Mr Snaith*	0	2	0
Item for 2 hogsh[eads]† of sack Dr Farmley*[206]	0	2	6
Item for cheeses Dr Smith*	0	2	0
Item for cheeses, cakes &c from Dr Manwayring*	0	7	0
Item to the gardner at Lambeth	0	9	3
Item to the bargemen	1	12	8
Item for 14 bush[els]† oates for the coach horses	1	13	3
Item for a bush[el]† of beanes	0	4	4
Item for 15 bush[els]† of oates for geldings	1	18	0
Item for nayling coach horses	0	1	0
Item spent in the kitchen this week ut patet p[er] libr[um]	31	8	6

Febr[uary] 16 1638

Item to the hetheman for bringing Mr Roses* 50 quarters of wheate with some other charges	3	5	9
Item to the porters for carrying it into the graynary	0	13	9
Item for 4 lamprey† pies from Mr Solicitor*	0	2	0
Item for yr G[races] offering	3	0	0
Item for a tun of claret from Sir Dudley Digges*	1	0	0
Item to Mr Levinthrop* for boathire	0	2	0
Item for a cake & puddings M[is]tr[es]s Dorman[207]	0	5	0
Item to the gardner at Croydon	1	3	0
Item to the bargemen	1	2	0
Item to the gardner at Lambeth	0	18	4
Item for pills for your Grace	0	2	0
Item for p[er]fumes Mr Southes*	0	2	0
Item to Sir William Beecher for a booke p[ayd] Mr Dell*	1	6	0
Item for boathires, letters &c	0	7	3
Item for pippins† &c Mr Denn*	0	2	6
Item for 2 lamprey† pies Judge Jones*	0	2	6
Item for a sallmon Mr Webb*	0	2	6
Item for puddings & apples D[uchess] of Richmond*	0	6	0
Item for a sallmon Mr Gent[208]	0	3	6
Item for 2 barr[els] of oysters Dr Aylett*	0	1	8
Item for 4 cheeses Dr Manwayring*	0	5	0

[fo. 64r]

Item a lamprey† pie Mr Mills[209]	0	1	0
Item a sallmon Mr Harfleet*	0	5	0

---

206 This entry probably relates to John Farmery*, civil lawyer.
207 This is the sole entry in the accounts for ‘Mistress Dorman’, whose identity remains elusive.
208 This is the sole entry in the accounts for ‘Mr Gent’, whose identity remains elusive.
209 See n. 155 above.

Item for 14 bush[els]† of oates for the coach horses	1	13	3
Item for a bush[el]† of beanes	0	4	4
Item for 16 bush[els]† of oates for geldings & colts	1	18	0
Item for nayling coach horses	0	1	0
Item for spent in the kitchen this week ut patet p[er] libr[um]	26	13	4
Some of this fortnight payd Febr[uary] 27 1638	89	15	6

Februar[y] 23 1638

Rec[eave]d 0–0–0

Inprimis lamprey† pyes from Alderman Robinson*	0	1	6
Item for lyninge yr Graces hatt p[ayd] Mr Rollston*	0	7	0
Item for shipp money for Lambeth[210]	9	0	0
Item for shipp money for Croydon[211]	5	0	0
Item to Mr Southes* for p[er]fumes	0	2	0
Item to the gardner at Croydon	1	5	6
Item to the bargemen	1	0	0
Item to the gardner at Lambeth	0	8	7
Item to Pallmer* for broomes	0	4	6
Item for fishe out of Ireland[212]	0	5	0
Item for a cheese & 2 lamprey† pies from Sir Rob[ert] Pie*[213]	0	6	0
Item for 14 bush[els]† of oates for coach horses at ij^{s} vj^{d}	1	15	0
Item for a bush[el]† of beanes	0	4	4
Item for 15 bush[els]† of oates for geldings at ij^{s} vj^{d}	1	17	6
Item spent in the kitchen this weeke ut patet p[er] libr[um]	31	1	2

March 2 1638

Item for a veale from Mr Farrant[214]	0	6	0
Item for a lamprey† pie Mr Jones of G[loucester][215]	0	1	6
Item to the Lo[rd] Treasurers* coachman	0	10	0
Item to a writt of Redding	0	5	0

---

210 See n. 20 above.

211 See n. 20 above.

212 This was probably the 'Lenten present' of salmon and eels from John Bramhall*, bishop of Derry. Laud wrote to thank Bramhall for the gift and reported that 'the herrings are not come'; *WWL*, VI, 518.

213 At the time of this gift, Sir Robert Pye* – in his capacity as executor for the estate of Buckingham, the assassinated royal favourite – had just renegotiated the wardship arrangements for the young George Villiers, Buckingham's son and heir. In particular, he had sought clarification as to whom certain incomes should be paid. As Laud reported to Wentworth, the matter was only resolved after Pye had appeared before the privy council on several occasions in late 1637 and early 1638; *WWL*, VI, 527, VII, 403–4, 409–10, 418.

214 See n. 115 above.

215 This is the sole entry in the accounts relating to 'Mr Jones of G.', whose identity remains elusive.

Item for boathires l[e]t[ter]s &c Mr Dell*	0	13	4
Item to Mr Braye* for a booke of the B[isho]p of Elyes[216]	2	5	0
Item to the bargemen	1	0	6
Item to the gardner at Lambeth	0	9	6
Item for 14 bush[els]† of oates for coach horses	1	15	0
Item for a bush[el]† of beanes	0	4	4

[fo. 65r]

Item for 16 bush[els]† of oates for the geldings at ij^{s} vj^{d}	2	0	0
Item for 2 newe shoes & removes	0	2	6
Item for 12 broomes	0	2	0
Item for an horses hire to Croydon	0	2	6
Item spent in the kitchen this week ut patet p[er] libr[um]	29	11	6
Some of this fortnight payd March 13 1638	92	6	9

March 9 1638

Receaved from Mr Roses* 50 quarters of barly	90	0	0
And for the Bill of Impost	24	0	0
Inprimis p[ay]d for bringing 2 barr of oysters Mr Cobb*	0	1	0
Item for 2 lamprey† pies Mr Subdean*	0	1	6
Item for a hogsh[eads]† of sack & another of claret Comp[any of] Vintners*	1	0	0
Item for 3 lamprey† pies Lo[rd] Saye*[217]	0	2	6
Item for bringing allmon butter	0	4	0
Item for North Downe ale from Mr Banks in the Ile of Thanett[218]	0	2	0
Item for a cake & cheeses Mr Ramsey*	0	1	0
Item to the gardner at Croydon	1	11	7
Item to the gardner at Lambeth	0	5	10
Item to the bargemen	1	1	0
Item to Mr Smiths[219] sone & porter p[ayd] Mr Dell* ut patet	1	2	0
Item to Mr Whitlocks* man with fish	0	10	0

216 Matthew Wren*, rather than Francis White, the previous incumbent of the diocese of Ely. White had died in Feb. 1638 and Wren was on the cusp of being translated to Ely; Timothy Wadkins, 'White, Francis (1563/4–1638)', *ODNB*.

217 This isolated gift from William Fiennes*, Viscount Saye and Sele, is curious. Saye was an arch-opponent of Laudian policy and associated with a circle of godly peers who opposed many of the prerogative fiscal measures of the 1630s. In addition, this gift came at a time when Saye was planning to emigrate to one of his plantations in New Hampshire, in the midst of the ship money case against John Hampden, with which Saye was centrally involved. Laud described Hampden in a letter to Wentworth as 'the very genius of those people who set themselves against the Government' and told the lord deputy that, in this, Hampden went even 'beyond the Lord Saye, which I for my part can hardly believe'; *WWL*, VII, 399.

218 Mr Banks, whose identity remains elusive, may have been a brewer, based in Thanet, Kent.

219 See n. 39 above.

Item for herrings & salmon out of Scotland	1	0	0
Item to Mr Rayltons* man	0	5	0
Item to him for boathire letters &c ut patet	0	5	6
Item to Mr Rylyes* man p[ayd] Mr Snaith*	2	0	0
Item for marking shirts & handkerchers &c ut patet	0	7	0
Item for his boathires &c ut patet	0	3	8
Item for 14 bush[els]† of oates for the coach horses at ij^{s} vj^{d}	1	15	0
Item for a bush[el]† of beanes	0	4	4
Item for 15 bush[els]† of oates for geldings	1	17	6
Item for 12 newe shoes & 5 removes	0	8	0
Item setting up the coach horses in the Charter House	0	3	0
Item spent in the kitchen this weeke ut patet p[er] libr[um]	30	14	11

For this quarter

Payd the brewer for 12 hogsh[eads]† of viij^{s} & 96 hogsh[eads]† of vj^{s} beere layd in this q[ua]rter	50	8	0
Item to M[is]tr[es]s Hoult* for this q[ua]rter	4	0	0
Item to Mr Squire* for this q[ua]rter	2	10	0

[fo. 66r]

Item to M[is]tr[es]s Whaly* for the rent of the slaughter house	0	12	6
Item to the mole catcher	0	5	0
Item to yr G[races] barber	0	10	0
Item for the footman	0	3	0
Item to the laundresse for ashes, soape, starch &c besides wages	4	10	0
Item for lynes & hooping tubbs	0	10	0
Item to Abbott* the sadler for shoeing geldings ut patet	4	2	10
Item to the armorer for making 25 footmans armor serviceable at xxvj^{s} a peece ut patet p[er] bill[220]	33	1	6
Item for a new harpsicon instrument[221]	20	0	0
Item for a frame for it	2	0	0
Item for 64 doz of candles taken in at iiij^{s} vj^{d} p[er] doz	14	8	0
Item to the vintner for 2 hogsh[eads]† of canary layd in for bill of impost	26	0	0

220 This is a curious entry, since Laud did not employ twenty-five footmen. The assumption is that this entry could well reflect the archbishop's contribution to the king's armoury, which was being reinforced in light of the growing sense of danger in London, where news was rife of the Scottish crisis. Armour was in short supply and senior crown servants, as well as other members of the nobility, were expected to assist the king (as they did in early 1639, when he was preparing for his first campaign against the Scots). The same week, one newsletter reported that 'the stirre in Scotland … is not yet quieted but rather seeming to burst out in to a flame'. Laud was also probably feeling the pressure, as a result of an incident involving the king's fool, Archibald Armstrong, who jibed at Laud, insinuating that he was responsible for the Scottish situation. When Laud complained about it to the king, Armstrong was promptly dismissed, leading to further gossip; TNA, C115/108 8623.

221 This instrument was kept in the parlour at Lambeth Palace. On Laud's death, it was bequeathed to John Cobb*, his organist; *WWL*, IV, 447.

Item for red wine, claret & maligo† to fill up the whels this yeare ut patet	4	3	8
and for signing the bill of impost	1	18	0
Item to the lynen drap for 17 ells† ½ of yd & broad cloth at ij^{s} p[er] ell† for cupboard cloths	2	12	6
Item for 32 ells† more at ij^{s} vj^{d} p[er] ell†	4	0	0
Item for 24 doz & 6 napkins at viij^{s} ix^{d} p[er] doz	10	14	4
Item for 6 doz & 3 napkins at xj^{s} vj^{d} p[er] doz	3	11	11
Item for making & marking the 25 cupboard & sideboard clothes at iij^{d} a peece	0	6	3
Item for making & marking the 30 doz & 9 napkins att xij^{d} p[er] doz	1	10	9
Item to William Duckett* for Mr Robinsons*[222] seales & chardges ut patet p[er] bill	18	11	4
Item to him for makinge upp cushins for the chappell &c ut patet	17	3	10
Item to him for John Cobb*	1	17	0
Item for the footman ut patet	0	12	2
Item for a tawney cloth for livryes sent 27 yards at xx^{s} iij^{d}	12	10	0
Item for an ell† ¾ of taffaty for x coates at xij^{s}	1	0	0

[fo. 67r]

Item p[ay]d Mr Watts* for a boate carridge of it to Croydon	3	7	0
Item to him for pigeons meale for this halfe yeare ut patet	1	16	10
Item to more to him for gravell & clensing the g[rea]t pond &c ut patet	1	2	6
Item to the pewterer for changing old pewter and for some newe ut patet p[er] bill	4	16	4
Item to Knight* & others for clensinge the watercourses and ditches about the marshes &c	12	3	6
Some total of this week payd	319	15	1
Some total of this quarters expenses and laying out cometh to	ix^{c} lxj^{l} xij^{s} vij^{d}		

All accompted & payd Adam Torlesse*

The Second quarter beginning March 16 1638

Receaved 0–0–0

Inprimis given to the 13 prisons against Easter	3	0	0
Item to the Lord Deputyes* man &c with a sadle &c[223]	2	2	0
Item to Mr Badger* for binding manuscripts &c ut patet	1	8	3

---

222 This is the sole entry in the accounts for 'Mr Robinson', as opposed to 'Alderman Robinson' or 'Anthony Robinson', for whom there are a number of entries respectively. It is likely that this entry relates to Hugh Robinson*.

223 By this stage, Laud had been anticipating the arrival of this 'rich saddle' with a 'Dutch pad' from Wentworth for some time. Writing in late Mar., he thanked the lord deputy and told him that he was keen to try it out, which he promised to do at 'the first opportunity I get to step to Croydon', although the archbishop expected that it might be 'too high'. The additional item/s referred to as '&c' in this entry, may well have been the lamp which Wentworth also sent; *WWL*, VII, 418.

Item to Mr Stones man & catermen &c with 2 pipes of canary[224]	1	16	6
Item to Pallmer* for broomes	0	5	2
Item to the gardner at Lambeth	0	9	4
Item to the bargemen	1	5	0
Item for basketts for coales and fish &c for the kitchen	0	4	4
Item for 14 bush[els]† of oates for coach horses at ij^{s} vj^{d}	1	15	0
Item for a bush[el]† of beanes	0	4	4
Item for 16 bush[els]† of oates for the geldings	2	0	0
Item for nayling coach horses	0	1	0
Item spent in the kitchen this week ut patet p[er] libr[um]	30	2	3

[fo. 68r]
March 23 1638

Item for 4 fleeches of bacon from Mr Wheate*[225]	0	6	0
Item for yr G[races] offeringe on Easter Day	3	0	0
Item to the prisons at yr G[race] going to the Charter House	0	2	0
Item to the boy at the garden gate	0	1	0
Item given to Mr Bostock* &c	1	5	0
Item for a bucke from yr Lord Peter*	1	1	0
Item for another from Sir Richard Newport*	1	0	0
Item for 2 lamprey† pies from Ald[erman] Robinson*	0	2	0
Item for bringing 2 pheasants	0	2	0
Item to the bargemen	1	5	0
Item to the gardner at Lambeth	0	4	8
Item to the 4 grooms and postilian to buy them bootes	2	10	0
Item for 14 bush[els]† of oates for the coach horsers at ij^{s} vj^{d}	1	15	0
Item for a bush[el]† of beanes	0	4	4
Item for 15 bush[els]† of oates for the geldings	1	17	6
Item for dressing Little Willmotts shoulder & foote	0	5	0
Item spend in the kitchen this weeke ut patet p[er] libr[um]	31	17	0
Some total of this fortnight payd Aprill 4 1638	91	10	8

March 30 1638

Receaved 0–0–0

Inprimis to Mr Cobb* for boathire to the Lady Dutchess of Buckingham*	0	1	0
Item to Mr Rollston* for boathires &c	0	2	6

224 Mr Stone's gift of wine – which is a classic example of a gift given for political purposes – came back to haunt Laud at his trial in 1644, since it was directly linked to a high commission case in which Stone had a vested interest. It is also a pertinent example of a gift related to a law suit, which was a common practice in the early modern period. *WWL*, III, 404, IV, 144. For gift-giving and legal cases, see Natalie Zemon Davies, *The gift in sixteenth century France* (Madison, 2000), p. 86.

225 This gift from William Wheate* is connected to the gift of wine mentioned in the note above.

Item to Mr Rayltons* brother-in-lawe for an harpe[226]	1	2	6
Item give the Lady Roes* man[227]	3	0	0
Item to the bargemen	1	0	0
Item to the gardner at Croydon ut patet	2	1	0
Item to the gardner at Lambeth	0	10	0
Item for 14 bush[els]† of oates for coach horses at ij^{s} vj^{d}	1	15	0
Item for a bush[el]† of beanes	0	4	4
Item for 14 bush[els]† of oates for geldings & colts at ij^{s} iij^{d}	1	11	9
Item for removing & nayling	0	1	2
Item spent in the kitchen this week ut patet p[er] libr[um]	34	12	4

[fo. 69r]
Aprill 6 1638

Item to John Newton* for 14 ducks	0	14	0
Item to Nutt* the slaughterman for bringing 65 Kent weathers† out of Kent ut patet	3	4	0
Item for herrings out of Ireland	0	6	0
Item for 3 lamprey† pies Dr Smith*	0	2	0
Item to the bargemen this weeke	1	0	0
Item given W[illiam] Loveday* the gardner[228]	1	0	0
Item to the weeders at Lambeth	0	10	0
Item for 2 loads of gravell for the sellers	0	2	8
Item for 14 bush[els]† of oates for the coach horsers at ij^{s} iiij^{d} p[er] bush[el]†	1	11	6
Item for a bush[el]† of beanes	0	4	4
Item for 14 bush[els]† of oates for the geldings	1	11	6
Item for 8 removes & naylings	0	1	8
Item spent in the kitchen this weeke ut patet p[er] libr[um]	33	2	2
Some total of this fortnight payd April 19 1638	89	11	5

Aprill 13 1638

Receaved for Mr Denns* barley	lxxx		
Inprimis for 4 cheeses from Dr Dodd[229]	0	4	0

226 William Raylton* had two brothers-in-law: Richard Bourne and Thomas Stirer. The former was the wife of Raylton's sister-in-law, Ann Bourne; the latter's exact relationship to Raylton is not known; TNA, Prob.11/231 quire 335, Prob. 11/332. My thanks to Dr Fiona Pogson for these references.

227 Sir Thomas Roe* had just been appointed ambassador extraordinary in Hamburg. Lady Eleanor Roe* wanted to join him on this embassy and petitioned Laud to be given leave to travel to her husband. In Aug. 1638, Laud wrote to Roe musing over the pros and cons of his wife joining him and it was not until the following spring that she eventually reached Hamburg; *WWL*, VII, 473.

228 Francis Loveday*, the gardener, was also known as William; LPL, TG1, fo. 28r.

229 Probably Dr Nathaniel Dodd (b. 1564), parson of Bennington in Hertfordshire, who had contributed funds for the repair of St Paul's cathedral in 1635; *Alumni oxonienses*, I, 410; TNA, SP 16/310, fo. 52.

Item for a letters Mr Southes*	0	0	6
Item for broomes & mopps Pallmer*	0	4	9
Item to the weeders at Lambeth	0	10	0
Item to the bargemen	1	0	0
Item to Mr Dell* ut patet	0	14	6
Item to the gardner at Croydon for weeders &c	1	7	3
Item for a p[aire] of g[rea]t bootes	1	6	0
Item for 14 bush[els]† of oates for the coach horses at ij^{s} iij^{d}	1	11	6
Item for a bush[el]† of beanes	0	4	4
Item for 14 bush[els]† of oates for the geldings & colts	1	11	6
Item for bleeding & drenching the 7 coach horses	1	1	0
Item spent in the kitchen this weeke ut patet p[er] libr[um]	29	13	5

Apr[il] 20 1638

Item payd for the shipp money for the court[230]	4	13	9
Item given Mr Bostock*	5	0	0
Item for boathires for musitians	0	2	0
Item for the E[arl] of Arundells* gent with MS p[ayd] Mr Dell*	2	0	0
Item to the watermen & porter	0	5	0
Item more p[ayd] to Mr Snaith* ut patet	1	10	0
Item to him for boathires ut patet	0	3	2

[fo. 70r]

Item for an horse from Mr Lowther* p[ayd] Mr Holford*	2	5	0
Item to him for boathires ut patet	0	7	0
Item to Mr Cobb* for boathires ut patet	0	1	0
Item to Mr Wrayes[231] men with 2 horses	6	0	0
Item to the bargemen	1	1	0
Item to Kingston for 6 dayes work about the 14 arr[ound] the park and the house	0	7	7
Item for an hogsh[eads]† of canary from Shrewsbury	0	15	0
Item for an hogsh[eads]† of claret from Mr Merryes of Dover[232]	0	8	0
Item for 3 doz of bottles & corks for the court	0	13	0
Item for 14 bush[els]† of oates for the coach horses at ij^{s} iij^{d}	1	11	6
Item for a bush[el]† of beanes	0	4	4
Item for 15 bush[els]† of oates for geldings & colts	1	13	9

230 This is the only occasion on which Laud made a ship money contribution related to his residence at court. Other payments of the levy, for Lambeth and Croydon, were made annually slightly earlier in the year. See n. 20 above.

231 This is the first of four entries in the accounts for 'Mr Wraye', whose identity remains elusive. Not to be confused with Sir Christopher Wray*, from whom one gift is recorded here.

232 This is the sole entry in the accounts relating to 'Mr Merryes of Dover', whose identity remains elusive.

Item for 4 new shoes & 12 removes for coach horses	0	4	4
Item spent in the kitchen this weeke ut patet p[er] libr[um]	31	16	7
Some total of this fortnight payd May 3 1638	100	5	9

Aprill 27 1638

Rec[eave]d for bay Newcastle[233]	17	0	0
For 3 ston[e]d horses†[234]	70	0	0
For the E[arl] of Thanetts* Wheate	28	0	0
In toto	cxv	0	0

Imprims p[ay]d for a p[aire] of gamashins† for yr Grace Mr Snaith*	0	9	0
Item for a p[aire] of shoes & boathire	0	5	0
Item to Mr Holford* for boathire	0	1	0
Item for musitians boathire	0	1	0
Item for a nagg† Earl of Newcastle*[235]	3	0	0
Item for a horse Mr Boswell*	2	0	0
Item for boathires to Mr Snaith*	0	3	6
Item to the groome butler & porter at the Star Chamber[236]	0	6	6
Item to a poore woman & a cake	0	4	6
Item to the gardner at Lambeth	0	7	2
Item to the bargemen	1	10	0
Item for 14 bush[els]† of oates for the coach horses at ij^{s} iij^{d}	1	11	6
Item for a bush[el]† of beanes	0	4	4
Item for 14 bush[els]† of oates for the geldings	1	11	6
Item for nayling coach horses	0	1	4
Item spent in the kitchen this week ut patet p[er] libr[um]	27	13	8

[fo. 71r]

Inprimis for a buck from Mr Dutton*	0	12	0
Item to Mr Solicitors* man Mr Dell*	2	0	0
Item to Pallmer* for broomes mopps & sweeping 2 chymneys	0	5	3

233 Newcastle had given this horse to Laud in Apr. 1637 (see n. 134 above) and it was now being sold on. In late Mar. 1638, Laud mentioned in a letter to Wentworth that 'my fine great horse which my Lord of Newcastle gave me and which you saw when you did me the honour to come to Croydon, is quite spoiled and gone with the fashions'; *WWL*, VII, 418.

234 The purchase of three new horses may have been to offset some recent losses in the archiepiscopal stables. Laud wrote to John Bridgeman*, bishop of Chester, in Aug. from Croydon, to inform him that the horse he had given the archbishop in May 1636 (see n. 50 above) had died of 'the Sleepie Disease and I was like to have lost two or three more with him'. In this same letter, Laud thanked Bridgeman for supplying him 'with another', although there is no record of this animal in the accounts; Staffordshire Record Office, D1287/18/2 (P/399/170).

235 In the context of the above note, this horse from the earl of Newcastle may have been a replacement for one of those which had recently succumbed to illness.

236 See n. 30 above.

Item to the gardner at Croydon	1	3	2
Item to the bargemen	1	0	0
Item to the gardner at Lambeth	0	13	11
Item to Rich[ard] the groome for sellinge bay Newcastle[237]	1	0	0
Item to Mr Snaith* for 2 p[aires] of shoes & a p[aire] of gamashins† for yr Grace	0	17	0
Item more to him for boathires	0	9	0
Item to Tho[mas] Sadler* for a suite & cloake for Jo[hn] Cobb* ut patet	4	5	6
Item to Mr Doylyes* man with cheeses, bacon &c	0	5	0
Item to Mr Woodalls* man with sugar and pepper	0	6	0
Item for 2 firkins†† of sturgeon from the Eastland Marchants*	0	6	0
Item for 14 bush[els]† of oates for coach horses	1	11	6
Item for a bush[el]† of beanes	0	4	4
Item for 13 bush[els]† of oates for geldings	1	9	3
Item for 13 shoes & 6 removes for coach horses	0	9	0
Item for 12 ropes to tye them	0	3	6
Item for 12 broomes	0	2	0
Item spent in the kitchen this weeke ut patet p[er] libr[um]	33	19	11
Some of this fortnight payd May 15 1638	96	13	10

Maye 11 1638

Rec[eave]d Mr Barton* in full payment of the last years woodsale	21	9	2
Item towards this years woodsale	100	0	0
Imprims for yr Graces offeringe at Whitsunday	3	0	0
Item to Mr Snaith* for boathires to the E[arl] of Northumberland* 6 days[238]	0	1	0
Item for a buck from Sir Robert Dormer*	1	0	0
Item for another Lo[rd] Newburgh*	1	0	0
Item for another Mr Wraye[239]	0	5	0
Item to the bargemen this week	1	5	0
Item to the gardner at Lambeth	0	11	8

237 'Richard' was possibly Richard Berridge, one of the coachmen at Lambeth Palace. The horse, given to the archbishop by the earl of Newcastle* in Apr. 1637 (see n. 134 above) had been sold just over a week before; LPL, TG1, fo. 28r.

238 On 13 Apr. 1638, Algernon Percy*, 10th earl of Northumberland, had been appointed lord admiral, the first time this office had been made since the assassination of the previous incumbent, Buckingham, in Aug. 1628. The appointment had the backing of both Laud and Wentworth. At the time of this payment, however, Northumberland was seriously ill and Laud told Wentworth that he was 'heartily sorry to write' that 'all hopes of his service are in danger, for he hath been in a high fever now these three weeks'. The archbishop was 'very fearful' that Northumberland might die. This explains the six visits – either by Laud or an emissary – to the earl to which this entry relates, as well as a further four the week after; *WWL*, VI, 526, VII, 453.

239 See n. 231 above.

Item for 14 bush[els]† of oates for the coach horses at ij[s] iij[d]	1	11	6
Item for a bush[el]† of beanes	0	4	4

[fo. 72r]

Item for 10 bush[els]† of oates for geldings	1	2	6
Item spent in the kitchen this week ut patet p[er] libr[um]	32	6	2

May 18 1638

Item to your G[race] for Mr Solicitors* fee	5	0	0
Item for Mr Harbords* fee	3	0	0
Item to Sir Humf[rey] Fosters* man	1	0	0
Item for your G[races] shoemakers boathire	0	2	0
Item to Mr Snaith* boathire to the E[arl] of Northumberland* 4 tymes	0	4	0
Item for Mr Crofts* boathire[240]	0	1	0
Item to the bargemen	0	14	4
Item to the gardner at Lambeth	0	12	2
Item for the horses meale & chardges into Kent	2	12	6
Item for Nicholas* chardges with a colt	0	8	6
Item for shoeing the 2 naggs†	0	3	0
Item to Alderman Robinson* for lamprey† pies this Lent	1	15	0
Item for letters & boathires Mr Dell*	0	7	0
Item for 14 bush[els]† of oates for the coach horses	1	11	6
Item for a bush[el]† of beanes	0	4	4
Item for 8 bush[els]† of oates for geldings	0	18	0
Item for 8 newe shoes & naylings	0	5	6
Item spent in the kitchen this weeke ut patet p[er] libr[um]	36	19	8
Some of this fortnight payd May 28 1638	98	10	8

May 25 1638

Rec[eave]d of Mr Barton* for wood	150	0	0
Item given to the E[arl] of Northumberlands* coachman p[ayd] Mr Snaith*[241]	0	6	0
Item for his boathires &c ut patet	0	7	0
Item given Nicholas* and John Mills* by yr Grace	1	0	0
Item for a bucke from the King	1	0	0
Item to Mr Snaith* for tape for yr Grace sleeves &c	0	3	6
Item to Mr Cobb* for boathire	0	1	0
Item to the gardner at Lambeth	0	8	6
Item to the bargemen	1	5	0

---

240 Herbert Croft* had recently been appointed chaplain to the earl of Northumberland.

241 See n. 238 above.

Item to the gardner at Croydon	2	5	0
Item for 4 trowts Mr Rylye*	0	2	6
Item for a buck Sir W[illiam] Killygree*	1	0	0
Item for 2 cheeses & birds Sir Nicholas Cary*	0	2	6
Item for 14 bush[els]† of oates for the coach horses	1	11	6
Item for a bush[el]† of beanes	0	4	4
Item for 12 bush[els]† of oates for geldings	1	7	0
Item for naylinge	0	1	0
Item spent in the kitchen this weeke ut patet p[er] libr[um]	32	10	1

[fo. 73r]
June 1 1638

Item to the hieman for the freight of Mr Roses* wheate at xiiij[d] p[er] q[ua]rter	3	3	3
Item to the porters for carrying it into the graynary at iij[d] p[er] q[ua]rter	0	13	3
Item for a buck & shoulders from Sir Morrice Bartley*	1	0	0
Item to Pallmer* for broomes and bowes for the chymney	0	7	0
Item for 4 staff pies from the Countesse of Newcastle*	0	15	0
Item for cheeses from Dr Smith*	0	1	0
Item to the gardner at Lambeth	0	9	2
Item to the bargemen	0	15	0
Item for 14 bush[els]† of oates for coach horses	1	11	6
Item for a bush[el]† of beanes	0	4	4
Item for 12 bush[els]† of oates for geldings	1	7	0
Item for removing & naylinge	0	2	6
Item for bayl at Greenwich	0	5	0
Item spent in the kitchen this weeke ut patet p[er] libr[um]	29	10	11
Some of this fortnight payd June 14 1638	83	19	10

June 8 1638

Receaved of Jo[hn] Newton* for Thanett haye	68	6	4
Inprimis given to the L[ord] Chamberlayns* gent &c with a nagg†	5	10	0
Item for a bucke Mr Craven[242]	0	10	0
Item for another Sir W[illiam] Killygree*	0	10	0
Item at the Star Chamber &c[243]	0	7	6

242 The identity of this 'Mr Craven' is unclear, but he should not be confused with 'Mr Craven of Trinity College', mentioned retrospectively by Laud in a letter to Charles I dated 6 Sept. 1628. This latter Craven was possibly William Craven (*c.* 1608–97), who matriculated from Trinity College, Oxford in 1623, who was knighted in 1627 and who served under Gustavus Adolphus V in Europe in 1632; *Alumni cantabrigienses*, part I, I, 414; *Alumni oxoniensis*, I, 346; Malcolm Smuts, 'Craven, William, earl of Craven (bap. 1608, d. 1697)', *ODNB*; *WWL*, VI, 17.

243 See n. 30 above.

Item for Winsor Earl of Newcastle*	0	14	0
Item for boathires Mr Snaith*	0	4	10
Item for 2 oxen Lo[rd] Sherwood*	3	5	0
Item to the hieman for bringing Mr Denns* 40 q[ua]rters of wheat	1	13	6
Item for 7 carts to carry it to Croydon	1	15	0
Item given to load and unload it	0	4	0
Item to the gardner at Lambeth	0	15	6
Item to the bargemen	0	15	0
Item for a sallmon Mayor of Portsmouth*[244]	0	5	0
Item for a sallmon pie Lady Chomley*	0	2	6
Item for a buck Lo[rd] Maynard*	1	0	0
Item for 2 bucks from Ford	1	5	0
Item for trowts from Fordwich	0	2	6
Item for a cake & cheeses from Mr Powell*	0	3	0
Item for 14 bush[els]† of oates for the coach horses	1	11	6

[fo. 74r]

Item for a bush[el]† of beanes	0	4	4
Item for 13 bush[els]† of oates for geldings	1	9	3
Item for a bayl for 12 horses at Greenwich	0	5	0
Item for bleedinge & drenching the coach horses	0	7	6
Item spent in the kitchen this weeke ut patet p[er] libr[um]	31	1	10

For this quarter

Payd the brewer of Putney for 10 hogsh[eads]† of viij^s & 52 hogsh[eads]† of vj^s beere layd in at Lambeth this q[ua]rter ut patet	29	8	0
Item to M[is]tr[es]s Hoult*	4	0	0
Item to Mr Squire*	2	10	0
Item to the Widd[ow] Whaly* for the slaughterhouse groome	0	12	6
Item to the mole catcher	0	5	0
Item to yr G[races] barber	0	10	8
Item for the footman	0	3	0
Item to the laundress for ashes, soape, starche & besides wages	4	10	0
Item for hoopinge tubs	0	9	6
Item for 2 flasketts† of cloth for 12 dresser clothes at xiiij^d	1	15	0
Item for 30 ells† of cloth at viij^s for 30 towells	1	0	0
Item for an ashe cloth	0	4	4
Item for making & marking	0	3	6
Item for making 12 p[aires] of shoes	0	11	0
Item p[ay]d the coachmaker for this yeare ut patet	16	7	0
Item to Mr Badger* for bringing manuscripts ut patet	14	11	0

244 Shortly before sending this gift, Thomas Beeston*, the mayor, along with other members of the town corporation, was summoned to appear before the exchequer court to 'pass their accounts for casual profits due to his Majesty'; *CSPD 1637–8*, p. 469, no. 66.

Item to Morris* the smith ut patet p[er] bill	6	1	0
Item to Abbott* the sadler for 12 livery sadles, furnish & clothes at xviij^{s} a peece	9	0	0
Item more to him for other things ut patet p[er] bill	9	18	8
Item to the harnessmaker for a lether coat &c ut patet	1	13	0
Item to Mr Browne* for the presse for coapes	8	0	0
Item to the wine coop[er] for port wine & hoopinge the vessels &c	12	18	3

[fo. 75r]

Item for 5 loads of straw layd in this q[ua]rter	3	1	6
Item for 12 glasses & 2 crewetts for Croydon	0	15	0
Item for 2 doz of bottles & corks for the court	0	12	6
Item to your G[races] taylor ut patet	23	3	10
Item to the appoticary for physicke ale Jo[hn] Cobb* footeman ut patet	4	18	2
Item for a new beare hide for court	3	5	0
Item for velvet lace &c for the padd	2	19	0
Item for yr lampe	0	18	0
Item for 5 foldinge chayres for the chappell	3	4	6
Item for 2 chaires & a stoole of velvett[245]	1	13	4
Item for portages, boathire &c	2	19	6
Item to Mr Watts* for carrying gravell & rubbish & cleansinge the moate	1	2	0
Item for 2 broomes mopps & sweeping the house this yeare	0	16	0
Item for graynes for the fish	0	7	0
Item for fishing nets	0	8	9
Item for pigeons meale	0	12	0
Item to the smith of Croydon for shoeing, bleedings and dressing horses at the park since Mich[ael]mas	2	7	9
Item to him for a baskett for the kitchen & other things about the house	2	9	3
Item to Jo[hn] Newton* for hedging and ditching since Mich[ael]mas last 5	18	4	
Item for threshing the corne	4	8	4
Item for 6 sacks	0	15	0
Item for killing moles this years	1	5	0
Item for hurt done by horses	1	0	0
Item for a p[aire] of dossers†	1	6	4
Item a new cart & ropes &c	1	10	10
Item for 2 ropes for the slaughterman	0	8	4
Item for mowing the walks &c	0	6	10
Item for plowinge corne & other chardges ut patet	44	9	7
Some of this weeke &c payd June 28 1638	399	8	2

245 An inventory of Lambeth Palace chapel, taken in May 1643, listed several items which matched the description of these; TNA, SP16/499, fo. 82.

Some total of this quarters expenses and laying out cometh to the some of	862	0	4

All accompted and p[ay]d June 28 1638 A[dam] T[orless]*

[fo. 76r]
Third quarter
beginning June 15 1638

Receaved for 2 oxen & for wheate & fier at consec[racion]	11	2	0
Imprims for yr Graces offering at the consecration[246]	3	0	0
Item for boathire Mr Cobb* and musitians	0	2	0
Item to the postilian at his going away	2	0	0
Item for a salmon pie Dr Parry*	0	2	6
Item for 2 does Sir Arth[ur] Capell*	1	0	0
Item for pies B[isho]p of Durham*	0	2	6
Item for bowes, mopps, broomes &c p[ayd] Pallmer*	0	7	6
Item for pippins† from Mr Mills[247]	0	1	0
Item to Mr Dell* for letters boathire &c	0	3	4
Item to the gardner at Lambeth	0	11	0
Item to the bargemen	1	1	0
Item to the gardner at Croydon 3 weekes	2	8	0
Item for 15 bush[els]† of oates for coach horses	1	13	9
Item for a bush[el]† of beans	0	4	4
Item for 14 bush[els]† for geldings	1	11	6
Item for 20 shoes & 8 removes	0	13	0
Item for a bayl for 12 horses at Greenwich	0	5	0
Item spent in the kitchen this weeke ut patet p[er] libr[um]	26	0	7

June 22 1638

Item to Mr Snaith* for boathire &c	0	3	8
Item for broomes and mopps p[ayd] Pallmer*	0	5	3
Item for a buck Mr Lumly[248]	0	10	0
Item for boathire Mr Levinthrop*	0	1	0
Item for bringing letters &c	0	2	6
Item for carts for removes Croydon	3	6	0
Item for 2 carts with wine	0	10	0
Item to the porter at the garden gate at Whitehall	0	10	0
Item to his man	0	5	0
Item for a buck and 2 fawnes	0	12	6

246 Brian Duppa* was consecrated bishop of Chichester on 13 June 1638 at Lambeth Palace, the previous encumbant, Richard Mountague*, having been translated to the see of Norwich in May.

247 See n. 155 above.

248 This is the first of two entries for ‘Mr Lumly’, whose identity remains elusive.

Item to the bargemen at Lambeth	0	15	0
Item to the gardner at Croydon	0	12	6
Item for 16 bush[els]† of oates for coach horses	1	17	0
Item for a bush[el]† of beans	0	4	4
Item for 13 bush[els]† of oats for geldings	1	12	6
Item for 2 new shoes and 6 removes	0	2	2
Item for hay for 13 horses 1 night at Greenwich at x^{d}	0	10	10
Item for 4 bush[els]† of oates & 7 pecke† of beanes	0	15	0
Item spent in the kitchen this weeke ut patet p[er] libr[um]	24	6	5
Some of this fortnight payd July 6 1638	78	18	8

[fo. 77r]
June 29 1638

Receaved for Mr Roses* mault	90	0	0
And for Mr Spratlings* barly	115	0	0
And for wood in Norwood	103	17	8
Inprimis for a stagg from the Kinge	2	0	0
Item for bringing a cake	0	2	6
Item to the gardner at Lambeth	0	18	10
Item to the gardner at Croydon	0	12	3
Item for a p[aire] of water bootes	1	6	0
Item for 16 bush[els]† of oates for the coach horses at ij^{s} vj^{d}	2	0	0
Item for a bush[el]† of beans	0	4	4
Item for 11 bush[els]† of oates for geldings at ij^{s} vj^{d} all spent	1	7	6
Item for bleedinge & drenching Naylor	0	3	0
Item for removing & naylinge	0	2	0
Item for 12 broomes	0	2	0
Item for hay for 14 horses at Greenwich on Satt[urday] night at x^{d}	0	11	8
Item for 4 bush[els]† of oates & 7 pecke† of beanes &c here	0	15	0
Item spent in the kitchen this week ut patet p[er] libr[um]	31	11	11

July 6 1638[249]

Item for bringing coolings	0	1	0
Item for a buck Sir H[umfrey] Styles*	0	12	6
Item for a stagg E[arl] of Lyndsey*	1	10	0
Item for 2 knives for your Grace	0	2	8
Item for mending shirts &c	0	1	6
Item to the gardner at Croydon	0	11	2
Item to the gardner at Lambeth	0	12	6

249 The household undertook its annual remove to Croydon on 5 July and Laud remained there for three months; *WWL*, VI, 530, VII, 487.

Item to Knight* & Constable* 3 days about Waddon Pond & graze	0	7	6
Item for 16 bush[els]† of oates for coach horses of yr G[races] owne	0	0	0
Item for a bush[el]† of beans	0	4	4
Item for 13 bush[els]† of oates for gelding	0	0	0
Item for removing & nayling	0	1	6
Item for 14 horses hay at court on Satturday night	0	9	4
Item for 4 bush[els]† of oates & 7 peck† of beans & other &c	0	13	8
Item for haye there on Tuesday	0	4	8
Item for oates &c home	0	6	10
Item spent in the kitchen this week ut patet p[er] libr[um]	27	8	11
Some of this fortnight p[ay]d July 18 1638	75	5	1

[fo. 78r]

Item for fencinge cuttinge & makinge & carridge of charcoales & wood this yeare ut patet p[er] libr[um]	157	19	10
Item for haymakinge at Lambeth this yeare ut patet	28	5	4
Item for haymakinge at Croydon this yeare ut finale patet	25	14	6
Some total for wood and haye payd July 18 1638	211	19	8

July 13 1638

Rec[eave]d	25–12–11	33	0	11
A cowe	5–8–0			
Hynds	2–0–0			
Inprimis for 2 bucks from Farnham		1	6	0
Item for apricocks Mr Wraye[250]		0	2	0
Item for Jo[hn] Newton's* charges att the Sessions &c		0	5	0
Item for driving a cowe to Smithfield		0	3	0
Item for broomes p[ayd] Pallmer*		0	4	0
Item for a buck & fish from Dr Burton*		0	10	0
Item to the gardner at Croydon		0	15	0
Item to the gardner at Lambeth		0	10	0
Item for 16 bush[els]† of oates for the coach horses		0	0	0
Item for a bush[el]† of beans		0	4	4
Item for 11 bush[els]† of oates for geldings		0	0	0
Item for 24 removes		0	4	0
Item for 14 horses haye at Greenwich one night at x^{d}		0	11	8
Item for 4 bush[els]† of oates & 7 pecke† of beans &c		0	15	0
Item spent in the kitchen this week ut patet p[er] libr[um]		28	14	0

250 See n. 231 above.

July 20 1638

Item for a buck from Farnham	0	15	0
Item for a cake, cheeses, cheesecakes &c from M[is]tr[es]s Turner*	0	3	6
Item for fillbirds† &c Sir John Tonstall*	0	2	6
Item for apricocks Mr Wraye[251]	0	2	0
Item to Tho[mas] Sadler* for the coachmans postilians cloaks ut patet p[er] bill	4	5	3
Item for sturgeon and partridges from Dr Howell*	0	3	6
Item to the gardner at Lambeth	0	11	8
Item to the gardner at Croydon	0	10	0
Item to the bargemen 3 dayes	1	2	6
Item for a stagg and a buck from the D[uchess] of Richmond*	2	5	0
Item to the gardner &c Somersett House[252]	0	3	0

[fo. 79r]

Item for 2 fawnes	0	6	0
Item for apricocks, mellons, cheeses &c p[ayd] ewry man†	0	6	0
Item for 16 bush[els]† of oates for the coach horses	0	0	0
Item for a bush[el]† of beans	0	4	4
Item for 11 bush[els]† of oates for geldings	0	0	0
Item for 2 payles for the stable	0	6	0
Item for 14 horses hay at Theobalds 1 night at viij^{d}	0	9	4
Item for 4 bush[els]† of oates & a pecke† of beans	0	18	6
Item for light for the coach	0	0	6
Item spent in the kitchen this week ut patet p[er] libr[um]	29	2	11
Some of this fortnight paid Aug[ust] 6 1638	76	2	8

July 27 1638

Receaved for Mr Spratlings* 30 q[ua]rters of wheate	63	5	0
Inprimis for a buck from Farnham Little Park	0	15	0
Item for mellons Sir Thomas Grymes*	0	3	6
Item given the butlers at court this progresse tyme[253]	0	10	0
Item for facing yr G[races] hatt	0	6	0
Item for Mr Crofts* boathire	0	1	0
Item to Mr Dell* for letters and boathire ut patet	0	6	0
Item for a buck Sir Tho[mas] Edmonds*	0	13	4
Item to the gardner at Lambeth	0	10	0
Item to the gardner at Croydon	0	10	0

251 See n. 231 above.

252 This entry suggests that there was an exchange of expertise between the gardeners at Lambeth and Somerset House, the queen's central London residence.

253 This entry suggests that Laud accompanied the king on royal progress this summer.

Item for 16 bush[els]† of oates for coach horses	0	0	0
Item for a bush[el]† of beans	0	4	4
Item for 22 bush[els]† of oates for geldings	0	0	0
Item for 24 new shoes & 4 removes for coach horses	0	14	8
Item for hay for 14 horses at court 2 nights at viij[d]	0	18	8
Item for 8 bush[els]† of oates & 2 pecke† of beans &c	1	8	6
Item spent in the kitchen this weeke ut patet p[er] libr[um]	28	9	7

August 3 1638

Item for a buck with shoulders Mr Myles[254]	1	0	0
Item for weekly bills & letters p[ayd]	0	2	0
Item for melons &c	0	4	6

[fo. 80r]

Item for pheas & part from Sir Anth[ony] Weldon*	0	3	6
Item to the gardner at Lambeth	0	10	0
Item to the gardner at Croydon	0	12	2
Item given a poore person	0	2	6
Item for 14 bush[els]† of oates for coach horses	0	0	0
Item for a bush[el]† of beans	0	4	4
Item for 8 bush[els]† of oates for geldings	0	0	0
Item for naylinge coach horses	0	1	0
Item for hay for 14 horses Weybridge 1 night at viij[d]	0	9	4
Item for 4 bush[els]† of oates and a pecke† of beans	0	15	6
Item spent in the kitchen this weeke ut patet p[er] libr[um]	27	10	4
Some of this fortnight paid Aug[ust] 14 1638	67	8	9

August 10 1638

Inprimis for a buck from the Little Park at Farnham	0	15	0
Item for peares &c Sir John Tonstall*	0	2	0
Item for a buck Earl of Cleveland	0	15	0
Item for a buck with the fees Lo[rd] Wimbledon*	1	0	0
Item to the gardner at Lambeth	0	15	6
Item to the gardner at Croydon	0	9	8
Item for bringing mellons &c	0	3	0
Item for 14 bush[els]† of oates for the coach horses	0	0	0
Item for a bush[el]† of beans	0	4	4
Item for 7 bush[els]† of oates for geldings	0	0	0
Item for 9 bayle of strawe at vj[d]	0	4	6

254 This is the sole entry in the accounts for 'Mr Myles', whose identity remains elusive.

Item for 14 horses hay at Weybridge one night at viij[d]	0	9	4
Item for 4 bush[els]† of oates & beans	0	17	0
Item spent in the kitchen this week ut patet p libris	32	3	0

August 17 1638

Item for a buck from the great park at Farnham	2	0	0
Item for an hyne from Mr Harvey*	0	1	0
Item to Mr Rollston* for yr G[race]	0	1	0
Item to Pallmer* for broomes	0	3	0
Item to Mr Snaith* for boathires & letters	0	1	2
Item for a buck Sir Nich[olas] Cary*	0	13	6
Item for 12 partr[idges] Sir Henry Snellgrave*	0	3	4
Item to the gardner at Lambeth (8 loads of gravell)	1	0	8
Item to the gardner at Croydon	0	15	9
Item to Mr Badger* for binding MS ut patet p[er] bill	7	6	8
Item for boathires at Putney	0	2	0
Item for 14 bush[els]† of oates for the coach horses	0	0	0
Item for a bush[el]† of beans	0	4	4

[fo. 81r]

Item for 9 bush[els]† of oates for geldings	0	0	0
Item for 4 shoes & 6 removes	0	3	4
Item for hay for 14 horses at Weybridge 1 night at viij[d] a peece	0	9	4
Item for 4 bush[els]† of oates & beans	0	17	0
Item spent in the kitchen this week ut patet p[er] libr[um]	28	8	4
Some of this fortnight payd Aug[ust] 30 1638	81	4	9

August 24 1638

Receaved of Mr Barton*

Inprimis for yr G[races] offeringe	3	0	0
Item for a stagg from Theobalds	1	2	6
Item for mending 14 bands & 18 paire of cuffes with tape &c for yr G[race]	1	4	0
Item for 4 ells† of Holland† for shirts, bootes, hose, socks, &c	1	4	0
Item to the gardner at Lambeth	0	10	0
Item to the gardner at Croydon	0	9	0
Item for 14 bush[els]† of oates for the coach horses	0	0	0
Item for a bush[el]† of beans	0	4	4
Item for 9 bush[els]† of oates for geldings	0	0	0
Item for bleedinge Watson &c	0	1	0
Item for a bayl at Putney for 15 horses	0	7	0
Item spent in the kitchen this weeke ut patet p[er] libr[um]	30	7	10

August ult 1638

Item given the 3 children at the chappell	0	15	0
Item to 4 men at Norwood	0	8	0
Item for Nich[olas]* chardges to Theobalds	0	2	0
Item to Mr Snaith* Lady Roe*	0	1	0
Item to the gardner at Lambeth	0	11	6
Item to the gardner at Croydon	0	14	0
Item for bringing a doe	0	10	0
Item for 2 bucks from Farnham	1	6	0
Item for a buck Sir Tho[mas] Edmunds*	0	15	0
Item for 14 bush[els]† of oates for coach horses	0	0	0
Item for a bush[el]† of beans	0	4	4
Item for 8 bush[els]† of oates for geldings	0	0	0
Item for 6 removes & nayling	0	1	4
Item for 14 horses hay 2 nights at court at viij^{d}	0	19	8
Item for 8 bush[els]† of oates & 2 pecke† of beans	1	8	6
Item spent in the kitchen this weeke ut patet p[er] libr[um]	31	2	0
Some of this fortnight payd Sept 14 1638	77	8	0

September 7 1638

Receaved for a red cowe	5	0	0
And for [Mr] Mattersheds*	4	0	0
Inprimis given the nurse & servants at Dr Turners*	1	10	0
Item for 10 cheeses Lady Sidley*	0	3	0
Item to the gardner at Lambeth	0	10	0
Item to the gardner at Croydon	0	13	8
Item to Pallmer* for broomes	0	5	8

[fo. 82r]

Item given to Gilbert at the park	0	1	0
Item for a buck from Marybone	0	15	0
Item for another Sir Tho[mas] Alsbury*	0	13	6
Item for another Lo[rd] Wimbleton*	0	13	6
Item for 14 horses hay at Weybridge 2 nights at viij^{d}	0	18	8
Item for 8 bush[els]† of oates & 2 pecks† of beans &c	1	5	10
Item for 14 bush[els]† of oates for coach horses at home	0	0	0
Item for a bush[el]† of beans	0	4	4
Item for 8 bush[els]† of oates for geldings	0	0	0
Item for 6 bush[els]† of oates for the B[isho]p of Oxfords* horses	0	0	0
Item for 20 new shoes & 8 removes for coach horses	0	13	0
Item for mending an iron	0	1	0
Item for 11 bayles of wheate strawe	0	7	6
Item spent in the kitchen this weeke ut patet p[er] libr[um]	30	7	11

September 14 1638

Item given the E[arl] of Newcastle's* gent with 2 mares	5	0	0
Item for a stagg Sir Arth[ur] Manwayring*	1	5	0
Item for a buck with all fees Sir John Epsley*	1	0	0
Item for another Mr Mynas[255]	0	15	0
Item for fish Mr Knight of New Romney[256]	0	6	0
Item to the gardner at Lambeth	0	10	0
Item to the bargemen	0	9	0
Item to the gardner at Croydon	0	12	1
Item given Mr Tompkins* by yr G[race]	1	0	0
Item to the La[dy] Styles* man grapes	0	2	0
Item for 14 horses haye at Kingston 2 nights at viij^d^	0	18	8
Item for 8 bush[els]† of beanes &c	1	5	5
Item for 14 bush[els]† of oates for coach horses at home	0	0	0
Item for a bush[el]† of beans	0	4	4
Item for xi bush[els]† of oates for geldings	0	0	0
Item for nayling coach horses	0	0	11
Item for broomes for the stable	0	1	0
Item for cutting 3 colts	0	10	0
Item spent in the kitchen this week ut patet p[er] libr[um]	30	2	6

for this quarter

Payd to the brewer for 1 hogsh[eads]† of x^{s} 32 hogsh[eads]† of viij^{s} and 123 hosghs of vj^{d} beare layd in this halfe yeare ut patet	75	6	0
Item to M[is]tr[es]s Hoult* for this q[ua]rter	4	0	0
Item to the Widd[ow] Whaly* for the rent of the slaughterhouse	0	12	6
Item to yr G[races] barber	0	10	0
Item for the footman	0	3	0
Item to the mole catcher at Lambeth	0	5	0

[fo. 83r]

Item to the laundress for ashes soape starch &c besides wages	4	10	0
Item for hoopinge tubbs	0	9	6
Item for a newe tubb	0	2	6
Item to William Duckett* for bedding &c ut patet	11	7	0
Item to him for John Cobb* ut patet	1	16	2
Item to him for the footman ut patet	0	9	10
Item to Morris* [the smith] for shoeing geldings &c ut patet p[er] bill	2	8	0
Item to Abbot* the sadler ut patet	2	19	0
Item to Comfort* the smith for shoeing geldings &c ut patet	4	1	3

255 This is the first of four entries for 'Mr Mynas', whose identity remains elusive.

256 This is the sole entry for Mr Knight of New Romney, whose identity remains elusive. Not to be confused with the 'Mr Knight' referred to in n. 8 above, or with Knight*, the household servant.

Item for household stuffe bought at the park ut patet	8	3	8
Item to Holland* for 6 dayes work paid by Jo[hn] Newton*	0	8	8
Item for pitch and tar to mark sheepe	0	0	8
Item to Knight* for cutting braks† and bryers† at the park xi dayes	0	12	10
Item to Holland* for raking and carrying braks† 5 dayes	0	5	10
Item to him for 7 dayes in clensinge the river &c at xiij^{d}	0	8	2
Item to Lane[257] for hedging 4 days	0	4	8
Item to Knight* for 6 dayes work at xiij^{d}	0	7	6
Item for a cuttinge knife for the park	0	3	0
Item for a mattock†	0	3	6
Item for 2 bills & an axe	0	4	6
Some total of this fortnight payd Septemb[er] 27 1638	204	3	3

Some total of this quarters expenses & laying out cometh to the some of

viij^{C} lxxij^{l} x^{s} x^{d}

All accompted and paid
Ada[m] Torlesse*

[fo. 84r]
Fourth quarter beginning September 21 1638

Rec[eave]d of Mr Barton*

Inprimis give to Sir Jo[hn] Epslyes* man with brawne and puddings at court	0	2	0
Item to Phillipp[258] for letters and weekly bills	0	2	6
Item to the gardner at Croydon	0	19	6
Item for carpes and peaches Mr Evelyn*	0	10	0
Item for puddings D[uchess] of Richmond*	0	2	6
Item for an hare Mr Harvey*	0	1	0
Item for 14 horses hay at Kingston 2 nights at viij^{d}	0	18	8
Item for 8 bush[els]† of oates and beans &c	1	5	8
Item for 14 bush[els]† of oates for coach horses at home of yr owne	0	0	0
Item for a bush[el]† of beans	0	4	4
Item for 14 bush[els]† of oates for geldings	0	0	0
Item for naylinge coach horses	0	0	10
Item spent in the kitchen this weeke ut patet p[er] libr[um]	31	14	8

257 This is the first of two entries for 'Lane', who was a hedger.

258 This is the second entry relating to letters delivered by 'Phillipp', the messenger. For the first, see n. 151 above.

September 28 1638

Item for cheeses from the Lady Parker[259]	0	2	0
Item for a cake Mr Webb*	0	2	6
Item for wallnutts Mr Bucknor*	0	2	0
Item to Fr[ancis] Loveday* for clensing the moate this yeare	2	0	0
Item for his paynes extraordinary	1	0	0
Item to Pitcher for bootes and fishing	1	0	0
Item to the woman at the park	1	0	0
Item to 2 mayds and a man there	1	5	0
Item to Mr Watts* man and mayd	0	15	0
Item sent yr G[race] by Mr Dade*	2	0	0
Item for a doe E[arl] of Northumberland*	0	12	0
Item for bringing 4 swans	0	5	0
Item for naylinge to remove stuffe	0	6	0
Item to Marqu[is of] Hambletons* footman[260]	**0**	**2**	**0**
Item to Mr Mabb* for letters, broomes, mopps and cleanings for house ut patet	0	19	6
Item to the gardner for this summer	0	8	0
Item to the groomes for the stable dunge att Croydon	1	0	0
Item for a doz of drinking glasse	0	14	0
Item for 7 carts for the removes Lambeth at vj^s per cart	3	0	0
Item for Pallmer* for broomes, moppps, stuffe for andirons†	0	10	2
Item to Knight* for 7 dayes worke &c	0	9	2
Item to the gardner at Lambeth for 2 weekes	0	6	0
Item for 12 partr[idges] from Mr Dale*	0	3	6
Item for brawne Mr Champneys[261]	0	6	0
Item for 2 pea hens Mr Munkton[262]	0	2	0
Item for a swan Mr Mills[263]	0	2	0
Item paid unto Mr Deane of Sarum*	20	0	0

[fo. 85r]

Item for a fleech of bacon Mr Parkinson[264]	0	2	0
Item for 40 bush[els]† of crabbs† to make 2 hogsh[eads]† of vargis† at iij^d p[er] bush[el]†	0	13	4

259 This is the sole entry in the accounts relating to a gift from 'Lady Parker', whose identity remains elusive. A possible candidate is the 'Lady Parker' who appealed to the privy council in 1622 for 'some present mayntenance' from her husband, Sir Henry Parker; *APC*, XXXVIII, 183.

260 The footman was probably delivering letters to Laud from his master, James, 3rd marquis of Hamilton*, who had been, somewhat reluctantly, despatched to Edinburgh in late May to negotiate with the covenanters on the king's behalf. Hamilton had 'suddenly and unexpectedly' come down to court in Aug. to update the king on the progress of his commission. The marquis had left again on 10 Sept.; *WWL*, VI, 538.

261 See n. 176 above.

262 See n. 91 above.

263 See n. 155 above.

264 See n. 6 above.

Item for making it and the 2 hogsh[eads]†	0	16	6
Item for coale baskets and shovell &c for the kitchen	0	6	6
Item for 14 horses hay at Kingston 3 nights at viij[d]	1	8	0
Item for 10 bush[els]† of oates and beanes &c	1	11	8
Item for 14 bush[els]† of oates for coach horses at home of yr owne	0	0	0
Item for a bush[el]† of beanes	0	4	4
Item for 14 bush[els]† of oates for geldings	0	0	0
Item for 3 bush[els]† D[ean] of Salisburys* horse	0	0	0
Item for removing & cloths	0	4	4
Item for a rope to tye the bales	0	5	0
Item spent in the kitchen this weeke ut patet p[er] libr[um]	33	5	5
Some of this fortnight payd Octob[er] 9 1638	113	17	11

Octob[er] 5 1638

Receaved 0–0–0			
Inprimis p[ay]d Tho[mas] Sadler* for 4 tawney coates for the 4 groomes ut patet p[er] bill	9	0	0
Item for a pike from Sir Paule Pider*	0	3	6
Item to the bargemen	0	5	0
Item for letters from the Marq[uis of] Hambleton*[265]	0	2	0
Item to the gardner at Croydon	0	14	6
Item for 2 cheeses Lo[rd] Harbert*	0	2	6
Item for grapes Lady Styles*	0	1	0
Item for pheasants & peares Sir Ant[ony] Welldon*	0	3	0
Item for 14 bush[els]† of oates for coach horses	0	0	0
Item for a bush[el]† of beanes	0	4	4
Item for 15 bush[els]† of oates for geldings	0	0	0
Item for 8 removes and naylinge	0	1	8
Item for a doz of broomes	0	2	0
Item spent in the kitchen this weeke ut patet p[er] libr[um]	35	10	5

October 12 1638

Item p[ay]d Dr Turner* for 6 gownes for 6 poore men in Redding ut patet p[er] bill	9	10	10
Item given Jo[hn] Lloyds[266] man at court	1	0	0

---

265 James, 3rd marquis of Hamilton* and Laud had been corresponding regularly since early June, when the marquis arrived in Edinburgh as king's commissioner to negotiate with the covenanters. The negotiations had reached a crucial point by late Sept.: the Scottish privy council had lukewarmly received the 'king's covenant', an alternative to the National Covenant, and the future of episcopacy in Scotland was in some doubt. The letters being delivered by the footman probably contained some of this news, since Hamilton wrote to Laud on 24 and 27 Sept., updating him of the latest developments; The National Records of Scotland, GD406/1/564, GD406/1/565; James, *Firebrand*, p. 138.

266 This is the sole entry in the accounts for 'John Lloyd', whose identity remains elusive.

Item for a g[rea]t cheese Captain Crispe*	0	6	0
Item for peares Mr Layfield*	0	2	0
Item to the gardner at Lambeth	0	3	7
Item to the bargemen this weeke	1	7	0
Item to Tho[mas] Sadler* for a suit cloake and gowne for John Cobb*	12	15	8
Item given a poore woman Redding and for letters boathires &c ut patet p[er] bill Mr Dell*	0	18	6
Item to Nutt* the slaughterman for his chardges with 121 Kent weachers out of Kent &c ut patet	3	17	0

[fo. 86r]

Item for bringing 3 barr[els] of oysters	0	2	0
Item for 6 turkeys 8 pheasants & 6 partr[idges] from Mr Williscott*	0	10	0
Item for 4 redd deare pies Sir Arth[ur] Ingram*	0	5	0
Item for a lamprey† pie Mr Mills[267]	0	1	0
Item for 14 bush[els]† of oates for coach horses	0	0	0
Item for a bush[el]† of beanes	0	4	4
Item for 15 bush[els]† of oates for gelds.	0	0	0
Item spent in the kitchen this week ut patet p[er] libr[um]	35	0	9

October 19 1638

Receaved 0–0–0

Inprimis to Mr Snaith* for boathire	0	1	6
Item for Nicholas* chardges into Kent and back with colts &c	1	7	6
Item given him by yr Grace	1	0	0
Item for an hare Mr Harvy*	0	1	0
Item for a brawne Mr Cartwright*	0	6	0
Item for partridges Lo[rd] Chamberlayne*	0	2	6
Item for a bottle to bringe Miller from Croydon	0	1	6
Item for 14 bush[els]† of oates for the coach horses	0	0	0
Item for a bush[el]† of beanes	0	4	4
Item for 6 bush[els]† of oates for geldings our own all spent	0	0	0
Item for 12 bush[els]† more bought at xxij^{d} p[er] bush[el]†	1	2	0
Item for bleedinge & drenchinge 7 coach horses at ij^{s} vj^{d}	0	17	6
Item for 4 shoes and 16 removes	0	5	0
Item spent in the kitchen this weeke ut patet p[er] libr[um]	27	7	8

Octob[er] 26 1638

Item to yr G[race] for Mr Solicitor* & Mr Harbort*	8	0	0
Item p[ay]d Mr Daniell Harvey* for manuscripts ut patet	50	0	0

267 See n. 155 above.

Item to Mr Snaith* for bootes for your Grace & boathires &c ut patet	0	13	6
Item to Pallmer* for broomes mopps &c	0	4	4
Item to the gardner at Lambeth	0	9	4
Item to the bargemen this weeke	1	4	0
Item to the gardner at Croydon for trees weeders &c ut patet	2	4	2
Item to Knight* for 4 dayes worke about the house	0	4	8
Item for mendinge hedges at the park stubbs 8 days[268]	0	8	0
Item for pitch and 2 salters	0	0	6
Item for pheas[ant] & partr[idge] & bacon from Mr Doyly*	0	6	0
Item for sugar Mr Harfleet*	0	5	0
Item for 2 pheasants Sir Rob[er]t Bannister*	0	2	6
Item to Mr Mabb* for the pasture of the park this summer	5	0	0

[fo. 87r]

Item to Mr Holford* for yr G[races]Watch	0	2	6
Item to the Lady Wakes* man Mr Dell*	0	10	0
Item for letters boathire &c	0	13	2
Item to Mr Cobb* for boathire from Croydon	0	0	6
Item for 2 barr of sallmon Londonderry	0	10	0
Item to Dr Paskes* man with a brawne & pheasants	0	10	0
Item for 14 bush[els]† of oates for coach horses at xxij^{d} p bush[el]†	1	5	8
Item for a bush[el]† of beanes	0	4	4
Item for 17 bush[els]† of oates for geldings	1	11	2
Item spent in the kitchen this week ut patet p[er] libr[um]	27	1	2
Some of this fortnight payd Novemb[er] 9 1638	135	16	0

Novemb[er] 2 1638

Receaved 0–0–0

Inprimis p[ay]d Mr Fettyplace* for Mr Pocock's* pension for 2 q[ua]rters ended at Mich[ael]mas last	20	0	0
Item to yr G[race] the Earl of Salisbury's* gent	1	0	0
Item to the keep &c for an hine	1	5	0
Item for a cocke pie & 4 cheeses from Sir Jo[hn] Peashall*	0	5	0
Item for dryde beife Lo[rd] Deputy*[269]	0	2	6

268 The hedges may have needed mending as a result of storm damage. On 26 Oct., Laud recorded in his diary that 'a most extreme tempest' had come up the Thames, which had hit the water while he was on his way back from star chamber 'between six and seven in the evening'. When he tried to land at Lambeth bridge, he was in 'great danger'. The previous week had been much the same and it was widely believed that it may have had something to do with the recent arrival in England of Marie de Medici, the mother of Henrietta Maria, which was the cause of some consternation. Apparently, the watermen on the Thames even referred to it as 'Queen Mother weather'; *WWL*, III, 230–1.

269 This gift came with a letter written by Thomas Wentworth* on 22 Oct., which was received on 2 Nov. and to which Laud replied immediately, because he had important information to impart to the lord deputy, concerning Wentworth's handling of Scottish presbyterians in Ireland; *WWL*, VII, 543.

Item for turkeys &c Mr Mills[270]	0	1	6
Item to the bargemen this week	1	7	0
Item for 14 bush[els]† of oates for the c[oach] horses at xxij[d] p[er] bush[el]†	1	5	8
Item for a bush[el]† of beanes	0	4	4
Item for 18 bush[els]† of oates for geldings & colts	1	13	0
Item for nayling coach horses	0	1	4
Item for a lantern for the stables	0	1	4
Item spent in the kitchen this week ut patet p[er] libr[um]	31	6	4

Novemb[er] 9 1638

Item for cheeses from Dr Smith*	0	1	0
Item for boathires for musitians	0	2	6
Item for a doe Sir Tho[mas] Alisbury*	0	11	0
Item for cheese Lady Foster*	0	2	0
Item for a gelt bucke E[arl] of Winchelsey*	0	11	0
Item to yr Grace for Mr Holloway*	1	0	0
Item to Mr Snaith* for boathires	0	5	0
Item for Mr Webbs* lodging &c	0	2	0
Item to the bargemen this week	1	8	6
Item to Pallmer* for broomes	0	3	6
Item for 6 pheasants Sir Ed[ward] Boys*	0	5	0
Item for a doe Sir Tho[mas] Edmunds*	0	10	0
Item for 13 partridges Mr Allnett[271]	0	3	0
Item for pepp[er] & sugar Mr Wooddall*	0	5	0
Item for 14 bush[els]† of oates for coach horsers at xxij[d] p[er] bush[el]†	1	5	8
Item for a bush[el]† of beanes	0	3	8
Item for 18 bush[els]† of oates for geldings & colts	1	13	0
Item for removing & naylinge	0	1	3
Item for bringinge 2 loads of oates from Croydon	0	12	0
Item for bringing 2 loads of sea coles Pitcher	0	8	0
Item spent in the kitchen this weeke ut patet p[er] libr[um]	25	8	4
Some total of this fortnight payd Novemb[er] 19 1638	93	14	5

[fo. 88r]

Receaved for Lutenor	14	0	0
For 10 q[ua]rters of wheate E[arl] of Thanett*	20	0	0

Inprimis to Capt[ain] Cartwright* man with 3 Arrabicke books	0	2	6

270 See n. 155 above.

271 This is the sole entry in the accounts relating to 'Mr Allnett', whose identity remains elusive.

Item to Stephen[272] for boathires	0	1	0
Item to Mr Southes* oysters and erringoes†	0	2	0
Item given at the Star Chamber[273] p[ayd] Mr Rollston*	0	10	6
Item to the gardner at Croydon for trees &c ut patet	2	17	4
Item to the bargemen this week	1	10	0
Item for 2 pies &c E[arl] of Lincoln*[274]	1	0	0
Item for salt sallmon out of Ireland	0	10	0
Item for a brawne Bail[i]ffe of Croydon[275]	0	5	0
Item to the baker St Clement[276]	0	10	0
Item to Mr Holfords* boathire &c	0	1	0
Item for 14 bush[els]† of oates for the coach horses at xxij[d]	1	5	8
Item for a bush[el]† of beanes	0	3	8
Item for 18 bush[els]† of oates for geldings & colts	1	13	0
Item for removinge & naylinge	0	2	0
Item for 12 broomes for the stable	0	2	0
Item spent in the kitchen this weeke ut patet p[er] libr[um]	28	16	7

Novemb[er] 23 1638

Item for 3 pheasants Lo[rd] Privy Seale*	0	7	0
Item for 2 cheddar cheeses Mr Egglefield*	0	6	0
Item for Katherine Laudes husband[277]	2	0	0
Item for boathires & letters Mr Dell*	0	13	10
Item for boathire &c Mr Southes*	0	2	0
Item for a present of fowle &c from the Deane of Winchester*	1	2	0
Item to Tho[mas] Sadler* for a suite, cloake & hatt &c for the footman	7	1	0
Item to him for a suite, cloake hatt &c for Thom[as] Webb* ut patet	5	7	3
Item to W[illiam] Duckett* for lynen & other new charges for him ut patet	9	1	3
Item give him &c by Mr Snaith*	1	5	0
Item for a hyne E[arl] of Lyndsey*	0	13	0
Item for a doe Lord Maynard*	0	10	0
Item to the bargemen this weeke	1	5	0
Item to the gardner at Lambeth	0	9	10
Item for 14 bush[els]† of oates for the coach horses at xxij[d]	1	5	8
Item for a bush[el]† of beanes	0	3	8

272 See n. 113 above.
273 See n. 30 above.
274 This is the sole entry in the account book for a gift from the earl of Lincoln.*
275 In Jan. 1638, Thomas Smith was appointed bailiff of the manor of Croydon by Laud; *Collectanea topographica et genealogica*, eds. Frederic Madden, Bulkeley Bandinel & John Nichols, II (London, 1838), p. 43.
276 See n. 80 above.
277 This is the sole entry in the accounts relating to 'Katherine Laude', who was probably one of the archbishop's paternal relations.

Item for 17 bush[els]† of oates for geldings & colts at xxij[d]	1	11	2
Item for naylinge coach horses	0	1	2
Item spent in the kitchen this week ut patet p[er] libr[um]	28	4	9
Some of this fortnight payd Dec[ember] 5 1638	107	6	4

[fo. 89r]

Receaved 0–0–0

Inprimis for a sugar loafe Mr Holloway*	0	2	6
Item for 2 sugar loaves B[isho]p of Landaff*	0	5	0
Item for 2 cheddar cheeses Dr Chaffin*	0	2	6
Item musitians boathire	0	1	0
Item for a brawne Guilford	0	1	0
Item for 2 pies from Sir Humf[rey] Foster*	0	2	0
Item for 4 cheshire cheeses from the Lady Savage*	0	6	0
Item for a cake B[isho]p of Rochester*	0	2	6
Item for 2 sugar loaves Dr Collyns* &c	0	2	6
Item to the gardner at Lambeth for 2 fares† of dunge and 8 carridges ut patet	2	8	0
Item to the bargemen this weeke ut patet	1	7	0
Item for a cocke pie Dr Parry*	0	3	6
Item for 3 pheasants Sir Ro[bert] Honeywood*	0	2	6
Item for oysters Dr Aylett*	0	1	0
Item for 14 bush[els]† of oates for coach horses at xxj[d] p[er] bush[el]†	1	5	6
Item for a bush[el]† of beanes	0	3	8
Item for 28 bush[els]† of oates for geldings	1	11	6
Item for 28 newe shoes for the 7 coach horses	0	16	4
Item spent in the kitchen this weeke ut patet p[er] libr[um]	29	4	9

Decemb[er] 7 1638

Item to Mr Southes* for the joyners and boathire	0	5	0
Item for glasses from Mr Padgett*	0	5	0
Item to Mr Dell* for boathires & letters ut patet	0	12	10
Item give a poore woman of Reddinge	0	10	0
Item for a cocke pie Mr Armestronge[278]	0	2	0
Item for 2 lambes B[isho]p of Oxon*	0	5	0
Item to the bargemen this weeke	1	0	0
Item to the gardner at Lambeth	0	8	4
Item to the gardner at Croydon	0	0	0

278 This is the sole entry in the accounts for 'Mr Armstronge', whose identity remains elusive. It would be a nice twist if the gift had been sent by Archibald Armstrong, the king's fool, who had been dismissed from office in Mar. 1638 (see n. 220 above), following public criticism of Laud, but this is merely conjecture.

Item for 14 bush[els]† of oates for coach horses at xxj^{d} p[er] bush[el]†	1	5	6
Item for a bush[el]† of beanes	0	3	8
Item for 18 bush[els]† of oates for gelds.	1	11	6
Item spent in the kitchen this weeke ut patet p[er] libr[um]	28	13	4
for this quarter			
Payd the brewer for 30 hogsh[eads]† of viij^{s} & 150 hogsh[eads]† of vj^{s} beare layd in at Lambeth since Midsomer	85	10	0
Item to M[is]tr[es]s Hoult* for this q[ua]rter	4	0	0
Item to M[is]tr[es]s Whaly* for the rent of the slaughterhouse	0	12	6
Item to the mole catcher	0	5	0
Item for yr G[races] barber	0	10	0
Item for the footman	0	3	0
Item to the laundress for ashes, soape, starche & besides wages	4	10	0
Item for hoopinge tubs &c	0	18	6
Item for 33 ells† of course towellinge at viij^{d} p[er] ell† for the kitchen & makings	1	4	0
Item for 3 cottons for the scullery	0	4	6
[fo. 90r]			
Item to Morris* [the smith] for shoeinge, dressinge & drenchinge geldings ut patet	4	19	10
Item to Abbot* the sadler for horse clothes, collars, bridles, sursingles† &c ut patet	10	17	2
Item to Bryan* the smith for a fier shovell, trivets &c for the kitchen	1	3	0
Item for changing brass for the kitchen	1	12	4
Item for 2 gross of trenchers†	0	14	0
Item for 100 doz of candles at iiij^{s} viij^{d} p[er] doz	23	6	8
Item for 8 bush[els]† of graynes for the ponds at Croydon &c	0	3	2
Item for 12 bush[els]† of oates for swans & pountry at xxj^{d} p[er] bush[el]†	1	1	0
Item for 14 loads of strawe at x^{s}	7	0	0
Item to William Duckett* for building &c ut patet p[er] bill	10	19	1
Item to him for the footman	2	15	8
Item to him for Rich[ard] Cobb*	1	8	6
Item for 500 of linges at ix^{l} p[er] C	45	0	0
Item for 600 of gabledines† at iij^{l} vj^{s} viij^{d}	20	0	0
Item for the charges by sea and land and layinge them in ut patet	3	11	6
Some total of this fortnight payd Decemb[er] 21 1638	306	1	4
Some total of this quarters expenses and layings out cometh to	viij^{c} lxix^{l}	viij^{s}	ix^{d}
Some of this years expenses & layings out cometh to	3569	12	6

All accompted and even Decemb[er] 21 1638

Adam Torlesse*

[fo. 91r]
December 14 1638

Receaved for lambe viij[l]			
Inprimis given to the 13 prisons against xxmas	3	0	0
Item to the poore of Lambeth	20	0	0
Item to the poore of Croydon	5	0	0
Item for an hogsh[eads]† of canary Stationers*[279]	0	10	0
Item for 5 tearses† of claret Sir Job Harby*	1	0	0
Item for fowle from Sir Humfrey Foster*	0	6	0
Item to the Citty Ingyneers	2	10	0
Item for putting a pin into yr G[races] watch	0	1	6
Item for a cake Dr Henry Kinge*	0	2	0
Item for an hogsh[eads]† of canary Redding	0	6	0
Item for a lanterne for the barge	0	2	0
Item for 2 sugar loaves Mr Wragg*	0	2	6
Item to Pallmer* for broomes, mopps, stuffe for andirons† &c	0	9	0
Item for a cheese & pippins† &c D[uchess] of Richmond*	0	5	0
Item for pheasants Sir Ed[ward] Gressom*[280]	0	2	6
Item to the postmasters man and tryminge 3 p[aires] of spurs Mr Snaith*	0	7	0
Item to the bargemen this week	1	2	0
Item to Knight* for clensing 33 redds at iij[d] &c at Croydon by the meadow	0	12	4
Item to Bunce and a labourer to lay in the boards &c 2 days[281]	0	3	0
Item for 3 cheeses and a cocke pie Judge Jones*	0	6	0
Item for a brawne Mr Dade*	0	5	0
Item for a sallmon Dr Fuller*	0	3	6
Item for a turkey Lady Cade[282]	0	2	0
Item for 4 capons Mr Hawk[283]	0	2	6
Item for 2 lambs Mr Dale*	0	5	0
Item for a doe Dutchess of Richmond*	0	10	0
Item for 14 bush[els]† of oates for coach horses	1	4	6
Item for a bush[el]† of beanes	0	3	8
Item for 18 bush[els]† of oates for geldings & colts at xxj[d]	1	11	6
Item given Martyn of Chislehurst for the great horse that dyed	0	10	0
Item for naylinge coach horses	0	1	2
Item spent in the kitchen this weeke ut patet p[er] libr[um]	27	11	6

279 The Company of Stationers*.

280 Shortly before sending this gift, on 26 Nov. 1638, Sir Edward Gresham* had petitioned Laud regarding a case which was soon to be brought to high commission. The case in question related to the marriage of Thomas, Gresham's son and heir against his father's will; *CSPD 1638–9*, p. 124, no. 54.

281 See n. 35 above.

282 See n. 86 above.

283 This is the first of three entries in the accounts for 'Mr Hawk' or 'Hawkes' whose identity remains elusive. Possibly the same person as 'Mr Hawkes of Upminster'.

Decemb[er] 21 1638

Item given Dr Crooks* man with fowle	0	13	6
Item for holly for the house	0	2	6
Item for sheepe from Croydon	0	2	0
Item for Mr Farrants[284] man and boy with leathers	0	13	6
Item to the brewers mens box	0	10	0
Item to the coachmakers mens box	0	5	0

[fo. 92r]

Item to Morris* the smiths men	0	3	6
Item to the harnessmakers men	0	2	0
Item to Bryan* the locksmiths men	0	2	0
Item to yr G[races] shoemakers men	0	5	0
Item for the weekly bills this yeare	1	0	0
Item to the groomes for selling 2 horses	1	0	0
Item for yr G[races] offeringe on xxmas daye	3	0	0
Item for the B[isho]p of Rochesters* man with xiij[l]	0	10	0
Item for a Spanish brawne D[eane] of Cant[erbury]*	0	6	0
Item to the gardner at Croydon	1	8	0
Item to the bargemen this weeke	0	12	0
Item to Tho[mas] Sadler* for apprel for yr Grace ut patet	5	8	0
Item to the E[arl] of Newcastles* footman	0	2	0
Item for 3 does Earl of Salisbury*	1	8	0
Item for 3 does B[isho]p of Winton*	1	0	0
Item for pepp[er], nuttmeggs, mace and cloves from the East India Company*	1	3	0
Item for sturgeon Westfalia tongue† from Dr Merrick*	0	7	0
Item for 2 pheasants D[uchess] of Richmond*	0	5	0
Item for fowle from Dr Sterne*	0	5	0
Item a doe Lo[rd] Cottington*	0	10	0
Item for lemons and pippins† D[uchess] of Richmond*	0	2	6
Item for 3 barr[els] of oysters Sir Jo[hn] Lucas*	0	2	0
Item for 2 lambes Sir And[rew] Jeynor*	0	5	0
Item for 14 bush[els]† of oates for coach horses	1	4	6
Item for a bush[el]† of beanes	0	3	8
Item for 18 bush[els]† of oates for geldings	1	11	6
Item spent in the kitchen this weeke ut patet p[er] libr[um]	33	0	8
Some of this fortnight payd Januar[y] 7 1639	127	17	0

284 See n. 115 above.

December 28 1638

Receaved for a pyed cowe and calf	v	0	0
Inprimis for yr G[races] New Years gift to the Kinge	40	0	0
Item to the household ut patet[285]	30	8	0
Item to M[is]tr[es]s Buckeridge* for a newe years gifte	5	0	0
Item for a lambe from Dr Ducke*	0	2	6
Item for W. Tillesley[286] with a sugar loafe	0	11	6
Item for a cupp & cover Mr Woodall*	1	0	0
Item for fowle E[arl] of Lyndsey*	1	2	0
Item for 2 hogsh[eads]† of claret Sir R[obert] Heath*	1	0	0
Item for a tun of claret B[isho]p of Chichester*	1	0	0
Item for a pipe of canary Comp[any] Vintners*	1	0	0
Item for 2 hogsh[eads]† of claret Marchant Taylors*	1	0	0
Item for cheeses & apples ewry man†	0	3	0
Item for 2 sugarloaves Mr Creswell*	0	3	6
Item for 6 small ones Burntwood	0	6	0
Item for a candlestick Turkey Marchants*	1	0	0
Item given wine coop[er]s & about wine	0	8	0
Item for a cupp and cove[r] Mr Attorney*	2	0	0
Item for a peece of sattyn Mr Dashwood[287]	1	0	0
Item to Lewes Harris[288] from the B[isho]p of St Asaph*	1	0	0
Item for a bason Sir Morris Abbot*	1	0	0

[fo. 93r]

Item to the boye at the garden stayres	0	2	6
Item for a candlestick March[ant] Advent[urers]*	1	10	0
Item for a cupp and cove[r] Sir Henry Gilford*	1	0	0
Item to Mr Dell* for boathires letters ut patet	0	11	4
Item for a Libel Cam. Registr. Advent.	0	10	0
Item to yr G[race] for Mr Snaith*	1	0	0
Item to the boy at the garden stayres	0	1	0
Item for boathires to the Lady Chomly* &c	0	1	6
Item for a present from her	0	5	0
Item for a present Mr Knight[289]	0	10	0
Item for a cupp and cov[er] p[ayd] Mr Longe[290]	2	0	0

285 See n. 14 above.

286 This entry may relate to the son of Richard Tillesley, whose name was John, mistakenly recorded as 'W'. See n. 193 above.

287 This is the sole entry in the accounts relating to 'Mr Dashwood', whose identity remains elusive.

288 This is the first of two identical entries for 'Lewes Harris' acting in some capacity for John Owens*, the bishop of St Asaph. Harris's identity is unclear, but he was unlikely to have been Lewes / Lewis Harris, under-sheriff of Oxford, who was removed from office in 1637 for irregularities in his collection of ship money in Oxfordshire; *CSPD 1636–7*, p. 78, no. 5; *CSPD 1637–8*, p. 235, no. 42.

289 See n. 8 above.

290 This is the sole entry in the accounts for 'Mr Longe', whose identity remains elusive.

Item for 6 lamprey† pies Mr Dutton*	0	5	0
Item for shirts &c Mr Henshawe*	1	0	0
Item for Glouc[e]s[ter] girdle M[is]tr[es]s Andrews[291]	0	10	0
Item for 2 swans Mr Hodges*[292]	0	3	6
Item to the scullery men yr G[race]	0	10	0
Item to the bargemen this week	0	11	0
Item to the gardner at Lambeth for trees &c ut patet p[er] bill	1	2	0
Item for a cake Lord North*	0	2	0
Item for 2 does B[isho]p of Winton*	1	0	0
Item for 2 lambs Mr Bartlett*	0	5	0
Item for 2 swans Dr Mountford*	0	5	0
Item for 4 pheas[ants] Sir Arth[ur] Manwaring*	0	5	0
Item for a sugar loafe Mr Turner*	0	2	6
Item for turkeys M[is]tr[es]s Buckeridge*	0	5	0
Item for 14 bush[els]† of oates for coach horses at xxij[d]	1	4	6
Item for a bush[el]† of beans	0	3	8
Item for 17 bush[els]† of oates for geldings	1	9	9
Item for naylinge coach horses	0	1	0
Item for 18 broomes for the stable	0	3	0
Item spent in the kitchen this weeke ut patet p[er] libr[um]	30	0	4
Januar[y] 4 1639			
Inprimis for a candlestick Capt[ain] Crispe*	1	0	0
Item to John Gore* for needles	0	10	0
Item to Pallmer* for broomes	0	4	3
Item for x sugarloaves Mr Washborn*[293]	0	10	0
Item for 2 p[aire] of shoes for yr Grace	0	9	0
Item to Mr Snaith* for boathire	0	2	6
Item for a case of knives for the poulter	0	11	0
Item for drivinge the pyed cowe from Croydon and into Smithfield	0	3	0
Item for lamprey† pies Sir Maur[ice] Bartlett*	0	2	0
Item to the bargemen this week	1	0	0
Item for 14 bush[els]† of oates for coach horses at xxi[d] p[er] bush[el]†	1	4	6
Item for a bush[el]† of beans	0	3	8
Item for 17 bush[els]† of oates for geldings & colts at xxj[d]	1	9	9
Item for naylinge coach horses	0	2	0
Item spent in the kitchen this weeke ut patet p[er] libr[um]	29	7	10
Some total of this fortnight payd Januar[y] 17	173	5	7

291 This is the sole entry in the accounts for 'Mistress Andrews', whose identity remains elusive.

292 This is the sole entry in the accounts for 'Mr Hodges', who should not be confused with George Hodges, the yeoman of the wine cellar at Lambeth. It is not possible to establish the identity of 'Mr Hodges' because, in 1638, someone with this name was resident in at least seven London parishes. *The inhabitants of London in 1638*, ed. T. C. Dale (London, 1931), *passim.*

293 Probably Benjamin Washborne*.

[fo. 94r]
Januar[y] 11 1639

Rec[eave]d for 14 bush[els]† of wheate & coales at the consecration	6	0	0
& for 50 q[ua]rters of barly from Mr Rose*	62	10	0
Inprimis paid for yr Graces offering at the consecration[294]	3	0	0
Item to the keep at the garden gate & his man p[ayd] Mr Holford*	0	12	6
Item for a tun of claret wine from the Soape Boylers	1	0	0
Item for 2 doz of bottles for the court	0	9	0
Item for 6 doz of corks for them	0	3	0
Item for 2 lambs Dr Higgs*	0	5	0
Item for 2 pheasants Mr Roberts[295]	0	2	6
Item to the bargemen this week	0	15	0
Item for 14 bush[els]† of oates for coach horses at xxj[d]	1	4	6
Item for a bush[el]† of beans	0	3	8
Item for 17 bush[els]† of oates for geldings and colts	1	9	9
Item for 28 removes for coach horses	0	4	8
Item spent in the kitchen this weeke ut patet p[er] libr[um]	27	12	7

Januar[y] 18 1639

Item paid Mr Browne* for the cases of the anatomy for work in yr Gr[aces] studdy &c ut patet p[er] bill	9	6	6
Item for cheeses from Mr Davyes[296]	0	2	0
Item for boathires Mr Cobb*	0	1	0
Item to the gardner at Lambeth	0	6	0
Item to the bargemen	1	0	0
Item to the gardner at Croydon	0	19	4
Item for 2 lambs Dr Higgs*	0	5	0
Item for fowle Dr Martyn*	1	2	0
Item for a lamprey† pie Mr Bartlett*	0	2	0
Item for 2 more from Judge Jones*	0	2	6
Item for 14 bush[els]† of oates for coach horses	1	4	6
Item for a bush[el]† of beanes	0	3	8
Item for 17 bush[els]† of oates for geldings	1	9	9
Item for mending 2 prongs	0	0	6
Item spent in the kitchen this weeke ut patet p[er] libr[um]	30	16	11
Some total of this fortnight payd Febr[uary] 5 1639	84	8	10

294 John Towers* was consecrated bishop of Peterborough on 13 Jan. 1639 at Lambeth Palace; John Fielding, 'Towers, John (d. 1649)', *ODNB*.

295 This is the sole entry in the accounts for 'Mr Roberts', whose identity remains elusive.

296 This is the first of two entries for 'Mr Davyes', who may be the same person as 'Mr Davyes the Chaplayne', although the precise identity of Davyes remains elusive.

Januar[y] 25 1639

Inprimis for a p[aire] of oyld bootes, boathire to the shoemaker for yr G[race]	0	15	6
Item for bringinge newes of the Q[ueen] beinge in labour[297]	0	10	0
Item for boathires Mr Snaith*	0	2	0
Item for a sword for Mr Webb*	0	16	0
Item for a belt for him	0	18	0
Item for a letter from the Kinge[298]	0	1	0
Item to Mr Buckeridge* for a beaver hatt for your Grace	4	10	0

[fo. 95r]

Item to Mr Southes* for boathire to the Q[ueen][299]	0	2	0
Item to the postmasters man with letters	0	2	0
Item to the gardner at Lambeth	0	2	8
Item to the bargemen this week	1	7	0
Item to Mr Dell* for boathires l[ette]rs &c ut patet p[er] bill	0	19	7
Item for a lamb and fowle B[isho]p of Bristol*	0	2	0
Item for bacon, puddings and pheas[ants] Mr Doyly*	0	5	0
Item for 3 wild goose pies Sir Lionel Tolln[age]*	0	5	0
Item for 14 bush[els]† of oates for coach horses	1	4	6
Item for a bush[el]† of beanes	0	3	8
Item for 16 bush[els]† of oates for geldings	1	8	0
Item for nayling coach horses	0	1	2
Item spent in the kitchen this weeke ut patet p[er] libr[um]	28	12	2

Februar[y] 1 1639

Item given Sir H[enry] Martyns* 2 men	2	0	0
Item for musitians boathire	0	2	0
Item given Pallmer* by yr Grace	0	10	0
Item to Mr Snaith* for boathires	0	2	4
Item for dyinge & lyning yr G[races] hatt	0	8	0
Item to the bargemen this week	1	5	0
Item to the gardner at Lambeth	0	4	8
Item for a brawne Mr Mills[300]	0	5	0
Item for pheasants, cake & cheese Mr Powell*	0	5	0
Item for 14 bush[els]† of oates for coach horses	1	4	6
Item for 16 bush[els]† of oates for geldings	1	8	0

297 Around 22 Jan., Henrietta Maria gave birth to a daughter 'who lived to be christened Princess Katherine, and then died'; *CSPD 1638–9*, p. 361, no. 8.

298 This letter from Charles I may have imparted the news of the queen's delivery of the baby, or of the baby's death.

299 Laud visited Henrietta Maria, who was recovering from the birth and death of her child. On 9 Feb., Laud wrote to Wentworth of 'the Queen's extremity, loss of her child and her happy gathering of strength since'; *WWL*, VII, 523.

300 See n. 155 above.

Item for 5 newe shoes & naylinge coach horses	0	4	0
Item spent in the kitchen this weeke ut patet p[er] libr[um].	31	2	6
Some of this fortnight payd Febr[uary] 23 1639	81	11	11

Februar[y] 8 1639

Receaved 0–0–0

Inprimis for 2 lamprey† pies Ald[erman] Robinson* of Glouc[e]s[ter]	0	2	0
Item to the groome porter and butler at the Star Chamber[301]	0	6	6
Item p[ay]d for ship money at Lambeth[302]	3	0	0
Item for ship money at Croydon[303]	1	16	0
Item to the bargemen this weeke	1	5	0
Item to the gardner at Lambeth	0	12	10
Item for 14 bush[els]† of oates for coach horses	1	4	6
Item for a bush[el]† of beanes	0	3	8
Item for 16 bush[els]† of oates for geldings and colts xxij[d]	1	8	0
Item for removinge & naylinge	0	1	0
Item for a bayl at Richmond for 12 horses	0	4	6
Item spent in the kitchen this weeke ut patet p[er] libr[um]	32	0	9

[fo. 96r]
Februar[y] 15 1639

Item p[ay]d to the hie man for bringing Mr Roses* 50 quarters of wheate & for carrying back the sacks	3	5	3
Item to the porters for carrying it into the graynary	0	13	2
Item to Mr Snaith* & Mr Baggott[304] for boathires	0	6	6
Item for musitians boathire	0	2	0
Item for a present from the Lady Norris*	1	0	0
Item for sheepe from Croydon	0	1	0
Item for 2 hogsh[eads]† vinegar Sir K[enelm] Digby*	0	10	0
Item for broomes & mopps	0	7	6
Item for a booke from an ambassador	1	10	0
Item to the gardner at Lambeth ut patet	0	17	10
Item to the gardner at Croydon ut patet	1	17	7
Item to the bargemen	1	7	6
Item for w[hy]t[e] & redd herrings from Yarmouth	0	10	0
Item for 8 pheas[ants] Sir Caple Beadell*	0	6	0
Item for 2 pheasants Lady Mildmay*	0	2	0

301 See n. 30 above.
302 See n. 20 above.
303 See n. 20 above.
304 This is the first of four entries relating to 'Mr Baggott', who provided boathire for the household.

Item for 4 cheeses Dr Manwayringe*	0	5	0
Item for 14 bush[els]† of oates for coach horses	1	4	6
Item for a bush[el]† of beanes	0	3	8
Item for 16 bush[els]† of oates for geldings & colts at xxij[d]	1	8	0
Item for 12 newe shoes for coach horses at vj[d] p[er] shoe	0	13	5
Item for bleedinge the coach horses	0	3	6
Item spent in the kitchen this week ut patet p[er] libr[um]	31	0	2
Some of this fortnight p[ay]d Februar[y] 27 1639	89	19	4

Februar[y] 22 1639

Receaved 0–0–0

Inprimis give Sir Anth[ony] Weldons* man with partridges &c	0	3	0
Item for 2 p[airs] of brass snuffers	0	2	6
Item to Mr Snaith* &c for boathires	0	4	6
Item to Mr Rayltons* man Mr Dell*	1	10	0
Item for bacon & a cheese Dr Worrall*	0	12	0
Item to the bargemen	1	0	0
Item to the gardner at Lambeth	0	4	3
Item for puddings pippins† &c D[uchess] of Richmond*	0	2	6
Item for 6 brand geese Dr Lewes*	0	5	0
Item for carpes and preserves Lo[rd] Newburgh*	0	3	6
Item for herrings from Sir Jo[hn] Lambe*	0	2	0
Item for 14 bush[els]† of oats for coach horses	1	4	6
Item for a bush[el]† of beanes	0	3	8
Item for 25 bush[els]† of oates for geldings & colts	1	6	3
Item for a bayl for 4 coach horses at the Charter House	0	1	6
Item spent in the kitchen this weeke ut patet p[er] libr[um]	31	12	7

March 1 1639

Inprimis p[ay]d Thomas Sadler* for apprell for yr Grace ut patet	31	8	8
Item to Mr Dell* for boathires letters &c ut patet	1	1	4

[fo. 97r]

Item given to the prisons &c at yr Graces going to the Charter House	0	6	0
Item to the gardner at Croydon ut patet	1	18	9
Item to the bargemen	0	15	0
Item to the gardner at Lambeth	0	5	0
Item for cakes and cheeses Dr Heywood*	0	2	6
Item to the Lady Chomleys* man	0	5	0
Item for a p[aire] of galoshers† for yr G[race]	0	4	0
Item for boathires Mr Snaith*	0	3	0
Item for 14 bush[els]† of oates for coach horses	1	4	6

Item for a bush[el]† of beanes	0	3	8
Item for 16 bush[els]† of oats for geldings & colts	1	8	0
Item for naylinge coach horses	0	1	4
Item spent in the kitchen this weeke ut patet p[er] libr[um]	28	10	4
Some of this fortnight payd March 14 1639	106	14	10

March 8 1639

Receaved for Mr Denn* for 40 q[ua]rters of barley	150	0	0
& for the bill of impost	24	0	0
Inprimis to Mr Dell* for MS from the Lord Scudamore*[305]	3	0	0
Item for 2 lamprey† pies Mr Subdeane*	0	2	0
Item to Pallmer* for broomes	0	5	6
Item to the bargemen	1	3	6
Item to the gardner at Lambeth	0	13	2
Item to the gardner at Croydon	2	18	8
Item for a veale from Mr Farrant[306]	0	6	0
Item for 6 pheas[ants] Sir H[umphrey] Foster*	0	2	6
Item for 2 barr[els] of oysters Mr Dade*	0	1	0
Item for 14 bush[els]† of oates for coach horses	1	4	6
Item for a bush[el]† of beans colt	0	7	4
Item for 16 bush[els]† of oates for gelds colts abot xij^{d} for xij bush	1	7	0
Item for removing & naylinge	0	1	6
Item spent in the kitchen this weeke ut patet p[er] libr[um]	25	12	10

For this quarter

Item p[ay]d the brewer for 18 hogsh[eads]† of viij^{s} & lxxxxj hogsh[eads]† of vij^{d} beare layd in this q[ua]rter ut patet	51	15	0
Item to M[is]tr[es]s Hoult* for this q[ua]rter	4	0	0
Item to the Widd[ow] Whaly* for the rent of the slaughterhouse	0	12	6
Item to the mole catcher	0	5	0
Item to yr G[races] barber	0	10	0
Item for the footman	0	3	0
Item to the laundress for ashes, soape, starche & besides wages	4	10	0
Item for hoopinge tubs	0	9	8
Item for 3 payles, a washing bowle, a piggin† and 2 beetles†	0	11	6
Item to Morris* the farrier for shoeinge and drenching geldings ut patet	4	2	0
Item to Abbot* the sadler for girths, bridles &c ut patet	2	9	2

305 This document, the details of which are unknown, may have been included in the consignment of manuscripts and coins sent by Laud to the University of Oxford in June 1639.

306 See n. 115 above.

[fo. 98r]

Item for vij loads of straw layd in at x^{d} p[er] load	3	10	0
Item for 100 doz of candles layd in at iij^{s} vj^{d} p[er] doz	22	10	0
Item to the furrier† for dressing & making upp yr martyn skyns†	5	15	0
Item to Will Duckett* for shirts for Rich[ard] Cobb* ut patet	2	0	0
Item to him for the footman	0	18	2
Item to him for packthread† letters &c	0	7	10
Item for red and clar[et] wine to fill the vessels this yeare	8	7	5
Item for an hogsh[eads]† of canary ut patet	13	9	4
Item for signinge the bill of impost	1	18	0
Item to the wine coop for rackinge wine and hooping vessels ut patet	8	7	0
Item for 5 bush[els]† of oates for swans and poultry at Lambeth at xxj^{d}	0	8	9
Item for 29 doz of flaxen napkins at xxij^{d} p doz	11	12	6
Item for makinge & markinge them at xij^{d} p doz	1	9	0
Item for facing 7 p[aires] of sheets	0	3	6
Item for repayring and new paynting the sundiall in the garden	2	0	0
Some total of this weeke payd March 30 1639	189	9	10

Some total of this first quarters expenses and laying out cometh to the some of viij^{c} liij^{l} vij^{s} iiij^{d}

All accompted and payd
A[dam] T[orless]* March 30 1639

Second quarter beginning March 15 1639

Receaved 0–0–0

Inprimis given for a salmon from Mr Harfleet*	0	6	0
Item for pikes peaches trouts and a salmon from Mr Whitlock*	0	11	0
Item for 2 barr[els] of oysters Mr Laud[307]	0	1	0
Item given the appoticarys man	0	2	6
Item for yr watch p[ayd] Mr Holford*	0	5	0
Item to the bargemen	0	5	0
Item to the gardner at Lambeth	0	18	6
Item for 14 bush[els]† of oates for coach horses	1	3	4
Item for a bush[el]† of beans	0	3	8
Item for 16 bush[els]† of oates for geldings	1	6	8
Item for a doz of broomes and naylinge	0	3	0
Item spent in the kitchen this week ut patet p[er] libr[um]	28	3	6

307 One of Laud's extended family, possibly related to Katherine Laud. See n. 277 above.

[fo. 99r]
March 22 1639

Itme for 2 lamprey† pies &c Glouc[e]s[ter]	0	2	0
Item to the beare and wine seller at court	0	10	0
Item p[ay]d Mr Badger* for bindinge MS and a bible ut patet[308]	5	19	8
Item to Sir Symon Baskerville* Mr Snaith*	1	0	0
Item more to him for boathires &c	0	5	0
Item to Mr Dell* for letters boathire &c ut patet	0	17	10
Item to the bargemen	1	5	0
Item to the gardner at Lambeth	0	7	6
Item for broomes	0	4	0
Item for 14 bush[els]† of oates for coach horses at xx[d]	1	3	4
Item for a bush[el]† of beans	0	3	8
Item for 16 bush[els]† of oates for geldings and colts xx[d]	1	6	8
Item spent in the kitchen this weeke ut patet p[er] libr[um]	26	10	6
Some total of this fortnight payd Apr[il] 4 1639	73	4	4

March 29 1639
Receaved 0–0–0

Inprimis p[ay]d for Mr Pococks* pensions for 2 q[ua]rters ended at the Lady Day last	20	0	0
Item for a cake Lady Chomly*	0	2	6
Item for books out of France	1	10	0
Item to the gardner at Croydon ut patet	3	2	6
Item to the bargemen	1	1	6
Item to the gardner at Lambeth ut patet	0	10	0
Item for a sallmon pie from Mr Bagnall	0	2	6
Item for a cake and cheese Deane of St Asaph*[309]	0	5	0
Item for 3 coale basketts for the kitchen	0	3	6
Item for fish bottomes for the kitchen	0	3	8
Item for 14 bush[els]† of oates for the coach horses at xx[d]	1	3	4
Item for a bush[el]† of beans	0	3	8
Item for 16 bush[els]† of oates for geldings and colts	1	6	8
Item for shoeinge coach horses	0	5	0
Item spent in the kitchen this week ut patet p[er] libr[um]	28	0	11

---

308 These documents may have been included in the consignment of manuscripts and coins sent by Laud to the University of Oxford in June.

309 This gift was received around the time that Andrew Morris*, dean of St Asaph, petitioned Laud for a transfer from the parsonage of Chiddingstone in Kent – a living in Laud's gift – to Llanwrst in Denbighshire; *CSPD 1638–9*, p. 208, no. 63.

Aprill 5 1639

Item given to the 13 prisons against Easter	3	0	0
Item given Eliz[abeth] Hoult*	1	0	0
Item to Mr Snaith* for boathires	0	4	6
Item given the groomes in the stable by your Grace	5	6	0
Item for Mr Solicitors* fee	5	0	0
Item to Tho[mas] Sadler* for 2 suites and a cloake for Rich[ard] Cobb*	8	2	8

[fo. 100r]

Item for a suite for the footman	4	3	6
Item for a tawney cloth for livryes with 3 q[ua]rters of an ell† of taffaty	16	1	0
Item to the gardner at Lambeth	0	19	0
Item to the bargemen ut patet	0	15	6
Item for a buck Sir Rich[ard] Newport*	0	16	0
Item for a buck E[arl] of Suffolk*	0	10	0
Item for a doz of carpes Mr Abbot*	0	10	0
Item for halfe a bucke Sir Tho[mas] Jerman*	0	12	0
Item for 14 bush[els]† of oates for coach horses	1	3	4
Item for a bush[el]† of beans	0	3	8
Item for 16 bush[els]† of oates for geldings	1	6	8
Item spent in the kitchen this week ut patet p[er] libr[um]	27	16	2
Some total of this fortnight payd April 19 1639	135	10	9

Aprill 12 1639

Receaved 0–0–0

Inprimis for yr Graces offering	3	0	0
Item to yr G[race] by Mr Dell* for Francis	2	0	0
Item to the gardner at Lambeth	0	8	4
Item to the bargemen	0	15	0
Item to Knight* for cuttinge nettles in the parke &c	0	2	6
Item to Pallmer* for broomes &c	0	8	8
Item for 14 bush[els]† of oates for coach horses at xx[d]	1	3	4
Item for a bush[el]† of beanes	0	3	8
Item for 15 bush[els]† of oates for geldings and colts	1	5	0
Item for naylinge coach horses	0	1	0
Item spent in the kitchen this weeke ut patet p[er] libr[um]	32	16	2

Aprill 19 1639

Item to yr Grace for Mr Harbords* fee	3	0	0
Item to the gardner at Croydon	2	0	4
Item to Mr Snaith* for boathire	0	1	6
Item to the bargement this weeke	1	2	0
Item for 14 bush[els]† of oates for coach horses at xx[d]	1	3	4

Item for a bush[el]† of beanes	0	3	8
Item for 15 bush[els]† of oates for geldings and colts at xx^d	1	5	0
Item spent in the kitchen this weeke ut patet p[er] libr[um]	31	11	10
Some total of this fortnight payd Maye 6 1639	83	0	6

[fo. 101r]
Aprill 26 1639

Rec[eave]d for a blind gelding	X		
Inprimis p[ay]d Mr Dell* for gratuities letters boathire &c ut patet	1	13	10
Item to the gardner at Lambeth	0	8	8
Item to the bargemen	0	11	0
Item for 14 bush[els]† of oates for the coach horses at xx^d	1	3	4
Item for a bush[el]† of beanes	0	3	8
Item for 13 bush[els]† of oates for geldings and colts	1	1	8
Item for nailing coach horses	0	1	2
Item spent in the kitchen this week ut patet p[er] libr[um]	30	17	7

May 3 1639

Item to Mr Browne* for making a cedar chest and facinge 5 planks &c ut patet p[er] bill	3	6	0
Item to Jo[hn] Josephs* brother for the mill &c in the bakehouse ut patet	2	16	0
Item for pippins† from Mr Mills[310]	0	2	0
Item to the gardner at Lambeth	0	12	6
Item to the bargemen	1	0	0
Item to the armorer for 9 light horsemens armour and 14 costlets† compleate ut patet p[er] bill[311]	52	1	6
Item for 14 bush[els]† of oates for the coach horses at xx^d	1	3	4
Item for a bush[el]† of beanes	0	3	8
Item for 13 bush[els]† of oates for geldings and colts at xx^d	1	1	8
Item for 24 shoes and 4 removes for coach horses	0	14	8
Item for 12 broomes for the stable	0	2	0
Item spent in the kitchen this weeke ut patet p[er] libr[um]	30	2	2
Some total of this fortnight payd May 18 1639	129	6	5

May 10 1639

Rec[eave]d of Mr Rose* for 50 q[uarters] mault	50	0	0
& the E[arl] of Thanett* for q[uarter] of wheate	16	0	0

---

310 See n. 155 above.
311 For a discussion of weaponry in the household, see 'Introduction', pp. xxx–xxxi above.

Inprimis for a buck from Sir Rob[er]t Dormer*	0	13	6
Item for another Sir Hatton Farmer*	0	10	0
Item to the ewry man† for glasses	0	12	6
Item to the gardner at Lambeth	0	10	6
Item to the bargemen	1	0	0
Item to the gardner at Croydon from 3 weeks and for seedes ut patet	2	5	1
Item for chickens &c from Mr Doyly*	0	5	0
Item for a cake & cheeses Mr Padgett*	0	2	6
Item for a lamprey† pie Mr Hawks[312]	0	1	0
Item for a bush[el]† of beanes	0	3	8
Item for 9 bush[els]† for geldings and colts	0	15	0
Item for the farryer for the baye stone colt	1	10	0
Item spent in the kitchen this weeke ut patet p[er] libr[um]	30	2	5

[fo. 102r]
May 17 1639

Item given 3 men for bringing 100 Welsh sheepe from Croydon	1	16	0
Item p[ay]d Mr Walker* for Mr Webbs* diett p Mr Snaith*	0	3	0
Item for 2 sheepes milke cheese from Mr Walker of Cheswick[313]	0	1	0
Item to the gardner at Lambeth	0	17	0
Item to the bargemen	1	5	0
Item for Nicholas* chardges into Ford and back with colts & 2 bucks ut patet	2	15	6
Item to Mr Snaith* for boathires ut patet	0	6	0
Item for a salmon from Sir Henry Wootton*	0	5	0
Item to Pallmer* for broomes and mopes	0	5	3
Item for 14 bush[els]† of oates for the coach horses	1	3	4
Item for a bush[el]† of beanes	0	3	8
Item for 9 bush[els]† of oates for geldings	0	15	0
Item 6 removes and naylinge	0	1	6
Item spent in the kitchen this weeke ut patet p[er] libr[um]	25	19	7
Some total of this fortnight payd May 30 1639	80	19	0

May 24 1639

Inprimis for a buck and a cake from Sir Robert Hatton*	0	13	0
Item for bringinge 83 weathers† out of Kent ut patet p[er] bill	3	6	0
Item to yr G[race] for Mr Holloway*	4	0	0

312 See n. 283.

313 A more precise identification of 'Mr Walker from Cheswick' remains elusive. Not to be confused with Thomas Walker*.

Item given at the Star Chamber[314] and cooks at the court Mr Rollston*	0	12	0
Item for cheeses from Dr Turner*	0	2	0
Item to Mr Dell* ut patet p[er] bill for this moneth	0	18	0
Item to the gardner at Lambeth	0	10	6
Item to the bargemen	0	10	0
Item for 14 bush[els]† of oates for the coach horses	1	3	4
Item for a bush[el]† of beanes	0	3	8
Item for 9 bush[els]† of oates for geldings	0	15	0
Item for naylinge coach horses	0	1	0
Item spent in the kitchen this weeke ut patet p[er] libr[um]	26	16	5

May ult

Item for your G[race] offering on Whitsunday	3	0	0
Item to the poore at the Savoye and Mr Rollston*	0	2	0
Item for cheeses Dr Smith*	0	1	6
Item for a pipe of canary B[isho]p of Derry*	1	0	0
Item to the bargemen	1	5	0
Item to the gardner at Lambeth	0	6	8
Item for boathire Mr Snaith*	0	2	0
Item for a buck from Sir Maurice Bartlett*	0	11	0
Item for 6 barr of herrings out of Ireland	0	10	0

[fo. 103r]

Item for 14 bush[els]† of oates for the coach horses	1	3	4
Item for a bush[el]† of beanes	0	3	8
Item for 7 bush[els]† of oates for geldings	0	11	8
Item for a shoe & 6 removes	0	1	7
Item spent in the kitchen this weeke ut patet p[er] libr[um]	28	15	9
Some total of this fortnight payd June 13 1639	77	5	1

June 7 1639

Rec[eave]d of Mr Barton* for wood	100	0	0
Inprimis for a buck from Ford	0	13	0
Item for powder from Mr Cordrey[315]	0	2	0
Item for redd canary Dr Featley*	0	5	0
Item for boathires Mr Holford*	0	1	0
Item to the bargemen this week	1	1	6
Item to the gardner at Lambeth	0	8	6
Item for broomes &c Mr Pallmer*	0	4	0

314 See n. 30 above.

315 This is the sole entry in the accounts for 'Mr Cordrey', whose identity remains elusive.

Item for a sallmon pie Dr Parry*	0	2	6
Item for a salmon Mr Abbott*	0	5	0
Item for a buck Lo[rd] Cottington*	0	15	0
Item for 3 dayes work Knight*	0	3	6
Item for 14 bush[els]† of oates for coach horses	1	3	4
Item for a bush[el]† of beanes	0	3	8
Item for 8 bush[els]† of oates for geldings	0	13	4
Item for removinge and naylinge	0	1	2
Item spent in the kitchen this weeke ut patet p[er] libr[um]	25	17	7

June 14 1639

Item for 2 barr of sturgeon Eastland Marchants*	0	12	0
Item for a fresh sallmon Lo[rd] Privy Seal*	1	0	0
Item a buck Mr Adr[ian] May*	0	16	0
Item for strawberries D[ean] of Sarum*	0	1	0
Item for a buck B[isho]p of Winton*	0	15	0
Item for a buck Mr Lumly[316]	0	5	0
Item for a barr of sturgeon Mr Edmonds[317]	0	2	0
Item for a bucke & a fawne from Ford	0	15	0
Item for 3 trowts Lo[rd] Finch*	0	5	0
Item to the gardner at Croydon for 5 weeks ut patet p[er] bill	5	0	0
Item to the bargemen this week	1	4	0
Item to the gardner at Lambeth	0	9	0
Item for a present from the Duchess of Richmond*	0	6	0
Item to Jo[hn] Mills* for washing the g[reat] horse	0	1	6
Item for 14 bush[els]† of oates for coach horses	1	3	4
Item for a bush[el]† of beanes	0	3	8
Item for 10 bush[els]† of oates for geldings	0	16	8
Item spent in the kitchen this week ut patet p[er] libr[um]	27	5	3

For this quarter

Item p[ay]d the brewer for 18 hogsh[eads]† of viij^{s} & 102 hogsh[eads]† of vj^{s} beare layd in att Lambeth this q[ua]rter	56	14	0
Item to M[is]tr[es]s Hoult* for her q[ua]rtridge	4	0	0
Item to M[is]tr[es]s Page* for this q[ua]rter	1	0	0
Item to the Widd[ow] Whaly* for the rent of the slaughterhouse	0	12	6
Item to the mole catcher	0	5	0
Item to yr G[races] barber	0	10	0

---

316 See n. 248 above.

317 This is the sole entry in the accounts for 'Mr Edmonds', whose identity remains elusive. Possibly William Edmunds, vicar of Rickmansworth, Hertfordshire, who acted as clerk to Laud's metropolitical visitation of the diocese of London, within which Hertfordshire was incorporated; *Alumni oxonienses*, II, 446; *WWL*, V, 500.

Item to the footman	0	3	0
Item to the laundress for ashes, soape, starch &c besides wages	4	10	0
Item for a newe washing tubb	0	8	0

[fo. 104r]

Item for hooping old tubs	0	7	8
Item for 30 ells† of cloth for 12 dresser cloths at xiij^d p[er] ell†	1	15	0
Item for 48 ells† of towelling for the kitchen & butlers &c at viij^d	1	12	0
Item for an ash cloth	0	4	8
Item for makinge & markinge dresser cloths & towells	0	4	2
Item to Morris* the smith for shoeinge & drenchinge geldings &c ut patet	3	11	0
Item to Abbott* the sadler for bridles, bitts, saddle cloths &c ut patet	4	12	0
Item to the harnessmaker for a sett of raynes and headstalls &c ut patet p[er] bill	5	7	10
Item to the coachmaker for 2 setts of newe wheeles and reparyinge the 2 coaches this yeare	22	5	0
Item for xij loads of strawe	6	0	0
Item for a turkey cock for the park	0	5	0
Item for 6 bush[els]† of oates for poultry at Lambeth	0	10	0
Item given to the yeoman of the wineseller for laying in wine at severall tymes	0	8	6
Item to Will[ia]m Duckett* for household stuffe &c ut patet p[er] bill	22	14	10
Item to him for Rich[ard] Cobb*	0	10	0
Item to him for the footman	3	11	0
Item to Mr Watts* for a newe net and mending the old one	2	1	8
Item for graynes and clensinge the pond this halfe yeare	0	9	0
Item for pigeons meale	0	8	6
Item for broomes and moppes this yeare	0	7	6
Item for 5 hurdles	0	2	6
Item for grubbing† in the cow pasture at Croydon	1	10	6
Item to Lane[318] and Holland* for hedging and ditching 140 redd at iiij^d p[er] redd betweene the cow pasture and Waterells ground	2	6	8
Item to them for 34 redds bewteene the cow pasture and Bushey Park	0	11	4
Item to them for 24 dayes worke in mendinge the hedges this springe	2	8	0
Item for killing moles & spreading the hills &c	1	5	0
Item for an axe tree and mentinge harnesses	0	5	0
Item for making 14 hurdles	0	3	0
Item for drenching 5 cowes	0	2	6
Item for washing 160 sheepe & for pitch to marke them	0	7	6
Item for shearinge them	0	10	0
Some total of this fortnight & quartridges paid Jul 1 1639	228	0	4

---

318 See n. 257 above.

Some total of this second quarters expenses and laying out cometh to viij vij vj v

[fo. 105r]
Third quarter beginninge June 21 1639

Receaved for Mr Spratlings* quarters of wheate sould at xxx[s] p[er] q[uarter]	45	0	0
Inprimis for bringinge a cake and cheeses from Mr Powell*	0	3	6
Item for a p[aire] of bootes for your Grace p[ayd] Mr Snaith*	0	12	0
Item to the keeper of the garden stayres at W[hi]t[e]hall for 2 q[ua]rt[e]rs	0	15	0
Item to the man & boye there	0	3	6
Item to the Lady Chomleys* man with cheeses	0	2	0
Item to the postm[a]st[e]rs man with letters	0	2	0
Item for Mr Snaiths* boathires ut patet	0	3	0
Item to the gardner this weeke ut patet Lamb[eth]	0	11	4
Item for a buck from the Lo[rd] Maynard*	0	15	0
Item for a buck & fawne Ford	0	10	0
Item for a buck Sir Charles Harbord*	0	15	4
Item for a buck B[isho]p of Winton*	0	15	0
Item for a salmon Mr Burfield[319]	0	2	6
Item for 14 bush[els]† of oates for coach horses at xx[d]	1	3	4
Item for a bush[el]† of beanes for them	0	3	8
Item for 10 bush[els]† of oates for geldings	0	16	8
Item for a shoe & 23 removes	0	4	6
Item for a doz of broomes for the stable	0	2	0
Item spent in the kitchen this weeke ut patet p[er] libr[um]	25	4	4

June 28 1639[320]

Item for a buck fawne winbles† and shoulders from Ford	0	15	0
Item for a grosse of corkes from the court bottles	0	4	0
Item to Pallmer* for broomes & mopps	0	6	6
Item for the fraight & chardges of Mr Spratling* 30 q[ua]rters of wheate	1	17	6
Item for carrying it into the granary by the ports at iijd p[er] q[ua]rt[e]r	0	13	2
Item to the gardner at Croydon for this fortnight ut patet	1	15	10
Item to the gardner at Lambeth	0	8	4
Item to the bargemen for this weeke	0	15	0

319 This is the sole entry in the accounts for 'Mr Burfield', whose identity remains elusive.

320 On 28 June, Laud, as vice-chancellor of the University, sent 'the remainder of my manuscripts to Oxford, being in number 576', around 'an hundred' of which were in Hebrew, Arabic and Persian. He also sent a collection of coins; *WWL*, III, 233, V, 225.

Item given at the Star Chamber[321] & p[ayd] Mr Rollston* ut patet	0	7	6
Item for a buck D[uchess] of Richmond*	1	0	0
Item for cheesecakes Dr Newell*	0	2	0
Item for hoopinge tubbs in the kitchen	0	3	0
Item for the smith at Croydon for 4 sieths† for pitcher &c ut patet	1	14	0
Item for 14 bush[els]† of oates for coach horses	1	3	4
Item for a bush[el]† of beanes	0	3	8
Item for 10 bush[els]† of oates for geldings	0	16	8
Item for bleedinge and scowringe 6 coach horses at iij[s]	0	18	0
Item for nayling them	0	1	4
Item to the smith at Croydon for shoeing bleedinge & drenching at the park since Mich[ael]mas last ut patet	2	8	3
Item spent in the kitchen this weeke ut patet p[er] libr[um]	25	19	11
Some of this fortnight payd July 16 1639	79	19	9

[fo. 106r]

Inprimis to Mr Snaith* for boathires & a letter	0	1	6
Item to the gardner at Lambeth	0	10	6
Item to the bargemen this week	1	1	0
Item for 2 bucks from Farnham	1	10	0
Item for cheesecakes Dr Newell*	0	2	0
Item p[ay]d Dr Turner* for his charges in xxinge the B[isho]p of Elyes* sonne[322]	2	10	0
Item for 14 bush[els]† of oates for coach horses	1	3	4
Item for a bush[el]† of beanes	0	3	8
Item for 10 bush[els]† of oates for geldings	0	16	8
Item spent in the kitchen this weeke ut patet p[er] libr[um]	26	17	7

July 12 1639

Item for a buck Sir Henry Wallopp*	0	15	0
Item given to a poor maultese	1	0	0
Item for brining a ticket for xxi chald[ers] of seacoales from Newcastle	1	0	0
Item to the lyterman† for bringing them upp at viij[d] p[er] chald[er] &c	0	14	0
Item to the porters for carrying them in at xvj[d] p[er] chald[er] & boathires	1	11	0
Item for 2 newe jacks & dressing 4 old ones for the butlers	0	11	6
Item to the gardner at Lambeth	0	11	2
Item to the bargemen	1	0	0
Item for a buck & fawne from Ford	0	10	0
Item for a buck Sir Tho[mas] Edmunds*	0	15	0

321 See n. 30 above.

322 Laud christened William Wren, the fourth son of Matthew Wren*, bishop of Ely, to whom he acted as godfather. In 1645, William Wren was bequeathed £100 in Laud's will; *WWL*, IV, 448.

Item for bringinge 40 q[ua]rters of wheat from Mr Denns*	2	9	0
Item to the porters for carrying it into the granary & carrying back the sacks	0	15	0
Item for 14 bush[els]† of oates for the coach horses	1	3	4
Item for a bush[el]† of beanes	0	3	8
Item for 8 bush[els]† of oates for geldings at xx[d]	0	13	4
Item for 2 bush[els]† of yr owne oates	0	0	0
Item for 10 removes & nayling	0	2	4
Item for a shovell for the stable	0	2	0
Item spent in the kitchen this weeke ut patet p[er] libr[um]	26	15	1
Some total of this fortnight payd July 27 1639	75	7	8

July 19 1639

Receaved 0–0–0			
Inprimis for 2 p[aires] of shoes for yr Grace & shoemakers boathire	0	9	0
Item for cittro[n] peeles Mr Snaith*	0	13	6
Item for boathire for him	0	2	0
Item for a booke Mr Alsopp*	0	0	6
Item to Mr Southes* for boathire	0	1	0
Item to the gent usher & man for boathire	0	4	0
Item to the gardner at Lambeth	0	9	4
Item to the bargemen	1	0	0
Item for a stagg from Theobalds	1	5	0
Item for a buck from Farnham	0	15	0
Item for 14 bush[els]† of oates for coach horses	0	0	0
Item for a bush[el]† of beanes	0	3	8
Item for 10 bush[els]† of oates for geldings	0	0	0
Item spent in the kitchen this weeke ut patet p[er] libr[um]	26	18	7

[fo. 107r]
July 26 1639

Item for cheeses and cheesecakes M[is]tr[es]s Turner*	0	2	0
Item for partridges Dr Howell*	0	2	6
Item for a buck Lady Norris*	0	13	0
Item for another from Farnham	0	15	0
Item to the gardner at Lambeth	0	7	6
Item to the bargemen	0	15	0
Item to the gardner at Croydon 4 weekes	0	19	8
Item to Palmer* for broomes stuffe for andirons† to carry to Croydon[323]	0	10	2

323 See n. 329 below.

Item for partr[idge] & apricocks Dr Bucknor*	0	1	6
Item for lobsters & cockles Dr Stanly*	0	1	0
Item for 10 meates tongue Mr Parkinson[324]	0	2	6
Item for 14 bush[els]† of oates for coach horses	0	0	0
Item for a bush[el]† of beanes	0	3	8
Item for 10 bush[els]† of oates for geldings	0	0	0
Item for 24 newe shoes & 4 removes	0	15	6
Item spent in the kitchen this weeke ut patet p[er] libr[um]	26	1	7
Some total of this fortnight payd August 6	64	12	2

August 2 1639

Receaved for wood sould 99–6–0			
And for corne &c 33–19–6	132	5	6
Inprimis to Knight* for mowing the park & backsides &c	0	4	6
Item for pippins† from Mr Mills[325]	0	2	0
Item for a doz of double bottles for wine	0	6	0
Item for 4 sheepes milk cheeses Mr Walker[326]	0	2	0
Item to Mr Levinthrope* for boathire	0	1	0
Item to Mr Badger* for binding books ink paper &c ut patet p[er] bill	2	9	0
Item to Mr Dell* for letters, boathires &c for the last month ut patet	0	9	1
Item for sheepe from Croydon	0	2	0
Item to the gardner at Lambeth	0	13	0
Item to the bargemen ut patet	1	5	0
Item for a buck from Farnham	0	15	0
Item for another & partridges Mr Knight[327]	0	4	6
Item for cheesecakes Dr Newell*	0	2	0
Item to the coop for work in the kitchen	0	3	0
Item for 14 bush[els]† of oates for coach horses	0	0	0
Item for a bush[el]† of beanes	0	3	8
Item for 10 bush[els]† of oates for geldings	0	0	0
Item spent in the kitchen this weeke ut patet p[er] libr[um]	27	17	10

August 9 1639

Item for a stagg from Theobalds[328]	1	7	0
Item for boathire Mr Snaith* ut patet	0	2	10

---

324 See n. 6 above.

325 See n. 155 above.

326 Possibly 'Mr Walker of Cheswick'. See n. 313 above.

327 See n. 8 above.

328 The king had very recently returned from his first, unsuccessful attempt to subdue the Scottish covenanters by force in the first Bishops' War. He arrived at Theobalds on 1 Aug. and reached Whitehall some days later. This gift was probably the result of a royal hunting trip; *WWL*, III, 233.

Item for 3 gross of trenchers† & 2 trencher† knives for Croydon	1	2	6
Item for 2 bottles potts & tapps	0	3	11
Item to the bargemen this weeke	0	15	0
Item to the gardner at Lambeth	0	14	0
Item to the gardner at Croydon ut patet	1	15	8
Item for 3 p[aires] of great water bootes	2	14	0
Item to Mr Watts* for a cowe	4	15	0
Item for bringing sheepe from Lambeth	0	1	0
Item for 14 bush[els]† of oates for coach horses	0	0	0
Item for a bush[el]† of beanes	0	3	8
Item for 10 bush[els]† of oates for geldings	0	0	0
Item for a pronge and a shovel for the stable	0	2	4
Item spent in the kitchen this weeke ut patet p[er] libr[um]	26	7	3
Some total of this fortnight payd Aug[ust] 22 1639	75	3	9

[fo. 108r]

Item p[ay]d for fencinge cuttinge makinge & carridge of charcoales & wood to Lambeth & Croydon this yeare ut patet	170	4	7
Item for haymakinge at Lambeth ut patet	26	7	10
Item for haymakinge at Croydon ut patet	24	4	7
Item for threshing barly wheate rye & oates ut patet	7	2	7
Item for plowinge & sowinge &c this yeare ut patet	24	7	9
Some total for wood haye corne &c payd Aug[ust] 22 1639	252	7	3

August 16 1639

Item for 12 cartes for the remove to Croydon[329]	2	15	0
Item for bringing a load of wine	0	5	0
Item for a basket for butter	0	1	4
Item for mending yr G[races] watch	0	2	0
Item for gloves for the gardner	0	1	0
Item to the gardner at Lambeth	1	4	6
Item to the bargemen	0	7	6
Item to the gardner at Croydon	0	11	0
Item for a shovel for the coale house & mendinge the almond tubb	0	1	8

329 This entry shows that the summer remove from Lambeth to Croydon took place much later than usual this year. Laud remained at Lambeth for much of the summer because the political climate required his presence beside the king who, in early Aug. 1639, had just returned south from his first failed campaign against the Scots (see n. 328 above). The archbishop's correspondence for July and Aug. each year was normally written from Croydon, but in 1639, however, he was certainly still in residence at Lambeth on 31 July, presumably waiting for the king to return (on 1 Aug.). No letters were sent from Croydon until 2 Sept. and he was back in Whitehall the following day; Historical Manuscripts Commission, *Hastings MSS*, IV, 82–4; TNA, SP 16/428/20; *WWL*, VI, 570.

Item for Pitcher for his ladyes	1	5	0
Item for a buck from Dr Heath*[330]	0	12	0
Item for a buck from Farnham	0	15	0
Item for another Sir Nicholas Cary*	0	15	0
Item for l[ette]rs to Oxon &c	0	0	9
Item for 12 bush[els]† of oates for coach horses	0	0	0
Item for a bush[el]† of beanes	0	3	8
Item for 10 bush[els]† of oates for geldings	0	0	0
Item for the carridge of x qu[a]rters of oates to Lambeth	0	6	8
Item for naylinge coach horses	0	1	6
Item spent in the kitchen this weeke ut patet p[er] libr[um]	24	19	4

August 23 1639

Item for partridges Mr Moore[331]	0	2	6
Item for cheesecakes & codlings† M[is]tress Barnard*	0	1	0
Item for a buck from Farnham	0	15	0
Item for another Mr May*	0	15	0
Item for turkeys & cheeses Lady Scott*	0	2	6
Item for letters to Oxon	0	0	6
Item to the gardner at Lambeth	0	13	8
Item to the bargemen	0	7	6
Item to the E[arl] of Newcastles* groomes Mr Dell*	1	0	0
Item for letters & boathires this month ut patet	0	8	9
Item for broomes p[ayd] Pallmer*	0	3	6
Item to the gardner at Croydon	0	18	0
Item for 12 bush[els]† of oates for coach horses	0	0	0
Item for a bush[el]† of beanes	0	3	8
Item for 10 bush[els]† of oates for geldings	0	0	0
Item for 6 broomes for the stable	0	1	0
Item for 1 shoe & 23 removes	0	4	5
Item spent in the kitchen this weeke ut patet p[er] libr[um]	24	10	2
Some total of this fortnight payd Septemb[er] 6 1639	64	15	1

[fo. 109r]
Receaved 0–0–0

Inprimis given Mr Mabbs* mayd for washing yr G[races] study &c	0	5	0
Item for cheeses from M[is]tr[es]s Turner*	0	2	6
Item for a buck from Farnham	0	15	0

330 Thomas Heath*, not to be confused with Sir Robert Heath*.
331 This is the sole entry in the accounts for 'Mr Moore', who may have been Francis Moore, yeoman of the wardrobe at Lambeth Palace; LPL, TG1, fo. 28r.

Item for another Mr Mynas[332]	0	15	0
Item for bringinge melons	0	3	0
Item the gardner at Lambeth	0	10	6
Item to the bargemen	0	18	6
Item to the gardner at Croydon	1	1	0
Item for 12 bush[els]† of oates for coach horses	0	0	0
Item for a bush[el]† of beanes	0	3	8
Item for 10 bush[els]† of oates for geldings	0	0	0
Item spent in the kitchen this weeke ut patet p[er] libr[um]	24	11	4

Septemb[er] 6 1639

Item for grapes & melons Mr Sidney[333]	0	2	6
Item to the workmen in the terrace at Lambeth	0	2	0
Item for cheeses Sir Kellem Digby*	0	2	6
Item to the gardner at Lambeth	0	10	6
Item to the bargemen	0	8	0
Item to the gardner at Croydon	0	13	6
Item for a buck from Farnham	0	15	0
Item for another Mr Mynas[334]	0	12	6
Item for 12 bush[els]† of oates coach horses	0	0	0
Item for a bush[el]† of beanes	0	3	8
Item for 10 bush[els]† of oates for geldings	0	0	0
Item for dressing 2 coach horses feete	0	5	0
Item for removing & nayling them	0	1	0
Item spent in the kitchen this weeke ut patet p[er] libr[um]	25	19	8
Some total of this fortnight payd Septemb[er] 17 1639	59	1	4

Septemb[er] 13 1639

Receaved 0–0–0

Inprimis for a stagg from Sir Arthur Manwayringe*	1	6	0
Item for a buck Sir Tho[mas] Alisbury*	0	15	0
Item for another from Marybone Park	0	15	0
Item for yr Graces offeringe on Sunday	3	0	0
Item to Mr Snaith* for boathire	0	1	0
Item to the gardner at Lambeth	0	8	10
Item to the gardner at Croydon	0	7	1
Item for carpes from Mr Evelinge*	1	0	0

332 See n. 255 above.

333 This is the sole entry in the accounts relating to 'Mr Sidney', whose identity remains elusive.

334 See n. 255 above.

Item for a stagg Mr Seamour[335]	1	5	0
Item for bringinge melons & damsons	0	4	6
Item to Knight* for 4 dayes worke about the hovells and river against the stubble	0	5	0
Item to Holland* for 7 dayes work about the hovells, river & carrying dunge from the garden	0	8	0
Item for 12 bush[els]† of oates for coach horses	0	0	0
Item for a bush[el]† of beanes	0	3	8
Item for 12 bush[els]† of oates for geldings	0	0	0
Item for nayling coach horses	0	1	5
Item spent in the kitchen this weeke ut patet p[er] libr[um]	24	18	9

[fo. 110r]
Septemb[er] 20 1639

Itme for bringinge a pie & peares	0	3	6
Item for a cake from Mr Webb* p Mr Rollston*	0	2	6
Item for boathire	0	1	0
Item to the gardner at Lambeth ut patet	0	10	10
Item to the bargemen	0	9	0
Item to the gardner at Croydon	0	12	6
Item to Pallmer* for broomes & mopps	0	4	0
Item for 12 bush[els]† of oates for the coach horses	0	0	0
Item for a bush[el]† of beanes	0	3	8
Item for 13 bush[els]† of oates for geldings	0	0	0
Item for 16 newe shoes for coach horses & naylinge	0	10	8
Item spent in the kitchen this weeke ut patet p[er] libr[um]	25	3	11
Some total of this fortnight payd October 4 1639	63	0	10

For this quarter

Item p[ay]d Putney brewer for xvj hogsh[eads]† of viij^s & Lxiij hogsh[eads]† of vj^s beare layd in at Lambeth this q[ua]rter	37	19	0
Item to the brewer of Croydon for xiiij hogsh[eads]† of viij^s & Lxx hogsh[eads]† of vij^s beare layd in since xxmas last	39	18	0
Item p[ay]d to the B[isho]pp of Oxford* for Mr Webb*	20	0	0
Item to M[is]tr[es]s Hoult* for this q[ua]rter	4	0	0
Item to M[is]tr[es]s Page* for this q[ua]rter	1	0	0
Item to M[is]tr[es]s Whaly* for the rent of the slaughterhouse	0	12	6
Item to the molecatcher at Lambeth	0	5	0
Item to yr Graces barber	0	10	0
Item to the laundress for ashes, soape, starch & besides wages	4	10	0
Item for hoopinge tubbs, payles, flaskets† & roses to Daye ut patet	1	0	10

335 See n. 10 above.

Item to Morris* the smith for shoeing geldings ut patet	1	14	10
Item to Abbott* the sadler for bridles, girths, halters &c ut patet	2	12	2
Item to Comfort* the sadler of Croydon for shoeing geldings & parke horses ut patet p[er] bill	2	11	0
Item for 4 loads of strawe for Lambeth	2	0	0
Item for an horse hire for the organ maker	0	2	0
Item to Tho[mas] Sadler* yr G[race]s taylor for apprell for your Grace ut patet	5	14	6
Item for 114 ells† of Gantish cloth at xx^{d} p ell† for xij p[aires] of sheetes allow 9 ells† vj to vii the paire	9	14	9
Item for xij ells† of Holland† at ij^{s} vj^{d} p[er] ell† for 12 pillowbeares	1	10	0
Item for makinge & markinge them	0	15	0
Item to William Duckett* for household stuff ut patet p bil	6	4	7
Item layd out by him for Richard Cobb* ut patet	1	10	0
Item for fringe canvas &c for the barge cloth tassels 5 yrds of cloth[336]	1	13	8
Item to the bargemaker for the hulke of the barge ut patet	20	0	0
Item to the joyner for the house of it	8	18	0
Item to the Master of the Barge for the old house	2	0	0
Item to the paynter for colouringe it	4	0	0
Item for 6 oares with xx^{s} chardges at the launching	3	5	0

[fo. 111r]

Item to Mr Watts* for clensing the g[rea]t pond this summer & for grayne for fishes	1	15	4
Item for pigeons meale & makinge cleane the house &c ut patet	0	9	0
Some total for this quarter payd Octob[er] 4 1639	186	5	2

Some total of this 3rd quarters expenses & layings out cometh to ix^{c} xx^{l} xiij^{s} o^{d}

All payd A[dam] T[orless]*

Fourth quarter beginning Septemb[er] 27 1639

Receaved CC of Mr Barker[337] for wood			
Inprimis to Francis Loveday* for cleansing the moate this yeare	2	0	0
Item for his extraordinary paynes	1	0	0
Item to Mr Watts* his man & mayd	0	15	0
Item for grapes Lady Styles*	0	2	0
Item for a catt &c	0	2	0
Item to the gardner at Lambeth	0	9	4
Item to the gardner at Croydon ut patet	1	3	2

336 This and the following five entries relate to the repair/rebuilding of Laud's barge which was launched in late Sept. 1639.

337 This is the sole entry in the accounts for 'Mr Barker', whose identity remains elusive.

Item to the bargemen	0	8	0
Item to Mr Dell* for this moneth ut patet	0	13	9
Item for 10 bush[els]† of oates for coach horses	0	0	0
Item for a bush[el]† of beanes	0	3	8
Item for 13 bush[els]† of oates for geldings	0	0	0
Item for naylinge coach horses	0	1	0
Item spent in the kitchen this weeke ut patet p[er] libr[um]	28	17	5

October 4 1639

Item for 12 carts for the remove to Lambeth at vj^{s} 2 yeare	3	6	0
Item to the gardner at Lambeth	0	10	0
Item to the gardner at Croydon	0	0	0
Item to the bargemen this weeke	0	10	0
Item to Knight* for moving the walkes att Croydon &c	0	8	4
Item for 10 bush[els]† of oates for coach horses	0	0	0
Item for a bush[el]† of beanes	0	2	6
Item for 12 bush[els]† of oates for geldings	0	0	0
Item for the carrydge of 2 loads of oates for Croydon	0	12	8
Item for a sawe for John Mills*	0	1	0
Item for a payle for the stable	0	3	2
Item for a doz of broomes	0	2	0
Item for naylinge coach horses	0	1	0
Item spent in the kitchen this weeke ut patet p[er] libr[um]	28	18	2
Some total of this fortnight payd Octob[er] 22 1639	70	16	2

[fo. 112r]

Receaved xxx^{l} vx^{s} x^{d}

Inprimis for 6 redd deare pyes from the Earle of Dorsett*	1	5	0
Item for 3 barr[els] of oysters Sir John Lucas*	0	2	6
Item for 6 pheasants 12 tongue & 6 hams of Westfalia bacon Dr Paske*	0	11	0
Item to the gardner at Lambeth	0	15	6
Item to the bargemen this weeke	1	6	6
Item for shoeing the colt & Nicholas* charges	0	11	0
Item for 10 bush[els]† of oates for coach horses	0	0	0
Item for a bush[el]† of beanes	0	2	6
Item for 9 bush[els]† of oates for geldings	0	0	0
Item spent in the kitchen this weeke ut patet p[er] libr[um]	27	8	1

October 18 1639

Item for a horse from Sir John Lambe*	1	0	0
Item for another Mr Boswell*	2	0	0
Item for Mr Pococks* pension for 2 qurters ended at Mich[ael]mas last	20	0	0

Item for mendinge yr watch & boy at garden gate	0	3	6
Item to Mr Snaith* for 2 p[aires] of shoes for yr Grace & boathires &c ut patet	0	14	0
Item to Palmer* for broomes & mops &c	0	10	9
Item to the yeoman of the wineseller for bottles & corks for the court	0	15	0
Item given the woman at the parke	0	10	0
Item to John Houlton[338] for boathire	0	1	0
Item to Mr Cobb* for boathire	0	1	0
Item to Dr Turner* for 7 poore mens gownes att Redding ut patet	10	16	6
Item to the gardner at Lambeth	0	8	10
Item to the bargemen	1	10	0
Item to the gardner at Croydon ut patet	1	19	6
Item for lamprey† pies from Ald[erman] Robinson* the last Lent	1	10	0
Item for 10 bush[els]† of oates for coach horses	0	0	0
Item for a bush[el]† of beanes	0	2	6
Item for 17 bush[els]† of oates for geldings	0	0	0
Item spent in the kitchen this weeke ut patet p[er] libr[um]	27	3	10
Some total of this fortnight payd Octob[er] 30 1639	109	8	6
Item for 500 of lynge† bought at Yarmouth at vx^{l} x^{s} p[er] 100	47	10	0
Item for 600 of gabberdines† att iij^{l} x^{s} p[er] 100	21	0	0
Item for the fraight & other chardges by sea and land ut patet	3	14	2
Some total payd October 30 1639	72	4	2

[fo. 113r]
October 25 1639

Receaved for Sherman sould for iiij^{l}			
Inprimis given to the 2 beare sellers at court	0	10	0
Item for a messengers boathire	0	1	0
Item to Mr Snaith* for boathire	0	1	0
Item for 2 gynny hens† Lo[rd] Privy Seale*	0	5	0
Item to the slaughterman for bringing 135 Kent weathers† out of Kent	4	4	0
Item for a doe Sir Nich[olas] Cary*	0	10	0
Item to the gardner at Lambeth	0	8	10
Item to the bargemen	1	6	0
Item to Mr Dell* for this moneth ut patet	1	12	7
Item for pheasants & puddings Sir John Shelly*	0	6	0
Item for brawne & puddings Sir John Epslye*	0	2	0
Item for 12 pheasants Mr Williscott*	0	6	0

338 This is the first of two entries for payments to 'John Houlton' for boathire. Mr Houlton's identity remains elusive.

Item for 3 gross of trenchers†	1	1	0
Item for a doz of glasses	0	9	6
Item for pipkins† for the kitchen	0	3	6
Item for 12 bush[els]† of oates for coach horses	0	0	0
Item for a bush[el]† of beanes	0	2	6
Item for 16 bush[els]† of oates for geldings	0	0	0
Item for 12 shoes & 12 removes	0	9	0
Item spent in the kitchen this weeke ut patet p[er] librum]	24	18	5

Novemb[er] 1 1639

Item to Mr Mabb* for the after pasture for the parke	3	0	0
Item to him for letters broomes mopps & clensinge the house ut patet	1	9	8
Item for 4 cheeses & angelotts† from the Lady Savage*	0	6	0
Item for a salmon pie Lady Seamour*	0	3	6
Item for angelotts† Mr Taylor*	0	2	0
Item for a pie & cheese Judge Jones*	0	3	6
Item for dryde beife Mr Garrett*	0	2	6
Item for a pie & 4 cheeses Sir John Peashall*	0	3	6
Item for a cheddar cheese Capt Crispe*	0	5	0
Item to the gardner at Lambeth	0	5	0
Item to the bargemen	1	5	0
Item to the gardner at Croydon	2	4	10
Item p[ay]d the appoticary for your Grace & household ut patet	2	11	6
Item for John Cobb*	1	1	3
Item for John Birkenhead*	0	19	0
Item for Mr Kinge* the porter	1	4	2
Item for Jo[hn] Joseph* the baker	0	11	3
Item for Richard Browne* at the granary	1	9	6
Item for John Mills*	0	3	6
Item for William Palmer*	0	6	6
Item for William Harman* the cooke	2	1	6
Item to Roger Parker* butler	5	18	0
Item for John Keely[339]	0	13	0

[fo. 114r]

Item for 12 bush[els]† of oates for coach horses of our owne	0	0	0
Item for a bush[el]† of beanes	0	2	6
Item for 17 bush[els]† of oates for geldings	0	0	0
Item for naylinge coach horses	0	0	9
Item spent in the kitchen this weeke ut patet p[er] librum]	27	5	1
Some total of this fortnight payd Novemb[er] 16 1639	90	14	4

339 See n. 178 above.

Novemb[er] 8 1639

Receaved xx[l] towards the organ			
xiij[l] v[s] viij[d] remained			
Inprimis p[ay]d Mr Burwood* for a newe organ sett upp in the chappell at Lambeth besides the old one ut patet	50	0	0
Item to Mr Babb* for gilding the organ ut patet[340]	13	6	8
Item for harvy apples Dr Eden*	0	2	0
Item to Knight* for 4 dayes worke about the causeway for the bardge &c	0	5	4
Item for a brawne Mr Cartwright*	0	6	0
Item for a doe from Farnham	0	10	0
Item for 4 pheas[ants] 2 pikes 2 carpes a collar of brawne & 2 doz of puddings	0	6	0
Item for a doe Sir Charles Harbord*	0	8	0
Item to the bargemen this weeke	1	18	0
Item to the gardner at Lambeth	0	7	4
Item for 12 bush[els]† of oates for c[oach]horses	0	0	0
Item for a bush[el]† of beanes	0	2	6
Item for 18 bush[els]† of oates for geldings and colts	0	0	0
Item for bringinge 7 c[artes] of oates from Croydon	0	6	0
Item spent in the kitchen this weeke ut patet p[er] libr[um]	26	14	8

Novemb[er] 15 1639

Item given the Lady Sherwoods[341] man with plate	2	0	0
Item for a barbary horse Earl of Newcastle*[342]	10	0	0
Item for 2 does Earl of Dorsett*	0	12	0
Item to Pallmer* for broomes & mopps &c	0	6	0
Item for a doe Sir Thomas Alisbury*	0	10	0
Item for another from Farnham	0	10	0
Item for a cocke pie Dr Parry*	0	3	6
Item for turkeys, partr &c Mr Doyly*	0	5	0
Item to the gardner at Lambeth	0	0	0
Item to the bargemen	1	10	0
Item to the gardner at Croydon	1	14	5
Item for 12 bush[els]† of oates for coach horses	0	0	0
Item for a bush[el]† of beanes	0	2	6
Item for 18 bush[els]† of oates for geldings & colts bought at x[s] iij[d] p[er] bush[el]†	1	7	0

340 Prior to painting the new one, Babb had worked on the old organ in Lambeth chapel. In Nov. 1635, he had carried out work on the pipes of the organ, which 'were richly gilded and the case … painted of wainscot colour'; *CSPD 1635*, p. 487, no. 9.

341 Lady Abigail Sherard, wife of William, Lord Sherard*.

342 This is the last recorded gift of a horse from Newcastle to Laud. For others, see nn. 134, 233 and 237 above.

Item for naylinge & a doz of broomes	0	3	0
Item spent in the kitchen this weeke ut patet p[er] libr[um]	25	11	11
Some total of this fortnight payd Decemb[er] 2 1639	139	7	10

[fo. 115r]
November 22 1639

Receaved 0–0–0			
Inprimis for a doe from Ford	0	10	0
Item to the baker on St Clement[343]	0	10	0
Item to Morris the waterman[344]	0	10	0
Item for a hyne Sir Ro[bert] Craford*	0	12	0
Item for a doe Lo[rd] Cottington*	0	10	0
Item for turkeys geese capons &c Dr Layfield*	0	6	0
Item for a tun of claret a jarr of oyle Sir Job Harby*	2	6	6
Item to the bargemen this weeke	1	10	0
Item to the gardner at Lambeth	0	3	10
Item for 12 bush[els]† of oates for coach horses at xviij^{d}	0	18	0
Item for a bush[el]† of beanes	0	2	6
Item for 17 bush[els]† of oates for geldings and colts at xviij^{d}	1	5	6
Item for 17 newe shoes & 4 removes for coach horses	0	10	7
Item spent in the kitchen this weeke ut patet p[er] libr[um]	25	1	10

Novemb[er] 29 1639

Item for 4 sugar loaves B[isho]p of Landaff*	0	5	0
Item for 2 potts of lamprey† E[arl] of Shrewsbury*	0	1	6
Item to the chamber keep[er]s man at court p[ayd] Mr Rollston*	1	0	0
Item given at the Star Chamber[345]	0	8	6
Item to Sir Jacob Ashlyes* man p[ayd] Mr Dell*	1	0	0
Item to him for letters, boathires &c this moneth ut patet	0	13	6
Item for citterne peeles† &c from Mr Seargeant Walthew*	0	4	0
Item to the gardner at Lambeth	0	12	2
Item to the bargemen this weeke	1	16	6
Item to the gardner at Croydon	0	0	0
Item for a brawne barrel of fishe	0	5	0
Item for a doe from Ford	0	10	0
Item for a sugar loaf Mr Holloway*	0	2	6
Item for 12 bush[els]† of oates for coach horses at xviij^{d}	0	18	0
Item for a bush[el]† of beanes	0	2	6

343 See n. 80 above.
344 Not to be confused with Mr Morris, the farrier*.
345 See n. 30 above.

Item for 17 bush[els]† of oates for geldings & colts at xviij[d]	1	5	6
Item spent in the kitchen this weeke ut patet p[er] libr[um]	27	18	1
Some total of this fortnight payd Decemb[er] 11 1639	71	19	6

Decemb[er] 6 1639

Inprimis to the Dutchess of Richmonds* gouldsmith with plate	1	0	0
Item for an hogsh[eads]† of canary from the Station[er]s*	0	10	0
Item for 6 sugar loaves Mr Harfleet*	0	5	0
Item for a p[aire] of swans for the millpond at Waddon	0	7	6

[fo. 116r]

Item for 2 lambes B[isho]p of Oxon*	0	5	0
Item for an hyne E[arl] of Lindsey*	0	16	0
Item for partridges Mr Dale*	0	3	6
Item for a cocke pie Mr Cooke[346]	0	5	0
Item for a lamprey† pie Sir Morr[ice] Bartlett*	0	2	0
Item for a brawne Clarke of the Checke[347]	0	6	0
Item to the bargemen this weeke	1	12	0
Item for 12 bush[els]† of oates for c[oach] horses	0	18	0
Item for a bush[el]† of beanes	0	2	6
Item for 17 bush[els]† of oates for geldings & colts at xviij[d]	1	5	6
Item spent in the kitchen this weeke ut patet p[er] libr[um]	29	18	7

December 13 1639

Item for 2 sugar loaves Dr Collyns*	0	3	6
Item for a brawne Bailiffe of Croydon[348]	0	5	0
Item for 2 pheasants Sir Roger Harfleet*	0	1	6
Item to Palmer* for broomes & mopes	0	7	6
Item for a doe from Farnham	0	10	0
Item for 2 cheeses Sir Randall Crew*	0	2	6
Item for a hyne from the Kinge	1	2	0
Item for spices East India Company*	1	5	0
Item to the gardner at Croydon 4 weekes	1	6	4
Item to the gardner at Lambeth 2 weekes	0	7	2
Item to the bargemen this weeke	1	9	0
Item for 12 bush[els]† of oates for coach horses	0	18	0
Item for a bush[el]† of beanes	0	2	6
Item for another for the gt horse	0	2	6

---

346 See n. 29 above.
347 See n. 70 above.
348 See nn. 39 and 275 above.

Item for 17 bush[els]† of oates for geldings and colts at xviij^{d}	1	5	6
Item for naylinge	0	1	6
Item spent in the kitchen this weeke ut patet p[er] libr[um]	27	5	5
For this quarter	74	11	6
Item p[ay]d the brewer for 20 hogsh[eads]† of viij^{s} & cx hogsh[eads]† of vj^{s} beeare layd in at Lambeth this q[ua]rter	61	10	0
Item to M[is]tr[es]s Hoult* for this q[ua]rter	4	0	0
Item to M[is]tr[es]s Page* for this q[ua]rter	2	0	0
Item to the Widd[ow] Whaley* for the rent of the slaughterhouse	0	12	6
Item to the molecatcher at Lambeth	0	5	0
Item to yr Graces barber	0	10	0
Item to the laundress for ashes soape starch & besides wages	4	10	0
Item for 51 ells† of towellinge for the kitchen pantry buttery &c at viij^{d}	1	14	0
Item for makinge & markinge them	0	3	0
Item for 3 yrds of cotton for the scullery	0	4	6
Item for a new washinge tubb 2 payles 2 beetles† lynes and hoopinge ut patet	1	11	6
Item for 6 towells for Rich[ard] Cobb*	0	7	0
Item to William Duckett* for a cushion carpet for the bardge a canopie &c ut patet	8	13	2
Item to him for apprell for Rich[ard] Cobb*	2	4	0
Item to Tho[mas] Sadler* for a suite & cloake for him ut patet	6	17	2
[fo. 117r]			
Item to Tho[mas] Sadler* for apprell for your Grace ut patet	14	3	0
Item to him for 12 wasecoates for 12 poore women ut patet	2	16	6
Item for 24 yrds of frize† at 22^{d} & an ell† of taffaty for coates	2	19	4
Item for a case of knives for the pantler†	0	12	0
Item for 100 doz of candlesticks layd in at iiij^{s} viij^{d} p[er] doz	23	6	8
Item to Morris* the smith for shoeing geldings & dressing lambe &c ut patet	5	3	0
Item to the smith of Croydon for shoeinge bleedinge & drenchinge geldings there	0	18	5
Item to Abbott* the sadler for bridles sadles girths clothes &c ut patet p[er] bill	13	7	0
Item for a light padd furnish[e]d for the barbary horse[349]	2	10	0
Item for a bitt with gilt bases	0	12	0
Item for 4 loads of straw layd in at viij^{s} p[er] load	1	12	0
Item for Christopher[350] for hedginge ditchinge at the pasture pond & for mending hedges about the ground	0	15	2

349 The barbary horse given to Laud byWilliam Cavendish, Earl of Newcastle a few weeks earlier. See n. 342 above.

350 Probably Christopher Hunt*, household servant.

Item for cuttinge rakinge & carrying the braks†	1	5	0
Item for gathering crabbs† making 1 hogsh[eads]† of vargis† and for vessells	1	5	10
Item for a fan and hooping tubbs	0	5	5
Some total of this fortnight & for this quarter payd Decemb[er] 30	241	4	8

Some total of this 4th quarters expenses & laying out cometh to vij^{c} lxxxxv^{l} ix^{s} ij^{d}

All accompted and payd
Ada^{m} Torlesse*

Some total of this years expenses & laying out cometh to ut patet	3376	15	11

All accompted and even

December 30 1639
Ada^{m} Torlesse*

[fo. 118r]

Inprimis given to the xii^{j} prisons agains xxmas	3	0	0
Item to the poore att Lambeth	20	0	0
Item to the poore at Croydon	5	0	0
Item to Dr Henshawes* man with shirts for your Grace	1	10	0
Item for fowle & sugar Dr Crooke* &c	1	1	0
Item to Mr Badger* for bindinge manuscripts ut patet	7	9	1
Item to the porter at the garden stayres for halfe an yeare	0	15	0
Item to the man there & bay	0	3	6
Item for cittro[n] peeles Mr Grant[351]	0	2	0
Item for 2 Holland cheeses Mr Jarvys[352]	0	2	6
Item for boathire Mr Rollston*	0	1	0
Item for your Graces oferinge	3	0	0
Item to the bargemen this weeke	1	13	6
Item for turkeys 2 pheas[ants] 6 partr[idges] from Dr Mountford*	0	5	0
Item for a turkey Lady Cade[353]	0	2	0
Item for turkeys Mr Hawkes of Upminster[354]	0	2	6
Item for halfe a stagg Sir Christopher Wray*	0	10	0
Item for pudding & partr[idge] &c Sir Jo[hn] Shelly*	0	5	0
Item for pipkins† pans strayners &c for the kitchen	0	4	0
Item for 12 bush[els]† of oates for coach horses	0	18	0
Item for a bush[el]† of beanes	0	2	0

351 This is the sole entry in the accounts for ‘Mr Grant’, whose identity remains elusive.
352 This is the sole entry in the accounts for ‘Mr Jarvys’, whose identity remains elusive.
353 See n. 86 above.
354 See n. 283 above.

Item for 17 bush[els]† of oates for geldings & colts 8 of them at xv^{d} p[er] bush[el]†	1	3	6
Item spent in the kitchen this weeke ut patet p[er] libr[um]	31	12	10

December 27 1639

Item for your G[races] new years gift to the Kinge	40	0	0
Item to the househould ut patet[355]	30	11	6
Item to M[is]tr[es]s Buckeridge*	5	0	0
Item to the brewers mens box	0	10	0
Item to the coachmakers men	0	5	0
Item to Morris* the smiths men	0	2	0
Item to the harnessmakers men	0	3	6
Item to Bryan* the locksmiths men	0	4	0
Item to yr G[races] shoemakers man	0	4	0
Item to Sir Henry Spillers* man with cheeses & sweetmeats	0	14	0
Item to the B[isho]p of Rochesters* man	0	10	0

[fo. 119r]

Item to the Deane of Rochesters* man	1	0	0
Item to Lewes Harris[356] from the B[isho]p of St Asaph*	1	0	0
Item for 6 sugar loaves from Burntwood	0	5	0
Item for Mr Knights son in lawe[357]	0	10	0
Item for the princes picture B[isho]p of Chichester*	1	0	0
Item to Mr Dell* for boathires letters &c last month ut patet	1	0	0
Item for plate Deane of Chichester*	1	0	0
Item for sattyn Mr Dan[iel] Harvye*	1	10	0
Item for 2 flagons Sir Nich[olas] Crispe*	2	5	0
Item for 2 hogsh[eads]† of claret Sir Robert Heath*	1	0	0
Item for sugar loaves &c Mr Pagett*	0	10	0
Item for a cand register of the Advent.	0	10	0
Item for boathire Mr Rollston*	0	1	0
Item to the scullery men	0	10	0
Item for a cupp and cover Prerogative	1	0	0
Item for a bason and ewer† March[ant] Advent[urers]*	2	0	0
Item for a warming pan Turkey Merchants*	2	0	0

355 A detailed breakdown of the servants in the royal household who benefited from this gift can be found in TNA, SP16/441, fo. 1. However, either this entry was entered incorrectly, or the manuscript contains an error. On the manuscript, in the translation from Roman to Arabic numerals, the writer may have misread the amount for shillings – seeing xvij^{s} for xj^{s} – thus converting it into Arabic £30 17s 6d, instead of the amount listed here of £30 11s 6d. Alternatively, since the following year's gift from Laud to the household is recorded in the accounts as £30 17s 6d, it may be that the date of '1639' on the manuscript was transcribed incorrectly and should really have been '1640'. See also n. 14 above.

356 See n. 288 above.

357 Probably the same 'Mr Knight' referred to in n. 8 above.

Item for a cupp & cover Mr Attorney*	2	0	0
Item for a cupp & cover Sir Henry Gilford*	1	0	0
Item for 3 beakers E[arl] of Newcastle*	3	0	0
Item to Sir Jo[hn] Lambes* man	1	0	0
Item for a possett pott & cover Lo[rd] Scudamore*	0	10	0
Item for a sweet bagg M[is]tr[es]s Burrows[358]	1	0	0
Item to Mr Snaith* for boathire Lord Keeper*[359]	0	2	0
Item to the gardner at Croydon	0	8	9
Item to the bargemen this weeke	1	4	0
Item for 2 lambs Sir Andr[ew] Jeynor*	0	6	0
Item for x sugar loaves Company of Clarks*	0	3	6
Item for vj sugar loaves Dr Merrick*	0	6	0
Item for a lamb & 2 turkeys Sir Tho[mas] Grymes*	0	5	0
Item for 2 sugar loaves Mr Creswell*	0	2	6
Item for 2 turkeys M[is]tr[es]s Buckeridge*	0	5	0
Item for 6 pheasants Lo[rd] Sherwood*	0	5	0
Item for fowle from Dr Sterne*	0	6	0
Item for 2 swans & partridges &c Mr Hay[360]	0	2	0
Item for 12 bush[els]† of oates for coach horses	0	15	0
Item for a bush[el]† of beanes	0	2	0
Item for 17 bush[els]† of oates for geldings & colts	1	1	3
Item for 4 shoes & 20 removes	0	5	8
Item for a doz of broomes for the stable	0	2	0
Item spent in the kitchen this weeke ut patet p[er] libr[um]	28	12	3
Some total of this fortnight payd Januar[y] 11 1640	221	3	4

Januar[y] 3 1640

Receaved 0–0–0

Inprimis given for a tun of claret & pipe of canary with carrier & porters from the Farmers of the Custome*	3	0	0
Item to the carrier & porters with 2 hogsh[eads]† of claret from Sir Rob[er]t Heath*	0	9	0
Item for a sugar loaf Mr Christopher Turner*	0	2	6
Item to the needles	0	10	0
Item to Palmer* for holly broomes & mopps	0	8	3
Item yr Grace for Sir Symo[n] Baskerfield*	5	0	0

358 This is the sole entry in the accounts for 'Mistress Burrows', whose identity remains elusive.

359 This entry suggests that Laud visited Thomas, Baron Coventry*, who was probably gravely ill at this stage. Coventry died on 14 January 1640 at Durham House in the Strand and was succeeded in the post of Lord Keeper by John Finch*.

360 This is the sole entry in the accounts for 'Mr Hay', whose identity remains elusive.

Item to the bargemen this weeke	1	0	0
Item for 2 lambs Mr Barrett[361]	0	5	0
Item to a poore dumbe man	0	5	0

[fo. 120r]

Item for 4 lamprey† pies	0	5	0
Item for 2 pheas & 2 partr[idges] Lo[rd] Cottington*	0	3	0
Item for 2 lambes Dr Oliver*	0	0	0
Item for 12 bush[els]† of oates for coach horses	0	15	0
Item for a bush[el]† of beanes	0	2	0
Item for 17 bush[els]† of oates for geldings & colts	1	1	3
Item spent in the kitchen this weeke ut patet p[er] libr[um]	29	3	1

Januar[y] 10 1640

Item for a present of fowle from Dr Martyn*	1	2	0
Item given for a tun of claret with carrier & porters from the Company of Soapboylers	1	10	0
Item for laying in the K[ings] printers & Dr Sheldons* wine	0	10	0
Item to the bargemen this weeke	1	0	0
Item for a doe Mr Morris*	0	10	0
Item for another Lo[rd] Chamberlayne*	0	11	0
Item for 3 grosse of trenchers†	1	1	0
Item 4 beare and wine glasses & crewetts	0	3	6
Item for 2 handbasketts for the kitchen	0	2	4
Item for a sack for salt	0	2	4
Item for 12 bush[els]† of oates for coach horses	0	15	0
Item for 2 bush[els]† of beanes for them & Barbary	0	4	0
Item for 17 bush[els]† of oates for geldings & colts at xi^d	1	1	3
Item for removinge & naylinge	0	1	6
Item spent in the kitchen this weeke ut patet p[er] libr[um]	26	18	10
Some total of this fortnight payd Januar[y] 24 1640	78	1	10

Januar[y] 17 1640

Receaved 0–0–0

Inprimis given Mr Browns* men	0	5	0
Item for Mr Holfords* boathire with money for St Paules 4 tymes[362]	0	4	0
Item to make upp Sir W[illiam] Penymans* money	0	10	0
Item for a cover for yr G[races] newe watch	0	10	0

361 This is the sole entry in the accounts for ‘Mr Barrett’, whose identity remains elusive.

362 This entry suggests that the collection of funds for the repair of St Paul’s cathedral was still underway in early 1640.

Item to Sir Symo[n] Baskervyles* ma[n] with a l[et]t[e]r p[ayd] Mr Snaith*	0	2	0
Item for boathires to the Lo[rd] Cottington*	0	1	8
Item to Sir Peter Witches* man	0	11	0
Item given the prisons in Southwark	0	2	0
Item to the gardner at Lambeth	0	8	9
Item to the bargemen	1	6	0
Item for 12 bush[els]† of oates for coach horses	0	15	0
Item for a bush[el]† of beanes	0	2	0
Item for 17 bush[els]† of oates for geldings & colts	1	1	3
Item spent in the kitchen this weeke ut patet p[er] libr[um]	29	13	5

Januar[y] 24 1640

Inprimis for 3 wild goose pies from Sir Lionell Tallnage*	0	3	6
Item for 3 lamprey† pies Mr Dutton*	0	2	6
Item for 2 turkeys 4 capons 12 partr[idges] from Dr Warren*	0	6	0
Item to Sir Henry Woottons* men with a picture[363]	1	0	0
Item p[ay]d Mr Browne* for the chardge of 3 cedar chests ut patet	4	5	0

[fo. 121r]

Item to the clark of the Soapboylers	1	0	0
Item to Sir Kellam Digbyes* man	2	0	0
Item to the postmasters man for letters	0	2	0
Item to Dr Stanleys* man	0	5	0
Item to Ald[erman] Clitheroes* man & porter	0	6	0
Item to Mr Dell* for letters boathires & this moneth ut patet	0	19	10
Item to the bargemen this weeke	1	7	0
Item to the gardner at Lambeth for poles for arbors &c ut patet	1	7	0
Item for 2 pheas[ants] Sir Stephen Scott*	0	2	6
Item for fowle B[isho]p of Bristol*	0	2	6
Item for 2 pheas Dr Aylett*	0	2	0
Item for 3 lamprey† pies Sir Ma[u]r[ice] Bartlett*	0	2	6
Item for 4 flitches of bacon Dr Stanly*	0	2	0
Item for 2 strayners & 2 coalbasketts for the kitchen	0	3	4
Item for 12 bush[els]† of oates for coach horses	0	15	0
Item for a bush[el]† of beanes	0	2	0
Item for 17 bush[els]† of oates for geldings and colts at vij^{d}	1	1	3
Item for nayling coach horses	0	1	0
Item spent in the kitchen this weeke ut patet p[er] libr[um]	26	14	0
Some total of this fortnight payd Februar[y] 10 1640	78	7	0

363 This was the painting of 'Divine Love', bequeathed by Sir Henry Wotton to Laud, on his death in Dec. 1639; Lawrence Pearsall Smith, *The life and letters of Sir Henry Wotton*, I (Oxford, 1907), 217.

Januar[y] ult 1640

Inprimis to Mr Snaith* Mr Bagott[364] &c for boathires	0	5	6
Item given Mr Harrisons man for weyinge yr G[races] robes[365]	0	2	6
Item for a pie Lady Chombley*	0	5	0
Item for a messengers boathire	0	1	0
Item to Palmer* for broomes &c	0	4	3
Item to the bargemen this weeke	1	5	0
Item for 2 lambs Dr Higgs*	0	5	0
Item for 7 lamprey† pies &c	0	7	6
Item for 12 bush[els]† of oates for coach horses	0	15	0
Item for a bush[el]† of beanes	0	2	0
Item for 17 bush[els]† of oates for geldings and colts at vj[d]	1	1	3
Item spent in the kitchen this weeke ut patet p[er] libr[um]	29	13	0

Februar[y] 7 1640

Item to the firemakers box	0	10	0
Item for boathires Mr Cobb* Mr Levinthrop*	0	2	0
Item for musicians boathires	0	5	0
Item for sheepe from Croydon	0	2	0
Item for a tubb for the butlers flagons	0	3	6
Item to the bargemen	0	16	0
Item to the gardner at Croydon ut patet	1	10	0
Item for 2 hogsh[eads]† of claret Marchant Adv[enturers]*	1	0	0
Item for 2 more Mr Croxly[366]	1	0	0
Item to the porters & carrymen	0	10	0

[fo. 122r]

Item for 2 lambes from Higgs*[367]	0	5	0
Item for boathires Mr Snaith*	0	4	0
Item for 4 cheeses Lady Chomly*	0	5	0
Item for 12 bush[els]† of oates for coach horses	0	15	0
Item for 2 bush[els]† of beanes	0	4	0
Item for 17 bush[els]† of oates for geldings and colts at vj[d]	1	1	3
Item for 24 newe shoes for coach horses	0	14	0

364 See n. 304 above.

365 This is the sole entry in the accounts for 'Mr Harrison', who may well have been Edmund Harrison (*c.* 1591–1667), the 'king's embroiderer', who was responsible for embroidering liveries, carpets and other fabric items in the royal household. This is based on the plausible assumption that 'Mr Harrison's man' was paid to stitch weights into the bottom hem of Laud's robes, rather than measuring the weight of the garments'; *CSPD 1635*, p. 576, no. 63; *CSPD 1637*, p. 8, no. 35.

366 This is the sole entry in the accounts relating to 'Mr Croxly', whose identity remains elusive.

367 The 'Dr' was missing from this entry, but it is safe to assume that the gift was given by Dr Griffin Higgs*.

Item spent in the kitchen this weeke	29	13	7
Some total of this fortnight payd Februar[y] 24 1640	73	8	2

Februar[y] 14 1640

Inprimis for brand geese &c Dr Lewes*	0	5	0
Item for 2 lamp[rey] pies Mr Subdeane*	0	2	0
Item for a brawne Mr Fox[368]	0	5	0
Item for 2 barr of herring Yarmouth	0	10	0
Item for a fresh salmon Mr Harfleet*	0	4	0
Item to the bargemen this weeke	1	15	0
Item to the gardner at Lambeth	0	6	3
Item for 12 bush[els]† of oates for coach horses	0	15	0
Item for a bush[el]† of beanes	0	2	0
Item for 16 bush[els]† of oates for geldings & colts	1	0	0
Item spent in the kitchen this weeke ut patet p[er] libr[um]	30	14	4

Februar[y] 21 1640

Item for a brace of pheas Sir Rob[er]t Bannister*	0	2	6
Item for a pipe of canary & 2 hogsh[eads]† of claret Ald[erman] Abell* & Company of Vintners*	1	0	0
Item for an hogsh[eads]† of claret & 6 fleetches of bacon Dr Farmory*	0	11	0
Item for dryed fish Lo[rd] Liftenant of Irel[and]*[369]	0	14	0
Item for sugar & pepper Mr Abbott*	0	6	0
Item to the gardner at Croydon ut patet	0	8	4
Item to the bargemen this weeke	1	5	0
Item to the gardner at Lambeth	0	7	6
Item for 12 bush[els]† of oates for coach horses	0	15	0
Item for a bush[el]† of beanes	0	2	0
Item for 15 bush[els]† of oates for geldings & colts	0	18	9
Item for naylinge c[oach] horses	0	1	0
Item for a doz of broomes for the stable	0	2	0
Item spent in the kitchen this weeke ut patet p[er] libr[um]	25	13	5
Some total of this fortnight	68	14	7

368 This is the sole entry in the accounts relating to 'Mr Fox', whose identity remains elusive.

369 Thomas Wentworth*, the lord deputy of Ireland, had been recalled to England by Charles I in Aug. 1639, to help resolve the Scottish crisis. He arrived in Sept. and was created lord lieutenant of Ireland in Jan. 1640, enabling him to continue governing *in absentia* through the appointment of his own deputy. His lengthy correspondence with Laud, which had continued since he arrived in Dublin in 1633, ceased now that he was back in England; Ronald Asch, 'Wentworth, Thomas, first earl of Strafford (1593–1641)', *ODNB*.

Februar[y] 28 1640

Inprimis for a cake Dr Haywood*	0	2	0
Item for 4 cheeses Dr Manwayringe*	0	5	0
Item to Mr Snaith* for boathires	0	3	8
Item given Watts* & Nicholas* p[ayd] Mr Dell*	1	0	0
Item to Mr Bemboe*	0	10	0
Item for letters &c this moneth ut patet	0	11	1
Item to the bargement this weeke	1	6	6
Item to the gardner at Lambeth	0	0	0

[fo. 123r]

Item for 3 doz of bottles & corks for wine	0	2	0
Item for 9 beare & wine glasses	0	8	0
Item for herrings Lo[rd] Conway*	0	2	0
Item for 12 bush[els]† of oates for coach horses	0	15	0
Item for a bush[el]† of beanes	0	2	0
Item for 15 bush[els]† of oates for geldings	0	18	9
Item spent in the kitchen this weeke ut patet p[er] libr[um]	27	16	11

March 6 1640

Item p[ay]d for Ship Money for Lambeth[370]	9	0	0
Item for Ship Money for Croydon[371]	5	0	0
Item given for an horse from the Bishop of Chester*	4	0	0
Item for broomes moppes & stuffe for andirons† p[ayd] Palmer*	0	7	6
Item to Mr Tynes[372] for bringinge over 2 candlesticks &c Mr Snaith*	0	5	6
Item to the gardner at Lambeth	0	7	6
Item to the bargemen	1	9	0
Item for 2 lamprey† pies from Gloucester	0	2	0
Item for 2 more from Sir H[enry] Spiller*	0	2	0
Item for bacon & 12 puddings Archdeacon Burges* &c	0	3	6
Item for 12 bush[els]† of oates for coach horses	0	15	0
Item for a bush[el]† of beanes	0	2	0
Item for 16 bush[els]† of oates for geldings & colts	1	0	0
Item for naylinge coach horses	0	1	6
Item spent in the kitchen this weeke ut patet p[er] libr[um]	29	12	4
Some total of this fortnight payd March 23 1640	87	2	9

370 See n. 20 above. This is the last, known ship money payment for Lambeth

371 See n. 20 above. This is the last, known ship money payment for Croydon.

372 This is the sole entry in the accounts for 'Mr Tynes', whose identity remains elusive.

March 13 1640

Receaved for 4 quart[ers] of barly Mr Denns* of Littlebourne xxxij[l]			
Inprimis for 3 barr[els] of oysters from Sir John Lucas*	0	3	0
Item given to a boy by Mr Cobb*	0	1	0
Item for 3 lamprey† pies from Gloucester	0	1	0
Item to the bargemen this week	1	11	0
Item to the gardner at Lambeth	0	10	6
Item to the gardner at Croydon	1	14	6
Item for a veale from Mr Farrant[373]	0	6	0
Item for a sallmon pie Mr Bagnell[374]	0	2	6
Item for 4 fleeches of bacon Mr Wheate*	0	7	0
Item to a tynker for mending brass &c in the kitchen	0	6	0
Item to Mr Snaith* for boathires	0	4	0
Item for 12 bush[els]† of oates for coach horses	0	15	0
Item for 2 bush[els]† of beanes	0	4	0
Item for 16 bush[els]† of oates for geldings & colts	1	0	0
Item for naylinge coach horses	0	0	8
Item spent in the kitchen this weeke ut patet p[er] libr[um]	26	16	3

for this quarter

Payd the brewer for 20 hogsh[eads]† of viij[s] & 99 hogsh[eads]† of vj[s] beare layd in at Lambeth this q[ua]rter	56	11	0
Item to M[is]tr[es]s Hoult* for this q[ua]rter	4	0	0
Item to M[is]tr[es]s Page for this q[ua]rter	2	0	0
Item to the Widd[ow] Whaly* for the rent of the slaughterhouse chambers	0	12	6
Item to the mole catcher at Lambeth	0	5	0

[fo. 124r]

Item to yr Grace barber	0	10	0
Item to the laundresse for ashes soape starch and besides wages	4	10	0
Item for hoopinge tubs	0	5	3
Item for lynes	0	3	0
Item to the lynen drap for 86 ells† of frize† & a broad cloth at iij[s] v[d] p[er] ell† for 16 tablecloths & 19 cupboard and sideboard cloths ut patet p[er] bill	14	12	6
Item for 24 doz & 5 napkins at vijs vjd p[er] dozen	10	7	6
Item for makinge & markinge the tablecloths & cupboard cloths at iij[d]	0	8	9
Item for makinge & markinge the 24 doz & 5 napkins at xij[d]	1	4	5
Item for cutting 4 tablecloths and facing 2 p[aires] of sheets	0	2	0
Item for stocking 3 bands for your Grace	0	1	0

---

373 See n. 115 above.

374 This is the sole entry in the accounts for 'Mr Bagnell', whose identity remains elusive.

Item to William Duckett* for a curtayne for the organists chamber	0	9	0
Item more to him for a bell roape & other things ut patet	0	14	3
Item for 4 shirts &c for Rich[ard] Cobb*	1	8	6
Item to Mr Fettyplace* for 2 q[ua]rters pensions to Mr Pococke* ended at the Ladyday	20	0	0
Item to Morris* the smith for shoeing bleedings & drenching geldings &c	5	5	2
Item to Abbot* the sadler for bridles, girths currycombs† &c ut patet	2	16	0
Item for 8 loads of strawe layd in at viij^{s} p[er] load	3	4	0
Item for 12 bush[els]† of oates for swans and poultry at Lambeth	0	15	0
Item for 100 doz of candles layd in at iiij^{s} vj^{d} p[er] doz	22	10	0
Item for grubbinge† in the cowe pasture at the park	2	12	0
Item for a p[aire] of dossers† for the park	0	6	0
Item to Mr Watts* for graynes & nets	0	15	6
Item to Tho[mas] Sadler* for facinge your G[races] consecration roabe & velvet for cap ut patet[375]	5	5	0
Item for yr servants halfe years wages ut patet	131	3	4
Item for 60 liveryes to be payd in money this yeare at xx^{s} ut patet	60	0	0
Some total of this weeke &c for this quarter payd April 2 1640	386	19	1

Some total of this first quarters expenses and laying out cometh to
ix^{c} lxxxxiij^{l} xvj^{s} ix^{d}

[fo. 125r]
Second quarter beginning March 20 1640

Inprimis given to the E[arl] of Newcastles* gent &c with a lampe	1	10	0
Item for a cake & cheeses Mr Powell*	0	2	6
Item given the prisons against Easter	3	0	0
Item to the poor at Lambeth for Lent	6	0	0
Item given Mr Page* by yr Grace	2	0	0
Item to the gardner at Lambeth	0	11	4
Item to the bargemen	1	10	0
Item for 12 bush[els]† of oates for coach horses	0	15	0
Item for a bush[el]† of beanes	0	2	0
Item 16 bush[els]† of oates for geldings & colts	1	0	0
Item spent in the kitchen this weeke ut patet p[er] libr[um]	29	19	7

375 Laud's robes were repaired in readiness for an episcopal consecration due to take place on 29 Mar. in Lambeth Palace chapel. See n. 377 below.

March 27 1640

Inprimis for bringinge cheeses	0	1	0
Item given Mr Wooddalls* sone p[ayd] Mr Dell*	0	10	0
Item for Pacius his Logick[376]	0	5	6
Item for letters, boathire &c this moneth	0	12	8
Item give yr Grace for 2 younge shellers	2	0	0
Item to Mr Farmerys* man	0	10	0
Item for yr Graces offering at the consecration[377]	3	0	0
Item for broomes & mopps	0	7	7
Item for lyninge your G[races] hatt Mr Snaith*	0	8	0
Item to the boy at the garden stayres	0	1	0
Item to the gardner at Lambeth	0	5	6
Item to the bargemen	1	9	0
Item for 2 barr[els] of herrings Lo[rd] Conway*	0	10	0
Item for 12 g[rea]t carpes Mr Abbott*	0	8	0
Item for a cake from a Redding woman	1	0	0
Item for a cake & 2 cheeses D[ean] of St Asaph*	0	2	6
Item for 2 lamprey† pies Glouces[ter]	0	2	0
Item for a buck Sir Rich[ard] Newport*	0	15	0
Item for 12 bush[els]† of oates for coach horses	0	15	0
Item for a bush[el]† of beanes	0	2	0
Item for 16 bush[els]† of oates for geldings & colts	1	0	0
Item for 24 removes & naylinge	0	4	6
Item spent in the kitchen this weeke ut patet p[er] libr[um]	25	15	11
Some total of this fortnight payd Apr[il] 8 1640	86	15	7

Aprill 3 1640

Receaved for yr bill of impost	24	0	0
for 50 q[uarts] of barly Mr Rose* at xvj^{s} p[er] q[ua]rt	40	0	0
Inprimis for your G[races] offering at Easter	3	0	0
Item to the gardner at Lambeth	0	4	10
Item to the bargemen	1	10	4
Item for 12 bush[els]† of oates for coach horses	0	15	0
Item for a bush[el]† of beanes	0	2	0
Item for 16 bush[els]† of oates for geldings & colts	1	0	0
Item spent in the kitchen this weeke ut patet p[er] libr[um]	28	4	10

376 This entry relates to the purchase of a book by Julius Pacius (*c.* 1550–1635), the philosopher and theologian.

377 Morgan Owen (*c.* 1584–1645) was consecrated bishop of Llandaff on 29 Mar. 1640, the previous encumbent William Murray* having died a month earlier.

[fo. 126r]
Aprill 10 1640[378]

Item to Mr Snaith* for 2 p[aires] of shoes for yr Grace & boathires	0	9	0
Item for MS from Capt[ain] Methall[379]	1	0	0
Item more to him for boathires	0	4	0
Item to the gardner at Lambeth	0	5	4
Item to the bargemen this week	2	3	6
Item to the gardner at Croydon	1	14	0
Item for a p[aire] of bootes for the moate	1	13	0
Item to the vintner for red & white wine & canary to fill the vessels this year	7	17	4
Item to the coop for rackinge & hoopinge this yeare ut patet	12	10	6
Item for signing the bill of impost by Mr Leachland*	1	18	0
Item for a salmon pie Lady Chomley*	0	3	0
Item for 12 bush[els]† of oates for coach horses	0	15	0
Item for a bush[el]† of beanes	0	2	0
Item for 16 bush[els]† of oates for geldings & colts	1	0	0
Item for 6 removes & naylinge	0	1	4
Item spent in the kitchen this weeke ut patet p[er] libr[um]	32	9	6
Some total of this fortnight payd May 7 1640	99	2	6

Aprill 17 1640

Rec[eave]d for Mr Spracklings* barly	49	10	0
For Mr Roses* mault	37	10	0
Inprimis for yr Grace for Mr Attorney*	5	0	0
Item for broomes & moppes	0	4	4
Item for 4 lamprey† pies from Gloucester this Lent	1	8	0
Item to the bargemen this weeke	2	0	0
Item the gardner at Lambeth	0	12	6
Item to the hyeman for bringing Mr Roses* 50 quart[ers] of wheate & sacks	3	3	3
Item to the porters for carrying it into the granary at iiij[d] p[er] q[ua]rter	0	13	2

378 This week, on 13 Apr., saw the opening of the Short Parliament: the first parliamentary session since Mar. 1629. The following day, as Laud recorded in his diary, 'Convocation began in St Paul's'. Parliament continued until 5 May. Traditionally, Convocation sat alongside parliament and was dismissed when the parliamentary session ended. On this occasion, however, as an exception, 'Convocation continued'. This was a highly controversial move – and one for which Laud was blamed – leading to the attempted ransack of Lambeth Palace by apprentices on 11 May; *WWL*, III, 234–5. For a discussion, see 'Introduction', p. xxx above.

379 Although it has not been possible to identify 'Capt. Methall', the fact that he delivered a manuscript to the Palace suggests that he may have been a merchant. He may have been the same Captain Methall who was involved in bringing a case to the Middlesex quarter sessions in 1657, against a colleague who had provided arms and money for the royalist cause; *CSPD 1649–60*, p. 384, no. 45.

Item for 12 bush[els]† of oates for coach horses	0	15	0
Item for a bush[el]† of beanes	0	2	0
Item for 16 bush[els]† of oates for geldings & colts	1	0	0
Item spent in the kitchen this weeke ut patet p[er] libr[um]	33	16	10

Aprill 24 1640

Item for a table book for yr Grace	0	2	0
Item p[ay]d Mr Bridgeman* for the Advowson of St Laurence at the signet & privy seale ut patet	9	16	8
Item for the fees at the broad seale	12	1	6
Item for the mortmane to Reddinge	3	16	8
Item for the fine with vellom ingrosmonts &c ut patet	6	2	6
Item to the gardner at Lambeth ut patet	0	11	4
Item to the gardner at Croydon	2	15	8
Item for Tho[mas] Arquin upon […][380]	1	5	0
Item for a buck Lo[rd] Chamberlayne*	1	2	6
Item for 12 bush[els]† of oates for coach horses	0	15	0
Item for a bush[el]† of beanes	0	2	0
Item for 16 bush[els]† of oates for geldings & colts	1	0	0
Item for naylinge coach horses	0	2	0
Item for 2 doz of broomes for the stable	0	4	0
Item spent in the kitchen this weeke ut patet p[er] libr[um]	32	19	7
Some total of this fortnight payd May 7 1640	123	8	6

[fo. 127r]
Receaved 0–0–0

Inprimis to Mr Dell* for letters boathires &c the last moneth ut patet	0	12	0
Item for cheeses Dr Griffin[381]	0	5	0
Item to Mr Levinthrope* for boathire	0	1	0
Item to the slaughterman for bringinge 40 Kent weathers† out of Kent	3	1	0
Item p[ay]d Mr Snaith* for yr G[races] entrance into the Parliament[382]	15	16	8
Item for a chamber pott there	0	2	6
Item to him for boathires &c ut patet	0	6	6

380 This entry relates to the purchase of a book by Thomas Aquinas (*c.* 1224–74), the ancient philosopher and theologian.

381 This is the sole entry in the accounts for 'Dr Griffin', who may have been William Griffith (1597–1648), lawyer. Griffith was appointed chancellor of the diocese of Bangor in 1635, entered the Doctors' Commons in 1636 and became master of chancery in 1637, a post he held until 1641; *Alumni oxonienses*, II, 613; Brian Levack, *The civil lawyers in England 1603–1641: a political study* (Oxford, 1973), p. 235.

382 This was the week in which the Short Parliament collapsed. The costs entered here related to Laud's entry to the House of Lords.

Item to the gardner at Lambeth	0	11	2
Item to the bargemen this weeke	1	16	0
Item for 12 bush[els]† of oates for coach horses	0	15	0
Item for a bush[el]† of beanes	0	2	0
Item for 16 bush[els]† of oates for geldings & colts	1	0	0
Item for cuttinge 3 colts	0	10	0
Item for 24 shoes & naylinge coach horses	0	14	6
Item spent in the kitchen this weeke ut patet p[er] libr[um]	31	7	1

May 8 1640

Item given to your G[race] for Captayne Hill[383]	7	0	0
Item to Mr Rollston* for boathire	0	6	0
Item for boathire to carry the rebells to the gatehouse at Westminster[384]	0	10	6
Item to the Lieutenant for 2 munitioning peeces wey[ing] 415l at 26^{s} p[er] 100	5	5	0
Item for the lynstocks† & carrying them to the water	0	3	0
Item for 2l of powder to trye them	0	2	8
Item for 100 w[eigh]t of shott & 2 barrells	0	16	0
Item to W[illiam] Duckett* for 13 skeanes† of match	1	4	6
Item for boathires about gettinge the musketeers &c ut patet	2	4	16
Item for bringing powder & match from the Tower	0	13	6
Item to Mr Snaith* for boathires ut patet	0	11	0
Item to the bargemen this week	1	11	0
Item to the gardner at Lambeth	0	10	10
Item for a buck Sir W[illiam] Russell*[385]	0	15	0
Item for a cake & cheeses Mr Doyly*	0	5	0
Item for a salmon pie	0	2	0
Item for 12 bush[els]† of oates for coach horses	0	15	0
Item for a bush[el]† of beanes	0	2	0
Item for 16 bush[els]† of oates for geldings & colts	1	0	0
Item spent in the kitchen this weeke ut patet p[er] libr[um]	23	16	0
Some total of this fortnight payd June 4 1640	104	14	3

383 Although it has not been possible to identify 'Captayne Hill', his sole appearance in the accounts during the week in which Lambeth Palace was stormed by apprentices strongly suggests that he was involved in the fortification of the Palace or in dispersing the crowd in the early hours of 11 May.

384 The 'rebells' referred to here were among the apprentices who attacked the Palace on 11 May. As Laud noted in his diary, 'at midnight, my house a[t Lambeth] was beset with 500 of these rascal routers'. Having been notified in advance that they were on their way, Laud managed to escape to his lodgings in Whitehall Palace before the attack; Heylyn, *Cyprianus anglicus*, p. 425; *WWL*, III, 235, 284.

385 This entry probably relates to Sir William Russell*, treasurer of the navy, rather than Sir William Russell, who was sheriff of Worcestershire in 1643 and governor of the city during the civil war.

May 15 1640

Rec[eave]d for x quarters of wheate from the E[arl] of Thanet* for Westwell	xxi		
Inprimis p[ay]d for 2 peeces of cambricke† cotton 12 ells† at viij[s] for 2 rotchetts for yr Grace	5	4	0
Item for making them with iij[s] for seaming lace for the necks	0	9	0

[fo. 128r]

Item for the carridge of the painters glass & Mr Burwoods* tooles from Croydon	0	5	0
Item to the watchmen at Westminster	0	3	0
Item more to them by Mr Levinthrope*	0	5	0
Item to 2 labourers about the house	0	3	0
Item to Ralphe the butler for bottles[386]	0	16	6
Item to Knight* for 6 dayes worke about the house & park	0	7	0
Item to Pallmer* for broomes & moppes	0	8	0
Item to the gardner at Lambeth	0	11	6
Item to the bargemen this weeke	1	10	0
Item for 12 bush[els]† of oates for coach horses	0	15	0
Item for a bush[el]† of beanes	0	2	0
Item for 16 bush[els]† of oates for gelds & colts	1	0	0
Item spent in the kitchen this weeke ut patet p[er] libr[um]	26	17	6

May 22 1640

Item for yr Graces offering at Whit Sunday	3	0	0
Item to Mr Dell* for Mr Holloway*	4	0	0
Item to Mr Maxwells* 2 men at the Parliament Mr Rollston*	0	5	0
Item to the groome, butler & porter at the Star Chamber[387]	0	6	6
Item to yr Grace for Mr Solicitors* fee	3	0	0
Item to a coachman to the Lo[rd] Lieutenant [of Ireland]*	0	5	0
Item for boathires &c Mr Snaith*	0	4	10
Item to Tho[mas] Sadler* for a suite & cloake &c for Rich[ard] Cobb*	6	2	0
Item for stockings garters shoestrings &c for the 2 footmen at the parliament	1	2	0
Item for a fresh salmon Mr Abbot*	0	5	0
Item for a buck Sir Rob[ert] Dormer*	0	15	0
Item to the gardner at Croydon	1	19	8
Item for a paire of bootes for the moate	1	14	0

386 This is the sole entry in the accounts for a butler called Ralphe. Not to be confused with Ralph Watts*, who was a groundsman at Lambeth and Croydon.

387 See n. 30 above.

Item to the bargemen this weeke	1	11	0
Item for 12 bush[els]† of oates for the coach horses	0	15	0
Item for a bush[el]† of beanes	0	2	0
Item for 8 bush[els]† of oates for geldings	0	10	0
Item for removing & curing one coach horse of a kenell nayle†	0	3	6
Item spent in the kitchen this weeke ut patet p[er] libr[um]	23	6	1
Some total of this fortnight payd June 4 1640	88	10	9

May 29 1640

Inprimis given by Mr Levinthrope* for the great seale for the consecration[388]	0	5	0
Item to the watchmen at Westminster and a coachman & boathire	0	5	0
Item to Mr Snaith* for a beaver hatt for your Grace	3	16	0
Item for him for boathires & watchmen	0	4	0

[fo. 129r]

Item p[ay]d Mr Burwood* for the organs at Croydon & Lambeth ut patet	13	15	9
Item p[ay]d Mr Bridgeman* for the signett & privy seale for Redding mortmain	9	16	8
Item given to his 2 clarks	3	0	0
Item to the Lo[rd] Chiefe Justice* clark by Mr Dell* ut patet	0	10	0
Item to a poore Scottishman	0	5	0
Item to 2 coachmen & footmen	0	11	0
Item to him for letters boathires &c this moneth	0	16	8
Item for the granadoes† with xd given the man that made & brought them	1	6	8
Item to 6 gunners for their attendance xij nights at xxx^{s} a peece	9	0	0
Item given divers watchmen in the towne &c ut patet	16	5	6
Item to the vintner for claret & sack ut patet	25	5	0
Item for a buck B[isho]p of Oxon*	0	7	6
Item for 6 cheeses B[isho]p of Chester*	0	3	0
Item to Roger* for boathires to and from the court	0	10	0
Item to the vintners at Croydon Monday	0	6	0
Item for cheesecakes Dr Newell*	0	1	6
Item for 2 firkins† of sturgeon Eastland Merchants*	0	11	0
Item for a buck Mr Adr[ian] May*	1	0	0
Item for a buck from the Kinge	1	1	0
Item for pease & a catt Lo[rd] Treasurer*	0	5	0
Item to Ra[lph] Merryfield* for boathires	0	2	0
Item to the bargemen this week	1	0	0

388 See n. 377 above.

Item to the gardner at Lambeth	0	12	6
Item for 3 pies & dry beife Lady Roe*	0	5	0
Item for 12 bush[els]† of oates for coach horses	0	15	0
Item for a bush[el]† of beanes	0	2	0
Item for 9 bush[els]† of oates for geldings	0	11	3
Item for 2 shoes & 22 removes	0	4	10
Item spent in the kitchen this weeke ut patet p[er] libr[um]	26	15	0

June 5 1640

Item p[ay]d to appoticary chirurgeon & honorable charges of porter	9	10	0
Item to Mr Snaith* for boathires	0	2	6
Item for dressing 2 beavers[389] for your Grace & boathire Mr Rollston*	0	11	0
Item for a messenger from Mr Attorney* Mr Snaith*	0	10	0
Item to Sir Tho[mas] Roes* man with a book	0	2	6
Item for gloves for your Grace	0	5	0
Item for his boathire	0	1	0
Item for Nicholas* chardges into Kent with 4 colts	1	2	0
Item to the gardner at Lambeth	0	11	7
Item to the bargemen this weeke	1	5	0
Item for 12 bush[els]† of oates for coach horses	0	15	0
Item for a bush[el]† of beanes	0	2	0
Item for 9 bush[els]† of oates for geldings	0	11	3
Item spent in the kitchen this weeke ut patet p[er] libr[um]	26	3	11
Some total of this fortnight payd June 18 1640	161	8	11

[fo. 130r]

Receaved for wheate rye & pease

Inprimis to Sir Abraham Williams* man with fish p[ayd] Mr Snaith*	0	2	6
Item to a coachman &c to the Lo[rd] Lieutenant*	0	5	0
Item for boathires	0	3	6
Item for sturgeon from Mr Edwards[390]	0	3	6
Item for a buck Lo[rd] Maynard*	0	16	0
Item for another Sir Morr[ice] Bartley*	1	0	0
Item for 2 bucks from Ford	1	0	0
Item for a buck B[isho]p of Winton*	0	15	0
Item for a buck Lo[rd] Newburgh*	0	15	0
Item bringing fresh herrings &c	0	3	0
Item to the gardner at Lambeth	0	10	0

389 The archbishop's 'beaver hatts', referred to elsewhere in the accounts.

390 This is the sole entry in the accounts for 'Mr Edwards', who was possibly John Edwards, formerly master of the Merchant Taylors' School, who was appointed proctor of St John's College, Oxford in Apr. 1635; *WWL*, V, 111.

Item to the bargemen	1	0	0
Item to the gardner at Croydon	1	11	0
Item for 14 bush[els]† of oates for coach horses	0	17	6
Item for a bush[el]† of beanes	0	2	0
Item for 9 bush[els]† of oates for geldings	0	11	3
Item for 2 shoes & 8 removes	0	2	6
Item for bleedinge 6 coach horses	0	3	0
Item spent in the kitchen this weeke ut patet p[er] libr[um]	24	17	6

for this quarter

Item p[ay]d the brewer for xij hogsh[eads]† of viij^s^ & lxxxvij hogsh[eads]† of vj^s^ beare layd in at Lambeth this q[ua]rter	4	0	0
Item to M[is]tr[es]s Hoult* for this q[ua]rter	4	0	0
Item to M[is]tr[es]s Page* for this q[ua]rter	2	0	0
Item to M[is]tr[es]s Whaly* for the rent of the slaughterhouse chambers	0	12	6
Item to the mole catcher	0	5	0
Item to yr Graces barber	0	10	0
Item to the laundresse for ashes soape starch & besides wages	4	10	0
Item for 30 ells† of cloth for 12 dresser cloths at xv^d^ p[er] ell†	1	17	6
Item for 36 ells† for towells at viij^d^	1	4	0
Item for 4 ells† for an ashe cloth at xv^d^	0	5	0
Item for payles baskets beetles† piggins† &c	0	8	10
Item for hooping tubbs	0	8	9
Item for makinge & markinge the dresser cloths & towells	0	3	6
Item to William Duckett* ut patet	0	16	9
Item to him for Richard Cobb* ut patet	2	4	6
Item p[ay]d Mr Bridgeman* for Oxford mortmane & inrolling & deeds	23	15	8
Item for 7 bush[els]† of oates for poultry there	0	8	9
Item to Mr Watts* for a newe trammell†	0	18	4
Item for bringing the E[arl] of Dorsetts* carpes	1	0	0
Item for mowinge & rollinge the walkes & greene & clensinge the pond	1	5	0
Item for broomes & moppes	0	7	6
Item for hedging & ditchinge at the park Stubbes & Norborowes	6	1	10
Item for killinge moles at the parke	0	5	0
Item for grossing the last years corne at the parke & pallace ut patet	9	4	0
Item for plowinge sowinge & oates for this years cropp ut patet	17	18	0
Item for washinge & shearinge 120 sheepe	0	15	0
Item for cuttinge braks†	0	9	0
Item to Knight* &c for 4 dayes work	0	5	0
Item for 9 loads of strawe for the stable at viij^s^ p[er] load	3	12	0
Item to Morris* the smith for shoeinge & bleedinge geldings ut patet	4	17	8

[fo. 131r]

Item to Abbott* the sadler for xij newe livery sadles with all furniture at xviij^s^ a peece	10	16	0

Item for gilding your G[races] styrrapps	1	2	0
Item for bitts bridles girths &c ut patet	4	9	0
Item for a postilian sadle	1	2	0
Item to the harnessmaker for a sett of harnesses for 6 horses with all furniture	14	0	0
Item for a sett of newe raynes for them	1	10	0
Item for oylinge coatches & harnesses this yeare ut patet	4	1	6
Item for 7 newe bitts	1	1	6
Item for spynning 140 l of wooll for xij p[aires] of blankets at vj^{d} p[er] l with v^{s} for seame	6	15	0
Item for weaving 120 yrds of cloth for blankets 1 yrd broad at vij^{d} p[er] yrd with other charges	4	1	6
Some total of this week & for the quarter p[ay]d July 3 1640	221	10	10

Some total of this second quarters expenses and layings out cometh to $viij^{c}$ lxxxx^{l} xj^{s} $iiij^{d}$

All accompted & payd A[dam] T[orless]*
July 3 1640

Third quarter beginning June 19 1640

Receaved of Mr Sumner* for wood $xxvij^{l}$

Inprimis for a tun of claret from the Master of the Rolls*	1	5	0
Item for a cake & cheeses Mr Powell*	0	4	0
Item for broomes & mopps Palmer*	0	4	6
Item to the groome butler & porter at the Star Chamber[391]	0	6	6
Item for cheeses Mr Williscott*	0	2	0
Item to Mr Secretarys* coachman &c	0	5	0
Item for a buck Lo[rd] Cottington*	0	15	0
Item for pippins† & charges Mr Mills[392] &c	0	6	0
Item to the bargemen this weeke	1	6	0
Item to the gardner at Lambeth	0	10	4
Item for 14 bush[els]† of oates for coach horses	0	17	6
Item for a bush[el]† of beanes	0	2	0
Item for 9 bush[els]† for geldings at xv^{d}	0	11	3
Item for 6 removes for coach horses	0	1	0
Item spent in the kitchen this weeke ut patet p[er] libr[um]	23	13	11

391 See n. 30 above.
392 See n. 155 above.

June 26 1640

Item given for bringinge 2 cowes for the B[isho]p of Bath & Wells*	2	0	0
Item for the fraight & charges of bringing & laying in Mr Spracklinges* 30 quarters of wheate	3	2	2
Item given Sir Abraham Williams* fishermen	0	2	0
Item to Mr Page* of the Chancery Mr Dell*	1	0	0
Item to Mr Taylor[393] the waterpoole	1	0	0
Item to Mr Dell* for boathires letters &c this moneth	1	5	0
Item for musitians boathires	0	3	0
Item for opening the garden stayres done this halfe yeare ut patet	0	9	6
Item for the graithf of Mr Denns* 42 quarters of wheate & sacks	2	12	6
Item for the carridge of it into the grandary at vj^{d} p[er] q[ua]rter	0	10	6
Item to the bargemen this week	1	0	0
Item to the gardner at Lambeth	0	9	0
Item for a buck Mr Lambe[394]	0	17	6
Item for 2 fawnes from Ford	0	7	0
Item for charges Mr Mills[395]	0	1	0
Item for a coop & tynke for the kitchen	0	3	10
Item for 14 bush[els]† of oates for c[oach] horses	0	17	6
Item for a bush[el]† of beanes	0	2	0
Item for 9 bush[els]† of oates for geldings	0	11	3
Item spent in the kitchen this weeke ut patet p[er] libr[um]	24	15	1
Some total of this fortnight payd July 9 1640	72	17	4

July 3 1640

Receaved 0–0–0

Inprimis to bringinge newes of the Queens deliverance[396]	0	10	0
Item given the poore for the fast dinner	3	0	0
Item to the bargemen this weeke	0	15	0
Item to the gardner at Lambeth	0	8	4
Item to the gardner at Croydon	2	11	9

393 The identity of this 'Mr Taylor' is unknown. Not to be confused with Jeremy Taylor*.

394 This is the sole entry for 'Mr Lambe', who has two possible identities. First, this may have been a mis-recorded entry relating to Sir John Lambe*, whose gifts feature throughout the accounts. Alternatively, he may have been William Lambe, an officer of the court of chancery, appointed in 1638; *Orders of the high court of chancery and statutes of the realm relating to chancery*, ed. George Sanders (London, 1845), I, 205.

395 See n. 155 above.

396 Henrietta Maria gave birth to Prince Henry on 8 July 1640 at Oatlands Palace 'about 6 of the clock in the evening'. Henry, who was created duke of Gloucester shortly after his birth, was the fourth, but third surviving son of Charles I and Henrietta Maria. Laud baptized the infant on 22 July. Gloucester died of smallpox in 1660; Stuart Handley, 'Henry, Prince, duke of Gloucester (1640–1660)', *ODNB*; *WWL*, III, 236.

Item for a buck Mr Parkinson[397]	0	7	0
Item for cheesecakes Dr Newell*	0	1	0
Item for 14 bush[els]† of oates for coach horses	0	17	6
Item for a bush[el]† of beanes for them	0	2	0
Item for 9 bush[els]† of oates for geldings	0	11	3
Item for 12 removes	0	2	0
Item spent in the kitchen this week ut patet p[er] libr[um]	23	14	1

July 10 1640

Item give Mr Bridgemans* man & for boathires &c Mr Rollston*	0	7	0
Item for the charges of 4 men & 2 mayds at the Session House 2 dayes	0	12	6
Item given M[is]tr[es]s Hoults* sone	1	0	0
Item to Mr Snaith* for boathires &c ut patet	0	4	0
Item to Pallmer* for broomes mopps &c	0	7	0
Item for a buck Sir Rob[ert] Hatton*	0	11	0
Item to the bargemen this week	0	15	0
Item to the gardner at Lambeth	0	9	4
Item for 14 bush[els]† of oates for coach horses	0	17	6
Item for a bush[el]† of beanes	0	2	0
Item for 9 bush[els]† of oates for geldings	0	11	3
Item for 20 shoes & 6 removes for coach horses	0	12	8
Item spent in the kitchen this weeke ut patet p[er] libr[um]	26	7	11
Some total of this fortnight p[ay]d July 27 1640	65	7	1

[fo. 133r]
Receaved 0–0–0

Inprimis given for a stagg from the Kinge[398]	1	10	0
Item for cheesecakes dryed beife &c from M[is]tr[es]s Turner*	0	3	0
Item for a gelt buck from Ford	0	10	0
Item for cheesecakes from Dr Mountford*	0	2	0
Item to John Flood* at the court	1	0	0
Item to the Lo[rd] Goringe* & housekeeps servants at Oatlands[399]	0	7	6
Item to Jo[hn] Houlton[400] for his boathire in London	0	1	0
Item to the hyeman for bringinge Mr Roses* 50 quarters of wheat at xiiij^{d} p[er] q[ua]rter with 4^{s} for the sacks	3	5	3
Item to the porters for carryinge it into the granary at iij^{d} p[er] q[ua]rter	0	13	3
Item to the gardner at Lambeth	0	10	8

397 See n. 6 above.
398 This was the final gift that Laud received from Charles I.
399 On 22 July, Laud recorded in his diary that he 'christened the king's young son, Henry, at Oatlands; *WWL*, III, 236. See n. 396 above.
400 See n. 338 above.

Item to the bargemen	0	11	0
Item for 14 bush[els]† of oates for c[oach] horses	0	17	6
Item for a bush[el]† of beanes	0	2	0
Item for 12 bush[els]† of oates for geldings	0	15	0
Item for 4 removes	0	0	8
Item for 15 horses hay & p[ro]vinder† at Kingston 3 nights	3	0	7
Item spent in the kitchen this week ut patet p[er] libr[um]	26	6	9

July 24 1640

Item for bringing 2 hogh[ead]s of canary from the B[isho]p of Londonderry*	1	0	0
Item to the carmen† & porters	0	8	0
Item to Mr Badger* for binding MS & for pay wax &c ut patet	4	12	3
Item to Mr Dell* for letters boathires &c for this moneth ut patet p[er] bill	1	4	10
Item to Mr Snaith* for boathires &c	0	7	6
Item to the bargemen this weeke	0	15	0
Item to the gardner at Lambeth	0	9	8
Item to the gardner at Croydon	2	0	4
Item for a buck from Farnham	0	15	0
Item for 4 melons Sir Tho[mas] Grymes*	0	5	0
Item for a bread grater for the kitchen	0	2	6
Item for a baskett & flasket†	0	6	6
Item for pipkins† & pans	0	6	0
Item for 2 new runletts for vinegar	0	3	0
Item for sheepe to & from Croydon	0	3	0
Item for broomes & mopps p[ayd] Palmer*	0	6	0
Item for 14 bush[els]† of oates for coach horses	0	17	6
Item for a bush[el]† of beanes	0	2	0
Item for 12 bush[els]† of oates for geldings	0	15	0
Item for naylinge & a shoe	0	1	5
Item for hay & p[ro]vinder† for 15 horses at Kingston 2 nights	2	1	2
Item for farriage at Sheppton	0	2	6
Item spent in the kitchen this weeke ut patet p[er] libr[um]	26	1	10
Some total of this fortnight payd August 10 1640	83	2	2

[fo. 134r]
July ult 1640

Inprimis p[ay]d for 13 carts for the removes to Croydon[401]	3	0	0
Item for a load of wine	0	5	0
Item given to Dr Turners* servants	1	7	0
Item given Sir Tho[mas] Reynolds*	2	10	0
Item to the Lo[rd] Keepers*[402] gent	1	0	0
Item to the wardrobe keeper at court for a bed & lynnen[403]	0	3	0
Item for 2 cheeses Sir Nich[olas] Carey*	0	1	0
Item for a buck Lo[rd] Cottington*	0	15	0
Item for 6 turkeys Sir Stephen Scott*	0	2	6
Item to the gardner at Lambeth ut patet	0	14	4
Item for 14 bush[els]† of oates for coach horses	0	17	6
Item for a bush[el]† of beanes	0	2	0
Item for 12 bush[els]† of oates for geldings	0	15	0
Item for 6 roapes for c[oach] horses	0	2	0
Item for 6 broomes	0	1	0
Item for haye & p[rov]inder† for 14 horses 1 night at Oatlands	1	2	4
Item spent in the kitchen this weeke ut patet p[er] libr[um]	24	16	1
Some total of this fortnight payd August 24 1640	73	17	3

August 14 1640

Receaved from Mr Sumner*	50	0	0
And for wood sould in Norwood	16	0	5
Inprimis for a buck from Farnham	0	15	0
Item to Sir Tho[mas] Reynolds* servants	2	10	0
Item give to Mr Solicitors* servant at court	0	2	6
Item for boathire Mr Snaith*	0	1	0
Item to yeoman of the wine seller for charges at court	0	6	0
Item to Mr Levinthrope* for beddinge &c at court	0	6	0
Item to the bargemen this week	1	11	0
Item to the gardner at Lambeth	0	11	4
Item to the gardner at Croydon	0	9	3
Item for another buck from Farnham	0	15	0

401 Although the household removed, as usual, to Croydon for the summer, Laud himself spent very little time at Croydon in the summer of 1640. He was certainly in temporary residence at Oatlands Palace in early Aug., passing through Croydon briefly around 14 Aug. and he was back in Lambeth again at the end of the month; *WWL*, V, 583, VII, 607–10.

402 John Finch*, who had taken over as lord keeper in January 1640, following the death of the previous postholder, Thomas Coventry*.

403 This entry confirms that Laud was in temporary residence at court, staying at Oatlands Palace, rather than Croydon, for much of August. He was one of a nucleus of courtiers and councillors who remained behind during the king's second campaign against the Scots.

Item for 14 bush[els]† of oates for coach horses	0	0	0
Item for a bush[el]† of beanes	0	2	0
Item for 11 bush[els]† of oates for geldings	0	0	0
Item for hay & p[rov]inder† for 14 horses at Oatlands 2 nights	1	19	6
Spent in the kitchen this weeke ut patet p[er] libr[um]	23	2	9

[fo. 135r]
August 21 1640

Inprimis to Mr Gallstons[404] man	0	2	6
Item to Pallmer* from broomes &c	0	5	0
Item given to the sellers & buttery at court	0	15	0
Item to the bargemen ut patet	0	15	0
Item to the gardner at Lambeth	0	7	7
Item to the gardner at Croydon	0	9	7
Item to him for seedes	0	8	11
Item for a buck from Farnham	0	15	0
Item for bringinge partridges &c	0	4	6
Item for a buck Sir Symo[n] Sewell[405]	1	0	0
Item for 14 bush[els]† of oates for c[oach] horses	0	0	0
Item for a bush[el]† of beanes	0	2	0
Item for 11 bush[els]† of oates for geldings	0	0	0
Item for hay & p[rov]inder† for 14 horses 1 night at Oatlands[406]	1	2	4
Item spent in the kitchen this weeke ut patet p[er] libr[um]	22	6	4
Some total of this fortnight payd Septemb[er] 3 1640	61	5	1
Item for fencinge cuttinge making & carryinge of charcoals & wood to Lambeth and Croydon this yeare ut patet	138	0	4
Item for haymakinge at Lambeth this yeare ut patet	21	12	10
Item for haymakinge at Croydon this yeare ut patet	17	4	7
Item to the armorer for makinge 19 carabyns† of 19 caliber barrells with flasks &c ut patet p[er] bill	20	13	10
Some total for wood coals hay &c p[ay]d Septemb[er] 3 1640	197	11	7

404 This is the sole entry in the accounts for 'Mr Gallston', whose identity remains elusive.

405 Despite extensive research, it has not been possible to come up with a conclusive identity for 'Sir Symo Sewell'.

406 Laud probably spent the night at Oatlands with the king before he departed, on 20 Aug., for Scotland to launch his second campaign against the Scots (the second Bishops' War); *WWL*, III, 237.

August 28 1640

Receaved from Mr Sumner* for wood	50	0	0
Inprimis for your Graces offering	3	0	0
Item to a poor workman	0	1	0
Item to Mr Dell* for this moneth ut patet	0	5	0
Item to Mr Mabbs* mayd Mr Rollston*	0	10	0
Item to the bargemen at Lambeth	1	3	0
Item to the gardner at Lambeth	0	11	6
Item to the gardner at Croydon	0	7	6
Item for a buck from Farnham	0	15	0
Item for halfe a stagg Sir Fr[ancis] Lea*	0	10	0
Item for 14 bush[els]† of oates for c[oach] horses	0	0	0
Item for a bush[el]† of beanes	0	2	0
Item for 11 bush[els]† of oates for geldings	0	0	0
Item spent in the kitchen this weeke ut patet p[er] libr[um]	22	3	10

Septemb[er] 4 1640

Item for a buck B[isho]p of Oxford*	0	10	0
Item for a stagg from Theobalds	1	5	0
Item for a buck from Farnham	0	15	0
Item for wheate eares Dr Burton*	0	6	0
Item to the bargemen	1	2	6
Item to the gardner at Lambeth	0	10	0
Item to the gardner at Croydon	0	14	0
Item for the liveridge of 2 brasse peaces from the Tower p[ayd] Hen[ry] Carelesse[407]	0	7	0
Item for 14 bush[els]† of oates for c[oach] horses	0	0	0
Item for a bush[el]† of beanes	0	2	0
Item for 12 bush[els]† of oates for geldings	0	0	0
Item for hay & provinder† for 14 horses at Kingston 1 night	1	9	8
Item spent in the kitchen this weeke ut patet p[er] libr[um]	26	18	2
Some total of this fortnight payd Septemb[er] 17 1640	63	8	2

[fo. 136r]

Receaved 0–0–0

Inprimis for a stagg from Sir Arth[ur] Manwayringe*	1	6	0
Item for a buck from Farnham	0	15	0

---

407 This is the sole entry in the accounts for 'Henry Carelesse', whose identity remains elusive. He may have been the Henry Carelesse who held a commission in the admiralty office in 1638 and who was possibly one of the king's creditors during the civil war; *CSPD 1637–8*, p. 488, no. 4b; *CJ*, IV, 681.

Item for another from Mr Mynas[408]	0	15	0
Item for another Sir Nich[olas] Carey*	0	15	0
Item to the bargemen this weeke	0	15	0
Item to the gardner at Lambeth	0	12	0
Item to the gardner at Croydon	0	11	3
Item for 14 bush[els]† of oates for coach horses	0	0	0
Item for a bush[el]† of beanes	0	2	0
Item for 13 bush[els]† of oates for geldings	0	0	0
Item for hay & p[rov]inder† for 14 horses at Kingston 1 night	1	1	0
Item spent in the kitchen this weeke ut patet p[er] libr[um]	22	18	2

Septemb[er] 18 1640

Item to Palmer* for broomes & mopps	0	5	4
Item to the bargemen this week	0	7	6
Item to the gardner at Lambeth	0	8	4
Item to the gardner at Croydon	0	12	6
Item to Henry Hore* for Raphes physic & lettinge him blood &c[409]	0	8	0
Item to the woman that attended him	0	5	0
Item to Knight* for burgamott peares &c	0	15	0
Item to him for mowinge the walks at Croydon this summer	0	10	0
Item for 14 horses meale at Kingston 1 night	1	0	8
Item for 14 bush[els]† of oates for coach horses	0	0	0
Item for a bush[el]† of beanes	0	2	0
Item for 12 bush[els]† of oates for geldings	0	0	0
Item spent in the kitchen this weeke ut patet p[er] libr[um]	25	3	7

For this quarter

Item to the brewer of Croydon for 13 hogsh[eads]† of viij^s^ & 74 hogsh[eads]† of vj^s^ beare layd in since xxmas last	41	2	0
Item for a salt	0	2	4
Item to the brewer of Putney for 12 hogsh[eads]† of viij^s^ & 78 hogsh[eads]† of vj^s^ beare layd in this q[ua]rter	42	6	0
Item to M[is]tr[es]s Hoult* for this q[ua]rter	4	0	0
Item to M[is]tr[es]s Page* for this q[ua]rter	2	0	0
Item for M[is]tr[es]s Whaly*s rent	0	12	6
Item to yr Graces barber	0	10	0
Item to the mole catcher	0	5	0
Item to the laundresse for ashes soape starch & besides wages	4	10	0
Item to her for hoopinge tubb &c	0	6	6
Item for roses for the lynnen	0	5	0

408 See n. 255 above.
409 Ralph Watts*, household servant.

Item for 108 ells† of white cloth at xvij^d p[er] ell† for 12 p[aires] of sheetes for servants 9 ells† to any p[aire]	7	13	0
Item for makinge & markinge them	0	12	0
Item for 3 grosse of trenchers† & 6 beare glasses	1	7	0
Item to William Duckett* for househould stuffe &c ut patet	6	2	2
Item layd out by him for Rich[ard] Cobb*	0	5	0

[fo. 137r]

Item p[ay]d Thomas Sadler* for apprell for your Grace ut patet p[er] bill	37	8	6
Item for 50 doz of candles layd in at iiij^s viij^d p[er] doz	11	13	4
Item to Abbot* the sadler for horse clothes halters &c ut patet	2	11	10
Item to Morris [the smith]* for shoeinge &c ut patet	1	19	0
Item to Comfort* the smith at Croydon for shoeinge bleedinge &c ut patet since xxmas	6	16	2
Item to the groomes for the dunge of the stable at Croydon for 2 yeares	2	0	0
Item for 5 loads of strawe at viij^s	2	0	0
Item for the charges of bringinge the harvest at Croydon this yeare ut patet	4	17	5
Item for cuttinge & carryinge braks† at the park	0	17	4
Item for yr G[races] servants halfe yeares wages ut patet	131	3	4
Some total of this fortnight & for the q[ua]rter payd Octob[er] 2 1640	372	13	9
Some total of this third quarters expenses & layings out cometh to All payd etc A[dam] T[orless]*	990	2	5

Fourth quarter beginning Septemb[er] 25 1640

Inprimis for xij carts for the remove to Lambeth at vj^s a peece	3	6	0
Item to Fra[ncis] Loveday* for the moate	2	0	0
Item for his extraordinary paynes	1	0	0
Item to Mr Watts* man & 2 mayds	1	0	0
Item to 8 men to helpe remove stuff & carry basins into the house	0	12	6
Item to Mr Mabb* for the after pasture of the park	3	0	0
Item to him for broomes mopps & cleaning the house	1	6	0
Item to Mr Dell* for letters messengers & this moneth ut patet	0	8	0
Item to the bargemen this weeke	1	2	6
Item to the gardner at Lambeth	0	12	4
Item to Pallmer* for broomes mopps &c	0	8	6
Item given Nicholas* for this halfe yeare	2	0	0
Item for a bush[el]† of oates for c[oach] horses	0	0	0
Item for a bush[el]† of beanes	0	2	0
Item for 14 bush[els]† of oates for geldings	0	0	0
Item for hay & p[rov]inder† &c for 14 horses at Kingston 1 night	1	0	8
Item spent in the kitchen this weeke ut patet p[er] libr[um]	24	10	10

[fo. 138r]
October 2 1640

Item for a p[aire] of shoes & liquoring your G[races] bootes p Mr Snaith*	0	6	6
Item for bringing a swan damsons &c	0	3	0
Item to the bargemen this weeke	0	6	0
Item to the gardner at Lambeth	0	10	0
Item to the gardner at Croydon	1	7	2
Item for halfe a doe Lo[rd] Newburgh*	0	5	0
Item for hens & cocks Sir Tho[mas] Reynolds*	0	3	0
Item for bringinge fresh herrings & oysters	0	3	0
Item for redd deares pies brawnes Lady Chomley*	0	6	4
Item for 14 bush[els]† of oates for coach horses	0	0	0
Item for a bush[el]† of beanes	0	2	0
Item for 14 bush[els]† of oates for geldings	0	0	0
Item for haye & p[rov]inder† for 14 horses at Kingston 1 night	1	0	8
Item spent in the kitchen this weeke ut patet p[er] libr[um]	28	2	2
Some total of this fortnight payd October 15 1640	75	4	2

October 9 1640

Receaved 0–0–0

Inprimis given the 2 mayds at the parke	0	3	6
Item for a lantherne & 4 skonces†	0	9	6
Item for 4 leather baskets for coals	0	7	0
Item for broomes &c p[ay]d Palmer*	0	6	6
Item to Mr Watts* for cleaning the pond & moate & mendinge the nets	0	9	8
Item for moweinge the walks and bowlinge greene	0	13	0
Item for pigeons meale	0	4	0
Item for cleaning the house	0	6	0
Item to Dr Turner* for 8 gownes for 8 poore men in Reddinge	12	10	0
Item to the wine coop for hoopinge & rackinge wine ut patet	1	12	3
Item to the Commissioners of Sewers for a tax of vj[d] p[er] arr for lvj arr	1	8	0
Item to the bargemen this weeke	0	15	9
Item to the gardner at Lambeth	0	12	0
Item for 500 of lyngs bought at Yarmouth at vx[l] iiij[s] p[er] 100	46	0	0
Item for 600 of gabberdines†at iij[l] x[s] the 100	21	0	0
Item for charges by sea & lande & laying them in ut patet p[er] bill	3	8	4
Item for 14 bushof oates for coach horses	0	0	0
Item for a bush[el]† of beanes	0	2	0
Item for 14 bush[els]† of oates for geldings	0	0	0
Item spent in the kitchen this weeke ut patet p[er] libr[um]	25	19	11

[fo. 139r]
October 16 1640

Inprimis to the slaughterman for his charges in bringing 125 Kent weathers† out of Kent ut patet	3	17	6
Item for letters from York	0	1	0
Item for pippins† from Mr Mills[410]	0	1	0
Item for 2 pheasants Mr Abbot*	0	2	6
Item for a cake & cheeses Mr Padgett*	0	2	6
Item for 5 collars of brawne Mr Champneys[411]	0	5	0
Item to the bargemen	0	15	0
Item to the gardner at Lambeth	0	9	8
Item to Nicholas* chardges for bringinge yr G[races] colt out of Kent	0	13	6
Item for 14 bush[els]† of oates for coach horses	0	0	0
Item for a bush[el]† of beanes	0	2	0
Item for 17 bush[els]† of oates for geldings	0	0	0
Item spent in the kitchen this weeke ut patet p[er] libr[um]	25	16	5
Some total of this fortnight payd October 28 1640	149	18	6

October 23 1640

Receaved 0–0–0			
Inprimis given Mr Burwoods* sone for mending the organ	0	5	0
Item to an old man at the park	0	1	0
Item for a cake Oxon carrier	0	1	6
Item for 9 pheasants Mr Williscott*	0	2	6
Item to the bargemen	0	16	0
Item to the gardner at Lambeth	0	8	10
Item for 14 bush[els]† of oates for coach horses	0	0	0
Item for a bush[el]† of beanes	0	2	0
Item for 17 bush[els]† of oates for geldings	0	0	0
Item for 12 broomes for the stable	0	2	0
Item for the carridge of 25 quar[ts] of oates from Croydon at viij^{d}	0	16	8
Item spent in the kitchen this weeke ut patet p[er] libr[um]	23	9	5

Octob[er] 30 1640

Item for a woodcock pie 4 cheeses &c Sir John Peashall*	0	7	0
Item for 8 p[aires] of bootes for the coachman & groomes at xiij^{s} vj^{d} a p[aire]	5	8	0
Item for lynings buttons & makinge 6 coates for 6 groomes ut patet	5	9	6

410 See n. 155 above.
411 See n. 176 above.

Item to the coachman in money for his coate	4	0	0
Item to the poore at Ludgate	0	1	0
Item to the bargemen this weeke	1	17	6
Item to the gardner at Lambeth	0	5	0
Item for parliament writts p[ayd] Mr Dell*[412]	0	10	0
Item more to him for letters boathires &c	0	17	6
Item for a doe Lo[rd] Newburgh*	0	10	0
Item for a brawne Mr Cartwright*	0	7	0
Item for 14 bush[els]† of oates for coach horses	0	0	0
Item for a bush[el]† of beanes	0	2	0
Item for 18 bush[els]† of oates for geldings	0	0	0
Item for bleedinge & drenchinge 7 coach horses	0	19	2
Item for newe shoeinge them &c	0	19	8
Item spent in the kitchen this weeke ut patet p[er] libr[um]	26	2	4
Some total of this fortnight payd Novemb[er] 16 1640	74	0	7

[fo. 140r]
Novemb[er] 6 1640

Receaved 0–0–0

Inprimis p[ay]d Mr Fettiplace* for Mr Pococks* halfe years pension ended at Mich[ael]mas past ut patet	20	0	0
Item for a cock pie Dr Merrick*	0	3	6
Item for a case of pistolls & furniture[413]	1	2	6
Item to the Lo[rd] Cottingtons* servant	0	2	6
Item to the younge porter at W[hi]t[e] Hall	0	1	0
Item to Mr Badger* for bindinge MS & for 3 of yr G[races] books	1	8	4
Item for sheepe from Croydon	0	1	0
Item to the bargemen this week	1	17	0
Item to the gardner at Lambeth	0	7	8
Item for a doe Lady Chomley*	0	10	6
Item for 10 bush[els]† of your owne oates for the c[oach] horses	0	0	0
Item for 4 bush[els]† more bought at xv[d]	0	5	0
Item for a bush[el]† of beanes	0	2	0
Item for 17 bush[els]† of oates for geldings at xv[d] p[er] bush[el]†	1	1	3
Item for settinge up 7 coach horses at London	0	1	6
Item spent in the kitchen this week ut patet p[er] libr[um]	29	14	4

412 On 3 Nov., the Long Parliament rose. The atmosphere around Westminster was tense. Having been defeated a second time by the Scots, the king was aware that this session would be difficult and 'he did not ride' through the streets of London but 'went by water to king's stairs and through Westminster Hall to the Church and so to the House'; *WWL*, III, 238.

413 The purchase of a case of pistols is particularly pertinent, given the political anxiety brought about by the king's failed Scottish campaigns and the new parliamentary session.

Novemb[er] 13 1640

Item for a doe Lo[rd] Cottington*	0	10	0
Item for a cock pie Judge Jones*	0	3	0
Item for dryd fishe E[arl] of Corke*	0	2	0
Item for a salmon Dr Mountford*	0	2	0
Item to Pallmer* for broomes &c	0	6	0
Item for mendinge lanthernes	0	2	0
Item to Mr Levinthrope* for boathires	0	1	0
Item to the bargemen this weeke	1	16	0
Item to the gardner at Lambeth	0	7	0
Item to the gardner at Croydon	1	4	3
Item to the poores box at parliament	1	10	0
Item given more at Westminster	0	10	0
Item to a poor man with Mr Bagott[414]	0	3	6
Item for pheasants brawne &c Mr Love[415]	0	6	0
Item for pheasants partridge & Mr Doyly*	0	5	0
Item for 14 bush[els]† of oates for c[oach] horses at xv^{d}	0	17	6
Item for a bush[el]† of beanes	0	2	0
Item for 18 bush[els]† of oates for geldings	1	2	6
Item for naylinge coach horses	0	1	6
Item spent in the kitchen this weeke ut patet p[er] libr[um]	27	17	2
Some total of this fortnight payd Novemb[er] 26 1640	94	6	6

[fo. 141r]
Novemb[er] 20 1640

Receaved for x quar[ters] of wheate E[arl] of Thanett* for Westwell	xvj		
Inprimis for a cock pie & cheese from the Lady Chomley*	0	5	0
Item to the baker on St Clement[416]	0	10	0
Item to the Lo[rd] Privy Seales* coachman &c	0	3	6
Item for boathires Mr Snaith*	0	2	0
Item to the bargemen this weeke	1	15	0
Item to the gardner at Lambeth	0	3	6
Item for a doe Lo[rd] Maynard*	0	10	0
Item for 4 pheasants Lady Sidley*	0	5	0
Item for 4 cheeses &c Lady Savage*	0	6	0
Item for a swan pie Lady Tollnage*	0	5	0
Item for 14 bush[els]† of oates for coach horses at xv^{d} p[er] bush[el]†	0	17	6

414 See n. 304 above.

415 This is the sole entry in the accounts for 'Mr Love', whose identity remains elusive. He may have been Nicholas Love (*c.* 1608–82) of Lincoln's Inn, who became a parliamentary clerk during the civil war and, later, an MP; Sean Kelsey, 'Love, Nicholas (*bap.* 1608, *d.* 1682)', *ODNB*.

416 See n. 80 above.

Item for a bush[el]† of beanes	0	2	0
Item for 9 bush[els]† of oates for geldings at xv[d]	0	11	3
Item for 8 more for them at xxij[d]	0	14	6
Item spent in the kitchen this weeke ut patet p[er] libr[um]	28	0	0

Novemb[er] 27 1640

Item p[ay]d Mr Badger* ut patet p[er] bill	14	11	0
Item for a sugar loafe Mr Holloway*	0	2	6
Item to the bargemen this weeke	1	15	6
Item to the gardner at Lambeth	0	3	4
Item for 3 loads of gravell for the wineseller & corkes &c ut patet	0	7	6
Item to Mr Dell* for boathires letters & this moneth ut patet	0	12	0
Item for 14 bush[els]† of oates for coach horses at xxij[d] p[er] bush[el]†	1	5	4
Item for a bush[el]† of beanes	0	2	0
Item for 18 bush[els]† of oates for geldings at xxij[d]	1	12	8
Item for naylinge c[oach] horses	0	1	2
Item for a doz of broomes	0	2	0
Item spent in the kitchen this weeke ut patet p[er] libr[um]	29	9	10
Some total of this fortnight accompted Decemb[er] 14 1640	84	15	1

December 4 1640

Inprimis p[ay]d for a poore woman upon petition	0	2	0
Item to Mr Southes* for boathire	0	4	6
Item to Mr Snaith* for cittron peeles†	0	3	0
Item to him for boathires	0	4	0
Item for broomes & moppes p[ayd] Palmer*	0	5	6
Item for a brawne Mr Denby[417]	0	5	0
Item for 4 pheasants Sir Ro[bert] Honeywood*	0	2	6
Item for a cocke pie Dr Parry*	0	2	6
Item for apples &c Mr Mills[418]	0	1	6
Item for 2 barr of oysters Mr Alsopp*	0	2	0
Item to the bargemen this weeke	1	15	0
Item to the gardner & man for hedges	1	10	0

[fo. 142r]

Item to the gardner at Lambeth p[er] bill	0	10	0
Item for 14 bush[els]† of oates for c[oach] horses	1	5	4
Item for a bush[el]† of beanes	0	2	0

417 This is the sole entry in the accounts relating to a gift from 'Mr Danby', whose identity remains elusive.

418 See n. 155 above.

Item for 19 bush[els]† of oates for geldings & colts	1	14	10
Item spent in the kitchen this weeke ut patet p[er] libr[um]	25	16	9

Decemb[er] 11 1640

Item for sugar from Mr Harfleett*	0	6	0
Item for fish 2 swans apples &c from Mr Buckeridge*	0	10	0
Item for boathires Mr Levinthrope*	0	1	6
Item for a cake Walt[er] Morris*	0	10	0
Item to the bargemen this week	2	1	0
Item to the gardner at Croydon	0	19	8
Item to Mr Snaith* for boathires	0	4	0
Item for 14 bush[els]† of oates for c[oach] horses	1	5	4
Item for a bush[el]† of beanes	0	2	0
Item for 18 bush[els]† of oates for geldings	1	13	0
Item for removinge the coach horses	0	5	0
Item spent in the kitchen this weeke ut patet p[er] libr[um]	28	13	10

For this quarter

Payd the brewer for 8 hogsh[eads]† of viij[s] and 118 hogsh[eads]† of vj[s] beare layd in at Lambeth house this q[ua]rter	57	18	0
Item to Mr Tho[mas] Webb* for this q[ua]rter	5	0	0
Item to M[is]tr[es]s Hoult* for this q[ua]rter	4	0	0
Item to M[is]tr[es]s Page* for this q[ua]rter	2	0	0
Item to M[is]tr[es]s Whaly* for the rent of the slaughterhouse chambers	0	12	6
Item to the mole catcher for this q[ua]rter	0	5	0
Item to yr Graces barber	0	10	0
Item to the laundresse for ashes soape starche & besides wages	4	10	0
Item for 4 doz of towells at viij[d] p[er] ell† with makinge & markinge them	1	12	8
Item for lynes & hooping tubbs &c	0	7	2
Item to Mr Compter for chardges at Croydon court more than was here	1	15	10
Item for 50 doz of candles layd in at iiij[s] viii[d] p[er] doz	11	13	4
Item to Abbot* the sadler ut patet p[er] bill	3	11	8
Item to Morris* the smith for shoeinge bleedinge & drenching geldings ut patet	4	4	8
Item to Comfort* the smith of Croydon for shoeing & bleedinge geldings &c there ut patet	0	14	8
Item to him for other worke ut patet	0	6	9
Item for 9 loads of straw at viij[s] p[er] load layd in this q[ua]rter	3	12	0
Item to Mr Watts* for clensing the river and pond &c ut patet	0	9	6
Item to the parke keep for mendinge hedges & horses harnesse &c	0	8	10

[fo. 143r]

Item for scowringe the ditches and drills in the stubbs	1	0	0

Item for 21 bush[els]† of oates for poultry and swans &c at Lamb[eth]	1	6	3
Item to the appoticary for purginge ale for servants for yr G[race] ut patet	2	11	2
Item for physick for Ra[lph] Merryfield* at Croydon	1	18	6
Item for John Mills* physicke	2	2	2
Item for Roger Parkers* physicke	0	6	0
Item given the appoticarys man	0	10	0
Item to William Duckett* for 2 fether bedd boulsters ruggs &c ut patet p[er] bill	13	11	2
Item to him for boots shoes lynen &c for Richard Cobb*	2	5	0
Item to Tho[mas] Sadler* for apprell for yr Grace ut patet p[er] bill	13	8	10
Item to him for a suite & cloake &c for Rich[ard] Cobb* ut patet	6	16	6
Item for xx wastcostes for 20 poore women in Lambeth	5	4	8
Item for 2 liverys for the 2 bargemen	1	0	0
Some total for this fortnight & q[ua]rter	226	10	7
Some total of this 4th quarterly expenses & laying out cometh to ut patet	700	15	5
Some total of this years expenses & laying out cometh to ut patet	3574	15	11

All accompted and payd etc Adam Torlesse*

[fo. 144r]
Incipit Anno
December 18 1640[419]

First quarter

Inprimis given to the xiij prisons against xxmas	3	0	0
Item to the poore at Lambeth	20	8	0
Item to the poore at Croydon	5	0	0
Item to Mr Snaith* & Mr Southes* for boathires	0	4	0
Item for boathires on Satturday	0	4	0
Item for a fee to Mr Sergeant Rolls[420]	2	0	0

419 On 18 Dec. 1640, the Scottish commissioners' articles against Laud were read out in the House of Commons and he was accused of high treason. He was committed to the custody of James Maxwell*, gentleman usher of the black rod, and placed under house arrest. The archbishop recorded in his diary that before going to Maxwell's house, he was 'permitted to go in his company to my house at Lambeth, for a book or two to read in, and such papers as pertained to my defence against the Scots'. Wishing to 'avoid the gazing of the people', Laud remained at Lambeth until after dark. As he left the archiepiscopal palace that night, he was waved off by 'hundreds of my poor neighbours' who 'prayed for my safety and return to my house'. He remained at Maxwell's lodgings in Charing Cross until 1 Mar. 1641, when he was transferred to the Tower, following his impeachment; *WWL*, III, 238–9.

420 This is the sole entry in the accounts for 'Mr Sergeant Rolls', whose identity remains elusive, but who was clearly delivering a legal document to Laud, probably relating to his impending impeachment. This postholder reported to the master of the rolls, an office which was held at the time by Sir Charles Caesar*.

Item for a fee to Mr Hearne*[421]	2	0	0
Item for boathires Mr Baggott[422] Rollston*	0	6	6
Item for 2 lambes B[isho]p of Oxon*	0	5	0
Item for 6 bush[els]† of oates for coach horses	0	11	0
Item for 10 bush[els]† for geldings at xxij^d	0	18	4
Item spent in the kitchen this weeke ut patet p[er] libr[um]	19	1	10

December 25 1640

Item for yr Grace offering on xxmas daye	3	0	0
Item to the brewers mens box	0	10	0
Item to the brewers men at Croydon	0	2	6
Item to the coachmakers men	0	5	0
Item to the farriers mens box	0	3	6
Item to the locksmiths men	0	2	0
Item for the weekly bills this yeare	1	0	0
Item for a doe from Ford	0	8	0
Item to Sir Tho[mas] Roes* man	0	1	6
Item for letters boathires & this moneth Mr Dell*	0	17	4
Item for a trunk & boathires W[illiam] Duckett*	0	10	9
Item for 6 bush[els]† of oates for c[oach] horses	0	11	0
Item for a bush[el]† of beanes	0	2	10
Item for 9 bush[els]† of oates for geldings	0	16	6
Item for a doz of broomes	0	2	0
Item spent in the kitchen this weeke ut patet p[er] libr[um]	17	15	0
Some total of this fortnight accompted A[dam] T[orless]*	80	10	1

Januar[y] 1 1641

Inprimis for the kings N[ew] Y[ears] gift	40	0	0
Item to the househould at court[423]	30	17	6
Item to Mr Subdeanes* man with sugar	0	2	0
Item to Mr Holfords* man with cake	0	2	0

[fo. 145r]

Item to M[is]tr[es]s Buckeridge* for a new years gift	5	0	0
Item to Mr Smiths[424] sone of Burntwood with sugar	0	3	6
Item p[ay]d Mr Compter by order from yr Grace	15	0	0
Item for fowle Dr Stearne*	0	6	0

421 John Herne* was appointed by Laud to act as counsel during his impeachment and later trial.
422 See n. 304 above.
423 This was Laud's last recorded payment to the royal household. See n. 14 above.
424 See n. 39 above.

Item for 2 lambes Dr Higgs*	0	5	0
Item for a doe Lady Eliz[abeth] Norris*	0	10	0
Item for 6 bush[els]† of oates for coach horses	0	11	0
Item for 10 bush[els]† for geldings & colts	0	18	4
Item spent in the kitchen this weeke ut patet p[er] libr[um]	15	2	5

Januar[y] 8 1641

Item for the last q[ua]rter at the garden stayres p[ayd] Mr Snaith*	0	18	6
Item to him for boathires &c	0	6	0
Item for boathires Mr Southes*	0	3	0
Item given John Floyds man[425]	1	0	0
Item to the Lady Levericks* man	0	2	6
Item for 6 bush[els]† of beanes	0	2	10
Item for a bush[el]† of beanes	0	2	10
Item for 9 bush[els]† of oates for geldings	0	16	6
Item for removinge & naylinge	0	0	10
Item spent in the kitchen this weeke ut patet p[er] libr[um]	15	1	6
Some total of this fortnight accompted A[dam] T[orless]*	128	0	5

Januar[y] 15 1641

Inprimis to Gregory Goodach[426] for worke at St Johns Coll[ege]	2	0	0
Item for sheepe from Croydon	0	3	0
Item to Palmer* for broomes & mopps	0	5	6
Item for boathires Mr Snaith*	0	3	6
Item to the clark of the Parliament for Oxford Mr Rollston*	1	0	0
Item to Stephen[427] for boathires	0	4	0
Item for 6 bush[els]† of oates for coach horses	0	11	0
Item for x bush[el]† for geldings & colts	0	18	4
Item spent in the kitchen this weeke ut patet p[er] libr[um]	15	9	5

Januar[y] 22 1641

Item for boathires & the boy at Mr Maxwells* Mr Snaith*	0	4	0
Item p[ay]d Mr Brigham*[428] the coachmaker ut patet p[er] bill for a yeare	0	13	4
Item for reeds to dress the barge	0	1	6

---

425 This is the sole entry in the accounts for John Floyd, whose identity remains elusive.

426 Given the nature of this entry, Gregory Goodach was probably a craftsman employed at St John's College, Oxford.

427 See n. 113 above.

428 See n. 119 above.

Item to the gardner for seeds	0	7	10
Item for 6 bush[els]† of oates for coach horses	0	11	10
Item for a bush[el]† of beanes	0	2	10
Item for 9 bush[els]† of oates for geldings	0	16	6
Item for a shoe & naylinge coach horses	0	1	0
Item spent in the kitchen this weeke ut patet p[er] libr[um]	14	18	5
Some total of this fortnight accompted A[dam] T[orless]*	38	11	2

[fo. 146r]

Inprimis given for a cake from the Clark of the Checke[429] Mr Snaith*	0	3	0
Item for a little booke	0	0	6
Item for boathires R[ichard] Cressall*	0	2	0
Item for apples Mr Mills[430]	0	2	0
Item for boathires Mr Rollston*	0	1	6
Item for a service booke Mr Dell*	0	7	0
Item for boathires &c by him	0	3	6
Item allowed Mr Sumner* for his paynes about the woods in Kent	10	0	0
Item for 6 bush[els]† of oates for coach horses	0	11	0
Item for x bush[el]† for geldings & colts	0	18	4
Item spent in the kitchen this weeke ut patet p[er] libr[um]	15	4	4

Februar[y] 5 1641

Item given Mr Keelinge yr G[races] Solicitor for a fee Mr Dell*	2	0	0
Item to Mr Bridgemans* man Mr Rollston*	2	0	0
Item for boathires & a band to Sir Thomas Dawes* & Sir Joh[n] Wolstenham*	0	6	6
Item given Mr Tho[mas] Webb* Mr Dell*	2	0	0
Item to Mr Hearne* for a fee Mr Dell*	2	0	0
Item to the gardner for seeds	0	7	6
Item for 6 bush[els]† of oates for coach horses	0	11	0
Item for a bush[el]† of beanes	0	2	10
Item for 9 bush[els]† of oates for geldings	0	16	6
Item for naylinge c[oach] horses	0	1	2
Item spent in the kitchen this weeke ut patet p[er] libr[um]	15	11	0
Some total of this fortnight accompted A[dam] T[orless]*	52	9	8

429 See n. 70 above.
430 See n. 155 above.

Februar[y] 12 1641

Inprimis given Mr Maxwells* cook[431]	2	0	0
Item to the clark of parliaments man with a petition	0	10	0
Item for boathires Mr Snaith*	0	3	0
Item for boathires garden	0	3	0
Item for a fee to Mr Hearne*	2	0	0
Item for broomes & mopps Pallmer*	0	6	6
Item for boathires &c Tho[mas] Sadler*	0	8	2
Item for 6 bush[els]† of oates for coach horses	0	11	0
Item for 11 bush[els]† for geldings & colts	1	0	2
Item for 18 newe shoes & 6 removes	0	11	6
Item spent in the kitchen this weeke ut patet p[er] libr[um]	14	18	8

Februar[y] 19 1641

Item to Mr Snaith* for cittron peeles†	0	15	0
Item to him for boathires	0	2	0
Item to Mr Lylle[432] for the bill of impost of xij tun at v^{s} p[er] tun	3	2	6
Item for signinge it at Mr Leachlands* at iij^{s} p[er] tun & entering it	1	18	0
Item to Mr Worrall[433] for red wine maliga to fill the vessels this yeare	5	8	0
Item to the yeoman of the wineseller for boathires	0	3	6

[fo. 147r]

Item for 6 bush[els]† of oates for c[oach] horses	0	11	0
Item for a bush[el]† of beanes	0	2	10
Item for 9 bush[els]† of oates for geldings	0	16	6
Item spent in the kitchen this weeke ut patet p[er] libr[um]	16	5	6
Some total of this fortnight accompted A[dam] T[orless]*	51	16	10

Februar[y] 26 1641

Inprimis to the lyterman† for carrying of goods to the Tower[434]	0	10	0
Item to Haycock* & Stephen[435] that day	0	7	0
Item to Knight* for helping them &c	0	3	0

---

431 Laud was ordered by the House of Commons to 'pay in fees for my diet and custody' while under house arrest at Maxwell's, the costs of which 'grew very heavy' over the course of his ten weeks there; *WWL*, III, 398.

432 This is the sole entry in the accounts for 'Mr Lylle', whose identity remains elusive.

433 This is the sole entry in the accounts for 'Mr Worrall', whose identity remains elusive. Not to be confused with Dr Thomas Worrall*.

434 Laud was impeached in the House of Commons on 23 Feb. and was moved to the Tower on 1 Mar. 1641. This entry indicates that his goods were conveyed to the Tower in advance of the archbishop's transfer there.

435 See n. 113 above.

Item to Mr Dell* for pamfletts &c ut patet	0	6	0
Item for 2 doz of bottles & corks for wine	0	7	0
Item for 12 pairs of gloves for Mr Edgar[436] p[ayd] Mr Snaith*	1	5	4
Item to him for boathires to the Lo[rd] Keep[er] Judge Bartley* Tower &c[437]	0	3	0
Item to the porter for removing stuffe from Mr Maxwells*[438]	0	4	0
Item to Stephen[439] for carridge &c	0	3	6
Item for a lamprey† pie B[isho]p of Glouc[e]s[ter]*	0	2	6
Item to the carmen† & wharfinger† for the stuffe & wood at the Tower	0	17	0
Item given labourers for carrying it in & cleaning the sellers &c	0	10	0
Item for earthenware a gymlett† & other new wares	0	5	6
Item for 2 candlesticks & a lantherne	0	6	6
Item to a joyner draymen† lemons &c	0	2	9
Item for mending locks & a brick layer for the kitchen	0	5	9
Item for 6 bush[els]† of oates for c[oach] horses	0	11	0
Item for 10 bush[els]† for geldings & colts	0	18	4
Item for naylinge c[oach] horses	0	1	0
Item for a doz of broomes	0	2	0
Item spent in the kitchen this weeke ut patet p[er] libr[um]	19	4	0

March 5 1641

Item to Mr Brown* & his man	0	5	0
Item to Mr Maxwells* porter a cake	0	2	0
Item for cords & boathires Tho[mas] Sadler*	0	2	0
Item to the lyterman† with coales & wood	0	5	0
Item to 5 carmen† at xx[d]	0	8	4
Item for wharfage at the Tower	0	0	10
Item for laying it in &c Knight*	0	2	0
Item for a coal shovell	0	1	6
Item for carrying away rubbish	0	4	0
Item to Mr Snaith* & Mr Duckett* boathires	0	4	0
Item for pipkins† lynes packthred†	0	2	2

436 This is the sole entry in the accounts for 'Mr Edgar', whose identity remains elusive.

437 The 'him' in this entry relates to George Snaith, who went by boat to visit Sir Edward Littleton*, the recently appointed lord keeper, the previous encumbant, Sir John Finch* having been removed from office in Jan. 1641. Snaith may also have visited Sir Robert Berkeley* – 'Judge Bartley' in this entry – who, the previous week, had been sequestered by James Maxwell, the gentleman usher, and placed under house arrest in the custody of a London sheriff. The purpose of both visits was almost certainly to seek legal opinion in relation to Laud's own impeachment and possible trial. www.historyofparliamentonline.org/volume/1604–1629/member/berkeley-robert-15845–1656; Louis Knafla, 'Finch, John, Baron Finch of Fordwich (1584–1660)', *ODNB*.

438 Laud was moved to the Tower from James Maxwell's* house in Charing Cross on 1 Mar., travelling in Maxwell's coach. From Cheapside to the Tower, the coach was 'followed and railed at by the prentices and rabble, in great numbers'. As the coach approached its destination, 'the number still increasing as they went … [and] the shouting was exceeding great'; *WWL*, III, 240, 436.

439 See n. 113 above.

Item for 6 bush[els]† of oates for c[oach] horses	0	11	0
Item for a bush[el]† of beanes	0	2	10
Item for 9 bush[els]† of oates for geldings	0	16	6
Item spent in the kitchen this week ut patet p[er] libr[um]	19	14	1
Some total of this fortnight			
Accompted A[dam] T[orless]*	49	16	5

[fo. 148r]
March 12 1641

Inprimis given Mr Farrants[440] man with a calfe	0	6	0
Item for 2 doz of q[ua]rt bottles	0	7	0
Item for 7 doz of pottle† bottles	0	3	6
Item for 7 grosse of corkes & boathire Mr Dell*	0	3	0
Item for a fee to Mr Hearne*	2	0	0
Item for boathires Mr Snaith*	0	1	0
Item for a skillet & 2 fish bottomes for yr Graces use	0	8	8
Item for a drippinge pan & pipkins†	0	6	0
Item for a cake & cheeses Mr Powell*	0	2	6
Item for a shovell & a payle	0	3	6
Item for a handbaskett & one for coals	0	2	0
Item for a spitt & a skypp	0	3	6
Item for 6 bush[els]† of oates for c[oach] horses	0	11	0
Item for naylinge them	0	1	0
Item for 10 bush[els]† for geldings & colts	0	18	4
Item spent in the kitchen this weeke ut patet p[er] libr[um]	15	8	0
For this quarter			
Payd the brewer for 65 hogsh[eads]† of vj^s beare layd in at Lambeth this q[ua]rter ut patet p[er] bill	29	5	0
Item to M[is]tr[es]s Hoult* for this q[ua]rter	4	0	0
Item to M[is]tr[es]s Page* for this q[ua]rter	2	0	0
Item to M[is]tr[es]s Whaly* for the rent of the slaughterhouse chambers	0	12	6
Item to the mole catcher	0	5	0
Item to yr Graces barber	0	10	0
Item to the laundress for ashes soape starch & besides wages	4	10	0
Item p[ay]d to Abbott* the sadler ut patet p[er] bill	1	1	0
Item to Morris* the farrier for shoeinge geldings &c ut patet	2	8	0
Item to the smith at Croydon for shoeinge drenchinge geldings &c ut patet	0	17	2
Item for 6 loads of straw at viij^s	2	8	0

440 See n. 115 above.

Item for 15 dayes work in mendinge hedges at the part at xij^{d}	0	15	0
Item for helpinge a cowe in calvinge	0	6	0
Item for 6 bush[els]† of oates for poultry at Lambeth at xxij^{d}	0	11	0
Item to Tho[mas] Sadler* for apprell for your Grace ut patet	2	1	0
Item to W[illiam] Duckett* for 2 old trunks	0	10	0
Item layd out by him for Rich[ard] Cobb*	0	2	6
Item to the hyman for bringinge 50 quarters of wheate from Mr Rose*	3	1	3
Item to the porters for carryinge it into the granary & other charges	1	4	11
Item for scowringe the ditches about the marshes	6	14	4

[fo. 149r]

Item for your Graces servants halfe years wages ut patet	129	13	4
Item for 62 liveryes att xx^{s} a peece	62	0	0
Some total of this weeke & for the quarter accompted	276	1	0

Some total of this first quarters expenses & laying out cometh to vj^{c} lxxviij^{l} v^{s} vij^{d}
All accompted and payd Adam Torlesse*

Second quarter beginning March 19 1641

Inprimis given to the jewell officers at the Mynt	1	17	6
Item for bringing a water for your Graces eye	0	2	6
Item for a cake from Mr Doyly*	0	2	6
Item to Palmer* for broomes &c	0	4	6
Item for 6 bush[els]† of oates for coach horses whereof 4 of your G[races] owne	0	3	8
Item for 9 bush[els]† of oates for geldings	0	0	0
Item spent in the kitchen this weeke ut patet p[er] libr[um]	16	15	0

March 26 1641

Item given Mr Reeves[441] sone for a box pewters to your Grace	2	0	0
Item to Mr Dell* for petitions Mr Pyms speech &c ut patet[442]	1	2	0
Item for getting a silver bason out of the well at the Tower	1	2	0
Item given the souldiers here	0	5	0
Item given an old man & Morris*[the smith]	0	7	0
Item for the kitchen & chamber 4 weekes at xx^{s} p[er] weeke p[ay]d Mr Badger*	4	0	0

441 See n. 23 above.

442 A number of the speeches given by John Pym in the House of Commons reached the press, but it is likely that this one concerned parliamentary case against Laud's friend and ally, Thomas Wentworth, earl of Strafford, delivered on 23 Mar.; *CJ*, II, 92.

Item for coales & wood	0	5	0
Item to 3 carmen† & wharfage	0	5	6
Item for laying them into the house	0	2	0
Item to W[illiam] Duckett* for the matts an hassock† & the bricklayer ut patet	0	7	0
Item spent 6 bush[els]† of oates for coach horses	0	0	0
Item for 10 bush[els]† of oates for geldings of yr G[races] owne	0	0	0
Item naylinge c[oach] horses	0	1	0
Item spent in the kitchen this weeke ut patet p[er] libr[um]	17	8	6
Some total of this fortnight accompted June 28 1641	46	13	6

[fo. 150r]
Aprill 2 1641

Inprimis given Mr Lieutenants man of the Tower* with carpes	0	5	0
Item to the workmen of the White Tower	0	5	0
Item for herrings a letter & boathires Mr Snaith*	0	3	0
Item given to see the park	0	2	0
Item to the muskett & halberd officers	0	5	0
Item for a salmon Mr Harfleet*	0	5	0
Item for a lamprey† pie B[isho]p of Glouc[e]s[ter]*	0	2	6
Item for 2 puddinge bags	0	1	6
Item for 6 bush[els]† of oates for coach horses	0	0	0
Item for a bush[el]† of beanes	0	2	10
Item for 9 bush[els]† of oates for geldings	0	0	0
Item spent in the kitchen this weeke ut patet p[er] libr[um]	16	17	0

Aprill 9 1641

Item to the armorers & gunners	0	5	0
Item to the gardner at Croydon for seedes digging bootes &c ut patet	1	0	2
Item to Nicholas* for this addition of wages	2	0	0
Item for 6 bush[els]† of oates for coach horses	0	0	0
Item for 10 bush[els]† of oates for geldings & colts	0	0	0
Item for 24 removes for c[oach] horses	0	4	0
Item spent in the kitchen this weeke ut patet p[er] libr[um]	17	7	2
Some total of this fortnight accompted June 28 1641	39	5	2

Aprill 16 1641

Inprimis given to the 13 prisons at Easter	5	0	0
Item to the poore at Lambeth	5	0	0
Item to the B[isho]p of Glou[cester]s* ma[n] with lamprey† pies	0	3	6

Item to Dr Layfields* man	0	2	6
Item for boathires &c Mr Rollston* &c	0	2	6
Item for water rubbish &c at the Tower	0	4	8
Item to Palmer* for broomes & mopps	0	5	6
Item to Tho[mas] Sadler* for apprell for Mr Webb* above his xij[l] ut patet p[er] bill	2	18	9
Item to the gardner at Lambeth for weeding	0	4	8
Item to Bunce[443] for work & nayles at the Tower	0	5	5
Item for 2 doz of bottles q[ua]rt & 5 doz of corks	0	8	4
Item to the lyterman† with coales & wood	0	5	0
Item for 4 carmen† at xxiij[d] & wharfage	0	11	8
Item for laying the coales & wood & for sand boathires &c ut patet	0	6	0
Item for 6 bush[els]† of oates for c[oach] horses	0	0	0
Item for a bush[el]† of beanes	0	2	10
Item for 9 bush[els]† of oates for geldings	0	0	0
Item spent in the kitchen this weeke ut patet p[er] libr[um]	17	17	9

Aprill 23 1641

Item given for your Graces offering at Easter	1	0	0
Item to Mr Davyes the Chaplayne[444]	1	0	0

[fo. 151r]

Item to the clark & sexton	1	10	0
Item to the Lieutenants* Servants[445]	1	6	0
Item for a padlock & key &c there	0	5	2
Item for a grosse of trenchers† there	0	4	6
Item for Ed[ward] Nutts* chardges out of Kent with 87 sheepe	3	8	0
Item given Mr Webb* in his purse at his going to Mr Bridgeman*	2	0	0
Item for 6 bush[els]† of oates for c[oach] horses	0	0	0
Item for x bush[els]† for geldings & colts	0	0	0
Item spent in the kitchen this weeke ut patet p[er] libr[um]	18	16	1
Some total of this fortnight accompted June 28 1641	61	18	10

April ult 1641

Inprimis given for lampreys† from the B[isho]p of Gloucester*	0	3	6

443 See n. 35 above.

444 See n. 296 above.

445 This ambiguous entry either related to a payment or gratuity to the servants of the lieutenant of the Tower, Sir William Balfour*, or to something similar for the servants of Thomas Wentworth*, lord lieutenant of Ireland, who was also imprisoned in the Tower, awaiting the outcome of his trial, which was still ongoing.

Item for a coppy of Mr Osbastons* order[446]	0	5	0
Item for boathires Mr Dell*	0	6	0
Item to W[illiam] Duckett* for boathires ut patet	0	5	0
Item for lamprey† B[isho]p of Glouc[e]s[ter]*	0	3	6
Item for 6 bush[els]† of oates for c[oach] horses	0	0	0
Item for a bush[el]† of beanes	0	2	10
Item for 7 bush[els]† of oates for geldings	0	0	0
Item spent in the kitchen this weeke ut patet p[er] libr[um]	20	17	7

May 7 1641

Item to a carpenter at the Tower[447]	0	5	0
Item to a smith for catches for casements	0	3	0
Item for boathires W[illiam] D[uckett]*	0	3	6
Item given the Lo[rd] Scudamores* man	0	5	0
Item for boathires &c Mr Snaith*	0	2	8
Item more to a carpenter p[ayd] W[illiam] D[uckett]*	0	1	6
Item to the woman in the kitchen	0	5	0
Item for boathires & porterages &c	0	4	8
Item for 6 bush[els]† of oates for c[oach] horses	0	0	0
Item for 7 bush[els]† for geldings	0	0	0
Item for naylinge c[oach] horses	0	2	0
Item for bleedinge them	0	3	0
Item for cuttinge 2 colts	0	10	0
Item spent in the kitchen this weeke ut patet p[er] libr[um]	17	14	9
Some total of this fortnight accompted June 28 1641	42	3	6

May 14 1641

Inprimis for a lamprey† pie Mr Staple*	0	2	0
Item for a cake & 2 cheeses Cl[erk] of Checke[448]	0	2	0
Item for cuttinge nettles in the park	0	2	6
Item for a powdering tubb† the Tower	0	10	9
Item to Pallmer* for broomes	0	5	8
Item for a lyter† with coales &c to the Tower	0	5	0
Item for carmen† wharfage &c	0	6	0
Item for laying in wood & coales	0	1	6
Item to the glazier there	0	5	0

---

446 On 26 May, shortly after this entry, Lambert Osbaston*, was pardoned by the king for having slandered Laud in 1639.

447 Since this was the week in which Wentworth was executed on Tower Hill, it would be a nice twist if this payment to the 'carpenter at the Tower' was a reward for having had the unpleasant task of assembling the scaffold just outside the Tower walls.

448 See n. 70 above.

Item for boathires Mr Snaith* Duckett* &c	0	5	2
Item given Mr Pigeon the Wardrobe keeper*	0	10	0

[fo. 152r]

Item to Tho[mas] Sadler* for a box and a key	0	2	10
Item for 6 bush[els]† of oates for c[oach] horses	0	0	0
Item for a bush[el]† of beanes	0	2	10
Item for 8 bush[els]† of oates for geldings	0	0	0
Item for 6 broomes for the stable	0	1	0
Item spent in the kitchen this weeke ut patet p[er] libr[um]	17	1	5

May 21 1641

Item for pippins† from Mr Mills[449] &c bought	0	2	6
Item to the carpenter at the Tower	0	1	6
Item to Mr Pigeons* man there	0	2	6
Item for boathires to Mr Maxwell* Mr Snaith*	0	1	0
Item for 6 bush[els]† of oates for c[oach] horses	0	0	0
Item for 6 bush[els]† for geldings	0	0	0
Item spent in the kitchen this weeke ut patet p[er] libr[um]	17	4	8
Some total of this fortnight accompted June 28 1641	37	15	10

May 28 1641

Inprimis for reeds to dress the barge	0	2	0
Item for fishinge at Waddon Mill	0	1	6
Item to Mr Dell* for boathires &c this moneth	0	10	6
Item to Dr Walkers* man with cheeses Tower	0	2	6
Item to Mr Lieutenants* man	0	1	0
Item for Mr Webb* for his boathires	0	2	0
Item for 3 bush[els]† of oates for coach horses	0	0	0
Item for a bush[el]† of beanes	0	0	0
Item for 4 bush[els]† of oates for gelds	0	0	0
Item for 20 shoes for 5 c[oach] horses & naylinge	0	12	0
Item spent in the kitchen this weeke ut patet p[er] libr[um]	13	11	1

June 4 1641

Item to Roger* for tapps & corkes	0	1	0
Item to the gardner for weeding & a syethe	0	11	3
Item given Mr Hores* man Tower	0	2	6

---

449 See n. 155 above.

Item for sheepe from Croydon	0	3	0
Item to Moore for a paper to your Grace Tower	0	3	0
Item for water to the kitchen & W[alter] Morris*	0	6	0
Item to Mr Powells* man with cheeses	0	2	0
Item for orringes	0	4	7
Item for a fee to Mr Hearne* Mr Dell*	2	0	0
Item for 3 bush[els]† of oates for c[oach] horses	0	0	0
Item for 4 bush[els]† for geldings	0	0	0
Item spent in the kitchen this weeke ut patet p[er] libr[um]	16	3	6
Some total of this fortnight accompted June 28 1641	35	1	3

June 11 1641

Item to the plummer at the Tower	0	6	0
Item for 6 fyne lynen capps for your Grace	0	10	6
Item given Walt[er] Morris* by your G[race]	0	10	0
Item for boathires &c W[illiam] Duckett*	0	6	0
Item for a Russia hide	0	14	0
Item to a lyterman† with coales & wood	0	5	0
Item to the carmen† & wharfage	0	6	6
Item for shootinge & laying it in	0	2	0
Item for 3 bush[els]† of oates for c[oach] horses	0	0	0

[fo. 153r]

Item for a bush[el]† of beanes for them	0	2	10
Item for 4 bush[els]† of oates for geldings	0	0	0
Item for naylinge coach horses	0	1	4
Item spent in the kitchen this weeke ut patet p[er] libr[um]	15	0	10

For this quarter

Item payd to the brewer of Putney for 4 hogsh[eads]† of viij^{s} & 64 hogsh[eads]† of vj^{s} beare layd in this q[ua]rter	31	4	0
Item to the brewer at the Tower for 26 barr of viij^{s} & 52 barr of vj^{s} beare layd in since the first of March	26	0	0
Item to M[is]tr[es]s Page* for this q[ua]rter	2	0	0
Item to your G[races] barber	0	10	0
Item to M[is]tr[es]s Whaly* for the rent of the slaughterhouse chambers	0	12	6
Item to the laundress for ashes soape starch & besides wages	4	10	0
Item for hoopinge tubbs	0	1	0
Item to Abbott* the sadler ut patet	0	13	6
Item to Morris* the smith for shoeinge bleedinge & drenching gelds &c ut patet	2	18	0
Item for 6 loads of straw this q[ua]rter	2	18	0

Item to Comfort* the smith at Croydon for shoeinge bleedinge &c horses ut patet	1	4	5
Item to the park keep for mendinge hedges & cattell & the cart &c ut patet	0	16	0
Item to Tho[mas] Sadler* for apprell for your Grace ut patet	4	11	0
Item to him for apprell for Rich[ard] Cobb* ut patet	8	6	10
Item to the vintner for redd wine maliga & rackinge wine ut patet	2	11	2
Item to Bryan* the smith for mendinge locks & keys &c ut patet	0	7	6
Item for this q[ua]rters rent of the roome at the stayres foote	0	5	6
Some of this weeke & for the quarter accompted June 28 1641	108	4	5

Some total of this second quarters expenses and laying out ut patet

iij[c] lxxij[l] ij[s] vj[d]

All accompted and payd June 28 1641
Adam Torlesse*

[fo. 154r]
Third quarter beginninge June 18 1641

Inprimis for a buck from the Lord Newburgh*	0	15	0
Item for 9 newe cappes & alteringe 3 others	0	16	0
Item for a cheese Mr Standen[450]	0	6	6
Item for pippins† charges & strawberries	0	6	8
Item for 3 bush[els]† of oates for coach horses	0	0	0
Item for 4 bush[els]† for geldings	0	0	0
Item spent in the kitchen this weeke ut patet p[er] libr[um]	14	16	11

June 25 1641[451]

Item given Sir Tho[mas] Ashtons* man with a book	1	0	0
Item to Palmer* for broomes & mopps	0	5	6
Item for a buck from Mr May*	1	0	0
Item for a cake Clerk of the Check[452]	0	2	6
Item to Mr Dell* for pamfletts & boathires	0	10	6
Item for a letter & bill from Baron Hendon*	1	0	0
Item for a coach from the E[arl] of Newcastle*	0	5	0
Item to Mr Duckett* for boathires &c	0	2	0
Item for 3 bush[els]† of oates for c[oach] horses	0	0	0
Item for a bush[el]† of beanes	0	2	10

450 This is the first of two entries in the accounts for 'Mr Standen', whose identity remains elusive.

451 Laud tendered his resignation as chancellor of the University of Oxford on 25 June, having first 'acquainted the king by my Lord of London [William Juxon*] that I would resign'; *WWL*, III, 242.

452 See n. 70 above.

Item for 3 bush[els]† of oates for geldings	0	0	0
Item spent in the kitchen this weeke ut patet p[er] libr[um]	14	16	5
Some total of this fortnight	36	5	4

July 2 1641

Item for the carridge of trunks &c	0	4	0
Item to the chirurgeon for Pattricks head	1	0	0
Item for a buck from Ford	0	12	6
Item for a bagg of salt & mendinge a pott	0	3	0
Item to Mr Badger* for pamphlets & books sent to your Grace to the vij of July	2	10	0
Item for knives bought at the Tower	0	5	6
Item given the B[isho]p of Glouc[e]s[ters]* man	0	2	0
Item for a shelfe in the seller &c	0	3	0
Item for boathires &c p[ayd] Will[iam] Duckett*	0	6	0
Item for 3 bush[els]† of oates for c horses	0	0	0
Item for 3 bush[els]† for geldings	0	0	0
Item for naylinge the coach horses	0	2	5
Item spent in the kitchen this weeke ut patet p[er] libr[um]	15	9	5

July 9 1641

Item to the hieman for bringinge Mr Denns* xxl quarters of wheate	1	1	0
Item for meatage porters &c	0	13	11
Item to Mr Morgan[453] & Mr Sanderson[454] for the arrerage of the acc in the xiiij arr for vij yeares at xxx^{s} p[er] yeare	10	10	0
Item for a buck from Ford	0	12	6
Item to the lyeman for bringinge 31 quarts of wheate at xij^{d} p[er] q[ua]rter	1	11	6
Item corkage meatage sillage groomidge &c ut patet	0	16	11
Item to the lyeman with it	0	5	10
Item to the porters into the graynary	0	8	0
Item for carrying back the sacks	0	1	6

[fo. 155r]

Item for lyteridge of wood & coales the Tower	0	5	0
Item to 4 carmen† wharfage &c	0	10	0
Item for 3 bush[els]† of oates for c[oach] horses	0	0	0
Item for a bush[el]† of beanes	0	2	10

453 See n. 144 above.
454 This is the sole entry in the accounts for 'Mr Sanderson', whose identity remains elusive.

Item for 4 bush[els]† of oates for geldings	0	0	0
Item spent in the kitchen this weeke ut patet p[er] libr[um]	14	15	11
Some total of this fortnight	53	7	9

July 16 1641

Item given Dr Birds* sones child W[illiam] Duckett*	0	10	0
Item for pippins† charges codlyns† &c	0	2	2
Item for his boathires	0	1	6
Item for a watering pott for the garden	0	4	0
Item for a buck Lady Norris*	0	12	0
Item for stringinge & mendinge yr Graces watch	0	4	0
Item for his boathire to Mr Maxwell*	0	1	6
Item more for charges pippins† boathire &c p[ayd] William Duckett*	0	6	8
Item for a buck from Ford	0	12	6
Item to the lyeman for bringing Mr Roses* 52 quar[t] of wheate	3	1	3
Item for meatage & filler ut patet	0	12	8
Item to the porters for carryinge it into the granary at iij[d] p[er] q[ua]rter	0	13	2
Item for carryinge back the sacks	0	3	6
Item for 3 bush[els]† of oates for c[oach] horses	0	0	0
Item for 3 bush[els]† more for geldings	0	0	0
Item for 20 removes for 5 c[oach] horses	0	3	4
Item spent in the kitchen this weeke ut patet p[er] libr[um]	14	8	4

July 23 1641

Item for halfe a buck from the B[isho]p of Winton*	0	0	0
Item to Palmer* for mopps broomes stuffe for andirons† &c	0	8	6
Item to Mr Staples* mayd pippins† W[illiam] Duckett*	0	2	0
Item more to him for a latch for your G[races] chamber &c ut patet	0	5	6
Item to Mr Tho[mas] Webb* for his journey into Kent	0	10	0
Item for cuttinge nettles in the park	0	1	6
Item for 3 bush[els]† of oates for coach horses	0	0	0
Item for a bush[el]† of beanes	0	2	10
Item for 4 bush[els]† of oates for geldings	0	0	0
Item spent in the kitchen this weeke ut patet p[er] libr[um]	15	14	11
Some total of this fortnight	39	1	10

July 30 1641

Inprimis given Davyes the messenger[455] p[ayd] Mr Dell*	0	5	0
Item to him for pamfletts	0	7	6
Item more for his boathires this moneth	0	8	0
Item for a doz of towells at viij^{d} p[er] ell† & makinge them	0	13	0
Item for hoopinge tubbs	0	2	0
Item for a buck from Mr Parkinson[456]	0	10	0

[fo. 156r]

Item for cherryes cheeses & beateroot the Tower	0	3	6
Item for turkys cheesecakes &c Dr Turner*	0	4	0
Item for 3 bush[els]† of oates for c[oach] horses	0	0	0
Item for 3 bush[els]† for geldings	0	0	0
Item for naylinge coach horses	0	1	4
Item spent in the kitchen this weeke ut patet p[er] libr[um]	15	1	1

August 6 1641

Item for halfe a buck B[isho]p of Winton*	0	7	0
Item for boathires to Fulham Lambeth &c Mr Snaith*	0	5	6
Item to the lyterman† with coales & wood the Tower	0	5	0
Item to 5 carriers wharfage &c	0	9	10
Item for shovelling & laying it in & boathires	0	3	6
Item for 3 bush[els]† of oates for c[oach] horses	0	0	0
Item for a bush[el]† of beanes	0	2	10
Item for 4 bush[els]† of oatesfor geldings	0	0	0
Item spent in the kitchen this weeke ut patet p[er] libr[um]	14	5	1
Some total of this fortnight	33	16	4

August 13 1641

Inprimis for money baggs &c at the Tower	0	2	6
Item to a reddinge woman & a poor lady	0	9	0
Item for bringinge sweete meates & apricocks	0	4	0
Item for boathires W[illiam] Duckett*	0	1	8
Item for sugar & pepper Mr Abbot*	0	10	0
Item for a grosse of trenchers†	0	5	0
Item for halfe a buck B[isho]p of Winton*	0	6	0
Item for bringinge calves from Croydon	0	8	0

455 This is the sole entry for 'Davyes the messenger' whose identity remains elusive. Not to be confused with 'Mr Davyes the Chaplayne'.

456 See n. 6 above.

Item for 3 bush[els]† of oates for c[oach] horses	0	0	0
Item for 3 bush[els]† for geldings	0	0	0
Item for 16 newe shoes & 5 removes & dressinge naylinge &c	0	13	4
Item spent in the kitchen this weeke ut patet p[er] libr[um]	13	18	7

August 20 1641

Item to the woman in the kitchen p[ayd] W[illiam] Duckett*	0	6	0
Item given to a souldier by your Grace	0	10	0
Item for a bin for bread	0	6	0
Item for a buck Mr Warwick*	0	10	0
Item for boathires p W[illiam] Duckett*	0	3	0
Item to yr G[race] for Dr Bathurst*	2	0	0
Item give a minister	0	10	0
Item for 3 bush[els]† of oates for c[oach] horses	0	0	0
Item for a bush[el]† of beanes	0	2	10
Item for 3 bush[els]† of oates for geldings	0	0	0
Item spent in the kitchen this weeke ut patet p[er] libr[um]	12	18	7
Some total of this fortnight	34	4	6

August 27 1641

Item for fencinge cuttinge makinge & carridge of wood & coales to Lambeth & Croydon this yeare	180	18	10
Item for haymakinge at Lambeth ut patet	15	8	6
Item for haymakinge at Croydon ut patet	9	8	8
Some total for wood coales haye &c	205	16	0

[fo. 157r]

Item to Mr Dell* for boathires last month	0	8	0
Item lost by Spanish money[457]	0	11	6
Item for a cheese Mr Standen[458]	0	6	0
Item for bringinge grapes &c and boathires p[ayd] Will[iam] Duckett*	0	6	10
Item for 3 bush[els]† of oates for c[oach] horses	0	0	0
Item for 3 bush[els]† for geldings	0	0	0
Item spent in the kitchen this weeke ut patet p[er] libr[um]	15	11	1

September 3 1641

Item to Palmer* for broomes & mopps	0	5	0

457 This was probably a card game.
458 See n. 450 above.

Item for a p[aire] of shoes & mendinge Rich[ard] Cobbs* apprell[459]	0	11	9
Item for 4 doz hogsh[eads]† & 3 runlets & caskinge 4 hogsh[eads]† of sack	1	12	0
Item given Mr Cales[460] man Tower	0	2	6
Item to Mr Bridgemans* man venison	0	5	0
Item to Mr French[461] for 6 plate &c	0	6	6
Item for boathire & peares W[illiam] Duckett*	0	2	0
Item for 3 bush[els]† of oates for c[oach] horses	0	0	0
Item for broomes for the stable	0	1	0
Item spent in the kitchen this weeke ut patet p[er] libr[um]	14	4	7
Some total of this fortnight	34	16	7

Septemb[er] 10 1641

Inprimis given to Mr Pigeons* man of the wardrobe at the Tower	0	5	0
Item for boathires & letters Mr Snaith*[462]	0	2	0
Item given to Mr Pigeons* maide ^grapes[463]	0	1	0
Item for a bottle of ink & paper W[illiam] Duckett*	0	0	10
Item given for peares & peches	0	2	0
Item given to Dr Merricks* man	0	2	6
Item litrage & bringing wood & coale to the Tower	0	17	6
Item for letters	0	0	3
Item given to M[is]tr[es]s Laniers[464] sonne ^grapes[465]	0	10	0
Item for boathires W[illiam] Duckett*	0	1	6
Item for 4 bush[els]† of oates for the c[oach] horses	0	6	4
Item for 4 bush[els]† of oates for the geldings	0	6	4
Item spent in the kitchen this weeke ut patet p[er] libr[um]	10	5	4

459 This is the first entry entered in the accounts by Walter Dobson*, who took over as steward on the death of Adam Torless*.

460 This is the sole entry in the accounts for 'Mr Cale', whose identity remains elusive, but who may have been the same 'Mr Cale' who was resident in the parish of St Mary-le-Bow, Cheapside, in 1638.

461 This is the sole entry in the accounts for 'Mr French', whose identity remains elusive. One 'Mr French' was recommended by George Abbot, Laud's predecessor, as master of Sutton's Hospital in Feb. 1625; *CSPD 1623–5*, p. 467, no. 22h.

462 The marginal note alongside this entry, in own Laud's hand, reads 'insert stewards death'.

463 This insertion is in Laud's own hand

464 This is the sole entry in the accounts for 'Mistress Laniers sonne'. Mistress Lanier herself may have been the wife of Nicholas Lanier (d. 1646), resident in the parish of St-Martin-in-the-Fields, London. An alternative identity is that she was Elizabeth Lanier, the wife of Nicholas Lanier (d. 1588–1666), court musician and art dealer. However, as there were no known children from this marriage, this makes the latter identity less plausible; Michael Wilson, 'Lanier, Nicholas (*bap.* 1588, *d.* 1666)', *ODNB*.

465 This insertion is in Laud's own hand.

Septemb[er] 17

Item for 2 bush[els]† of oates for c[oach] horses	0	3	2
Item for 6 bush[els]† of oates for geldings	0	9	6
Item spent in the kitchen this weeke ut patet p[er] libr[um]	6	5	2
Some total of this fortnight	19	18	5

For this quarter

Item p[ay]d to the brewer of Putney for 2 hogsh[eads]† of xiij^{s} & 67 hogsh[eads]† of vj^{s} beare layd in this q[ua]rter	31	7	0
Item to the brewer at the Tower for [...] barr of vii^{s} & [...] barr of vj^{s} beare layd in ynned by W: Duckett* W: Cant[466]			
Item to M[is]tr[es]s Whaly* for the rent of the slaughterhouse this q[ua]rter	0	12	6
Item to the laundresse for ashes, soape starch besides other wages given by her	4	10	0
Item to Abbott* the sadler ut patet p[er] bill	1	15	2
Item to Morris* the farrier for shoeing, bleeding and drenching of geldings &c ut patet	3	5	10
Item to Comfort* the smith of Croydon for shoeing bleeding &c ut patet	1	10	7
Item to Tho[mas] Sadler* for apprell for your Grace ut patet p[er] bill	2	18	4
Item to Haycock* yr Gr[aces] bargeman for reeds	0	5	6

[fo. 158r]

Item to the park keeper at Croydon for mending the hedges there &c 8 dayes work	0	8	0
Item for 5 loades of straw layd in this q[ua]rter	2	10	0
Item for your Graces servants at Lambeth house their wages this halfe yeare ut patet	55	16	8
Item spent this q[ua]rter, 15 bush[els]† of oates for poultry at Lambeth & Tower, whairof 9 bush[els]† were bought at xx^{d} p[er] bush[el]†	0	14	3
Some total of this fortnight for this quarter	120	12	3
Some total of this third quarters expenses & layings out cometh to	558	0	7

Hitherto this book payed W: Cant

466 This insertion is in Laud's own hand.

Fourth quarter beginning Septemb[er] 24 1641[467]

Inprimis for 2 bush[els]† of oates for the c[oach] horses at j^{s} vij^{d} p[er] bush[el]†	0	3	2
Item for 5 bush[els]† of oates for the geldings	0	7	11
Item 1 bush[els]† for poultry of the same	0	1	7
Item spent in the kitchen this weeke ut patet per libr[um]	5	12	1

October 1 1641

Item to Palmer* for broomes & mopps sent to the Tower	0	7	0
Item given the groome for clensing the motes from woods	0	1	6
Item for 2 bush[els]† of oates for c[oach] horses	0	3	2
Item for 4 bush[els]† for the geldings	0	6	4
Item for 1 bush[el]† of oates for poultry	0	1	7
Item spent in the kitchen this weeke ut patet p[er] libr[um]	5	11	8
Some total of this fortnight	12	16	0

October 8 1641

Inprimis the gardners bill at Lambeth	0	2	6
Item for 2 bush[els]† of oates for the c[oach] horses	0	3	2
Item for 4 bush[els]† for the geldings	0	6	4
Item 2 bush[els]† for the poultry at the Tower &c	0	3	2
Item spent in the kitchen this weeke ut patet p[er] libr[um]	5	11	10

October 15 1641

Item to Edw[ard] Nutt* for his charges bringing 51 Kent sheepe out of Kent ut patet p[er] bill	2	15	4
Thus far payd and remains in my hands 25 Octob[er] 1641 the some of CCCx^{l} vj^{s} iiij^{d}			
Ita e/t Walt[er] Dobson*			
Item for 2 bush[els]† of oates for c[oach] horses bought at j^{s} vij^{d} the bush[el]†	0	3	2
Item 5 bush[els]† for geldings whereof 2 bush[els]† is at j^{s} vij^{d} the other 3 at j^{s} vj^{d} in total	0	8	5
Item for 2 new shoes & 6 removes for c[oach] horses	0	2	2
Item 12 broomes for the stables	0	2	0

467 On 23 Sept., Adam Torless* – Laud's 'ancient, loving and faithful servant' – died after forty-two years' service for the archbishop. Laud recorded his 'great loss and grief' in his diary. The post was immediately filled by Walter Dobson*; *WWL*, III, 242.

Item spent in the kitchen this weeke ut patet p[er] libr[um]	5	14	6
Some total of this fortnight	15	14	4

[fo. 159r]
October 22 1641[468]

Inprimis for 2 bush[els]† of oates for c[oach] horses at j^{s} vi^{d} p[er] bush[el]† bought	0	3	6
Item for 5 bush[els]† of the same for geldings	0	8	9
Item for 2 bush[els]† of the same for poultry	0	3	6
Item spent in the kitchen this weeke ut patet p[er] libr[um]	5	6	11

October 29 1641

Inprimis p[ay]d for the Armourer Foster* his halfe yeares wages due at Mich[ael]mas past not afore sett down	3	6	8
Item given to Haycock* for his man by yr Graces direction	1	0	0
Item for a baskett to send bread to the Tower	0	2	0
Item for a sack for salt	0	2	4
Item for a buckett & a bowle for the baking use	0	2	0
Item 2 bush[els]† of oates for the c[oach] horses bought at j^{s} ix^{d} the bush[el]†	0	3	6
Item 5 bush[els]† of the same for the geldings	0	8	9
Item 2 bush[els]† of the same for the poultry	0	3	6
Item spent in the kitchen this weeke ut patet p[er] libr[um]	5	12	11
Some total of this fortnight	17	4	4
Payd & now remains in my hands Walt[er] Dobson*	286	10	0

November 5 1641

Inprimis p[ay]d to your Grace of the foresaid 286^{l} 10^{s} the some of fiftie pounds being p[ar]t of Mr Sumners* money for woodsale this yeare	50	0	0
Item p[ay]d to Knight* for mending the wharfe by Stangate & for nailes & spikes	0	3	0
Item for 2 bush[els]† of oates for c[oach] horses bought at j^{s} ix^{d} the bush[el]†	0	3	6
Item for 5 bush[els]† of the same for geldings	0	8	9

468 On 23 Oct., Laud's archiepiscopal jurisdiction was sequestered and he was thereafter prohibited from making any ecclesiastical appointments without first acquainting parliament with and seeking parliamentary approval for them; *WWL*, III, 242.

Item for 2 bush[els]† of the same for poultry	0	3	6
Item spent in the kitchen this weeke ut patet p[er] librum]	5	15	4

November 12 1641

Item paid for bringing 5 skeenes† from Croydon	0	1	0
Item for 2 bush[els]† of oates for c[oach] horses bought at j^s ix^d the bush[el]†	0	3	6
Item for 5 bush[els]† of the same for geldings	0	8	9
Item for 3 bush[els]† of the same for poultry	0	5	3
Item spent in the kitchen this weeke ut patet per Libra	5	16	8
Some total of this fortnight	63	9	3

Hitherto payd & remaines in my hands 223–0–9

November 19 1641

Inprimis for a doe from the Lo[rd] B[isho]p of Winton* 19 Novemb[er]	0	10	0
Item given to the baker at Lambeth for St Clements night[469]	0	10	0
Item p[ay]d for mending Mr Rich[ard] Cobb* windows of his chamber	0	0	8
Item for 2 bush[els]† of oates for 5 c[oach] horses bought at 1^s 9^d the bush[el]†	0	3	6
Item for 5 bush[els]† of the same for the geldings	0	8	9
Item for 3 bush[els]† of the same for the poultry	0	3	6

[Unfoliated page]

Item spent in the kitchen this weeke ut patet p[er] librum]	5	11	2

Decemb[er] 3 1641

Item p[ay]d to Mr Dell* for boathires &c since Mr Stewards death	0	10	0
Item to Palmer* for broomes & mopps	0	5	2
Item for 2 bush[els]† of oates for c[oach] horses bought at xxj^d the bush[el]†	0	3	6
Item for 5 bush[els]† of the same for geldings	0	8	9
Item for 1 bush[el]† of the same oates for colts	0	1	9
Item for 2 bush[els]† of the same oates for poultry	0	3	6
Item for 8 new shoes for the geldings	0	4	8
Item spent in the kitchen this weeke ut patet p[er] libr[um	7	0	7
Some total of this fortnight	16	5	6

Hitherto p[ay]d & remains in my hands 206–15–3

469 The archiepiscopal household continued its annual celebration of St Clement's night, despite the imprisonment of the head of the household. See n. 80 above.

Decemb[er] 10 1641

Inprimis for 2 bush[els]† of oates for c[oach] horses bought xxj^d the bush[el]†	0	3	6
Item for 5 bush[els]† of the same for the geldings	0	8	9
Item for 2 bush[els]† of the same oates for the poultry at Lambeth	0	3	6
Item for one bush[el]† for the swans	0	1	9
Item spent in the kitchen this weeke ut patet p[er] libr[um]	5	9	9

Decemb[er] 17 1641

Item p[ay]d the gardner at Lambeth his bill for nailes &c to tack up 5 vines & other trees	0	2	8
Item carrying out 1 hogsh[eads]† of beare to the bonfyre 5th Novemb[er]	0	0	6
Item for 2 bush[els]† of oates for c[oach] horses bought at 1s 9d the bush[el]†	0	3	6
Item for 5 bush[els]† of the same for geldings	0	8	9
Item for 1 bush[el]† of the same for colts	0	1	9
Item for 2 bush[els]† for 5 poultry at Lambeth bought as aforesayd	0	3	6
Item spent in the kitchen this weeke ut patet p[er] libr[um]	5	19	5
Some total of this fortnight	13	7	4

Thus far all payd and remaines in my hands the some of 193 -7 -11
Walt[er] Dobson*

December 24 1641

Inprimis for 6 sugarloaves from Mr Harfleet*	0	5	0
Item to Palmer* for broomes	0	2	6
Item for 2 bush[els]† of oates for c[oach] horses bought at js viijd the bush[el]†	0	3	5
Item for 5 bush[els]† of the same for gelds	0	8	6
Item for 2 bush[els]† of the same for poultry at Lambeth	0	3	5
Item for 1 bush[el]† of the same oates for swans	0	1	8
Item for 4 removes & for c[oach] horses	0	0	8
Item spent in the kitchen this weeke ut patet p[er] libr[um]	5	11	5

For this quarter

Item p[ay]d to the brewer for 25 hogsh[eads]† of vjs beare layd in this q[ua]rter	11	5	0

[fo. 160r]

Item p[ay]d to Mr Whaley* for the rent of chambers by the slaughterhouse this q[ua]rter	0	12	6

Item p[ay]d the laundresse for ashes soape & starch this quaerter besides wages	2	10	0
Item to the farrier Morris* for shoeinge & drenchinge horses &c at Lambeth	1	7	4
Item p[ay]d to Comfort* the smith at Croydon for shoeinge &c of gelds & mares there ut patet	0	19	10
Item to Northop bricklayer at Croydon for worke at the parke & pallace there ut patet	0	12	1
Item p[ay]d the park keeper at Croydon his wages for this q[ua]rter	5	0	0
Item for 4 loads of straw layd in this q[ua]rter	2	0	0
Item for 41 doz of candles taken in at iiij^{s} viij^{d} the doz	9	11	4
Item to Tho[mas] Sadler* the taylor for your Grace ut patet p[er] bill	1	14	6
Item to him more for aprell for Richard Cobb* ut patet	7	12	6
Item p[ay]d more to him for 20 wastcotts for 20 poore women at Lambeth	5	4	8
Item p[ay]d the laundresse for hooping the tubbs mending of pales	0	3	0
Item for 8 bush[els]† of oates bought & spent at the park upon poultry there ut patet	0	13	4
Item for mendinge the hedges at the parke xiij dayes	0	13	0
Item to Holland* bringing apples from Croydon	0	1	0
Item p[ay]d to Mr Watts* for a new net & for other worke done at Croydon and for killing moles there xxv^{s} for the yeare past ut patet p[er] bill	6	7	6
Some total of this weeke and for the quarter is	83	5	9

Some total of this 4th quarters expenses and layings out cometh to j^{c} lxxij^{l} ij^{s} vj^{d}

Some total of this years expenses and layings out cometh to j^{m} vij^{c} lxxx^{l} xj^{s} ij^{d}
Hitherto is all accompted for and payd, so remaines in my hands the some of 110–2–2

Walt[er] Dobson*

[fo. 161r]
Incipit Annus
December 24 1641
First quarter

Inprimis given to the xiij prisons against xxmas	3	0	0
Item give to the poore of Lambeth against xxmas	20	0	0
Item given then to the poore of Croydon	5	0	0
Item given to old Giles King* from your Grace	1	0	0
Item given to the poore woman in the kitchen at Lambeth	0	10	0
Item for fowle from Doctor Sterne*	0	6	0
Item for 2 sugar loaves from Mr Creswell*, Proctor of the Arches	0	2	6
Item for 2 bush[els]† of oates for coach horses bought at xx^{d} the bush[el]†	0	3	5

Item for 5 bush[els]† of the same oates for geldings	0	8	6
Item for 1 bush[el]† of the same oates for colts	0	1	8
Item for 2 bush[els]† of the same for poultry at Lambeth	0	3	5
Item for 1 bush[el]† thereof for swans	0	1	8
Item spent in the kitchen this weeke ut patet p[er] libr[um]	7	19	11

31 Dec[ember] 1641

Item for the Kings N[ew] Years gift[470]	40	0	0
Item for the fees at the Jewell House and for a purse x^s^ in toto	4	5	0
Item given to the brewers mens box	0	10	0
Item to Mr Morris* the farriers mens box	0	3	6
Item for the weekly bills this yeare	1	0	0
Item for 2 bush[els]† of oates for c[oach] horse bought at xx^d^ the bush[el]†	0	3	5
Item for 5 bush[els]† of the same oates for gelds	0	8	6
Item for 2 bush[els]† of the same for poultry at Lambeth	0	3	5
Item for 1 bush[el]† thereof for swans at Lambeth	0	1	8
Item spent in the kitchen this weeke ut patet p[er] libr[um]	7	2	5
Some total of this fortnight	92	15	2

Januar[y] 7 1642

Inprimis for 3 grosse of trenchers†	0	2	6
Item for a flower bagg for the Tower	0	1	6
Item for pudding baggs	0	1	8
Item for 2 bush[els]† of oates for c[oach] horse bought at xx^d^ p[er] bush[el]†	0	3	5
Item for 5 bush[els]† of the same for geldings	0	8	6
Item for 1 bush[el]† thereof for coults	0	1	8
Item for 2 bush[els]† thereof for poultry at Lambeth	0	3	5
Item for 1 bush[el]† thereof for swans	0	1	8
Item spent in the kitchen this weeke ut patet p[er] libr[um]	5	13	4

Januar[y] 14 1642

Item for 2 bush[els]† of oates for c[oach] horses bought at xx^d^ p[er] bush[el]†	0	3	5

470 This is the last, known gift given by William Laud to Charles I. The date of the entry suggests that the gift's arrival at court probably coincided with the king's attempt to arrest five members of the House of Commons, on 4 Jan. 1642. The attempt on the five members, which failed catastrophically, escalated the political crisis which led to civil war in England later in the year. Laud would remain in the Tower until his execution on 10 Jan. 1645.

Item 5 bush[els]† of the same for geld[ing]s	0	8	6
Item 2 bush[els]† thereof for poultry at Lambeth	0	3	5
Item 1 bush[el]† thereof for swans	0	1	8
Item 6 removes c[oach] horses	0	1	0
Item 12 broomes for the stables	0	2	0

[fo. 162r]

Item spent in the kitchen this weeke ut patet p[er] libr[um]	5	10	2
Some total of this fortnight	13	8	8

Hitherto all accompted for and payd so remaines in my hands 3–18–11

Walt[er] Dobson*

Appendix I: Glossary of names

The following glossary of names includes every identifiable person whose name appears in the manuscript, as denoted with an asterisk in the edition. Each name is accompanied by all variant spellings occurring in the accounts, with the standard spelling in bold. The standard spelling is that which has been commonly adopted by modern scholars or that which occurs most frequently in sources coeval with the accounts. Where the standard spelling of a name does not occur in the manuscript – either because the name is spelt differently there or because the person is identified only by their title, official *rôle* or surname – it is placed in square brackets below. A brief biographical profile of each person is given beneath their name, detailing the most significant formal office and title held in the period broadly synchronous with the accounts, as well as any known association with Laud.

Abbot, [**Maurice**] / Morris (1565–1642), merchant and politician. A founder member – and later, governor – of the East India Company, Abbot was the younger brother of George Abbot, Laud's predecessor. Resident in Coleman Street, London – a parish dominated by puritans – Abbot held a number of civic offices during his career, acting as alderman for Coleman Street ward from 1631 and as mayor of London in 1638.[1]

Abbot / Abbott, [**William**] (fl. 1631–40), the saddler, who supplied the archbishop's stables with leather horse tack, including equipment such as bridles, reins, saddles and bits.[2]

Abell, [**William**] (*c.* 1584 – *c.* 1655), vintner and local politician. Abell was appointed an alderman of London in 1636 and became master of the Company of Vintners a year later. In 1637, Abell was pricked as sheriff of London and it was in this capacity that he gained notoriety for his *rôle* in the violent arrest of the puritan minister, Henry Burton.[3]

Alsbury / Alisbury / [**Aylesbury**], **Thomas** (*c.* 1580–1658), patron of mathematics and naval official. In 1625, Aylesbury was appointed surveyor-general and served as secretary to Buckingham during his tenure as lord high admiral. In addition to the office of master of requests, which he held from at least 1627, Aylesbury was commissioner for the Mint from 1635. In 1634, one of his daughters – Frances

1 Andrew Thrush, 'Abbot, Sir Maurice (1565–1642)', *ODNB*.
2 LPL, TG1, fo. 28v.
3 Dagmar Freist, 'Abell, William (*b. c.* 1584, *d.* in or after 1655)', *ODNB*.

– married Edward Hyde, later earl of Clarendon. Aylesbury was, therefore, great-grandfather to both Queen Mary (1662–94) and Queen Anne (1665–1714).[4]

[**Alsope**] / Alsopp, **John** (fl. 1639–45), a household servant. In his will, Laud bequeathed to Alsope one of his watches.[5]

Apslye, John – see Hippesley, John.

[**Arundel**] / Arundell, earl of – see Howard, Thomas.

Ashlye / [**Astley**], **Jacob** (1579–1652), royalist commander. Astley, who began his military career in the late 1590s, had active service in the Thirty Years' War, under both Christian IV of Denmark and Gustavus Adolphus of Sweden. Astley was recalled by Charles I in 1639 and commanded a regiment under the earl of Northumberland at the battle of Newburn in 1640. He joined the king at Nottingham in August 1642.[6]

Ashton / [**Aston**], **Thomas** (1600–46), courtier and politician. Aston's career was mostly devoted to local politics, although he had been appointed to the position of gentleman-extraordinary of the king's privy chamber by 1635, the year in which he was also made high sheriff of Cheshire, which gave him responsibility for the collection of ship money. In the early Long Parliament, Aston wrote a tract against the Laudian bishops.[7]

Attorney, **Mr** – see Bankes, John.

Aylett, [**Robert**] (*c.* 1582–1655), poet. In 1628, Aylett was appointed to the court of high commission by Laud, with specific responsibility for tackling puritanism and ensuring the implementation of Laudian reforms in Essex. He was appointed to the advisory *rôle* of master in chancery in the House of Lords in 1638. When Laud was impeached in February 1641, Aylett was named as one of his circle, although he continued to work in the House of Lords until 1649.[8]

Babb, [**Thomas**] (fl. 1635–9), painter. Babb carried out works at Lambeth, including painting the new organ installed in the palace chapel in November 1639, four years after he had renovated the old one. Babb was also employed at Croydon, painting the benches in the grounds.[9]

Badger, [**Richard**] (1585–1641), Laud's house-printer and related to him by

4 Colin Alsbury, 'Aylesbury, Sir Thomas, baronet (1579/80–1658)', *ODNB*.
5 *WWL*, IV, 444.
6 *CSPD 1638–9*, p. 436; Ian Roy, 'Astley, Jacob, first Baron Astley of Reading (1579–1652)', *ODNB*; *WWL*, VII, 514, 542.
7 Edward Vernon, 'Aston, Sir Thomas, first baronet (1600–1646)', *ODNB*.
8 Matthew Steggle, 'Aylett, Robert (*c.* 1582–1655)', *ODNB*.
9 *CSPD 1635*, p. 487, no. 9.

marriage. Badger's appointment as master printer was endorsed by Laud in March 1629 and he retained close associations with Laud's household until his death in 1641.[10]

[**Balfour**, **William**] (d. 1660), parliamentarian army officer. Balfour was lord lieutenant of the Tower of London from 1630 until late 1641 and, as such, was responsible for the Tower during Laud's first year of imprisonment.[11]

[**Bancroft**, **John**] (1574–1641), Church of England bishop. Bancroft, Laud's friend and ally, was promoted to the see of Oxford in 1632 at Laud's behest. Bancroft also held the vicarage of Cuddesden near Oxford and used the income from this living to fund the building of an episcopal palace in the parish, which Laud visited in 1636 *en route* to Oxford for the formal opening of the Canterbury quadrangle at St John's College.[12]

Bangor, bishop of – see Griffith, Edmund; Roberts, William.

Banister / [**Banastre**] / Bannister, **Robert** (d. 1649), local politician. Banastre was sheriff of Northamptonshire from 1637 and, in this capacity, collected ship money contributions for the county. Little is known of Banastre's connexions with Laud, but his restoration of the parish church at Passenham, which featured an altarwise, railed-in communion table, speaks to his sympathy to Laudianism.[13]

[**Bankes**, **John**] (1589–1644), judge. Appointed attorney general to Charles I in August 1634, Bankes was responsible for investigating legal precedents for prerogative fiscal initiatives, including ship money, and, in 1637, he also initiated, on the king's behalf, the legal suits in star chamber against Burton, Bastwick and Prynne. In January 1641, he was removed from this office to become chief justice of the common pleas, a post he held until his death.[14]

[**Bargrave**, **Isaac**] (*c.* 1586–1643), royal chaplain and dean of Canterbury. Bargrave was appointed chaplain to Prince Charles in 1622, a post in which he continued after Charles became king in 1625. The same year, Bargrave was admitted to the deanery of Canterbury cathedral, at the behest of Buckingham. A staunch supporter of the crown, Bargrave's moderation as dean brought him into conflict with Laud in 1635, when the archbishop insisted that French Huguenots were forced to conform to anglican ceremonial, against the wishes of the dean and chapter.[15]

---

10 Peter McCullough, 'Print, publication and religious politics in Caroline England', *HJ*, 51 (2008), 285–313.

11 Edward Furgol, 'Balfour, Sir William (d. 1660)', *ODNB*.

12 Nicholas Cranfield, 'Bancroft, John (1574–1641)', *ODNB*.

13 *CSPD 1637*, p. 40, no. 138, p. 53, no. 14; Fielding, 'Arminianism in the localities', p. 106; Fincham and Tyacke, *Altars restored*, pp. 260–1.

14 Christopher Brooks, 'Bankes, Sir John (1589–1644)', *ODNB*; *WWL*, IV, 105.

15 Sidney Lee, 'Bargrave, Isaac (*bap.* 1586, *d.* 1643)', rev. Stephen Bann, *ODNB*.

[**Barnard**, **Samuel**] (1610–42), vicar of Croydon during the 1630s, through whom Laud planned to found a hospital in Reading, if his estate on his death amounted to £3,000. 'Mistress Barnard', whose gifts appear in Laud's accounts, may well have been the wife of Samuel.[16]

[**Barrett**, **Edward**] (1581–1644), created Lord Barrett of Newburgh in the Scottish peerage in 1626; appointed chancellor of the exchequer from 1628; and chancellor of the duchy of Lancaster from 1629. Barrett sat on the privy council from 1628 until his death and was a member of court of high commission for Canterbury province from 1629 until 1641, when he was impeached by the Long Parliament as a privy councillor. Despite this, Barrett continued to act as assistant in the House of Lords.[17]

[**Barrington**, **Henry**] (fl. 1637), mayor of Colchester. Barrington, who was an active member of the godly community in Essex, was appointed mayor of Colchester in 1637, having previously been bailiff of the town. He came under fire in the same year, for his refusal to pay the Colchester ship money contribution.[18]

Bartlett / Bartley / [**Berkeley**, **Maurice**] / Morrice / Morris, (1599–1654). Berkeley was a Gloucestershire MP who refused to subscribe or implement the forced loan in 1626, facing a spell in Marshalsea prison as a consequence. A colonist and member of the Virginia Company from 1623, Berkeley also appeared before the high commission in the 1630s following financial difficulties. He became a royalist in the civil war.[19]

Bartley / [**Berkeley**, **Robert**] (1584–1656), judge. Berkeley sat as a judge on the king's bench from 1632 and was commissioner for ecclesiastical causes in the province of Canterbury from 1633. He is perhaps best known for his ruling in favour of the king on the legality of ship money during Hampden's case in 1637. Berkeley was arrested, imprisoned and impeached in February 1641, shortly before Laud was moved to the Tower. His 1643 trial resulted in a hefty fine, but he escaped further punishment, spending the remainder of his life in retirement in the country.[20]

Barton, [**Francis**] (fl. 1635), steward of the archbishop's manors in Kent. Barton, trained as a lawyer in the middle temple, was appointed in November 1635 and held the stewardship jointly with John Crane.[21]

Baskerfield / [**Baskerville**] / Baskervyle, Symon / **Simon** (*c.* 1574–1641), royal

---

16 *WWL*, III, 254.
17 Richard Wisker, 'Barrett, Edward, Lord Barrett of Newburgh (1581–1644/5)', *ODNB*.
18 *A history of the county of Essex*, IX, ed. Janet Cooper and Charles Elrington (London, 1994), pp. 374–81; John Walter, *Understanding popular violence in the English revolution – the Colchester plunderers* (Cambridge, 2004), p. 110.
19 www.historyofparliamentonline.org/volume/1604–1629/member/berkeley-maurice-1599–1654.
20 Sheila Doyle, 'Berkeley, Sir Robert (1584–1656)', *ODNB*.
21 LPL, TK16.

physician to both James I and Charles I. Baskerville, educated at Exeter College, Oxford, practised in the city before moving to London in the mid-1610s. He became a popular and wealthy physician, and Laud was one of his patients. He was knighted by the king at Oxford in August 1636.[22]

Bath and Wells, bishop of – see Piers, William.

Bathurst, [**Theodore**] (*c*. 1587–1652), Church of England clergyman. In his early career, Bathurst was a protégé of Lancelot Andrewes, Laud's mentor, obtaining several livings in the diocese of Ely after Andrewes's promotion to the bishopric in 1609. He was rector of Orton Waterville in Huntingdonshire from 1618 until his death.[23]

[**Baylie**, **Richard**] (*c*. 1585–1667), Church of England clergyman. In 1633, Baylie – related to Laud by marriage – was elected president of St John's College, Oxford, where he later implemented the Laudian statutes at the university as vice-chancellor in 1636 and 1637. Baylie, appointed to the deanery of Salisbury in 1635, also acted as domestic chaplain to the archbishop during the 1630s. He was sole executor of Laud's will, with responsibility for all the archbishop's surviving 'papers and paper-books'. Baylie may well have introduced Richard Badger to Laud.[24]

Beadell / Beadle / [**Bedell**], **Capell** (1602–43), politician. Bedell sat as MP for Huntingdon in the 1628 parliament and again in 1640. During the 1630s, he held a range of offices in local government, including sitting on the peace commission for Huntingdon and Northamptonshire. He was appointed gentleman of the privy chamber extraordinary in 1639.[25]

[**Becher**] / Beecher, **William** (*c*. 1580–1651), diplomat and clerk to the privy council. A client of Buckingham, through whom he was appointed council clerk in 1623, Becher's office involved him in many aspects of government business. Becher was clerk to several of the significant council sub-committees of which Laud was a member, including the treasury commission – established in March 1635 on the death of Richard Weston, lord treasurer – and the council committee for Irish affairs, through which he became associated with Richard Boyle, 1st earl of Cork.[26]

[**Beeston**, **Thomas**] (fl. 1638), mayor of Portsmouth in 1638.[27]

---

22 Thompson Cooper, 'Baskerville, Sir Simon (*bap.* 1574, *d.* 1641)', rev. Brian Nance, *ODNB*.

23 William Kelleher, 'Bathurst, Theodore (*c.*1587–1652)', *ODNB*; *WWL*, III, 286.

24 Andrew Ducarel, *The history and antiquities of the archiepiscopal palace of Lambeth: from its foundation to the present time* (London, 1885), Appendix, p. 21; Andrew Hegarty, 'Baylie, Richard (1585/6?–1667)', *ODNB*.

25 www.historyofparliamentonline.org/volume/1604–1629/member/bedell-sir-capell-1602–1643.

26 Sabrina Baron, 'Becher, Sir William (*bap.* 1580, *d.* 1651), *ODNB*.

27 *CSPD 1637–8*, p. 469, no. 66.

[**Belhaven**] / Bellhaven, Lord – see Douglas, Robert.

Bemboe, Mr (fl. 1637–40). Little is known of 'Mr Bemboe', who was resident in St Paul's churchyard within the parish of St Faith's under St Paul during the 1630s. He was a neighbour of 'Mr Bostock' and 'John Egglefield', who also gave gifts to Laud.[28]

[**Bertie, Robert**] (1582–1642), 1st earl of Lindsey, privy councillor and naval officer. Having served under Buckingham in the naval escapades of the late 1620s, Lindsey was appointed lord great chamberlain in 1626 and lord lieutenant of Lincolnshire in 1629. He returned to naval affairs in 1635, when he was made admiral of the first ship money fleet; he was appointed governor of Berwick in 1639 and briefly lieutenant-general of the king's army in August 1642. He died as a result of a wound sustained at Edgehill in October 1642.[29]

Bird / [**Byrd**, **Andrew**] (b. *c*. 1618), son of Dr Andrew Byrd, physician and schoolmaster. Byrd's father, appointed master of Reading School in 1610, died in November 1636. Little is known of the younger Byrd, although when writing to the corporation of Reading shortly afterward the death of Byrd senior, Laud commended the 'great deal of pains … and great deal of service' done to the town by him.[30]

Birkenhead, **John** (1617–79), journalist and poet. Birkenhead first came to Laud's attention during the royal visit to Oxford in 1636, when Birkenhead carried out scribal duties. He was employed as a scribe at Lambeth in the late 1630s, but returned to Oxford after the archbishop's imprisonment in 1641. It was here that, in 1643, Birkenhead launched *Mercurius Aulicus*, the royalist newsbook. In late 1644, Laud wrote to Birkenhead asking him to ensure that his bequests were distributed after his death.[31]

Bohemia, queen of – see Stuart, Elizabeth.

[**Borough**] / Burroughs, **John** (d. 1643), antiquary, herald and keeper of the ancient records in the Tower of London. Born in Kent, Borough was consulted by crown servants on all matters of historical precedent, including ship money and other Caroline fiscal measures.[32]

Bostock, Mr (fl. 1636–8), resident in the parish of St Faith's under St Paul during the 1630s. Bostock was a neighbour of 'Mr Bemboe' and 'Mr Egglefield', who also gave gifts to Laud.[33]

---

28 'Inhabitants of London in 1638: St. Faith's', in *The inhabitants of London in 1638*, ed. Dale, p. 57.

29 Andrew Thrush, 'Bertie, Robert, first earl of Lindsey (1582–1642)', *ODNB*.

30 *Original letters and other documents relating to the benefactions of William Laud, archbishop of Canterbury to the county of Berks*, ed. John Bruce (London, 1841), p. 8; *WWL*, VI, 470.

31 LPL, Comm. I/145; Charles Doyle, 'Birkenhead, Sir John (1617–1679), *ODNB*.

32 Sabrina Baron, 'Borough, Sir John (*d.* 1643)', *ODNB*.

33 'Inhabitants of London in 1638: St. Faith's', in *The inhabitants of London in 1638*, ed. Dale, p. 57.

Boswell, [**Thomas**] (fl. 1642), member of the Kentish gentry, knighted by Charles I in May 1642, just before the civil war.[34]

[**Boughton**, **Stephen**] (b. 1573), Church of England clergyman. Little is known of Boughton, who was appointed sub-dean of the chapel royal in 1623.[35]

[**Bowle**, **John**] (d. 1637), Church of England bishop. Appointed to the bishopric of Rochester in early 1630, Bowle kept a relatively low profile during the 1630s, although he did preach at George Abbot's funeral in September 1633. He died in October 1637 and was succeeded by John Warner.

[**Boyle**, **Richard**] (1566–1643), 1st earl of Cork, lord justice and lord treasurer of Ireland. Of Kentish origins, Boyle rose to prominence in Ireland as a magnate and politician, chiefly through investment in Protestant plantation and other mercantile projects, but his power was opposed by Wentworth, the lord deputy, after 1633. In 1634, Laud demanded the removal of the earl's family tomb from the east end of St Patrick's cathedral, Dublin, to make way for an altarwise communion table.[36]

Boys, **Edward** (1579–1646), Kentish MP and magistrate. Based in Nonington, Kent, Boys was MP for Sandwich in 1626, a Kent magistrate from 1632 and returned for Dover in both the Short and Long Parliaments. After Laud's death and the abolition of the episcopate, Boys was responsible for surveying, on behalf of parliament, all former archiepiscopal lands.[37]

[**Bramhall**, **John**] (*c*. 1594–1663), Church of Ireland bishop. A Yorkshireman by birth, Bramhall's enthusiasm for the forms of the English church gained him the support of Laud and Sir Thomas Wentworth, whom he accompanied to Dublin in 1633 as chaplain. Bramhall was promoted to the bishopric of Derry a year later and was instrumental in assisting Wentworth in the material and financial reconstruction of the Irish church. His regular correspondence with Laud kept the archbishop well informed of events across the Irish Sea. He was appointed archbishop of Armagh in 1660.[38]

[**Bramston**, **John**] (1577–1654), judge. Appointed lord chief justice of the king's bench in April 1635, Bramston soon became involved in the political and judicial controversies surrounding the levying of ship money. Bramston was one of the seven judges whose votes confirmed the king's right to implement the levy in 1637. He remained in post until the early Long Parliament when he was deprived of his office, but was reappointed in 1643.[39]

---

34 *Knights of England*, II, 213.
35 Rimbault, *The old cheque book or book of remembrance of the chapel royal*, pp. 12, 48.
36 *WWL*, VII, 116.
37 LPL, Comm XIIa/23, fo. 242.
38 John McCafferty, 'Bramhall, John (*bap*. 1594, *d*. 1663)', *ODNB*.
39 Christopher Brooks, 'Bramston, Sir John, the elder (1577–1654)', *ODNB*.

Bray / Braye, [**William.**] (d. 1643), Church of England clergyman. Bray, who was appointed chaplain to Laud in the late 1620s, held the prebendary of St Paul's from 1632 and was made canon of Canterbury in 1637. Bray's *rôle* as licenser brought him before the House of Lords in early 1641.[40]

Brent, **Nathaniel** (*c.* 1573–1652), vicar-general to George Abbot from 1629 and to Laud from 1633. Laud came to trust Brent, whom he described in 1636 as 'an honest man'. Relations soured in 1638, however, during Laud's visitation of Merton College, Oxford, where Brent was warden.[41]

Brichain / [**Brechin**], bishop of – see Whitford, Walter

[**Bridgeman**, **John**] (*c.* 1577–1652), Church of England. Appointed to the bishopric of Chester in 1619, Bridgeman showed an early inclination for the preferences for the 'beauty of holiness' which became characteristic of Laudian policy in England during the 1630s.[42]

Bridgeman, [**Orlando**] (1609–74), son of John Bridgeman, bishop of Chester. Bridgeman, a staunch royalist and supporter of Laudian innovations in the church, nevertheless survived the civil war and Interregnum to become lord chief baron of the exchequer, chief justice of the common pleas in 1660, famously presiding over the trials of the regicides and officiating during Clarendon's downfall in 1667.[43]

Bristol, bishop of – see Skinner, Robert.

Brown / **Browne**, **Mr** (fl.1633–1640), carpenter, who provided woodwork for Lambeth Palace, including the renovations to the palace chapel when Laud became archbishop in September 1633 and refurbishment of Laud's barge in 1639. Browne also carried out joinery at St John's College, Oxford.[44]

Browne, **Richard** (fl. 1635–42), household servant, who worked in the granary at Lambeth Palace.

Bryan, [**William**] (fl. 1635–42), household servant, who acted as locksmith at Lambeth and Croydon.

Buckeridge, [**Anthony**] (1596 – *c.* 1669), *alumnus* of St John's College, Oxford, and later resident of Lambeth. Buckeridge was the nephew of John Buckeridge, bishop of Ely (*c.* 1562–1631), formerly Laud's tutor at St John's. It is likely that entries in the

---

40 Ducarel, *Archiepiscopal palace*, Appendix, p. 21; Arnold Hunt, 'Bray, William (*d.* 1643)', *ODNB*; *WWL*, III, 241.

41 Andrew Hegarty, 'Brent, Sir Nathanael (1573/4–1652)', *ODNB*; *WWL*, VII, 268.

42 Peter Yorke, 'Bridgeman, John (*bap.* 1577, *d.* 1652)', *ODNB*.

43 Howard Nenner, 'Bridgeman, Sir Orlando, first baronet (1609–1674)', *ODNB*; *WWL*, IV, 148.

44 TNA, SP 16/246, fo. 169.

accounts for 'Mistress Buckeridge' relate to Anthony Buckeridge's wife, Constance, whom he married in 1626, rather than John Buckeridge's mother, Elizabeth, who was still alive in 1631, but who was probably dead by the mid-1630s.[45]

Buckingham, duchess of – see MacDonnell, Katherine (née Manners)

[**Buckner**] / Bucknor, **Thomas** (1591–1644), Church of England clergyman. Buckner, who was chaplain to George Abbot, held the living of Chevening in Kent from 1633 until his death in 1644. He was also prebend of Winchester from 1635. In 1633, he was brought before the court of high commission for his *rôle* in licensing William Prynne's *Histriomastix.* Despite Laud having 'a great mind to spare him', Buckner was fined £50 and imprisoned temporarily.[46]

Burges / [**Burgess**], **Elizeus** (1595–1652), Church of England clergyman. Burgess was an *alumnus* of Laud's *alma mater* St John's College, Oxford, and, as archdeacon of Rochester (1625–46) was responsible for settling the deanery of Malling which was 'very much out of order'.[47]

Burton, [**Edward**] (b. 1596), Church of England clergyman. Burton was appointed chaplain to Charles I in the late 1620s and held the livings of Sedlescombe and Westham in Sussex from 1628 and 1638 respectively.[48]

Burton, **Henry** (fl. 1603–40), created knight of the bath in 1603, Burton was a neighbour of Laud when at Croydon Palace, after having purchased land in Carshalton, Surrey, in late 1637 or early 1638.[49]

Burwood, [**John**] (fl. 1635–40), carpenter. Burwood, described as 'late carpenter to the Great James', a vessel in Charles I's navy, carried out carpentry services at both Lambeth and Croydon, including installing a new organ in Lambeth chapel in November 1639.[50]

Caesar, **Charles** (1590–1642), judge. During his distinguished legal career, Caesar focused mainly on ecclesiastical and admiralty law. He was a member of the court of high commission under George Abbot, Laud's predecessor, after whose suspension in 1627, Caesar was a commissioner appointed to exercise his ecclesiastical jurisdiction. Caesar held the office of master of the rolls from 1639 until his death, a post previously held by his father, Sir Julius.[51]

---

45 *Alumni oxonienses*, I, 204; *Biographical Register of SJC*, p. 25; Peter McCullough, 'Buckeridge, John (*d.* 1631)', *ODNB.*

46 Cyndia Clegg, *Press censorship in Caroline England* (Cambridge, 2008), p. 142; *WWL*, VI, 234.

47 *Visitation articles and injunctions of the early Stuart church,* ed. Kenneth Fincham (Church of England Record Society, I, 1998), pp. 74–9; *WWL*, V, 319.

48 *Alumni oxonienses*, I, 217.

49 *CSPD 1637–8*, p. 119, no. 167; *Knights of England*, I, 156.

50 *Calender of state papers colonial, East Indies and Persia 1630–1634*, VIII, ed. Noel Sainsbury (London, 1892), 533.

51 L. M. Hill, 'Caesar, Sir Charles (1590–1642)', *ODNB.*

Canterbury, archdeacon of – see Kingsley, William.

Canterbury, [**deane**] of – see Bargrave, Isaac.

Capell, **Arthur** (1585–1653), gentleman of the privy chamber extraordinary. Capell, who stood as MP for Hertfordshire in 1624, was retained in Charles I's household from 1625, having also served under James I. In 1636, following a duel with Sir Thomas Leventhorpe, in which the latter was killed, Capell was found guilty of manslaughter but pardoned subsequently by the king.[52]

[**Carew**] / Carey / Cary / Carye, **Nicholas** (*c.* 1567–1644). Born Nicholas Throckmorton, Carew changed his name in the early 1600s, after having been adopted by his uncle, Sir Francis Carew. As MP for Surrey from 1621, Nicholas Carew served as collector for both the 1622 palatinate benevolence and the 1626 forced loan. In 1642, he held a commission of array for the king.[53]

Carlisle, countess of – see Hay, Lucy.

[**Carteret**] / Cartwright, [**George**] (*c.* 1610–80), naval officer and administrator. Carteret, who is referred to as 'Captain Cartwright' in the accounts, held the post of comptroller of the navy in the late 1630s. In this capacity, he helped to fortify the Channel Islands for the king during the civil war and was knighted in 1645. After the Restoration, Carteret became a privy councillor and treasurer of the navy.[54]

Cartwright, [**William**] (1611–43), Church of England clergyman and playwright. Cartwright, one of whose plays, *The royal slave*, was performed at Christ Church College, Oxford, during the royal visit in August 1636, was mooted to be in the running for the post of licensor of the press at the university in 1637. He was never appointed, but Laud nevertheless saw him as 'so well deserving for this or a better place'.[55]

[**Cavendish, Elizabeth**] (1599–1643), countess of Newcastle. Little is known of Elizabeth, who married William Cavendish, in 1618. She certainly helped to entertain Charles I at Welbeck, one of the Cavendish family homes, en route to Edinburgh for his Scottish coronation in the summer of 1633.[56]

[**Cavendish**, **William**] (1593–1676), 1st earl of Newcastle and later royalist army officer. Cavendish, an *alumnus* of St John's College, Oxford, enjoyed a long friendship with Laud. The earl's equestrian interest and prowess was well known

---

52 www.historyofparliamentonline.org/volume/1604–1629/member/capell-sir-arthur-1585–1653.

53 www.historyofparliamentonline.org/volume/1604–1629/member/carew-sir-nicholas-1567–1644.

54 *CSPD 1639–40*, p. 325, no. 100; Charles Firth, 'Carteret, Sir George, first baronet (c. 1610?–1680)', rev. C. S. Knighton, *ODNB*.

55 Dennis Flynn, 'Cartwright, William (1611–1643), *ODNB*; *WWL*, V, p. 170.

56 Lynn Hulse, 'Cavendish, William, first duke of Newcastle upon Tyne (*bap.* 1593, *d.* 1676)', *ODNB*.

and the horses that he gave to Laud as gifts are recorded in the accounts. He was bequeathed the archbishop's 'best diamond ring, worth 140*l*' in his will.[57]

[**Cecil**, **Edward**] (1572–1638), politician. A nephew of Sir Robert Cecil, principal minister to James I, Cecil's association with the disastrous naval raid on Cadiz of 1626, led by the duke of Buckingham, clouded the later years of his career, much of which was spent as lord lieutenant of Surrey (from 1626) and as privy councillor (from 1628). A committed Protestant, Cecil's only documented involvement with Laud came in 1637, when the lease for the rectory of Wimbledon was due for renewal.[58]

[**Cecil**, **William**] (1591–1668), 2nd earl of Salisbury and the son of Robert Cecil, secretary of state to Elizabeth I and lord treasurer under James I. Salisbury was lord lieutenant of Hertfordshire from 1612, and privy councillor from 1626. He was appointed captain of the king's gentleman pensioners in 1635, but most of his time from the mid-1630s onwards was spent in improving his estates. Like Laud, he employed John Tradescant to design his gardens.[59]

Chaffin / [**Chafin**, **Thomas**] (d. 1648), Church of England clergyman. Appointed prebendary of Warthacwm, Llandaff in 1630, little is known of Chafin's relationship with Laud.[60]

[**Chamberlain**] / Chamberlayne / Chamberlyn, Lord – see Herbert, Philip.

Chester, bishop of – see Bridgeman, John.

Chichester, bishop of – see Mountague, Richard; Duppa, Brian.

chief justice, lord – see Bramston, John.

[**Cholmley**] / Chomlye, [**Hugh**] (1600–57), politician and later royalist army officer. Cholmley represented Scarborough in all the parliaments from 1621 until 1643. Following a bitter falling-out with Thomas Wentworth, lord deputy of Ireland, over Cholmley's refusal to participate in the first Bishops' War in 1639, Cholmley joined the parliamentary opposition to the king. In 1643, however, he saw the error of his ways and became a royalist.[61]

57 ibid; *WWL*, IV, p. 443.
58 Roger Lockyer, 'Cecil, Edward, viscount Wimbledon (1572–1638)', *ODNB*; *WWL*, VI, 488.
59 George Owen, 'Cecil, William, second earl of Salisbury (1591–1668)', *ODNB*.
60 *Alumni oxoniensis*, I, 255; *Fasti*, II, 269; *A survey of the cathedral church of Landaff*, ed. Browne Willis (London, 1719), p. 91.
61 www.historyofparliamentonline.org/volume/1604–1629/member/cholmley-hugh-1600–1657; Jack Binns, 'Cholmley, Sir Hugh, first baronet (1600–1657)', *ODNB*.

[**Cholmley**] / Chombley / Chomley / Chomly / Chomlye, [**Elizabeth**] (1600–55), wife of Sir Hugh Cholmley and daughter of Kentish MP, Sir Roger Twysden.

[**Chute**] / Chyte, **George** (d. 1649), resident of Lambeth and Stockwell. Little is known of Chute, although he may have had Kentish origins. In September 1629, Charles I purchased a property in Lambeth, 'wherein Sir George Chute hath lately dwelt'. Chute was certainly resident in Stockwell in 1638 and was buried in Lambeth church in 1649.[62]

Cleaveland / **Cleveland**, earl of – see Wentworth, Thomas.

[**Clinton**, **Theophilus**] (1600–67), 4th earl of Lincoln. Clinton was the 'most extreme' aristocratic opponent of the forced loan, involving himself in local meetings in Lincoln to obstruct the collection of the loan by royal commissioners, earning himself a stint in the Tower in March 1627. He spent relatively little time at court during the 1630s and emerged as an opponent of Charles I after 1640.[63]

Clitheroe / [**Clitherow**], **Christopher** (*c.* 1577–1641), merchant and politician. In the 1610s and 1620s, Clitherow was involved in the activities of the Ironmongers' Company, the Eastland Company, the Virginia Company and the Company of Merchant Adventurers, but his most prestigious appointment was held in the East India Company, to which he was appointed governor in 1638. Clitherow, who was knighted in January 1636, was also active in civic politics, being appointed lord mayor of London for 1635–6. A critic of Charles I, Clitherow has nevertheless been described as one of a group of London-based 'Arminian sympathisers'.[64]

Cobb, **John** (fl. 1635–45), a servant of the archiepiscopal household, was highly regarded by Laud. Cobb, who was probably the archbishop's organist, also took up an instrumental post in the chapel royal in 1638. Cobb was left the most valuable, material bequest to any servant in Laud's will – 'my organ that is at Croydon, my harp, my chest of viols and the harpsico in the parlour at Lambeth'. He was also left a significant lump sum of £50 – more than double the sum left to William Dell – suggesting his value as a household servant.[65]

Cobb, **Richard** (fl. 1635–45), a household servant and brother of John Cobb. Cobb attended Laud during his early imprisonment in the Tower, although he was not one of the two servants who remained with Laud throughout his incarceration. The archbishop's regard for Cobb is testified by his bequests of £50, a further annual sum

62 *CSPD 1629–31*, p. 48, no 11; Ducarel, *Archiepiscopal palace*, Appendix, p. 56; A. Pearman, 'The Chutes of Bethersden, Appledore and Hinxhill', *Archaologia Cantiana*, 18 (1889), 62.
63 Richard Cust, *Charles I and the aristocracy, 1625–1642* (Cambridge, 2013), pp. 51, 83.
64 Andrew Thrush, 'Clitherow, Sir Christopher (1577/8–1641), *ODNB*; Tyacke, *Anti-Calvinists*, p. 221.
65 Rimbault, *The old cheque book or book of remembrance of the chapel royal*, pp. 12, 48; *WWL*, IV, p. 446.

of £50, together with £100 from the lease of Winchester cathedral, on its renewal. Cobb was also promised a further £50 'if he deal truly with' Laud's estate'.[66]

[**Coke**, **John**] (1563–1644), politician. As secretary of state to Charles I from 1625 until 1640, Coke was in regular contact with Laud, whom he clearly saw as an ally. Having stood as MP for Cambridge in the 1626 and 1628 parliaments, Coke held a range of senior posts during the 1630s. During the royal visit to Oxford in 1636, Coke gave a lengthy oration praising Laud's achievements in the churches in all three of Charles I's kingdoms. The ageing secretary was forced to resign his post in early 1640, to be replaced by Sir Henry Vane.[67]

Colchester, mayor of – see Barrington, Henry.

[**Collins**] / Collyns, [**Samuel**] (1578–1651), regius professor of divinity at Cambridge from 1617. Collins undertook the beautification of King's College chapel during the 1630s, including adorning the communion table with candlesticks, crucifixes and tapers, and investing in a velvet communion cloth. By 1640 – and in the face of increasing criticism for his ceremonialism – Collins had begun to make remedial changes, moving the altar back to its former tablewise position and scaling down the adornments. Nevertheless, he was removed from office in 1644.[68]

Comfort, **Mr** (fl. 1635–41), the blacksmith and saddler, who provided farriage and leather horse tack at Croydon.

Company of Clarks – see Parish Clerks' Company.

[**Company of**] **Merchant Adventurers** – established in 1407 by royal charter, the Company was set up to govern the export of wool from England's flourishing cloth trade to the Low Countries. In 1629, the Company protested against Charles I's unparliamentary levy of tonnage and poundage, by refusing to ship cloth, although it was forced to raise loans to the king money to fund his campaigns against Scotland in 1639 and 1640.[69]

[**Company of**] **Merchant Taylors** – receiving its first royal charter in 1327, the Company served as an affiliation of artisan clothiers. Given Laud's background as the son of a Reading clothier, this organization was close to his heart. He became a freeman of the Company in 1632 and helped them appoint a headmaster, William Staple, in 1634.[70]

---

66 *WWL*, IV, 447–8.

67 Michael Young, 'Coke, Sir John (1563–1644)', *ODNB*; *WWL*, V, 126–32.

68 Nicholas Cranfield, 'Collins, Samuel (1576–1651)', *ODNB*.

69 Valerie Pearl, *London and the outbreak of the puritan revolution – city government and national politics 1625–1643* (Oxford, 1961), pp. 77, 101.

70 *Biographical register of SJC*, p. 141; *The further correspondence of William Laud*, ed. Fincham, p. 7 n. 7; *WWL*, VI, 367.

Company of Stationers – see Stationers' Company.

Company of Vintners – see Vintners' Company.

Confections, Seargeant / [**Sergeant**] – see Walthew, Robert.

Constable, [**William**], a carpenter who carried out works at Croydon. Constable, who had been retained by the household since at least 1631, enjoyed a long service under successive archbishops, being appointed bailiff of the manor of Croydon by William Juxon, Laud's successor, in November 1660.[71]

Conway, [**Edward**] (*c.* 1594–1655), 2nd Viscount Conway and 2nd Viscount Killultagh. Conway was, like Laud, a renowned bibliophile. He was appointed general of the horse at Newburn in 1640 and corresponded with Laud regularly throughout the second Bishops' War, whom he used to communicate to the king essential details about the campaign.[72]

Cork / Corke, earl of – see Boyle, Richard.

Cottington, [**Francis**] (1579–1652), diplomat, politician and courtier. A former client of Buckingham, Cottington was appointed chancellor of the exchequer in 1629 and clashed several times with Laud thereafter, including over the soap monopoly and the prosecution of John Williams, bishop of Lincoln. Despite his mutual animosity with Laud, Cottington remained an ally of Thomas Wentworth, lord deputy of Ireland, throughout the 1630s.[73]

[**Courten**] / Curtane, **William** (*c.* 1568–1636), merchant and financier. Courten, knighted by James I in 1622, was in the closing stages of his career by the mid-1630s. The final enterprise in which he was involved came in the form of a royal commission to challenge the East India Company's interests in Asia in early 1636. This ambitious project, which collapsed in 1638 having achieved very little and in which Courten, through illness, was unable actively to participate, probably hastened his demise, which came in May 1636.[74]

[**Coventry, Thomas**] (1578–1640), lawyer. Appointed to the post of lord keeper in 1625, Coventry was a client of Buckingham but, after his patron's assassination in 1628, while he remained in post, he took a more detached approach to court life in the 1630s. He died in office in January 1640.[75]

---

71 LPL, TG1, fos. 23v, 28v, TK31.

72 James Knowles, 'Conway, Edward, second Viscount Conway and second Viscount Killultagh (*bap.* 1594, *d.* 1655)', *ODNB*; *WWL*, VII, 601, 602, 604, 605–10.

73 Fiona Pogson, 'Cottington, Francis, first Baron Cottington (*c.* 1579–1652)', *ODNB*.

74 John Appleby, 'Courten, Sir William (*c.* 1568–1636)', *ODNB*; *Knights of England*, II, 179.

75 Richard Cust, 'Coventry, Thomas, first Baron Coventry (1578–1640), *ODNB*.

Craford / [**Crayford**], **Robert** (fl. 1624–39), knight. Little is known of Crayford, who originated from Kent, except that he was created knight bachelor by James I in July 1624.[76]

Crane, [**John**] (fl. 1635), steward of the archbishop's manors in Kent. Crane, a lawyer trained in Clifford's Inn, was appointed in November 1635. He held the stewardship jointly with Francis Barton.[77]

Cressall, Richard (fl. 1641–5), a household servant, who often arranged boathire for the archbishop's water-borne journeys. Cressall was bequeathed £10 in Laud's will.[78]

Creswell, Mr, little is known of Creswell, who is recorded as 'Proctor of the Arches' in the accounts in August 1641. At the same time, a 'Mr Creswell' was ordered by the Commons to be examined in the Lords as a witness in the case against Laud. Creswell was among the few people whose gifts continued beyond the archbishop's impeachment and imprisonment in February 1641.[79]

Crew / [**Crewe**], Randall / [**Randolph**] (*c.* 1559–1646), judge. Crewe, who sat as MP for Saltash in the 1614 parliament, was appointed chief justice of the king's bench in 1625. The following year, he was promptly dismissed by the king, after heading a delegation of judges who collectively refused to endorse the forced loan. Despite attempting to regain royal favour, even asking the royal favourite Buckingham to intervene on his behalf, Crewe spent most of the rest of his life in retirement.[80]

[**Crisp**] / Crispe, **Nicholas** (*c.* 1599–1666), merchant, alderman and sheriff of London, described by Laud in 1639 as 'a man that I have been long acquainted with, and is a forward servant of the king's to his utmost power'. Certainly, Laud and Crisp were already acquainted in 1629. Crisp received a knighthood in January 1640 for his services to the crown.[81]

Croft, [**Herbert**] (1603–91), Church of England clergyman. Croft, who benefited from Laud's patronage, was appointed chaplain to Algernon Percy, 10th earl of Northumberland during his Scottish campaign in 1638 and became a royal chaplain a year later. Croft, who was a staunch royalist, became bishop of Hereford in 1661.[82]

[**Croke**] / Crooke, [**Henry**] (*c.* 1598–1642), Church of England clergyman. Croke held the post of professor of rhetoric at Gresham College from 1619 to 1627. A year

---

76 *Knights of England*, II, 185.
77 LPL, TK16, fo. 695.
78 *WWL*, IV, 446.
79 *CJ*, II, 233.
80 www.historyofparliamentonline.org/volume/1604–1629/member/crewe-ranulphe-1559–1646; Wilfrid Prest, 'Crewe, Sir Randolph (*bap.* 1559, *d.* 1646)', *ODNB*.
81 Robert Ashton, 'Crisp, Sir Nicholas, first baronet (*c.* 1599–1666)', *ODNB*; *WWL*, VII, 25, 30, 567.
82 *Alumni oxonienses*, I, 351; William Marshall, 'Croft, Herbert (1603–1691)', *ODNB*; *WWL*, IV, 230.

later, he became canon of Wells and in 1636, held the same post at Lincoln.[83]

[**Crymes**] / Grymes, **Thomas** (1574–1644), justice of the peace and deputy lieutenant of Surrey. Crymes was an active commissioner for the collection of the forced loan in 1627 and, in the 1630s, was collector and commissioner for knighthood compositions for Surrey. In 1642, he was removed from his post as deputy lieutenant of the county. The following year, he led a commission of array for the king, although it is not clear whether he was particularly active on behalf of the royalist cause.[84]

[**Culpeper**] / Colepeper, **Thomas** (*c.* 1575–1662), politician and writer. Culpeper acquired Leeds Castle, Kent, in 1622 and was returned as MP for Tewkesbury in 1628. Culpeper carried letters from Elizabeth of Bohemia to Laud in October 1635.[85]

[**Curll, Walter**] (1575–1647), Church of England bishop. Translated to Winchester in 1632 at Laud's behest, Curll was an active supporter of some aspects of Caroline ecclesiastical policy during the 1630s, although he was not as vigorous in the pursuit of conformity as some of his episcopal colleagues. This may explain why Curll was one of the few bishops to escape censure by the Long Parliament.[86]

Customs Farmers, the syndicate of officials responsible for administering customs duties on behalf of the crown. Brought in under James I in the early 1600s, customs farming was intended to increase royal revenue from customs duties, while the 'farmers' themselves invariably also made a personal profit.

[**Dade**] / Dayd, [**Henry**] (*c.* 1582–1653), civil lawyer. Dade, returned as MP for Dunwich in Suffolk for the 1614 parliament, acted as commissary for the archdeaconry court of Suffolk from 1617. In this *rôle*, he came under fire for his oppression of puritans in the Ipswich area and in 1637 was forced to resign from both this position and his *rôle* on the admiralty court for Suffolk.[87]

Dale, [**Christopher**] (b. 1569), Church of England clergyman. Dale, who was appointed proctor of Merton College, Oxford, in 1603, held a number of livings in Kent from the early 1600s until at least 1638. He was appointed prebendary of Rochester in 1625.[88]

Dawes, Thomas (d. 1655), collector for customs and gentleman-in-ordinary of the king's bedchamber from 1640. In January 1640, Dawes was responsible for

---

83 *Alumni oxonienses*, I, 352.

84 A. McConnell, 'Culpeper [Colepeper], Sir Thomas (1577/8–1662), *ODNB;* www.historyofparliamentonline.org/volume/1604–1629/member/crymes-sir-thomas-1574–1644.

85 www.historyofparliamentonline.org/volume/1604–1629/member/culpeper-thomas-1575–1662; *WWL*, VII, 185.

86 M. Dorman, 'Curll, Walter (1575–1647)', *ODNB*.

87 *CSPD 1635–6*, p. 51, no. 49; *CSPD 1637*, p. 109, no. 66; *WWL*, IV, 130–2.

88 *Alumni oxonienses*, I, 367; *WWL*, IV, 318.

administering the repayment to Laud of his loan to the king of £4,000 to fund the king's first campaign against the Scots.[89]

Dell, [**William**] (*c.* 1603–48), household servant and *alumnus* of St John's, Oxford. Dell was probably appointed as one of Laud's two personal servants during his presidency of the College (1611–21). Later, Dell played a central *rôle* as Laud's secretary and *amanuensis* and was one of three servants who usually accompanied Laud to court. Dell was bequeathed £20 in Laud's will. A different William Dell held the post of master of Gonville and Caius College, Cambridge, from 1649.[90]

[**Denn** / **John**] (fl. 1635–9), yeoman retainer to the archiepiscopal household. Denn, who lived in Littlebourne, Kent, supplied wheat and barley to Lambeth Palace. Denn was already retained under Abbot by 1631 and may have been supplying the household under Bancroft, Abbot's predecessor.[91]

Deputy / Deputye, Lord – see Wentworth, Thomas.

Derry, bishop of – see Bramhall, John.

Digby / Digbye / Kellam / [**Kenelm**] (1603–65), courtier. Having converted from Catholicism to the Church of England by 1630, in early 1636, Digby informed Laud of his reconversion to Catholicism. Laud responded that he was 'not a little troubled' by this, but that they would remain friends, which they did.[92]

Digges / Diggs, **Dudley** (1582/3–1639), Kentish MP and justice of the peace during the 1620s. Digges enjoyed two separate spells in prison, first for maligning Buckingham in the 1626 parliament and, shortly afterwards, for speaking out against the forced loan. He recovered his position and was appointed master of the court of chancery from 1631 to 1637, and master of the rolls from 1636 to 1639.[93]

Dobson, Walter (fl. 1631–45), a household servant and keeper of the archiepiscopal accounts from September 1641, following the death of Laud's steward, Adam Torless. Dobson, who may have served George Abbot from as early as 1612, usually attended Laud when he was at court and was bequeathed £20 by the archbishop.[94]

Dormer, Robert (*c.* 1610–43), courtier, royalist army officer and, later, 1st earl of Caernarvon. Dormer died at the first battle of Newbury in September 1643.[95]

---

89 *CSPD 1639–40*, p. 337.
90 Hugh Trevor-Roper, 'William Dell', *EHR*, 62 (1947), 377–9; *WWL*, IV, 344, 445.
91 LPL, TG1, fos. 23v, 28v, TB1, fo. 60r.
92 Michael Foster, 'Digby, Sir Kenelm (1603–1665)', *ODNB*; *WWL*, VI, 454.
93 Sean Kelsey, 'Digges, Sir Dudley (1582/3–1639)', *ODNB*.
94 Ducarel, *Archiepiscopal palace*, Appendix, p. 52; *WWL*, IV, 344, 445.
95 Ian Roy, 'Dormer, Robert, first earl of Carnarvon (1610?–1643)', *ODNB*.

[**Dorset**] / Dorsett, countess of – see Sackville, Mary.

[**Dorset**]/ Dorsett, earl of – see Sackville, Edward.

[**Douglas**, **Robert**] (*c*. 1573–1639), politician. Douglas, who had served as master of the horse to Prince Henry, was appointed gentleman of James I's bedchamber in 1612 on the prince's death. He continued in this *rôle* after the accession of Charles I, being appointed master of the royal household. Douglas, who was admitted to the Scottish privy council in 1631, was created Viscount Belhaven in June 1633 during the king's coronation visit to Edinburgh and, despite his blindness, signed the 'king's covenant' in 1638, the royal alternative to the Scottish National Covenant.[96]

Downer, [**Thomas**] (b. 1583), Church of England clergyman. Downer, an *alumnus* of St John's College, Oxford, was vicar of Charlbury, Oxfordshire, from 1623. In May 1637, he asked Laud to mediate on his behalf in a tithes dispute with Sir Henry Calthrop, but there is little else to link Downer to the archbishop.[97]

Doyly / Doylye, [**John**] (1602–60), politician. Doyly, who was appointed sheriff of Oxford in 1639, became MP for the town in 1646, but was ejected during Pride's Purge in 1648.[98]

Duck, [**Arthur**] (1580–1648), civil lawyer. Duck's associations with Laud dated back to the early 1620s when Duck was chancellor of the diocese of Bath and Wells when Laud was diocesan bishop. Duck was appointed to the court of high commission by Laud in 1633, although he failed to support Laud in the St Gregory's case later that year.[99]

Duckett, **William** (fl. 1635–45), a household servant and one of the two men permitted to remain with Laud throughout his imprisonment in the Tower. Duckett was rewarded for his endeavours with a bequest of £40 a year from the renewed lease of Winchester cathedral.[100]

[**Duppa**, **Brian**] (1588–1662), Church of England bishop. Although Duppa was promoted to the bishopric of Chichester in 1638 during Laud's archiepiscopate, he had a reputation for moderation and was not close to Laud. He was translated to the see of Winchester in 1660.[101]

Durham, bishop of – see Morton, Thomas.

---

96 G. F. R. Barker, 'Douglas, Robert, Viscount Belhaven (1573/4–1639)', *ODNB*.
97 *Alumni oxonienses*, I, 419; *CSPD 1637*, p. 121, no. 120.
98 *Alumni oxonienses*, I, 421; *CSPD 1639*, p. 6, no. 6; W. Williams, *The parliamentary history of the county of Oxford including the city and the University of Oxford* (Oxford, 1899) p. 118.
99 Peter Stein, 'Duck, Arthur (1580–1648)', *ODNB*.
100 *WWL*, IV, 447.
101 Ian Green, 'Duppa, Brian (1588–1662)', *ODNB*.

Dutton, [**John**] (1594–1657), lawyer and politician. Returned as MP for Gloucestershire in the 1624 and 1625 parliaments, Dutton also stood again in the Short Parliament. Despite having been an opponent of the forced loan in 1627, Dutton nevertheless retained links with the court, serving on the commission for the repair of St Paul's cathedral in 1632. One gift from 'Mistress Dutton' recorded in the accounts may have been from Dutton's wife, Elizabeth (1606–38) daughter of Sir Matthew Baynton.[102]

East India Company – founded by royal charter in 1600, the East India Company was originally established predominantly to share in the East Indian spice trade, hitherto dominated by Spain and Portugal. Only later did it play a significant part in British commercial expansion and imperial activity.

Eastland [**Company**] / Marchants / Merchants– founded by royal charter in 1579, the Eastland Company was established primarily to trade cloth with the Baltic. It was smaller in scale than the Merchant Adventurers' Company, although there was some overlap of membership.[103]

Eden, [**Thomas**] (d. 1645), civil lawyer and politician. Eden, who served as MP for the University of Cambridge in the parliaments of 1624, 1628 and 1640, was active in the ecclesiastical courts in London during the 1630s, serving on the high commission from 1633 until 1641. Eden was also chancellor of the diocese of Ely from 1630. For his *rôle* in the case against John Bastwick, Eden was originally named in the impeachment articles against Laud in 1641, but he was not prosecuted.[104]

Edmonds / **Edmondes** / Edmunds, **Thomas** (d. 1639), diplomat. A staunch supporter of Charles I, Edmondes's final diplomatic mission was to Paris in 1629, to negotiate peace with France. Edmondes had connexions with Oxford, having been elected MP for the University in 1625 and 1626, which may explain his associations with Laud. Edmondes also voted for the appointment of Sir John Finch as speaker of the Commons in March 1628.[105]

Egglefield, [**John**] (fl. 1638). Little is known of Egglefield, who was resident in the parish of St Faith's under St Paul during the 1630s. His neighbours, 'Mr Bemboe' and 'Mr Bostock' also gave gifts to Laud.[106]

[**Ely**] / Elye, bishop of – see Wren, Matthew.

---

102 Jan Broadway, 'Dutton family (per. 1522–1743)', *ODNB*; Alison Wall, 'Baynton family (per. 1508–1716)', *ODNB*; www.historyofparliamentonline.org/volume/1604–1629/member/dutton-john-1594–1657.

103 *The acts and ordinances of the Eastland Company*, ed. Maud Sellers (London, 1906), pp. x, xxxix.

104 *Alumni cantabrigienses*, part II, I, 84; Brian Levack, 'Eden, Thomas (*d.* 1645)', *ODNB*; *WWL*, IV, 148.

105 *WWL*, VII, 28.

106 'Inhabitants of London in 1638: St. Faith's', in *The inhabitants of London in 1638*, ed. Dale, p. 57.

Epsley / Epslye, John – see Hippesley, John.

Evelinge / **Evelyn**, [**Richard**] (d. 1640), sheriff of Surrey from 1634 and father of the diarist, Sir John Evelyn.[107]

[**Fane**, **Mary**] (née Mildmay) (*c.* 1581–1640), dowager countess of Westmorland. In 1599, she married Sir Francis Fane, who became 1st earl of Westmorland in December 1624. Her eldest son, Mildmay Fane, became 2nd earl on his father's death in 1629. In October 1637, a gift of 'a hynde from ye Countesse of Westm.land' is recorded in Laud's accounts and it is safe to assume that this gift came from the dowager countess, since Fane's first wife, Grace, died in 1636 and he did not remarry until June 1638.[108]

Farmer / [**Fermor**], **Hatton** (*c.* 1580–1640), local politician. Little is known of Fermor, who acted as sheriff of Northamptonshire in the 1610s. On his death in 1640, Fermor was succeeded as baronet by his son, William, who served as a royalist commander at Edgehill in 1642.[109]

Farmers of the custom – see Customs Farmers.

Farmery / Farmley / Farmory, [**John**] (d. 1648), civil lawyer and politician. Although unpopular within the diocese of Lincoln, where he was chancellor from 1621, Farmery was useful to Laud in trying to achieve conformity with royal policy. He acted as a justice of the peace for Lincoln from 1620 to 1632 and sat as MP for the city in the Short Parliament.[110]

Featley, [**Daniel**] (1585–1645), Church of England clergyman. Featley, who was chaplain to George Abbot from 1619, held the living of All Saints, Lambeth, close to the archiepiscopal palace. In the late 1620s, Featley's puritan sympathies enabled him, as ecclesiastical licensor, to secure the publication of several anti-Arminian books and tracts. He fell out with Laud in 1634 for publishing anti-Catholic material and gave evidence at Laud's trial about it in 1644. Featley was buried in Lambeth church in 1645.[111]

[**Fell**, **Samuel**] (*c.* 1584–1649), royal chaplain. Holding chaplaincies to James I from 1619 and to Charles I from 1625, Fell was appointed Lady Margaret professor of theology at Oxford from 1626. Under pressure from Laud for neglecting lectures in

---

107 *CSPD 1635*, p. 285, no. 18; Douglas Chambers, 'Evelyn, John (1620–1706)', *ODNB*.

108 Stephen Wright, 'Fane, Mildmay, second earl of Westmorland (1602–1666)', *ODNB*; *Newsletters from the Caroline court 1631–1638: Catholicism and the politics of the personal rule*, ed. Michael Questier (Camden Fifth Series, XXVI, 1985), p. 212 n. 996.

109 *Complete baronetage*, II, 143.

110 Levack, *Civil lawyers*, p. 229; *WWL*, V, 369.

111 Ducarel, *Archiepiscopal palace*, Appendix, p. 62; Arnold Hunt, 'Featley, Daniel (1582–1645)', *ODNB*.

1631, he was replaced by Thomas Lawrence, an anti-Calvinist, in 1638. Possibly to compensate, Fell was awarded the deanery of Lichfield in 1637, although the prize he really sought – the bishopric of Rochester – eluded him.[112]

Fettiplace / Fettyplace, [**Charles**] – see under Pocock / Pococke, Edward.

[**Field**, **Theophilus**] (1575–1636), Church of England bishop. Field owed his promotion to the bishopric of Llandaff in 1619 to the royal favourite, Buckingham, who used Field to deliver letters to Laud in 1626. Field was translated to the bishopric of Hereford in December 1635.[113]

[**Fiennes**, **William**] (1582–1662), 1st Viscount Saye and Sele, politician. Fiennes was closely associated with a group of godly divines who emerged as opponents of the policies of Charles I's personal rule. An active member of the Providence Island Company, established in 1630 to foster the Protestant colonization of North America, Fiennes was alienated from court during the 1630s for his opposition to extra-parliamentary taxation. It was Fiennes who wanted to be brought to court to test the legality of ship money, but the king, wishing to avoid a high-profile case, instead chose to proceed against John Hampden.[114]

Finch, [**John**] (1584–1660), speaker of the House of Commons and judge. As speaker, a position he held from 1628, Finch was, famously, forced back into the speaker's chair by Denzil Holles and others while trying to adjourn the session on behalf of the king in February 1629. Finch held several senior judicial posts during the 1630s, including that of chief justice of the common pleas (1634–40) and lord keeper (1640–1) and he was actively involved in the business of star chamber with Laud.[115]

[**Finch**, **Thomas**] (1578–1639), 2nd earl of Winchelsea and Kentish MP. Finch, who acquired the earldom of Winchelsea in 1634 on the death of his widowed mother, Elizabeth, was elected MP for Kent with the backing of Sir Edwin Sandys, a client of Buckingham, but did not play a significant part in parliamentary politics. This is in marked contrast to his younger brother, Sir Heneage Finch, who held the post of speaker of the House of Commons in 1626.[116]

Flood / Floodd / [**Flud**], **John** (fl. 1631–45), the archbishop's chamber-keeper, to whom Laud left £5 in his will.[117]

[**Forster**] / Foster, **Humphrey** (*c.* 1595–1663), 1st baronet. Forster, whose country

---

112 Hegarty, 'Fell, Samuel (*bap.* 1584, *d.* 1649)', *ODNB*; *WWL*, V, 186.
113 Ian Atherton, 'Field, Theophilus (*bap.* 1575, *d.* 1636)', *ODNB*; *WWL*, III, 193.
114 Smith, 'Fiennes', *ODNB.*
115 Knafla, 'Finch, John, Baron Finch of Fordwich (1584–1660)', *ODNB.*
116 www.historyofparliamentonline.org/volume/1604–1629/member/finch-sir-thomas-1578–1639.
117 *WWL*, IV, 446.

seat was in Aldermaston, Berkshire, appeared before the court of high commission in February 1634. Forster was also proceeded against in star chamber in April 1635 for continuing to reside in London against the king's proclamation ordering the gentry to return to their country seats.[118]

Foster, **John** (fl. 1631–41), armourer to the archiepiscopal household, who was employed in this capacity from at least 1631.[119]

Fuller, [**William**] (1579/80–1659), Church of England clergyman. Fuller held the vicarage of St Giles Cripplegate, London and was appointed dean of Ely in July 1636. Fuller was controversial within his parish, for pluralism (he retained St Giles after being promoted to Ely) and because of his adherence to 'popish' ceremonies, such as bowing to and the railing in of the communion table.[120]

[**Garrard**] / Garrett, **George** (1579 – *c.* 1650), politician and aristocratic chaplain. Garrard sat as MP for Preston in 1628 and Hindon in 1640. He is perhaps best known for his lengthy correspondence with Sir Thomas Wentworth during the latter's tenure as Irish lord deputy during the 1630s. Appointed master of Charterhouse School in 1635, Garrard appears to have had Laud's approval and may have used the archbishop to procure this appointment. Garrard was also appointed household chaplain to Algernon Percy, 10th earl of Northumberland, in 1635.[121]

Garrowaye / [**Garway**], [**Henry**] (*c.* 1575–1646), merchant and politician. A member of the Drapers' Company, Garway was appointed alderman of the City of London in 1627, a position he retained until 1639, when he was elected lord mayor of London. Garway, who was also governor of the Levant Company from 1635 to 1643, was involved in the suppression of the attack on Lambeth by apprentices in May 1640.[122]

George, **Robert** (fl. 1635–7), an occasional household servant, who acted as messenger to Lambeth Palace.

Gilford / [**Guildford**], **Henry** (fl. 1634–42), local politician. Guildford, who lived at Hempstead Place in Kent, was probably the same 'Sir Henry Guildford' who was proceeded against in the exchequer court in 1639, 'touching the soap business'.[123]

Glascoe / Glasgow, archbishop of – see Lindsay, Patrick.

---

118 *CSPD 1633–4*, p. 149, no. 1; *Extinct and dormant baronetcies*, pp. 204–5; *Historical collections, 1629–38*, II, ed. John Rushworth, (London, 1721), p. 291.

119 LPL, TG1, fos. 23v, 28v.

120 Gordon Goodwin, 'Fuller, William (1579/80–1659)', rev. Nicholas Cranfield, *ODNB*.

121 www.historyofparliamentonline.org/volume/1604–1629/member/garrard-george-1579–1650.

122 Anita McConnell and Robert Brown, 'Garway, Sir Henry (*bap.* 1575, *d.* 1646)', *ODNB*; *The aldermen of the City of London temp Henry III to 1912*, II, ed. Alfred Beaven (London, 1908), p. 65.

123 *CSPD 1639–40*, p. 193; *Extinct and dormant baronetcies*, p. 231.

Gloucester, bishop of – see Goodman, Godfrey.

Goad, [**John**] (1616–89), *alumnus* of St John's College, Oxford. As an undergraduate, Goad performed in 'Love's Hospital' before the king and Laud at St John's during the royal visit in the summer of 1636. Later, he became a meteorologist and, in 1661, was appointed headmaster of the Merchant Taylors' School.[124]

[**Goodman**, **Godfrey**] (1583–1656), Church of England bishop. Goodman was appointed to the see of Gloucester in 1624, but was dogged by suspicions of being a Roman Catholic throughout his career. Disappointed in his wish to be translated to the bishopric of Hereford in 1633 – having apparently only accepted Gloucester on the promise of Hereford when it next became vacant – Goodman's relations with Laud were strained throughout the 1630s.[125]

Googe / [**Gouge, William**] (1575–1653), Church of England clergyman and author. Gouge was, until the early 1630s, a leading member of the 'feoffees for impropriations', a voluntary organization which sought to reclaim for the church tithes which had been acquired by the laity. Laud suspected the feoffees of puritan subversion and succeeded in having them dissolved in the exchequer court in February 1633.[126]

Gore, **John** (fl. 1631–39), household servant, who acted as almoner of the hall at Lambeth under both Abbot and Laud.

[**Goring**] / Goringe, **George** (1585–1663), Baron Goring and later 1st earl of Norwich. Goring's career as a diplomat and courtier was defined by his membership of the queen's, rather than the king's household, in which he acted as vice-chamberlain from 1626, having played an instrumental *rôle* in her arriving in England in 1625. It was not until 1639 that Goring held his first major position within the king's household and was appointed to the privy council.[127]

[**Gresham**] / Gressom, **Edward** (*c.* 1590–1647), gentleman. Little is known of Surrey-based Gresham, except that he petitioned Laud in 1638 regarding the marriage of his own son Thomas, against Gresham's will. The case reached the court of high commission in 1638 and later came back to haunt Laud during his trial in 1644, when Gresham's son (his father having died in 1639) demanded repayment of the damages to which he had been earlier made liable.[128]

[**Griffith**, **Edmund**] (1570–1637), Church of England bishop. Griffith was

124 Patrick Curry, 'Goad, John (1616–1689)', *ODNB*; *WWL*, V, 153.
125 Nicholas Cranfield, 'Goodman, Godfrey (1583–1656)', *ODNB*; *WWL*, VII, 62.
126 Brett Usher, 'Gouge, William (1575–1653)', *ODNB*; *WWL*, III, 217.
127 Barbara Donagan, 'Goring, George, first earl of Norwich (1585–1663)', *ODNB*.
128 *CSPD 1638–9*, p. 124, no. 54; *Knights of England*, II, 167; *WWL*, IV, 142.

consecrated bishop of Bangor at Lambeth in February 1634, but died in May 1637. During his brief tenure in the diocese, Griffith was criticized by his parishioners for taxing them to fund cathedral repairs and for failing to appoint preaching ministers.[129]

Grymes, Thomas – see [Crymes, Thomas]

Gwyn / [**Gwynne**, **Thomas**] (fl. 1594–1638), Church of England clergyman. As precentor of Salisbury and chancellor of Llandaff, Laud was in contact with 'Dr Gwin' in February 1638 regarding the endowment of Jesus College, Oxford, from the impropriate rectory of Holyhead.[130]

[**Hacket**] / Hackett, [**John**] (1592–1670), royal chaplain. A moderate Calvinist, Hacket was appointed to the archdeaconry of Bedford in 1631 by John Williams, bishop of Lincoln – Laud's arch-nemesis – to whom he had earlier acted as household chaplain. Although Hacket approved of some of the religious policies of the personal rule, including Book of Sports and use of the liturgy, his association with Williams meant that he was never on good terms with Laud. In March 1641, Hacket was appointed to a sub-committee of the Lords to investigate religious grievances. He was promoted to the bishopric of Coventry and Lichfield in 1661.[131]

[**Hamilton**, **Elizabeth**] (1620–59), noblewoman. Married to William Hamilton, later 2nd duke of Hamilton (brother of James Hamilton), Elizabeth became countess of Lanark in 1639, when her husband was granted the earldom. Little is known of her life, although she outlived her husband, who died following an injury sustained at the battle of Worcester in 1650.[132]

Hambleton / [**Hamilton**, **James**] (1606–49), 3rd marquis and later 1st duke of Hamilton. Hamilton, who held the prestigious position of master of the horse and gentleman of the king's bedchamber from 1632, was one of the most senior figures at the court of Charles I after the death of Buckingham. Although based predominantly in London during the 1630s, Hamilton did not sever his ties with his native Scotland and in May 1638, he was sent to Edinburgh to act as the king's commissioner. He played a key *rôle* in negotiating with the Covenanters until the collapse of the Glasgow assembly in December and corresponded with Laud throughout his commission.[133]

Harbart / Harbert / **Harbord** / Harbort / Herbert, **Charles** (1596–1679), surveyor-general to Charles I and MP for Launceston, Cornwall, after the Restoration.[134]

---

129 Gwynfor Jones, 'Griffith, Edmund (1570–1637)', *ODNB*; *WWL*, VI, 389–90.

130 *WWL*, VI, 519–20. Cf *Memorials of Oxford*, I, ed. James Ingram (Oxford, 1837), p. 14.

131 Brian Quintrell, 'Hacket, John (1592–1670)', *ODNB*; *WWL*, III, 438.

132 *Survey of London*, XVIII: *The Strand: the parish of St Martin-in-the-Fields, part II*, ed. G. H. Gater and E. P. Wheeler (London, 1937), p. 5.

133 James, *Firebrand*, pp. 112–45; John Scally, 'Hamilton, William, second duke of Hamilton (1616–1651)', *ODNB*; *WWL*, VI, 547–8.

134 www.historyofparliamentonline.org/volume/1660–1690/member/harbord-sir-charles-1596–1679.

Harby, Job (*c.* 1590–1663), London merchant. In December 1635, Harby was employed on behalf of the crown in attempts to sell the king's jewels on the continent. In 1636, he was involved in transferring to the admiralty office, the ship money payments collected by the sheriffs of Cornwall.[135]

Harbye / **Harvey** / Harvy / Harvye, **Daniel** (d. 1650?), merchant. Harvey, like Laud, was a Reading man and frequently visited the archbishop at Croydon, close to which Harvey had a country house. A member of the East India and Levant Companies in the late 1630s, Harvey introduced Laud to Edward Hyde, later earl of Clarendon in 1635.[136]

Harfleet / Harfleett / [**Harflett**], **Roger** (fl. 1621–1641), keeper and 'howsekeeper' of Bekesbourne manor, Kent.[137]

Harman, William, the cook at Lambeth Palace, to whom Laud left £40.[138]

Harrison, Richard (1584–1655), local politician. Harrison was appointed high sheriff of Berkshire during the 1630s and returned as MP for Windsor in the Short Parliament. Evidence of Laud's associations with Harrison can be traced back to the beginning of Charles I's reign.[139]

Hart, [**Richard**] (fl. 1632–45), lawyer. The son of John Hart (d. 1635) of Fulham a neighbour of Laud, the younger Hart was active in the London courts as an advocate from 1634 to 1640. Hart was also probably the 'Mr Harte' listed as acting as solicitor to the archiepiscopal household in 1632. Hart was expelled from the Doctors' Commons in 1632 for recusancy, but subsequently agreed to receive the sacraments according to the forms of the Church of England and was readmitted. In responding to charges of popery in the prelude to his trial, Laud cited Hart as among twenty people whose religion he had 'either converted or settled'. [140]

Hatton, Robert (1582–1653), politician. Hatton, who served as MP for Sandwich in all the parliaments of the 1620s, was steward to Laud's archiepiscopal predecessor, George Abbot, from 1612 to around 1626. Serving as a JP for Cambridge, Ely and Northamptonshire during the 1630s, Hatton spent the majority of his time on his estates in Northamptonshire, before acting as royalist commissioner of array in the county in 1642.[141]

---

135 *CSPD 1635*, p. 565, no. 21e, p. 582, no. 90, p. 583, no. 92; *CSPD 1635–6*, p. 324, no. 28i.

136 Edward Hyde, *The life of Edward, earl of Clarendon written by himself* (Oxford, 1761), p. 21; Alfred Wood, *A history of the Levant Company* (Oxford, 1935), p. 128.

137 LPL TG1, fo. 28v.

138 *WWL*, IV, 446.

139 *WWL*, III, 169, 176.

140 LPL, TG1 fo. 31; *WWL*, IV, 65; Levack, *Civil lawyers*, p. 236.

141 www.historyofparliamentonline.org/volume/1604–1629/member/hatton-robert-1582–1653.

[**Hay**, **Lucy**] (1599–1660), countess of Carlisle, courtier and lady-in-waiting to Henrietta Maria. Hay was one of the most politically active women at the court of Charles I, although she had little direct contact with Laud. In 1637, however, Hay relinquished to Laud her right to certain rooms at Hampton Court – an act for which he conveyed his gratitude to her through their mutual correspondent Thomas Wentworth, lord deputy of Ireland – and in the following year, she also enlisted Laud's help when trying to sell her monopoly on Irish wines.[142]

Haycock, **William** (fl. 1631–41), a bargeman, retained by the household for occasional use. Haycock had carried out this *rôle* since at least 1631.[143]

Haywood /Heywood, [**William**] (*c.* 1599–1663), Church of England clergyman. In 1631, Heywood was appointed domestic chaplain to Laud, as bishop of London, and a canon of St Paul's. In 1637, he left Laud's service to become a royal chaplain and a year later, he was appointed canon of Westminster.[144]

Hearne / [**Herne**] [**John**] (*c.* 1593–1649), lawyer. Herne played an important part in several state trials of the 1630s and 1640s. Paradoxically, he served as counsel for William Prynne in 1634 during his star chamber trial for the publication of the controversial *Histriomastix;* and in 1641, he was appointed as counsel in Laud's impeachment and, later, his trial.[145]

Heath, **Robert** (1575–1649), chief justice of the common pleas from 1631. Heath's removal from the office of chief justice in September 1634 has been attributed to Laud, ostensibly because Heath did not share the archbishop's *penchant* for ceremonialism and because Heath was not in Laud's clique at court. However, Heath regained favour in 1637, being appointed king's serjeant. He stood for election as MP for Reading in 1640, but failed to win a single vote.[146]

Heath, [**Thomas**] (1598–1680), lawyer and Church of England official. Heath, an *alumnus* of St John's College, Oxford, was appointed chancellor of Peterborough diocese in 1637. As proctor, he attended the 1640 Convocation and, in early 1643, visited Laud in the Tower in an attempt to persuade the archbishop to confer the living of Chartham, Kent on Edward Corbet, parliament's chosen candidate. Although the archbishop refused, this event resulted in his authority being annulled and Corbet being appointed by parliamentary ordinance.[147]

---

142 Roy Schreiber, 'Hay, Lucy, countess of Carlisle (1599–1660)', *ODNB*; *WWL*, VI, 499, 513; VII, 329, 406, 408, 417.

143 LPL, TG1, fos. 23v, 28v.

144 Arnold Hunt, 'Haywood, William (1599/1600–1663)', *ODNB*; Ducarel, *Archiepiscopal palace*, Appendix, p. 21; *Alumni oxonienses*, II, 683.

145 Alan Orr, 'Herne, John (*c.* 1593–1649)', *ODNB*; *WWL*, III, 437.

146 Barnes, 'Cropping the Heath'; Paul Kopperman, 'Heath, Sir Robert (1575–1649)', *ODNB*; Paul Kopperman, *Sir Robert Heath: Window on an Age* (London, 1989).

147 *CSPD 1639*, p. 340, no. 48; Mark Bell, 'Corbet, Edward (1601x3–1658)', *ODNB*; *WWL*, III, 248, 287.

[**Henden**] / Hendon, [**Edward**] (1567–1644), politician and lawyer. Henden, who served as MP for Rye in 1614, was JP and assizes judge for Kent for several decades until 1642. He was steward to the archiepiscopal household under George Abbot. Created baron of the exchequer in 1638, Henden acted as an assistant in the house of lords during the trial of Strafford.[148]

[**Henshaw**] / Henshawe, [**Joseph**] (1603–1689), Church of England clergyman. Henshaw was personal chaplain to George Villiers, duke of Buckingham at the time of the latter's assassination in 1628 and later that year, was appointed prebendary of Chichester. In 1663, Henshaw was consecrated bishop of Peterborough, a position he held until his death.[149]

[**Herbert, Philip**] (1584–1650), 4th earl of Pembroke courtier and privy councillor. Pembroke held the prestigious post of Lord Chamberlain of the king's household from 1626 until 1641. Like his royal master, he was an avid patron of the arts, although his godly Protestantism meant that he was increasingly isolated from court as the 1630s progressed and may explain his allegiance to parliament after 1640. In May 1641, Pembroke was appointed chancellor of Oxford University when Laud resigned from the office, having been narrowly defeated by Laud to secure the chancellorship, on the death of the previous incumbent, Pembroke's father.[150]

Hereford, bishop of – see Field, Theophilus.

Higgs, [**Griffin** / Griffith] (*c.*1589 – 1659), Church of England clergyman. Higgs was an *alumnus* of St John's College, Oxford, and a longstanding associate of the archbishop. He was chaplain to the exiled Queen Elizabeth of Bohemia from 1627 until 1638, who used her influence with Laud to secure Higgs's appointment to the precentorship of St Davids in 1631 and the deanery of Lichfield in 1638. Higgs went on to become chaplain-in-ordinary to the king in 1639.[151]

[**Hippesley**] / Apslye / Epsley / Epslye /, **John** (d. 1655), politician and JP. Hippesley, a client of Buckingham, was appointed deputy warden of the Cinque Ports and lieutenant-general of Dover Castle in 1624. Having acted as commissioner for the forced loan in Kent and Middlesex in 1626, and as MP for Dover in the parliaments of 1625 to 1628, Hippesley was mostly occupied in local government during the 1630s, finding little favour at court. In 1636, he visited Laud at Croydon and offered to entertain him *en route* to Oxford, but the archbishop declined.[152]

---

148 *LJ*, IV, 260; P. Rapid de Thoyras, *The history of England by Mr Rapin de Thoyras*, IV, part II (London, 1747), p. 260; *CSPD Addenda, 1625–1649*, p. 465, no. 73.I.

149 William Sheils, 'Henshaw, Joseph (1603–1679)', *ODNB*; *Alumni oxonienses*, II, 694.

150 David Smith, 'Herbert, Philip, first earl of Montgomery and fourth earl of Pembroke (1584–1650)', *ODNB*; *WWL*, III, 242.

151 Pat Bancroft, 'Higgs, Griffith (*bap.* 1589, *d.* 1659)', *ODNB*; *WWL*, IV, 298, VII, 590.

152 www.historyofparliamentonline.org/volume/1604–1629/member/hippisley-sir-john-1655; *WWL*, VII, 277.

[**Hoare**] / Hore, **Henry** (fl. 1631–41), retained at Croydon, who may also have acted as an apothecary.[153]

Hodges, **George** (fl. 1631–6), yeoman of the wine cellar at Lambeth, who had been in post since at least 1631.[154]

Holford, [**Benjamin**] (fl. 1631–45) a household servant, who carried out sundry duties for Laud, including tipping the servants at court, giving money to the poor and arranging boathire. Holford was left £20 by Laud.[155]

Holland, **Mr** (fl. 1636–41), a household servant, whose duties involved heavy manual labour in the grounds of Lambeth and Croydon.

Holloway, [**John**] (d. 1675), official to the archdeacon of Berkshire. Little is known of Holloway. His son, Richard, became a judge after the Restoration and was knighted in 1683. Not to be confused with the John Holloway who acted as comptroller of the customs during the 1630s and who died in 1636.[156]

[**Holt**] / Hoult, **Elizabeth**, a household servant and the daughter of Laud's sister, Bennett, was bequeathed £50 on the archbishop's death.[157]

Honeywood / [**Honywood**], **Robert** (1601–86), diplomat and translator. Kentish by birth, Honywood was appointed servant to Queen Elizabeth of Bohemia in 1627 and his duties included acting as messenger to her allies in England, including the king and Laud.[158]

[**Howard**, **Theophilus**] (1584–1640), 2nd earl of Suffolk, courtier and local politician. Suffolk held a range of senior positions at court and in the localities under both James I and Charles I, including the lord lieutenancy of Cumberland, Westmoreland, Northumberland, Dorset, Suffolk and Cambridgeshire. In 1639, when Charles I needed to strengthen the borders in the face of the Scottish crisis, Suffolk resigned his northern lieutenancies.[159]

[**Howard, Thomas**] (1585–1646), 14th earl of Arundel, 4th earl of Surrey and, later, 1st earl of Norfolk. Arundel was a senior member of the privy council under Charles I, a diplomat and an enthusiastic art collector, and can be counted among the king's

153 LPL, TG1, fos. 28r, 31r.
154 LPL, TG1 fos. 28r, 31v.
155 *WWL*, IV, 445.
156 *Alumni oxonienses*, II, 734; *CSPD 1633–4*, p. 233, no. 32; Stuart Handley, 'Holloway, Sir Richard (*bap.* 1627, *d.* 1699)', *ODNB*; *WWL*, VII, 242. For John Holloway, the customs official (d. 1636), see *CSPD 1611–18*, p. 175, no. 76a; *CSPD 1633–4*, p. 104, no. 20.
157 *WWL*, IV, 444.
158 Gillian Wright, 'Honywood, Sir Robert (1601–1686)', *ODNB*; *WWL*, VII, 244.
159 Victor Stater, 'Howard, Theophilus, second earl of Suffolk (1584–1640)', *ODNB*.

circle of true friends. A Catholic, Arundel sat on several privy council committees with Laud.[160]

Howell, [**Thomas**] (1588–1650), Church of England clergyman. Howell acted as chaplain to Charles I during the 1630s and was appointed canon of Windsor in November 1636. The last bishop to be consecrated in England until after the Restoration, Howell's tenure as bishop of Bristol from 1644 was brief. Within a year, the city had been surrendered to parliament and all royalist clergy were ejected.[161]

Huchenson / **Hutchinson**, [**William**] (1592–1643), Church of England clergyman. An *alumnus* of St John's College, Oxford, Hutchinson was archdeacon of Lewes from 1629 until his death in 1643.[162]

[**Hunt**], **Christopher** (fl. 1639), household servant with unspecified duties. Hunt received a bequest of £5 in Laud's will.[163]

Ingram, **Sir Arthur** (*c*. 1571–1642), financier and politician. Ingram was secretary of the council of the north in York from 1613 to 1633, when he resigned his post after a quarrel with Wentworth over the farm of the northern recusancy fines. As MP for New Windsor and Callington in the Short and Long Parliaments, Ingram was opposed to the religious policies of the 1630s and also gave evidence against Thomas Wentworth at his trial in 1641.[164]

[**Jenoure**] / Jeynor, **Andrew** (d. 1690), local politician. Based in Great Dunmow, now in Essex, Jenoure acted as JP after the Restoration, but little is known of his activities during the 1630s.[165]

Jerman / [**Jermyn**], **Thomas** (*c*. 1573 – *c*. 1645), soldier and courtier. Jermyn held a number of senior administrative offices during the 1630s, in addition to his membership of the privy council. In 1628, he was vice-chamberlain of the queen's household; in 1631, he became non-resident governor of Jersey; from 1638, he was lord lieutenant of Suffolk; and he was appointed comptroller of the king's household in 1639, a position he had been seeking for a decade.[166]

Jones, Judge – see Jones, William.

---

160 Malcolm Smuts, 'Howard, Thomas, fourteenth earl of Arundel, fourth earl of Surrey, and first earl of Norfolk (1585–1646)', *ODNB*.
161 Geoffrey Browell, 'Howell, Thomas (1588–1650)', *ODNB*.
162 *Alumni oxoniensis*, II, 779.
163 *WWL*, IV, 446.
164 Simon Healy, 'Ingram, Sir Arthur (b. before 1571, d. 1642)', *ODNB*.
165 *Complete baronetage*, II, 429.
166 *CSPD Addenda 1625–1649*, p. 425, no. 67; Diarmaid MacCulloch, 'Jermyn, Sir Thomas (*bap*. 1573, *d*. 1644/5)', *ODNB*.

Jones, [**William**] (1566–1640), judge. Transferred to the king's bench from the common pleas in 1624, Jones was a loyal supporter of the crown throughout the 1620s and 1630s, upholding the monarch's right to imprison the forced loan refusers in 1627 and to levy ship money in 1637. Jones, who also operated on the Oxford assize circuit, sat in star chamber with Laud and entertained the archbishop on his return from the royal visit to Oxford in August 1636.[167]

Joseph, **John**, baker to the archiepiscopal household. Joseph was already in post in 1632 under Abbot.[168]

Joyner, [**Henry**], a household servant, to whom Laud left £40 on his death.[169]

[**Juxon**, **William**] (1582–1663), Church of England bishop and lord treasurer. Juxon became bishop of London after Laud's translation to Canterbury in August 1633 and lord treasurer from March 1636. Traditionally regarded as Laud's protégé, Juxon has more recently been viewed as a possible rival candidate for the lord treasurership, which had been in commission since the death of the previous incumbent, Sir Richard Weston, in March 1635.[170]

keeper, lord – see Coventry, Thomas; Finch, John; Littleton, Edward.

Kellygree / [**Killigrew**] / Killygree, **William** (*c.* 1606–95), courtier and politician. Returned as MP for Penryn, Cornwall, in 1628, Killigrew shortly after acquired the governorship of Pendennis Castle in the county. Although involved in fen drainage projects in Lincolnshire from 1633, Killigrew spent the majority of the 1630s in the west of England. Killigrew was involved in attempts to secure support for the king after his attempt to arrest the five members in January 1642 and distinguished himself as a royalist officer at Edgehill later that year.[171]

King / Kinge, **Giles** (fl. 1639–1645), an 'old' household servant, who served as porter at Lambeth under both Abbot and Laud and to whom the latter left £5 in his will.[172]

King / Kinge, [**Henry**] (1592–1669), Church of England clergyman and, later, bishop. King served as chaplain to Charles I and sat on the court of high commission until 1633. A keen writer of poetry and a loyal servant of the crown, King was appointed to the deanery of Rochester in February 1639 and to the bishopric of Chichester in October 1641.[173]

---

167 Christopher Brooks, 'Jones, Sir William (1566–1640)', *ODNB*; *WWL*, V, 155.
168 LPL, TG1, fo. 28r.
169 *WWL*, IV, 446.
170 Brian Quintrell, 'Juxon, William (bap. 1582, d. 1663)', *ODNB*; Quintrell, 'The church triumphant?'.
171 Jean Pierre Vander Motten, 'Killigrew, Sir William (bap. 1606, d. 1695)', *ODNB*.
172 LPL, TG1, fo. 28v; *WWL*, IV, 445.
173 Mary Hobbs, 'King, Henry (1592–1669)', *ODNB*.

[**Kingsley**, **William**] (1584–1647), Church of England clergyman. Kingsley, who held a number of livings in Kent in the 1610s, was appointed to the archdeaconry of Canterbury in 1619, a position he held until his death.[174]

kitchen, clerk of the – see Shelton, Thomas.

Knight _ (fl. 1636–41), a household servant, whose duties included manual labour in the park and grounds around both Lambeth and Croydon.

Lamb / **Lambe**, **John** (1566–1646), civil lawyer. Lambe was promoted to the deanery of the Arches by Laud in 1633. As a member of the court of high commission, Lambe was responsible for enforcing many of the most unpopular policies with which Laud was associated, such as altar policy and the Book of Sports. Lambe was also involved in most of the high-profile prosecutions of the 1630s, including that of Burton, Bastwick and Prynne in 1637.[175]

[**Lanark**] / Leverick, countess of – see Hamilton, Elizabeth.

Landaff / Landaffe / Llandaff, bishop of – see Murray, William.

Layfield, [**Edward**] (1604–80), Church of England clergyman. An *alumnus* of St John's College, Oxford, and the son of Laud's sister Bridget, Layfield was appointed by the archbishop to a prebendal seat at St Paul's in 1633 and also acted as his domestic chaplain during the 1630s. Later, he was appointed archdeacon of Essex and was the executor and a beneficiary of Laud's will.[176]

Lea / Lee / [**Leigh**], **Francis** (1598–1653), politician, courtier and later 1st earl of Chichester. Leigh was married to a niece of Buckingham and it was through Buckingham that Leigh owed his rise at court. Serving as a JP for Surrey from 1631 to 1642, Leigh emerged as an opponent of the crown in the Short Parliament of 1640 as MP for the county. He was involved in a tithe dispute with Laud in late 1636.[177]

Leachland, [**William**] (fl. 1635–41), merchant. Leachland, who lived in Mincing Lane, handled the imposts of wine for the archiepiscopal household, as well as for the household of Sir John Lambe.[178]

[**Lenthrop**] / Levinthrop / Levinthrope, [**Edward**] (fl. 1617–40), a household servant, whose duties included arranging boathire, fetching and carrying goods and acting as

---

174 *Alumni oxonienses*, II, 855; *WWL*, VII, 269.
175 John Fielding, 'Lambe, Sir John (*c*. 1566–1646)', *ODNB*.
176 *WWL*, VII, 138, IV, 446, 448; Ducarel, *Archiepiscopal palace*, Appendix, p. 21; cf. McCullough, 'Print, publication and religious politics', 298 n. 46.
177 *CSPD 1636–7*, p. 404; Thomas Seccombe, 'Leigh, Francis, first earl of Chichester (d. 1653)', rev. Sean Kelsey, *ODNB*; *WWL*, VII, 304.
178 *CSPD 1627*, p. 452, no. 530; *CSPD 1635–6*, p. 198, no. 80.

messenger. Lenthrop, who was employed in the household under Abbot, disappears from the household accounts just before Laud's house arrest in December 1640. [179]

Levant Company – an English mercantile company originally founded in 1581 by royal charter as the 'Turkey Company' – with the sole right to trade with the Ottoman Empire – the Levant Company was granted a new charter in 1592, extending its scope to Venice and the Levant. The Company was opposed to Charles I's use of impositions and tonnage and poundage, refusing to implement an increased impost on currants.

Lewes / [**Lewis, William**] (*c.* 1591–1667), Church of England clergyman. An ally of Laud, Lewis was master of the hospital of St Cross, Winchester, and served as royal chaplain to Charles I from the mid-1630s until 1644, when he was stripped of his preferments by parliament.[180]

Lichfield / Litchfield, dean of – see Fell, Samuel; Higgs, Griffin.

lieutenant of the Tower – see Balfour, William.

liftenant / lieutenant of Ireland, lord – see Wentworth, Thomas.

Lincoln, earl of – see Clinton, Theophilus.

[**Lindsay, Patrick**] (1566–1644). Lindsay was promoted to the archbishopric of Glasgow from the see of Ross in August 1633, and was an active supporter of the Perth Articles, as well as other ecclesiastical reforms implemented under Charles I, including the Scottish liturgy.[181]

Lindsey / Lyndsey, earl of – see Bertie, Robert.

[**Littleton, Edward**] (1589–1645), politician, judge and Lord Keeper. As MP for Leominster and the borough of Caernarvon in the parliaments of the 1620s, Littleton was an active politician, often sitting on over forty committees in a session. In addition to the office of solicitor-general, which he held from 1634 to 1639, his plethora of legal appointments included acting as counsel to the University of Oxford in 1631 and membership of the court of high commission in 1633. At Laud's behest, Littleton was admitted to the privy council in 1640 and he also signed the writ for the continuation of the 1640 Convocation after the dissolution of the Short Parliament.[182]

---

179 *WWL*, IV, 30.

180 Stephen Wright, 'Lewis, William (1591/2–1667)', *ODNB*.

181 Stevenson, 'Lindsay, Patrick (1566–1644)', *ODNB*.

182 www.historyofparliamentonline.org/volume/1604–1629/member/littleton-edward-ii-1590–1645; Christopher Brooks, 'Littleton, Edward, Baron Littleton (1589–1645)', *ODNB*; *WWL*, IV, 286.

Lloyd, **Marmaduke** (1585–1651), lawyer. The nephew of Marmaduke Middleton, bishop of St David's from 1590 to 1592, Lloyd was a devoted royalist who had a successful career as a circuit judge in Wales and the Marches, being appointed chief justice for Glamorgan, Brecon and Radnor in 1636.[183]

Londonderry, bishop of – see Bramhall, John.

Loveday, **Francis**, the gardener at Lambeth and, later, at Croydon.

Lowther, [**William**] (*c.* 1612–88), merchant. Lowther was a JP for Yorkshire from 1632 and was admitted to the Company of Merchant Adventurers in March 1635. Although he owned lands in Yorkshire, Lowther also resided variously in London and Hamburg. Despite not having taken up arms for the royalist cause after 1642, in 1646 he was charged with having raised a loan to help the king's northern forces. He was knighted after the Restoration.[184]

Lucas, **John** (1606–71), local politician. After his appointment as sheriff of Essex in 1636, Lucas made a significant contribution to the collection of ship money in the county, for which he was rewarded with a knighthood in 1638. Lucas's patronage of ceremonially inclined ministers earned him enemies, particularly in his locality, the home of Robert Rich, 2nd earl of Warwick. In 1642, following his attempt to provide the king with men and horses, Lucas's property was attacked and he was imprisoned, although he later served in the royalist army.[185]

Mabb, [**Edward**] (fl. 1631–45), a household servant, appointed housekeeper of Lambeth in June 1631 by Abbot, and may have continued in that capacity under Laud. His specific duties after 1635 are unclear and he was not remembered in Laud's will, but was still alive in 1645.[186]

[**MacDonnell, Katherine**] (née Manners) (*c.* 1603 – 1649), duchess of Buckingham and widow of the royal favourite, George Villiers, 1st duke of Buckingham. During the height of her husband's power, Katherine was the most influential woman at court after the queen. Despite her remarriage in April 1635 to Randall MacDonnell, son of the Catholic earl of Antrim, Katherine continued to use her former title. The second marriage was controversial and Laud, whose patronage from and loyalty to Buckingham is well known, was 'more troubled at the thing than any other friend she hath'.[187]

---

183 *Knights of England*, II, 178.

184 Christine Churches, 'Lowther, Sir William (*bap.* 1612, *d.* 1688)', *ODNB*.

185 *Knights of England*, II, 205; John Walter, 'Lucas, John, first Baron Lucas of Shenfield (1606–1671)', *ODNB*.

186 LPL, TG1, fo. 28r.

187 Jane Ohlmeyer, 'MacDonnell, Katherine, duchess of Buckingham and marchioness of Antrim (1603?–1649)', *ODNB*; *WWL*, VII, 133.

[**Mainwaring**] / Manwaring / Manwaringe / Manwayringe, **Arthur** (*c*. 1580–1648), politician and member of the royal household. Mainwaring was appointed lieutenant of Windsor Castle and forest in 1628 and was returned as MP for Huntingdon in the parliaments of the 1620s. He was listed as a member of the privy chamber as late as 1643.[188]

[**Mainwaring**] / Manwaringe / Manwayring, **Philip** (1589–1661), government official. Mainwaring was appointed as Irish secretary to Wentworth in 1634 following a period at court in which he acted as a contact for provincial gentry but for the remainder of the 1630s, he remained in Dublin, only returning to court in 1641 after Wentworth's fall.[189]

Manwaring / Manwayringe / Maynwaring, [**Roger**] (*c*. 1589–1653), Church of England clergyman. As dean of Worcester until late 1635 and consecrated bishop of St David's by Laud in early 1636, Manwaring was a strong supporter of *jure divino* monarchy and had been attacked by the committee for religion in the 1628 parliament. Controversially, he was subsequently pardoned by the king and given further preferment.[190]

Marchant / Merchant Adventurers – see Company of Merchant Adventurers.

Marchant / [Merchant] Taylors – see Company of Merchant Taylors.

[Marshal] / Marshall, Lord – see Howard, Thomas.

[**Marten**] / Martyn, **Henry** (*c*. 1561–1641), civil lawyer, judge and dean of the arches when Laud acquired the see of Canterbury in August 1633. Marten was involved in the controversial St Gregory's case concerning the position of the communion table, due to be heard before the court of arches but diverted to the privy council in November 1633 at the king's request. Having supported the parishioners rather than the crown, Marten was removed from the office of dean shortly afterwards and replaced by Sir John Lambe.[191]

[**Martin**] / Martyn, [**Edward**] (d. 1662), Church of England clergyman. Martin was serving as Laud's chaplain by 1628 and was elected president of Queen's College, Cambridge (his *alma mater*), in 1631. Martin was a staunch Laudian, whose 'Arminian' sermons at Paul's Cross were vilified during the archbishop's trial. In the archbishop's will, Martin was bequeathed his 'ring with a hyacinth in it'.[192]

---

188 www.historyofparliamentonline.org/volume/1604–1629/member/mainwaring-sir-arthur-1580–1648.
189 Fiona Pogson, 'Mainwaring, Sir Philip (1589–1661)', *ODNB*.
190 Vivienne Larminie, 'Maynwaring, Roger (1589/90?–1653)', *ODNB*.
191 James Hart, 'Marten, Sir Henry (*c*. 1561–1641), *ODNB*.
192 Anthony Milton, 'Martin, Edward (d. 1662)', *ODNB*; *WWL*, IV, 296, 444.

Master of the Rolls – see Digges, Dudley; Caesar, Charles.

Mattershed / [**Mottershed, Thomas**] (b. 1602), lawyer. Mottershed was registrar of the court of high commission and receiver of ecclesiastical fines and forfeitures. Briefly committed to the Fleet prison in the mid-1630s after an altercation with a master in Convocation, Mottershed was later released, quite possibly with Laud's help.[193]

Maxwell, [**James**] (fl. 1620–44), gentleman usher of the black rod in the House of Lords. When Maxwell was given the black rod in 1629, he was also awarded the custodianship of Windsor Little Park, an office which was annexed to the black rod by Charles I in perpetuity at the same time. Laud was held in custody at Maxwell's house in Charing Cross from 18 December 1640 to 1 March 1641, when he was escorted to the Tower in Maxwell's coach. Laud noted Maxwell's 'love and care' towards him during his house arrest.[194]

May, Adrian (b. 1604), courtier. May, an *alumnus* of St John's College, Oxford, was already acting as groom of the king's privy chamber by 1628 and in January 1638, was appointed clerk of the statutes.[195]

May, Hugh (d. 1636), government official. An *alumnus* of St John's College, Oxford, May served as clerk of the market, a treasury post for at least two decades until his death in early 1636. He also undertook duties for the dean and chapter of Rochester.[196]

May, [**Thomas**] (b. 1570), lawyer. An *alumnus* of St John's College, Oxford, May trained in the middle temple in the 1590s. Described by Laud as his 'ancient friend', May was bequeathed the archbishop's 'ring with an emerald, in which only my arms are cut'.[197]

Maynard, [**William**] (1592–1640), local politician. Maynard held a range of positions under both James I and Charles I and played an active part in implementing crown policy. In the Essex locality, Maynard encouraged the gentry to contribute to the 1626 benevolence and the 1627 forced loan, and in the early 1630s, he was responsible for collecting knighthood fines, another source of royal revenue. In 1635, he was appointed joint lord lieutenant of Essex. Maynard, an Arminian, enjoyed a long friendship with Laud.[198]

---

193 *CSPD 1635*, p. 80, no. 17.1; *CSPD 1635–6*, p. 458, no. 29.2, p. 468, no. 21; *WWL*, IV, 347, V, 80.

194 R. Tighe and J. Davis, *The annals of Windsor Castle, being a history of the castle and town*, II (London, 1858), p. 178; *WWL*, III, 240, 437.

195 *Alumni oxonienses*, III, 992; *CSPD 1637–8*, p. 173, no. 23a.

196 *Alumni oxonienses*, III, 993; *CSPD 1635–6*, p. 3, no. 18.

197 *WWL*, IV, 444.

198 www.historyofparliamentonline.org/volume/1604–1629/member/maynard-sir-william-1586–1640.

[**Mennes**] / Mynce, [**Margaret**] (*c.* 1598 – *c.* 1635), daughter of John Steward, 1st earl of Carrick, who was himself the illegitimate son of James V of Scotland. Little is known of Margaret's life, although she was married to Sir Matthew Mennes by 1630. Her exact date of death is unknown too, although she is believed to have died shortly after 1635.[199]

[**Mennes**] / Mynce / **Matthew** (1593–1648), gentleman. Mennes, of Sandwich, Kent, gained a reputation as an aggressive and litigious man during the 1630s. Parishioners in Ash, near Sandwich, petitioned Laud in June 1640 to replace Mennes with someone less severe in imposing tithes, but Mennes retained his right to collect them. From 1631, Mennes also acted as housekeeper for the archiepiscopal manor at Ford, Kent.[200]

Merrick / Merricke / [**Meyrick**], **William** (1595/6 – 1669), civil lawyer. Meyrick was one of the judges whom Laud assigned to act as counsel on his behalf following his impeachment on 23 February 1641. Meyrick was appointed judge of the prerogative court of Canterbury in October 1641 by Laud, at the time imprisoned in the Tower, although this was contested by Dr Arthur Duck, who claimed that the archbishop had in fact issued him with a patent for the office.[201]

[**Merrifield**] / Merryfield, **Ralph** (fl. 1640–5), a household servant at Croydon, who was bequeathed £40 in Laud's will.[202]

Mildmay, Anne – see under Mildmay, Henry.

Mildmay, **Henry** (*c.* 1594 – *c.* 1644), courtier and politician. A former client of Buckingham, Mildmay was returned as member for Maldon, Essex, in the parliaments of the 1620s and the Short and Long Parliaments in 1640. Mildmay participated in the attacks on Arminianism in the 1629 parliament and gave evidence against Laud at his trial in March 1644. During the 1630s, he had a number of prominent *rôles*, including that of master of the king's jewels, a position he held from at least 1625 until 1642. His wife – Lady Anne – was the daughter of William Halliday, a London alderman and governor of the East India Company.[203]

Mills, **John** (fl. 1636–40), a household servant, whose duties are largely unspecified.

[**Montagu**, **Henry**] (*c.* 1564–1642), 1st earl of Manchester, judge and government official, appointed lord keeper of the privy seal in 1628, a post he held until his death. Montagu was the chief architect of the revised Book of Orders, finalized in

---

199 Timothy Raylor, 'Sir Matthew Mennes', *HR*, 61 (1988), 118–22, at 121.
200 *CSPD 1640*, p. 316, no. 59; LPL, TG1, fos. 23v, 28v; Raylor, 'Sir Matthew Mennes', 118–22.
201 Stuart Handley, 'Meyrick, Sir William (1595/6–1669)', *ODNB*; *WWL*, III, 450.
202 *WWL*, IV, 446.
203 *CSPD 1625–6*, p. 157, no. 24a; *CSPD 1641–3*, p. 292, no. 59; Jason Peacey, 'Mildmay, Henry (c. 1594–1664/5?)', *ODNB*; *WWL*, IV, 46, 206–7.

early 1631 and which represented the cornerstone of Caroline social policy. Montagu may have been warned by Laud to stay away from a privy council meeting in 1637 at which he criticized sharply Catholic conversions around the queen, including Montagu's son.[204]

Moorton / [**Morton**, **Thomas**] (*c.* 1564–1659), Church of England bishop. A mainstream Calvinist, Morton's first episcopal appointment came in 1616, when he was consecrated bishop of Chester, where he remained until 1619. Thence he was translated to Coventry and Lichfield until 1632, when he moved to Durham. As the 1630s progressed, Morton was increasingly out of touch with court, despite having entertained the king's party en route to Edinburgh for his Scottish coronation in June 1633.[205]

[**Moreton**] / Morton, [**Edward**] (*c.* 1599–1675). Moreton was the son of William Moreton of Morton, Cheshire, and married to Margaret, daughter of Laud's uncle Sir William Webbe (d. 1599), and therefore the archbishop's cousin.

[**Morris**, **Andrew**] (d. 1654), Church of England clergyman. Appointed dean of St Asaph in August 1634, the only known interaction between Morris and Laud occurred in early 1639, when Morris petitioned the archbishop, unsuccessfully, for a transfer from the parsonage of Chiddingstone, Kent, to Llanwrst, Denbighshire. Morris was appointed rector of Llanycil, Merionethshire, in 1640. Not to be confused with either of the following entries.[206]

Morris, **Mr** (fl. 1636–41) blacksmith, who provided farriage for the archiepiscopal stables for the duration of the accounts.

Morris, **Walter** (fl. 1631–45), a household servant, who carried out duties in the scullery under Abbot from at least 1631, may well have continued in this *rôle* under Laud. Morris was left £5 in Laud's will.[207]

[**Mountague**, **Richard**] (*c.* 1575–1641), Church of England bishop. Mountague was no stranger to religious controversy during the 1620s, especially after the publication of his works *A new gagg for an old goose* (1624) and *Appello Caesarem* (1625). Despite being attacked in parliament earlier that year for his publications, Mountague was appointed bishop of Chichester in July 1628.[208]

Mountford, [John] (d. 1652), Church of England clergyman. Appointed prebend of St Paul's in 1618, Mountford joined the commission for the repair of the cathedral in

204 Brian Quintrell, 'Montagu, Henry, first earl of Manchester (*c.*1564–1642), *ODNB*; *WWL*, III, 229.
205 Brian Quintrell, 'Morton, Thomas (bap. 1564, d. 1659)', *ODNB*.
206 *Fasti*, I, 83; *CSPD 1638–9*, p. 208, no. 63; *Alumni oxoniensis*, III, 1034.
207 LPL, TG1 fo. 28r; LPL, Comm XIIa/23, fos. 64–6; *WWL*, IV, 445.
208 John Macauley, 'Mountague, Richard (bap. 1575, d. 1641)', *ODNB*.

1631. He went on to hold a number of livings in Hertfordshire during the 1630s and early 1640s, before being ejected in 1643.[209]

[**Murray, William**] (d. 1640), Church of England bishop. Little is known of Murray, but as bishop of Llandaff from 1627, his annual diocesan reports to Laud suggest that he was a moderate, who only occasionally took action against nonconformity. Murray did, however, implement the metropolitical order regarding communion table, advocating the altarwise and east-end position.[210]

Mustard, John (fl. 1631), merchant and gentleman. The brother of Thomas Mustard (d. 1636) – who was a member of the Levant and East India Companies – John Mustard originated from Kent and lived in Deptford during the 1630s.[211]

Mynne, [**Jane**] (fl. 1635–8), the wife of Sir Henry Mynne, who was accused of having been a popish recusant by William, Lord Sherard in 1635. The ensuing quarrel between the two families, in which Mynne responded by slandering Sherard, resulted in a star chamber case being brought against Sherard by Mynne in February 1638, in which Laud was involved.[212]

[**Neile, Richard**] (1562–1640), Church of England archbishop. Appointed archbishop of York in 1632 after presiding over six different episcopal dioceses, Neile enjoyed a long association with Laud, who had acted as Neile's chaplain in 1608.[213]

Newburgh, Lord – see Barrett, Edward.

Newcastle, countess of – see Cavendish, Elizabeth.

Newcastle, earl of – see Cavendish, William.

Newdigate, [**John**] (1600–42), gentleman of leisure and diarist. Following a spell as sheriff and JP in Warwickshire, Newdigate moved to Croydon in 1633, where he lived until his death. Despite his godly background, and his younger brother Richard's involvement in Laud's impeachment and trial, Newdigate's circle for much of the 1630s included Laudian clergy.[214]

Newell, [**Robert**] (1576–1642), Church of England clergyman. Newell, who was step-brother to Richard Neile, archbishop of York, held the position of archdeacon of Buckingham from 1614 and prebend of Westminster from 1620. Newell, who was part

---

209 TNA, SP 16/188 f.15; *Alumni cantabrigienses,* part I, III, 224.
210 Davies, *Caroline captivity*, p. 218; *WWL*, V, 321, 329, 334, 354.
211 Brenner, *Merchants and revolution*, p. 71.
212 *CSPD 1637–8*, p. 241, no. 65.
213 Foster, 'Neile, Richard (1562–1640)', *ODNB*.
214 *WWL*, IV, 166; *Alumni oxonienses*, III, 1060; Vivienne Lamarnie, *Wealth, kinship and culture: the seventeenth-century Newdigates of Arbury and their world* (London, 1995), p. 157.

of a group of clergy which effectively ran Westminster Abbey after the sequestration of John Williams in 1637, was committed to ceremonialism, particularly surrounding communion.[215]

Newport, **Richard** (1587–1651), local politician and 1st Baron Newport. Returned as MP for Shropshire in 1625 and 1626, Newport was appointed sheriff in 1627 and became a councillor in the Marches of Wales. During the civil war, Newport became a royalist army officer, although in the 1630s, he was generally a moderate in political and religious terms.[216]

Newton, **John** (fl. 1631–41), a household servant who carried out the duties of a 'husbandman' in the grounds around Lambeth from at least 1631. Newton was not remembered in Laud's will.[217]

Nicholas – see Tasker, Nicholas

Norris, **Elizabeth** (d. 1645), wife of Sir John Jephson.[218]

North, [**Dudley**] (*c*. 1582–1666), nobleman and poet. Having spent some years as an active participant at the Jacobean court, North came close to financial ruin and mental breakdown and, thus, spent most of the 1630s on his estates in Cambridgeshire. His chief political activity was as a member of the House of Lords, where he sat on various parliamentary committees. An advocate of moderate religious reform in the Long Parliament, North was tangentially involved in the case against Laud from 1644 to 1645.[219]

Northumberland, earl of – see Percy, Algernon.

Nutt, **Edward** (fl. 1631–45), the slaughterman at Lambeth, whose duties included driving sheep and cattle to and from the palace. Nutt, who had served under Abbot, was left £5 in Laud's will.[220]

Oliver, [**John**] (*c*. 1600–61), Church of England clergyman. Oliver was appointed domestic chaplain to Laud in 1639, shortly after receiving his doctorate, hence he can be found referred to as both 'Mr' and 'Dr Oliver' in the accounts.[221]

---

215 *WWL*, IV, 228; VI, 585.

216 Stephen Wright, 'Newport, Richard, first Baron Newport (1587–1651)', *ODNB*.

217 LPL, TG1, fo. 28r.

218 Jodocus Crull, *The antiquities of St Peters or the abbey church of Westminster* (London, 1722), p. 88.

219 Victor Stater, 'North, Dudley, third Baron North (*bap*. 1582, *d*. 1666)', *ODNB*; *WWL*, III, 437; IV, 413–17.

220 LPL, TG1, fo. 31r; *WWL*, IV, 446.

221 *Alumni oxonienses*, III, 1089; Ducarel, *Archiepiscopal palace*, Appendix, p. 21; Stephen Wright, 'Oliver, John (1600/01–1661)', *ODNB*.

[**Osbaldeston**] / Osbaston, [**Lambert**] (1594–1659) schoolmaster and Church of England clergyman. Osbaldeston, a good friend of John Williams, bishop of Lincoln, one of Laud's nemeses, was brought before star chamber with the bishop in 1639 for slandering Laud. Osbaldeston escaped harsh punishment – a £5,000 fine payable to both Laud and the king, and the nailing of his ears to the pillory – by going into hiding in London until the opening of the Long Parliament. Shortly afterwards, in 1641, he was pardoned.[222]

Oxford / Oxon, bishop of – see Bancroft, John.

[**Owen**] / Owens, **John** (1580–1651), Church of England bishop. Created bishop of St Asaph in 1629, Owen was locally popular and his tenure as bishop was relatively uncontroversial. He was one of five bishops who did not enforce altar policy in his diocese, although this did not prevent him from facing parliamentary impeachment and imprisonment in the Tower in 1641.[223]

Padgett / **Pagett**, [**Ephraim**] (1574–1646), Church of England clergyman and writer. Pagett secured Laud's approval for exporting to the continent one of his best-known works *Christianographie* (1635), several editions of which appeared during the 1630s and all of which were dedicated to Laud.[224]

Page, [**John**] (fl. 1636–48), lawyer. Page, who served as master of chancery during the 1630s, was also involved in 1643 in preparing for Laud's trial.[225]

Page, **Mistress**, a household servant, whose function is unclear, although she was paid every quarter for the duration of the accounts.

Palmer / Pallmer, [**William**] (fl. 1635–41), a household servant, who was responsible for cleaning and preparing the fireplaces, sweeping the chimneys and providing brooms, mops and fireside equipment for the archiepiscopal household.

[**Parish Clerks' Company**] – established by royal charter in 1442, the Company comprised all parish clerks in the cities of London and Westminster and their suburbs. The charter was renewed in 1636 by Charles I, following a petition to Laud by the Company.[226]

Parker, **Roger** (fl. 1631–40), one of two butlers at Lambeth, who had previously served under Abbot.[227]

---

222 Thompson Cooper, 'Osbaldeston, Lambert (1594–1659)', rev. C. S. Knighton, *ODNB*; *WWL*, VII, 525.
223 Davies, *Caroline captivity*, p. 218; Glanmor Williams, 'Owen, John (*bap.* 1580, *d.* 1651)', *ODNB*.
224 S. C. Dyton, 'Pagett, Ephraim (1574–1646)', *ODNB*; *WWL*, IV, 125.
225 TNA, ACC/0276/367; *WWL*, IV, 45; *LJ*, IV, 130.
226 TNA, SP/16/299, fo. 130; *CSPD 1635–6*, p. 252.
227 LPL, TG1, fo. 28r.

Parry, [**George**] (*c*. 1601–70), civil lawyer. Active in the London law courts from 1635 to 1639, Parry served as chancellor for Exeter diocese from 1624 until at least the mid-1650s. He stood as MP for St Mawes in Cornwall in both the Short and Long Parliaments, during which he defended the canons of 1640.[228]

Paske, [**Thomas**] (d. 1662), Church of England clergyman. Paske's appointment as prebendary and sub-dean of Canterbury in 1625 was followed a year later with the archdeaconry of London, positions he held until his death. He was also chaplain to James, 3rd marquis of Hamilton.[229]

[**Paul**] / Pawle, [**William**] (1599–1665), Church of England clergyman and, later, bishop. Paul, rector of Brightwell Baldwin in Oxfordshire from 1632, a living he continued to hold until at least 1652. Appointed chaplain to Charles I in 1635, Paul's third wife was Rachel, daughter of Christopher Clitherow, and may have been part of a London-based group of Arminian sympathizers. He was appointed bishop of Oxford in 1663.[230]

Pearce / **Pearse**, [**Thomas**] (d. 1666), chorister in the chapel royal, who had sung previously in Westminster Abbey.[231]

Peashall / [**Peshall**], **John** (1562–1646), local politician. Peshall served as sheriff of Staffordshire in the 1610s and, having been brought before his local assizes in 1626 for non-attendance at church, was thereafter returned to good favour. He seems to have been involved in local affairs, rather than national politics, during the 1630s.[232]

[**Pennyman**] / Penyman, **William** (*c*. 1606–43), politician. Pennyman had been appointed JP for Yorkshire by the mid-1630s and sheriff in 1635, probably through his business associations with Wentworth. Pennyman was commander of a regiment of Yorkshire-trained bands during the first Bishops' War in 1639 and sent Laud 'a fair and discreet letter' while camped at Berwick. He repeated this commission again in the second Bishops' War. Serving as MP for Richmond, Yorkshire in 1640, Pennyman was called to give evidence at Strafford's trial a year later, but refused the sign the bill of attainder.[233]

[**Percy**, **Algernon**] (1602–68), politician and courtier. Percy, who held an array of posts, including the lord lieutenancy of Northumberland, Westmorland and

---

228 Levack, *Civil lawyers*, p. 261.

229 *Alumni cantabrigienses*, part I, III, 316; *Fasti*, I, 52, II, 324; Charlotte Fell-Smith, 'Paske, Thomas (d. 1662)', rev. S. L. Sadler, *ODNB*.

230 *Alumni oxonienses*, III, 1128; Vivienne Larminie, 'Paule, William (1599–1665)', *ODNB*; Tyacke, *Anti-Calvinists*, p. 221.

231 Rimbault, *The old cheque book or book of remembrance of the chapel royal*, p. 203.

232 *Complete baronetage*, I, 101, *CSPD 1625–6*, p. 374, no. 68i.

233 Charles Firth, 'Pennyman, Sir William, baronet (1606/7–1643)', rev. R. M. Armstrong, *ODNB*; *WWL*, VII, 572.

Cumberland, became 10th earl of Northumberland in 1632. Percy was appointed admiral of the ship money fleet in 1636 and lord admiral in 1638, the first appointment to this post since the assassination of Buckingham a decade earlier. Percy's promotion to this pivotal *rôle* owed much to the lobbying and patronage of Laud and Wentworth. Laud clearly valued Percy's acquaintance, confiding to Wentworth in 1636 that 'if I have got him, I hope I shall be able to keep him'.[234]

Peter / [**Petre**, **Robert**] (1599–1638), nobleman. The Petres were a prominent Catholic family based in Essex, who held large swathes of land, but their religion prevented them from ever properly gaining high office. Succeeding to the title 3rd Baron Petre on his father's death in 1637, Petre survived for a mere year before himself dying.[235]

[**Phelips**] / Phillipps, **Robert** (*c.* 1586–1638), politician. Phelips, who sat as MP for Somerset in the parliaments of the 1620s, was pricked as sheriff for the county in 1625, thereby preventing him from sitting in parliament, following disagreements over crown policy towards Spain. Phelips's opposition to Arminianism and other aspects of the personal rule prevented him from gaining preferment at court. As sheriff of Somerset, he was at the forefront of objections to ship money.

Pider / [**Pindar**], **Paul** (*c.* 1565–1650), merchant and diplomat. In 1623, Pindar returned to court from his embassy in Constantinople, and during the 1630s, accumulated significant wealth by virtue of his position as customs farmer, particularly while Portland was lord treasurer. Pindar helped to fund the king's campaigns against the Scots in 1639 and 1640.[236]

Pie / [**Pye**], **Robert** (*c.* 1585–1662), politician and exchequer official. A former client of Buckingham, in whose household he served in the late 1610s, Pye held a range of offices during the 1630s, including posts in the exchequer and on the committee for the repair of St Paul's cathedral and acting as JP for London, Middlesex and Surrey. In 1637, in Pye's capacity as executor of Buckingham's will, he crossed Laud's path over arrangements for the wardship of the former favourite's son, George, later 2nd duke of Buckingham.[237]

[**Piers, William**] (*c.* 1580–1670), Church of England bishop. Having acted as vice-chancellor of Oxford University from 1621 to 1624, Piers was translated from the diocese of Peterborough, where he had been bishop since 1630, to Bath and Wells in 1632. He was among the most stringent members of the Caroline episcopal bench

---

234 George Drake, 'Percy, Algernon, tenth earl of Northumberland (1602–1668)', *ODNB*; WWL, VII, 294.

235 Christopher Clay, 'The misfortunes of William, Fourth Lord Petre (1638–1655), *British Catholic History*, 11 (1971), pp. 86–116.

236 Robert Ashton, 'Pindar, Sir Paul (1565/6–1650)', *ODNB*.

237 www.historyofparliamentonline.org/volume/1604–1629/member/pye-robert-1586–1662; Gerald Aylmer, 'Pye, Sir Robert (bap. 1585, d. 1662)', *ODNB*; *WWL*, VII, 403–4, 410–11.

when it came to enforcing Laudian reforms. He was the first bishop to enforce the 1633 St Gregory's ruling regarding the east-end location of the communion table and he courted controversy by his rigorous enforcement of the Book of Sports in his diocese.[238]

Pigeon, [**John**] (fl. 1641), servant of the royal household. Little is known of Pigeon, who worked as keeper of the wardrobe at the Tower of London.[239]

Pocock / **Pococke**, [**Edward**] (1604–91), Church of England clergyman and oriental scholar. Having previously acted as chaplain to the Levant Company in London from 1630, Pococke was the first professor of Arabic at the University of Oxford, a post established by Laud in 1636 during his tenure as chancellor. By the time of his appointment, Pococke had already been commissioned by the archbishop to collect Greek coins and manuscripts as part of the enrichment of the Bodleian Library. The intermediary between Laud and Pococke was Charles Fettiplace, who features in the accounts as 'Mr Fettiplace' or 'Mr Fettyplace'.[240]

Portsmouth, mayor of – see Beeston, Thomas.

Powell, [**Edward**] (b. 1614), schoolmaster. An *alumnus* of St John's College, Oxford, Powell was the son of John Powell of Southwark. He was funded through university by the Mercers' Company of London and was appointed sub-usher of St Paul's School (possibly his *alma mater*) in 1640 and became surmaster of the School a year later. He resigned the post in 1647.[241]

privy seal / seale, lord – see Montagu, Henry.

[**Ramsay**] / Ramsey [**David**] (d. 1642), gentleman of the privy chamber to Charles I. Ramsay, brother of Sir James Ramsay, groom of the bedchamber to Prince Henry, also served in the prince's bedchamber until the latter's death in 1612. Despite involvement in a high-profile dispute with Lord Reay which reached the court of chivalry in the early 1630s, he was still in the king's privy chamber in 1633.[242]

Raylton, [**William**] (d. 1653), agent to Thomas Wentworth, lord deputy of Ireland. Raylton was indispensable to Wentworth while in Dublin, not only in the transaction of business, but through acting as his master's 'eyes and ears at court'. He regularly conveyed letters and information from Wentworth to Laud and had, by at least 1636, moved 'beyond the conventional duties of an agent', in regularly discussing Irish affairs with the archbishop.[243]

---

238 M. Dorman, 'Piers, William (bap. 1580, d. 1670)', *ODNB*; *WWL*, VI, 319.
239 TNA, E115/315/141.
240 Gerald Toomer, 'Pococke, Edward (1604–1691)', *ODNB*.
241 *Alumni oxonienses*, III, 1190; *Biographical register of SJC*, p. 396.
242 Stephen Wright, 'Ramsay, David (*d.* 1642)', *ODNB*.
243 Fiona Pogson, 'The career of William Raylton', *HR* (2011), 84, 53, 58.

Reeves / [**Ryves, Thomas**] (d. 1652), civil lawyer. Ryves acted as advocate general to Charles I and extraordinary master of requests from 1626. He was placed on a commission to visit schools and churches in the diocese of Canterbury in 1634 and was knighted by Charles I in March 1644.[244]

Reynolds / [**Reynell**], **Thomas** (*c.* 1590–1665), courtier and politician. Reynell, who married a daughter of Sir Henry Spiller, served as cupbearer in the household of Charles I prior to his accession and was in the king's privy chamber from 1625 to 1646. Reynell was returned as MP for Morpeth in parliament from 1624 to 1628, but did not take up his seat after 1640.[245]

Richmond, duchess of – see Stuart, Frances.

[**Roberts**, **William**] (1585–1665), Church of England bishop. Roberts, who was cousin of Godfrey Goodman, bishop of Gloucester, was a keen supporter of Laud. He was elected bishop of Bangor in June 1637 and was consecrated in September.[246]

Robinson, [**Anthony**] (*c.* 1582–1641), alderman of Gloucester. Robinson, who served as MP for Gloucester in 1621 and 1624, was appointed to the post of alderman in 1626 and appears to have held the post until his death in 1641. In 1634, he petitioned Laud on behalf of the city in favour of a puritan lecturer, John Workman. From 1635, he was appointed deputy lieutenant of Gloucestershire.[247]

Robinson, [**Hugh**] (1583/4–1655), Church of England clergyman and schoolmaster. Having held various rectories in Wales, Hampshire and Buckinghamshire in the late 1610s and early 1620s, Robinson was appointed canon of Lincoln cathedral in 1625 and collated to the archdeaconry of Gloucester in 1634. Laud approved of Robinson's 'grave and fitting' approach to his archdiaconal duties.[248]

Robinson, **John** (*c.* 1615–80), merchant, financier and local politician. Robinson, who acted as alderman of the city of London during the 1630s, was the son of Laud's half-brother, William Robinson. After the Restoration, he became lord mayor of London and lieutenant of the Tower of London.[249]

Rochester, bishop of – see Bowle, John; Warner, John.

Rochester, dean of – see King, Henry.

Roe, [**Eleanor**] (d. 1675), wife of Sir Thomas Roe, who accompanied him on some

---

244 David Davies, 'Ryves, Sir Thomas (d. 1652)', *ODNB*.
245 Mary Wolffe, 'Reynell family (per. 1540–1735)', *ODNB*.
246 Gwynfor Jones, 'Roberts, William (1585–1665)', *ODNB*.
247 www.historyofparliamentonline.org/volume/1604–1629/member/robinson-anthony-1582–1641.
248 Rosemary O'Day, 'Robinson, Hugh (1583/4–1655)', *ODNB*; *WWL*, V, 359.
249 Paul Seaward, 'Robinson, Sir John, first baronet (bap. 1615, d. 1680)', *ODNB*.

of his diplomatic missions, and who secured Laud's support to join her husband during his mission to Hamburg in 1639, when it was clear that he would not be returning to England.[250]

Roe, **Thomas** (1581–1644), diplomat. Roe served James I and Charles I in India, Turkey, the Baltic and northern Europe. After a stint as chancellor of the order of the garter at Windsor in 1636, Roe resumed ambassadorial duties in 1638. He pursued Laud's friendship from the mid-1630s, possibly to further his quest for a peerage as a reward for diplomatic service and extant correspondence supports this, although more than once Laud berated Roe for his extensive use of cipher, which was 'extreme hard and … ill expressed'.[251]

Roger – see Parker, Roger

[**Rolleston**] / Rollston [**Simon**] (fl. 1635–45), a household servant. Rolleston was bequeathed £50 in Laud's will.[252]

Rose, [**Ambrose**] (fl. 1631–41), 'gentleman retayner' to the archiepiscopal household. Rose, a farmer and landowner, provided barley, malt and wheat to the household, from his lands in Chislet, near Canterbury.[253]

Russell, **William** (*c.* 1575–1654), merchant and naval administrator. Acting as treasurer of the navy from 1618, Russell held this position almost until his death. From 1639 until late 1641, he was assisted as joint treasurer by Sir Henry Vane the Younger.[254]

[**Ryley**] / Rylye, [**William**] (d. 1667), herald. Ryley, who held various heraldic posts during the 1630s, under the supervision of Sir John Borough. Ryley was admitted to Lincoln's Inn in 1638 and joined the king at Oxford in 1642.[255]

[**Sackville, Edward**] (1590–1652), courtier and politician. Sackville, 4th earl of Dorset, came into conflict with Laud on a number of occasions in the 1630s, not least because of his fierce loyalty to Henrietta Maria, to whom he acted as lord chamberlain from the mid-1630s. He held the same position for the king in exile from 1644.[256]

[**Sackville, Mary**] (1586–1645), countess of Dorset and wife of Sir Edward Sackville, 4th earl of Dorset, and governess to the royal children from the late 1630s until close to her death.[257]

---

250 Michael Strachan, 'Roe, Sir Thomas (1581–1644)', *ODNB*; *WWL*, VII, 548, 558.
251 ibid; *WWL*, VII, 460.
252 *WWL*, IV, 445.
253 Canterbury Cathedral Archives, DCb/j/j/56/194; LPL, TG1, fo. 28v.
254 Andrew Thrush, 'Russell, Sir William, first baronet (*c.* 1575–1654)', *ODNB*; *WWL*, V, 351; VII, 145.
255 Stuart Handley, 'Ryley, William (*d.* 1667)', *ODNB*.
256 David Smith, 'Sackville, Edward, fourth earl of Dorset (1590–1652)', *ODNB*.
257 David Smith, 'Sackville, Mary, countess of Dorset (bap. 1586, d. 1645)', *ODNB*.

Sadler, **Thomas** (fl. 1636–45), the archbishop's tailor, who also crafted clothing for other household servants. Sadler was left £10 in Laud's will.[258]

St Asaph, bishop of – see Owen, John.

St Asaph, dean / deane of – see Morris, Andrew.

Salisbury / Sarum, dean / deane of – see Baylie, Richard.

Salisbury, earl of – see Cecil, William.

Sands / [**Sandys**] **George** (1578–1644), writer, traveller and gentleman of the privy chamber. Sandys was heavily involved in the Virginia Company during the 1610s and 1620s, but returned to England in 1625 following a four-year spell as treasurer for the colony. On his return, he was appointed to Charles I's privy chamber and, in 1638, he joined the sub-committee for foreign plantations under Laud.[259]

Sands / [**Sandys**], **William** (*c*. 1607–69), politician. Serving as MP for Evesham in the Short and Long Parliaments, Sandys had become a servant of Henrietta Maria by 1648. He had some dealings with Laud during the 1630s, regarding the rights of patronage to two parsonages which were donated to St John's College, Oxford.[260]

Savage, [**Elizabeth**] (1581–1651), courtier and lady of the bedchamber to Henrietta Maria. In November 1635, on the death of her husband – Thomas Savage, chancellor to the queen – Elizabeth Savage inherited estates in Chester and Lancashire. Both she and her husband were associated with crown policy during the 1630s and this, combined with their religion – they were Catholic – made Elizabeth an inevitable target for popular protest after the outbreak of civil war in 1642.[261]

Saye, Lord – see Fiennes, William.

Scott, **Stephen** (d. 1658), local politician. Appointed sheriff of Kent in 1648, Scott, whose country seat was in Hayes, also served as gentleman pensioner to Charles I. His wife, 'Lady Scott' appears in the accounts as a gift-giver.[262]

Scudamore, [**John**] (1601–71), diplomat and politician. Prior to a brief sojourn in Paris as English ambassador from 1635 to 1536, John, 1st Viscount Scudamore spent

---

258 *WWL*, IV, 446.

259 James Ellison, 'Sandys, George (1578–1644)', *ODNB*.

260 www.historyofparliamentonline.org/volume/1660–1690/member/sandys-william-1607–69; *WWL*, VII, 307, 434.

261 John Walter, 'Savage, Elizabeth, suo jure countess Rivers (1581–1651)', *ODNB*; *WWL*, VII, 206.

262 *CSPD 1648–9*, p. 234, no. 81(a); *The history and topographical survey of the countuy of Kent*, ed. Edward Hasted (Canterbury, 1797), I, p. 206; *The environs of London – the counties of Herts, Essex and Kent*, ed. Daniel Lysons (London, 1796), IV, 496.

much of the early 1630s renovating churches in his native Herefordshire, including Dore, the consecration of which occupied an entire day in March 1635, and which epitomized the 'beauty of holiness'. Scudamore's close association with Laud, to whom he looked up as a quasi-paternal figure, is well known, as is his attachment to Laudianism.[263]

Seamour / [**Seymour**, **Dorothy**] (fl. 1626–77), member of Henrietta Maria's household. Little is known of Seymour, appointed as one of the queen's maids of honour in 1626, although she remained in post beyond 1641, even if she may not have accompanied the queen to Oxford in 1642. Seymour was still alive in 1677, having successfully petitioned three debtors for the reimbursement of a personal loan.[264]

Secretary, Mr – see Coke, John.

[**Sedley**] / Sidley, [**Elizabeth**] (*c.* 1595 – *c.* 1651.). Little is known of Elizabeth, who appears in the accounts as 'Lady Sidley'. She was, however, the mother of Henry, an undergraduate at St John's College, Oxford, in the late 1630s. In 1639, Elizabeth appealed to Laud for his assistance in ensuring that her son was 'entertained … with more than ordinary respect' by the College. The following year, she also sought his help in acquiring land in Oxford for the sum of £500.[265]

Selden, [**John**] (1584–1654), scholar and lawyer. Selden, who was imprisoned after the collapse of the 1629 parliament for his part in giving constitutional advice to the Commons' leaders, had restored his reputation with the king by 1635. The publication of *Mare Clausum* defended British sovereignty of the seas. Neither did Selden's former opposition to Buckingham in the 1620s prevent him from forming a friendship with Laud during the mid-1630s, dedicating two of his works to the archbishop.[266]

Sheldon, [**Gilbert**] (1598–1677), Church of England clergyman and, later, archbishop of Canterbury. Sheldon, who held a number of livings in Oxfordshire during the 1630s, was elected warden of All Souls College, Oxford, in 1635, having the previous year acted as vice-chancellor to the university, a post to which he returned in 1640. In 1639, he became a royal chaplain. Possibly a protégé of Laud, Sheldon was certainly a Laudian sympathizer.[267]

[**Shelley**] / Shelly, **John** (fl. 1630–9), local politician. Appointed grand collector of ship money for Arundel, Sussex, in 1637, Shelley's severe ill health caused the

---

263 Ian Atherton, 'Scudamore, John, first Viscount Scudamore (1601–1671)', *ODNB*; *WWL*, VI, 336.

264 Durham Record Office, D547M/T27; Sara Wolfson, 'Aristocratic women of the household and court of Queen Henrietta 1625–1659', Ph.D. dissertation, Durham University, 2010, pp. 78, 147, 272.

265 *Alumni oxonienses*, IV, 1332; *CSPD 1639–40*, p. 508, no. 9; *WWL*, VII, 558.

266 Paul Christianson, 'Selden, John (1584–1654)', *ODNB*.

267 John Spurr, 'Sheldon, Gilbert (1598–1677)', *ODNB*; *WWL*, VI, 444.

county sheriffs to appeal to the king for a replacement. His wife, about whom little is known, was Lady Jane Shelley and his son William, who died in 1637, was married to Christiana Maria, a chamberer to Henrietta Maria, known as Lady Christiana Shelley.[268]

Shelton, **Thomas** (fl. 1631–8), a household servant, who acted as clerk of the kitchen at Lambeth from at least 1631.[269]

[**Sherard**] / Sherwood, [**William**] (d. 1640), local landowner. Knighted by James I in 1619, Sherard was an Irish peer, some of whose lands in Rutland neighboured on those of Sir Henry Mynne. At the Oakham assizes in 1635, Sherard accused Mynne's wife, Lady Jane, of being a recusant, leading to a protracted dispute between both families, in which Mynne retaliated by casting aspersions on Sherard's aristocratic title. By 1638, it had led to cases in both the court of chivalry and star chamber, with Laud officiating in the latter case.[270]

Shrewsbury, earl of – see Talbot, John.

Skinner, [**Robert**] (1591–1670), Church of England bishop. Promoted to the bishopric of Bristol in 1636, Skinner showed a preference for Arminianism. He was translated to the see of Oxford in November 1641 but, shortly afterwards, was among the group of twelve bishops imprisoned in the Tower for protesting against their exclusion from the House of Lords.[271]

Smith / [**Smyth**, **Henry**] (fl. 1625–35), vice-chancellor of the University of Cambridge in 1625, 1626 and 1635.

Snaythe / **Snaith** / Snaithe, [**George**] (fl. 1635–45), a household servant, was responsible for fetching and carrying, and arranging and paying for boathire for Laud's journeys along the Thames. Snaith frequently accompanied Laud to court. Snaith was left £50 in Laud's will, to which he was also one of the five signatories in January 1644.[272]

[**Snelgrove**] / Snellgrave, **Henry** (fl. 1626–38), local politician. Little is known of Snelgrove, except that he was created knight bachelor by James I in 1617 and was deputy lord lieutenant of Hampshire in 1626.[273]

---

268 *CSPD 1634–5*, p. 597, no. 37; *CSPD 1636–7*, p. 105, no. 76, p. 365, no. 10; *CSPD 1637*, p. 522, no. 43d; *CSPD 1637–8*, p. 92.

269 LPL, TG1, fos. 23v, 28v.

270 *CSPD 1637–8*, p. 241, no. 65; Cust, *Charles I and the aristocracy*, pp. 148–9; *Cases in the high court of chivalry*, ed. Cust and Hopper, p. 257; TNA, C115/8854.

271 Larminie, 'Skinner, Robert (1591–1670)', *ODNB*; *WWL*, III, 243.

272 *WWL*, IV, 344, 445, 450.

273 *Knights of England*, II, 165; TNA, PC2/34, fo. 61.

Solicitor, Mr – see Littleton, Edward.

Southes / Sutches, [**James**] (fl. 1631–45), a servant of the archiepiscopal household, who performed regular tasks for Laud, such as arranging and paying for boathire, delivering letters and settling routine payments. Southes, whose father, William, was a master mason and goldsmith, was rewarded for his services with a bequest in Laud's will of £50.[274]

Spellar / **Spiller**, **Henry** (*c.* 1570–1649), politician. Returned for Middlesex in 1628, Spiller held a number of offices during the 1630s, including JP, commissioner for sewers and the soap monopoly and clerk to the exchequer. He was also appointed commissioner for collecting the forced loan in 1627 and for the repair of St Paul's cathedral in 1631. Spiller was suspected of Catholicism and was placed in custody in late 1640, later serving as royalist commissioner during the civil war.[275]

Sprackling / Spracklinge / Spratling / Spratlinge, [**Adam**] (fl. 1636–1640), yeoman retainer in the archiepiscopal household. Sprackling, whose lands were in Fordwich, Kent, supplied wheat, malt and barley to Lambeth. Unlike John Denn and Ambrose Rose, who played a similar part in the life of the household, there is no evidence that Sprackling carried out this *rôle* under Abbot.[276]

Squire, **Mr** (fl. 1636–41), a household servant, whose duties are unclear, but who was paid every quarter for the duration of the accounts and lived in the household.

Stanley / Stanly, [**Edward**] (*c.* 1598–1662), Church of England clergyman and schoolmaster. In September 1630, Stanley, who had been headmaster of Winchester College since 1627, was nominated for the wardenship of the College by Laud, when the latter was bishop of London. Stanley, already Laud's chaplain, was recommended as 'a good able scholar'. In the event, Stanley was passed over in favour of John Harris but he remained headmaster of Winchester until 1642.[277]

Staple, [**William**] (1597–1650), Church of England clergyman and schoolmaster. An *alumnus* of St John's College, Oxford, Staple acted as servant or agent to Sir John Scudamore during the 1620s. He was appointed master of the Merchant Taylors' School, London, in 1634 at Laud's behest.[278]

Stationers' [**Company**] – founded in 1403 and given its royal charter in 1557, the Stationers' Company worked very closely with the archbishops of Canterbury and the bishops of London in the business of licensing works for the press. In some

274 Ducarel, *Archiepiscopal palace*, Appendix, p. 47; *WWL*, IV, 446.
275 www.historyofparliamentonline.org/volume/1604–1629/member/spiller-henry-1570–1649.
276 Canterbury Cathedral Archives, DCb/PRC/18/13/35.
277 *WWL*, VI, 278.
278 *Biographical register of SJC*, p. 141; *The further correspondence of William Laud*, ed. Fincham, pp. 7 n. 7, 25; *WWL*, VI, 367.

instances, the Company helped to bring to the attention of the archbishop – and the courts -unlicensed material.

Stearne / **Sterne**, [**Richard**] (1595/6–1683), Church of England clergyman and, later, archbishop of York. Sterne was appointed to the rectory of Yeovilton, Somerset by Laud in 1634, a year after he became one of the archbishop's domestic chaplains. Sterne was close to Laud, being present on the scaffold when the archbishop was executed.[279]

[**Stewart**, **John**] (*c.* 1599–1659), privy councillor and lord high treasurer of Scotland from 1636. Stewart's career flourished considerably after the accession of Charles I in 1625 and he was created 1st earl of Traquair during the royal visit to Scotland in June 1633. His prominence in Scottish affairs from the mid-1630s led to his being identified closely with the implementation of the controversial prayer book in Scotland in 1637, despite his own personal distrust of the Scottish bishops. After Laud's imprisonment in 1641, the archbishop referred to the earl as having 'played fast and loose with me', despite their having contracted a successful working relationship during the previous decade.[280]

[**Stuart**, **Elizabeth**] (1596–1662), Queen of Bohemia and electress of Palatine, daughter of James I and sister of Charles I. Brought up a Calvinist and married (in 1613) to Frederick V, count palatine of the Rhine and elector of the Holy Roman Empire, Elizabeth's position became central to European dynastic and confessional politics after 1619, when her husband accepted the crown of Bohemia. Elizabeth was on good terms with Laud's archiepiscopal predecessor, George Abbot, but had a more distant relationship with Laud, although they corresponded during the 1630s.[281]

[**Stuart**, **Frances**] (née Howard) (1578–1639), dowager duchess of Richmond and Lennox. Frances married Edward Seymour, earl of Hertford in 1601 and on Hertford's death in 1621, married Ludovick Stuart, 3rd duke of Lennox. In 1623, Lennox was also given the title duke of Richmond but he died the following year. Thereafter, Frances remained unmarried (although very rich) until her own death in October 1639. Frances's associations with Laud are not well known, but a range of gifts were sent to the archbishop, until shortly before her death.[282]

[**Style**] / Styles, **Humfrey** (d. 1659), courtier and royal servant. Style, a resident of Langley in Kent, was created baronet in 1627. He held the office of cupbearer to Charles I during the 1630s, having previously acted as gentleman of James I's

279 Ducarel, *Archiepiscopal palace*, Appendix, p. 21; A. F. Pollard, 'Sterne, Richard (1595/6–1683)', rev. John Spurr, *ODNB*; *WWL*, IV, 424, 437.

280 Jared Sizer, 'Stewart, John, first earl of Traquair (*c.* 1599–1659)', *ODNB*; *WWL*, III, 314, VI, 409, 438–40, 491–6, 504–6.

281 Ronald Asch, 'Elizabeth, Princess (1596–1662)', *ODNB*.

282 Donald Foster, 'Stuart, Frances, duchess of Lennox and Richmond (1578–1639)', *ODNB*.

bedchamber. Little is known of his wife, Elizabeth, Lady Style, although she also sent gifts to Laud.[283]

Subdean / Subdeane, Mr – see Boughton, Stephen.

Suffolk, earl of – see Howard, Theophilus.

Sumner, [**George**] (fl. 1631–41), a wood-reeve listed as a 'yeoman retayner' at Lambeth from 1631. Sumner was responsible for overseeing woods on the archiepiscopal estate, including those in Kent.[284]

[**Talbot**, **John**] (1601–54), local politician. The openly Catholic 10th earl of Shrewsbury, Talbot was on the periphery of court life during the 1630s. He did, however, attend the council of peers at York in August 1640 and was a royalist after the outbreak of civil war in 1642.[285]

Tallnage / [**Tollemache**] / Tollnage, **Elizabeth** (d. 1661). The daughter of Sir John Stanhope of Harrington, Northamptonshire, Elizabeth married Sir Lionel Tollemache in 1612.

Tallnage / [**Tollemache**] / Tollnage, **Lionel** (1591–1640), politician. Returned as MP for Orford in 1628, Tollemache held a number of local appointments during the 1620s and 1630s. He acted as forced loan collector for Norfolk and Suffolk in 1626–7, collector of knighthood fines in 1630–1 and JP for Suffolk until *c.* 1637. By 1636, Tollemache had also been appointed gentleman extraordinary of the king's privy chamber.[286]

[**Tasker**], **Nicholas (**fl. 1637–45 a servant attached to the household, whose duties mainly involved moving horses from the archiepiscopal manors in Kent to Lambeth. Tasker was bequeathed £10 in Laud's will.[287]

Taylor, [**Jeremy** / Jeremiah] (*c.* 1608–67), Church of England clergyman. A rising star in the church, Taylor was appointed domestic chaplain to Laud in 1636 and, later, to Charles I. His appointment to the rectory of Uppingham in Rutland in 1638 took him away from the limelight, but he may have had to resume royal service in 1642, when he was supposedly with the king at Nottingham.[288]

---

283 William Betham, *The baronetage of England or the history of the English baronets*, I (London, 1805), 295.

284 LPL, TG1, fos. 23v, 28v.

285 Cust, *Charles I and the aristocracy*, pp. 83, 314.

286 www.historyofparliamentonline.org/volume/1604–1629/member/tollemache-sir-lionel-1591–1640.

287 *WWL*, IV, 446.

288 *Alumni oxonienses*, III, 1459; Ducarel, *Archiepiscopal palace*, Appendix, p. 21; John Spurr, 'Taylor, Jeremy (*bap.* 1613, *d.* 1667)', *ODNB.*

Terringham, [**Thomas**] (fl. 1616–37), ranger of Windsor Great Park during the 1610s, who also served as master of the privy pack of buckhounds at Windsor between 1633 and 1637. In this capacity, Terringham was responsible for organizing royal hunting trips.[289]

Thanet / Thanett, earl of – see Tufton, John.

[**Tomkins**] / Tompkins, [**Nathaniel**] (1599–1681), Church of England clergyman and musician. Tomkins was appointed canon of Worcester cathedral by Laud in 1629 and allegedly later acted as informant for the archbishop against bishop John Williams of Lincoln. Tomkins was certainly not in favour with the bishop of Worcester, who reportedly 'hated' Tomkins, following an altercation in Worcester cathedral in 1637, which was reported to Laud.[290]

[**Torless**] / Torlesse, **Adam** (1585–1641), household servant and *alumnus* of St John's, Oxford. Described by Laud as his 'ancient, loving and faithful servant', Torless served the archbishop for 'full forty and two years' until his death, acting as steward to the household for the duration of the accounts. On his steward's demise, in September 1641, the archbishop attested to their longstanding friendship, pronouncing that Torless had been 'almost the only comfort of my affliction, and my age'.[291]

[**Towers, John**] (d. 1649), Church of England bishop. Described as 'the most combative of the Laudian bishops', Towers was consecrated bishop of Peterborough by Laud at Lambeth in January 1639. He went on to enforce the full range of Laudian reforms in his visitation articles.[292]

[**Tradescant**, **John**] (d. 1638), royal gardener and collector. Tradescant, who joined the service of Buckingham in 1623, moved to south Lambeth after the duke's assassination in 1628. Known for collecting exotic plants and curiosities, Tradescant designed the bowling green at Oatlands Palace and may have contributed to the gardens at Lambeth, close to which he resided.[293]

[**Traquair**]/ Traquare, earl of – see Stewart, John.

treasurer, lord – see Juxon, William.

Tonstall / [**Tunstall**], **John** (fl. 1619–38), local politician and resident of Croydon. Tunstall, a Catholic, was knighted by James I in 1618, and in 1630, was named

289 Jane Roberts, *Royal landscape: the gardens and parks of Windsor* (New Haven, 1997), p. 14.

290 *CSPD 1636–7*, p. 390, no. 107; John Irving, 'Tomkins, Thomas (1572–1656)', *ODNB*.

291 *Alumni oxonienses*, IV, 1497; *WWL*, III, 449.

292 John Fielding, 'Towers, John (d. 1649)', *ODNB*.

293 Arthur MacGregor, 'Tradescant, John, the Elder (d. 1638)', *ODNB*.

among six men to attend the infant Prince Charles (later Charles II) at St James's Palace. Tunstall was also present in the royal party when the king and queen were hosted at St John's College, Oxford, by Laud in August 1636 and he acted as JP for Surrey in the 1630s.[294]

[**Tufton, John**] (1608–64), local politician. Knighted by Charles I in 1627, Tufton became 2nd earl of Thanet on the death of his father, Nicholas, in 1631. Local affairs occupied much of Tufton's time during the 1630s, where he secured the purchase of Bodiam Castle, Kent, in 1639. He was called upon to provide horse and men for the king's first Scottish campaign in 1639 and became a staunch royalist during the civil war.[295]

Turkey Merchants / Marchants – see Levant Company.

Turner / [**Turnor**], **Christopher** (1607–1675), lawyer. Turner joined the inns of court in 1633 and was made joint receiver-general of south Wales in March 1639. He was knighted by Charles II in 1660.[296]

Turner, **Margaret** (née Windebank) (*c.* 1607–92). By 1637, Margaret Windebank had married Dr Thomas Turner (see above), a client of her father, Sir Francis Windebank (*c.* 1582–1646), secretary of state to Charles I.

Turner, [**Thomas**] (*c.* 1592–1672), Church of England clergyman. Turner, who held the living of St Olave, Southwark, during the 1630s, had been appointed chaplain and licenser to Laud, as bishop of London, by 1629. By 1633, he was chaplain-in-ordinary to Charles I and accompanied the king on his coronation visit to Scotland in June 1633. In Laud's will, Turner was bequeathed the archbishop's 'ring with a diamond, and the garter about it'.[297]

[**Van Dyck**] / Vandike / Vandyke, **Anthony** (1599–1641), Dutch artist and court painter to Charles I from 1632.

Venn, **Lady**, the wife of Sir Richard Venn, lord mayor of London in 1637.[298]

Vintners' Company – established in 1383 by royal charter, the Vintners' Company originally had the monopoly on all imports of wine from Gascony, although its status was in decline by the seventeenth century.

---

294 *CSPD 1629–31*, p. 331; *CSPD 1636–7* pp. 407, 457; *Knights of England*, II, 172; *Newsletters*, ed. Questier, p. 289.

295 *CSPD 1635–6*, p. 396, no. 93; *CSPD 1638–9*, p. 466, no. 139; *Knights of England*, II, 193.

296 Stuart Handley, 'Turnor, Sir Christopher (1607–1675)', *ODNB*.

297 Ducarel, *Archiepiscopal palace*, Appendix, p. 21; Elizabeth Allen, 'Turner, Thomas (bap. 1592, d. 1672)', *ODNB*; *WWL*, IV, 444.

298 *CSPD 1639–40*, p. 463, no. 47.

Wake, [**Anna**] (1593–1642), widow of Sir Isaac Wake (1580/1–1632), English ambassador to Venice, Turin and France during the early 1630s. Lady Wake, born Anna Bray, was half-sister to Sir Edward Conway and procured his assistance to alleviate the dire financial straits into which she was plunged on the death of her husband in 1632.[299]

Walker, [Thomas], (d. 1665), Church of England clergyman and *alumnus* of St John's College, Oxford. During the 1630s, Walker was master of University College, Oxford. In his will, Laud bequeathed to Walker, his 'kinsman', his 'ring with a sapphire in it'.[300]

Wallop / Wallopp, **Henry** (1568–1642), local politician. Wallop was returned as MP for Hampshire in all the parliaments from 1626 to 1640. An opponent of the forced loan, Wallop was pricked as sheriff in 1629 and was in trouble again in 1631, when he was fine £200 for failing to call in distraint of knighthood fines. Wallop appeared before star chamber in 1633 for a range of misdemeanours.[301]

[**Walthew, Robert**] (fl. 1632), lawyer. Little is known of Walthew, who had Kentish origins, except that he was in post as 'Sergeant of the Confectionary' in 1632 and may have been appointed under James I.[302]

Warner, [**John**] (1581–1666), Church of England bishop. Having been rector of Hollingbourne in Kent, Warner became bishop of Rochester in late 1637. Warner was among the royal chaplains who accompanied Charles I on his coronation visit to Scotland in 1633 and as bishop, was associated with enforcing controversial religious policies (such as the railing in of the communion table).[303]

Warren, [**Robert**] (fl. 1636), Church of England clergyman. Little is known of Warren, who acted as standing commissioner for Matthew Wren, bishop of Ely, in 1636. Warren was also rector of Long Melford, Suffolk, during the 1630s.[304]

Warwick, [**Philip**] (1609–83), politician and historian. Warwick, secretary to William Juxon after the latter's appointment as lord treasurer in Mar. 1636, also served as clerk of the signet from the same year. As secretary to Charles I from 1647, Warwick's personal proximity to the monarch informed his *Memoires of the reign of King Charles I*, published posthumously in 1701. Having served as MP for Radnor in the Long Parliament – a position from which he was ejected in 1645 – Warwick survived the Interregnum and was knighted by Charles II in 1660.[305]

---

299 Vivienne Larminie, 'Wake, Sir Isaac (1580/81–1632)', *ODNB*.
300 *Alumni oxonienses,* IV, 1558; *WWL*, IV, 444, 447; VII, 424.
301 www.historyofparliamentonline.org/volume/1604–1629/member/wallop-sir-henry-1568–1642.
302 *CSPD 1606*, p. 211, no. 403; *CSPD 1631–3*, p. 399, no. 17; *Alumni oxonienses*, IV, 1566.
303 Ian Green, 'Warner, John (bap. 1581, d. 1666)', *ODNB*.
304 *Visitation articles*, p. 163.
305 David Smith, 'Warwick, Sir Philip (1609–1683)', *ODNB*.

Washborn / [**Washborne, Benjamin**] (fl. 1638), little is known of Washborne, who was resident in the parish of St Mary Colechurch, London, during the 1630s. His donation of £1 towards the cost of repairing his local church in 1638 suggests that he may have been a supporter of some of the Laudian reforms.[306]

Watts, [**Ralph**] (fl. 1631–45), a household servant, who was responsible for working in the grounds of Lambeth Palace, cleaning the moat and clearing the gardens. Watts, who served under Abbot, was bequeathed £10 in Laud's will.[307]

Webb, **Thomas** (fl. 1637–41), the son of Sir William Webb, and great-grandson of Laud's uncle, also Sir William Webb, was placed by the archbishop with 'a careful divine', John Bancroft, bishop of Oxford for tutelage. Payments for Webb's clothing, lodgings, food and upkeep are recorded in the accounts.[308]

[**Weldon**] / Welldon, **Anthony** (*c*. 1583–1648), Kentish politician and former member of the royal household. Weldon, who accompanied James I on his visit to Scotland in 1617, resigned his post as clerk of the green cloth and kitchen in 1623 for reasons which are unclear, but which may be linked to his purported authorship of the anti-Jacobean tract *The court and character of James I*, published in 1650.[309]

[**Wentworth**, **Thomas**] (1593–1641), lord deputy and later lord lieutenant of Ireland and 1st earl of Strafford. Wentworth's association with Laud, transacted primarily through frequent correspondence between Dublin and London from 1633 until Wentworth's return to support the king in autumn 1639, was perhaps his closest political association, despite their geographical distance from one another.[310]

[**Wentworth**, **Thomas**] (1591–1667), earl of Cleveland and lord lieutenant of Bedfordshire from 1625. Distantly related to Thomas Wentworth, earl of Strafford, Cleveland had been a patron of Buckingham in the 1620s and served with the duke at La Rochelle in 1627. He went on to lead royal forces during the civil war, including at the second battle of Newbury in October 1644.[311]

Westmoreland, countess of – see Fane, Mary

Whaley / [**Whaly**], **Mistress**, **Widdow** (fl. 1635–41), a household servant, who managed the slaughterhouse within the grounds of Lambeth Palace. It is possible that an initial reference to 'Old Whaley' refers to Mistress Whaly's husband (who

---

306 People in Place project, 'Vestry minutes, St Mary Colechurch: 1638–72', in *St Mary Colechurch: vestry minutes 1613–72* (London, 2011), British History Online www.british-history.ac.uk/no-series/vestry-mins-colechurch-1613–72/vestry-minutes-1638–72.

307 *WWL*, IV, 445.

308 *WWL*, VII, 64.

309 Joseph Marshall and Sean Kelsey, 'Weldon, Sir Anthony (bap. 1583, d. 1648)', *ODNB*.

310 Asch, 'Wentworth, Thomas, first earl of Strafford (1593–1641)', *ODNB*.

311 David Smith, 'Wentworth, Thomas, earl of Cleveland (1591–1667)', *ODNB*.

then died, as she is sometimes referred to as 'Widdow'); and that later references to 'Mr Whaley' relate to her second husband or possibly her son.[312]

Wheate, [**William**] (b. 1595), lawyer. Wheate, an *alumnus* of St John's College, Oxford, whom Laud described as having been 'bred under me', entered the middle temple in 1620. He was related by marriage to Richard Baylie, who was himself related by marriage to Laud.[313]

Whitaker / **Whittaker**, [**Laurence**] (*c.* 1578–1654), local politician and government official. Whittaker, who stood as MP for Peterborough in the parliaments of 1624 to 1629 and for Okehampton in 1641, acted as clerk extraordinary of the privy council from 1624 to 1642. He was also collector of the forced loan in Middlesex in 1626 and the following year, was appointed JP for the county, a post he held until 1642. Whittaker also acted as commissioner for the repair of St Paul's in 1631.[314]

[**Whitford**, **Walter**] (d. 1647), Church of Scotland bishop. Whitford became bishop of Brechin in 1635 and was an active member of the reinvigorated Scottish court of high commission, established in 1634. As bishop, Whitford was an enthusiastic supporter of the liturgical changes put in place by Charles I and Laud and was threatened with physical violence in 1637 for announcing his intention to read the new service book. In 1641, although now in the Tower, Laud used his influence to place Whitford's son, John, in the rectory of Northamptonshire.[315]

Whitlock, [**Bulstrode**] (1605–75), lawyer and politician. Whitlock, who stood for Stafford in the 1626 parliament and for Marlow in the Short Parliament, was a JP for Oxfordshire from 1633. Although his leniency towards puritans almost lost him the post in 1634, he remained a JP until 1642. His career prospered during the Interregnum and only suffered after the Restoration.[316]

Witche / [**Wyche**], **Peter** (d. 1643), diplomat. A protégé of Buckingham, Wyche received his knighthood in 1628, when he left England to serve as English ambassador in Constantinople. During his tenure, which lasted until 1641, Wyche kept a keen eye on works of art to add to the royal collection. When Edward Pococke visited on a research trip in 1637, Wyche entertained him.[317]

Williams, **Abraham** (d. 1654), resident in New Palace Yard, Westminster. Agent and diplomatic correspondent to Queen Elizabeth of Bohemia, Williams' house was

312 For instance, fos. 5r, 160r.

313 *Alumni oxonienses*, IV, 1608; *WWL*, IV, 143, 402.

314 *Alumni oxonienses*, IV, 339; *CSPD 1629–31*, p. 342, no. 36; *CSPD 1631–3*, p. 66, no. 4; www.historyofparliamentonline.org/volume/1604–1629/member/whitaker-laurence-1578–1654.

315 Edward Carlyle, 'Whitford, Walter (d. 1647)', rev. Sean Kelsey, *ODNB*.

316 *Alumni oxonienses*, IV, 1620; Ruth Spalding, 'Whitelocke, Bulstrode (1605–1675)', *ODNB*.

317 Liane Saunders, 'Wyche, Sir Peter (d. 1643)', *ODNB*.

often used to entertain foreign ambassadors and for accommodating figures involved in high profile political events, such as the trial of Charles I.[318]

Williams, Henry (*c.* 1579–1636), local politician. Williams, who stood for Brecon in the 1621 and 1624 parliaments and was Justice of the Peace from 1603, held a range of other posts in the locality under Charles I. He was collector for the forced loan in 1626–7, collector of knighthood fines in 1630–1 and commissioner for the repair of St Paul's cathedral in 1634.[319]

Williscot / Williscott, [**William**] (fl. 1637–1644), Church of England clergyman. Williscot was appointed Warden Estcot of Wadham College, Oxford, in 1637. In the prelude to his trial, Laud described Williscot as 'continuing in conformity to the Church of England'.[320]

Willmott / [**Wilmot**], **George** (b. 1604?). Little is known of Wilmot, from Charlton, Berkshire, except that he graduated from Queen's College, Oxford in 1619 and was knighted by Charles I in September 1628.[321]

Willson / [**Wilson, Aaron**] (*c.* 1588–1643), Church of England clergyman. Wilson was rector of St Stephen Walbrook, London, for a decade from 1625 and was appointed prebendary and archdeacon of Exeter cathedral in 1634 and canon of the cathedral in 1641.[322]

Wimbledon / Wimbleton, Lord – see Cecil, Edward.

Winchelsey / Winchelsea, earl of – see Finch, Thomas.

Winchester, dean of – see Young, John.

Windebank, [**Edith**] (1582–1646), wife of Sir Francis Windebank, secretary of state to Charles I from 1632. Of obscure origins, Lady Edith appears to have been well regarded by Laud, and vice versa, until the breach between her husband and the archbishop in 1635.[323]

Winter, **John** (*c.* 1600 – *c.* 1676), Catholic courtier and ironmaster. Despite being in favour at court, Winter fell foul of the king in 1634 for illegal cutting and charcoaling

---

318 *Knights of England*, II, 188.
319 www.historyofparliamentonline.org/volume/1604–1629/member/williams-sir-henry-157980–1636.
320 Robert Gardiner, *The registers of Wadham College, Oxford from 1613 to 1719* (London, 1889), p. 134; *WWL*, IV, 65.
321 *Alumni oxonienses*, IV, 1653; *Knights of England*, II, 195.
322 Kathleen Menzie Lesko, 'Wilson, John (*bap.* 1626, *d.* 1695?)', *ODNB.*
323 *WWL*, VII, 44.

in the forest of Dean. In 1638, Winter was appointed as the queen's private secretary and master of requests, a position he held until 1669.[324]

Winton / Winchester, bishop of – see Curll, Walter.

Wolstenham / [**Wolstenholme**], **John** (*c.* 1596–1670), politician and customs official. Wolstenholme – a member of the East India Company, the Virginia Company and the North West Passage Company – was also a commissioner for the collection of customs, including impositions and tonnage and poundage from 1619 to 1639. In July 1632, Laud consecrated Wolstenholme's newly built chapel at Stanmore Magna in Middlesex, an action which came back to haunt him during his trial, since it was urged against him as one of a few 'popish' chapel consecrations. [325]

Wood, **Basil** (d. 1644), civil lawyer. Wood, active in the London law courts from 1630 to 1641, also sat on the high commission from 1633 and acted as chancellor to the diocese of Rochester from 1630 to 1644.[326]

Woodall / Wooddall / [**Woodhall**], **Edmund** (*c.* 1580–1639), lawyer. During the 1630s, Woodhall acted as principal registrar of the prerogative court of Canterbury.[327]

Wootton / [**Wotton**], **Henry** (1568–1639), diplomat and writer. Having served as ambassador to Venice in 1616 and 1621, Wotton was appointed provost of Eton College in 1624 and was returned as MP for Sandwich in 1625. A keen patron of the arts, on his death in 1639, Wotton bequeathed to Laud a 'picture of Divine Love, rarely copied from one in the king's Galleries ... beseeching him to receive it as a pledge of my humble reverence to his great Wisdom'.[328]

Worrall, [**Thomas**] (d. 1639), Church of England clergyman and prebendary of Holborn, London.[329]

Wragg / Wragge, [**John**] (fl. 1635–1639), royal servant. As messenger in the king's chamber, Wragg also carried out similar duties for the court of high commission.[330]

Wray, **Christopher** (*c.* 1601–46), politician. Married to Albinia Cecil, daughter of Edward Cecil, viscount Wimbledon, Wray was MP for Grimsby in the 1628 and 1640 parliaments. Wray successfully resisted ship money in 1636 and was part of

---

324 *A history of the county of Gloucestershire*, Victoria County History, ed. C. Currie and N. Herberts (London, 1996), III, 54–377.

325 www.historyofparliamentonline.org/volume/1604–1629/member/wolstenholme-john-1596–1670; *WWL*, III, 216; IV, 250.

326 Levack, *Civil lawyers*, p. 280.

327 *Alumni cantabrigienses*, part I, IV, 456; *CSPD 1665–6*, p. 175, no. 61.

328 Pearsall Smith, *The life and letters of Sir Henry Wotton*, I, 217; Albert Loomie, 'Wotton, Sir Henry (1568–1639)', *ODNB*; *WWL*, VII, 361.

329 *Fasti*, II, 393

330 *CSPD 1638–9*, p. 601, no. 23.

the parliamentary committee which presented the Grand Remonstrance to the king in 1641.[331]

[**Wren**, **Matthew**] (1585–1667), Church of England bishop. As bishop of Norwich from 1635 and Ely from 1638, Wren gained a reputation for severity, showing a ruthless determination to clamp down on puritanism and, in particular, to promote altar policy, being one of only two bishops to fully implement the metropolitical order for railing, east-end location, altarwise position and receiving at the rails. Wren was impeached by the Long Parliament in late 1641 and spent almost eighteen years there, only being released after the Restoration.[332]

Wright, [**Abraham**] (1611–90), Church of England clergyman. Wright, an *alumnus* of St John's College, Oxford, participated in the royal visit to the university in August 1636, giving a speech in the library at his *alma mater*. He was minister of St Olave, Silver Street, in London from 1655 to just before the Restoration.[333]

York, archbishop of – see Neile, Richard.

[**Young**, **John**] (1585–1654), dean of Winchester. Appointed to the deanery of Winchester in 1616, Young was well supported at the Jacobean court, being the son of James I's former tutor and brother of Patrick Young, the royal librarian. Under Charles I, Young fared less well – although there were rumours that he was in the running for the new bishopric of Edinburgh in 1634 – remaining in the deanery of Winchester until at least 1644.[334]

[**Young**] / Younge, **Patrick** (1584–1652), scholar and royal librarian to James I and Charles I. As the king's librarian until 1649, Young was responsible for setting the foundations for the later establishment of the British Library, expanding and reorganizing the royal collection, as well as compiling inventories of manuscripts at the Bodleian Library in Oxford. Young was also responsible for reorganizing the libraries at several other English cathedrals and had been appointed treasurer and prebend of St Paul's cathedral in 1621.[335]

---

331 Andrew Hopper, 'Wray, Sir Christopher (bap. 1601, d. 1646)', *ODNB*.

332 Nicholas Cranfield, 'Wren, Matthew (1585–1667)', *ODNB*; Davies, *Caroline captivity*, p. 218.

333 *Alumni oxonienses*, IV, 1685; Stephen Wright, 'Wright, Abraham (1611–1690)', *ODNB*; *WWL*, V, 152.

334 Kenneth Fincham, 'Young, John (1585–1654)', *ODNB*.

335 Elizabethanne Boran, 'Young, Patrick (1584–1652)', *ODNB*; *WWL*, VI, 342–3.

Appendix II: Glossary of words

Definitions of archaic words, which occur in the accounts but are no longer in use, have been included below, taken from the *Oxford English Dictionary*. Square brackets are used to denote the modern spelling of the word in question (according to the OED), where it is still in use, but does not appear thus in the main text.

Amberly trout / trowt – trout from Amberley, a village in Sussex, which lies on the river Arun.

andiron – an iron stand, typically one of a pair, used for supporting wood burning in a fireplace, with a horizontal length of metal which extends to the back of the fireplace, and a vertical post at the front, the latter usually featuring some ornamental detail.

[angelot] / angelott – a small, rich cheese made in Normandy; also the name of a French gold coin, the imprint of which was often stamped into the cheese.

beetle – an implement with a large or heavy head, usually made of wood, used for driving, ramming or hammering pegs or wedges; also used for crushing things,

[brack] / brak – a short form of the word 'bracken', a tall fern.

[briar] / bryer – a prickly, thorny bush.

bushel – a unit of capacity of dry goods, usually corn or wheat (approx. 8 gallons).

cabistone / [capstan] – taken from the French – '*cabestan*' – a winch mechanism used for lifting heavy items.

[cambric] / cambricke – a type of fine white linen, originally made in Cambray in Flanders. Often used for napkins and handkerchiefs.

carabyn / [carbine] – a small firearm, shorter than a musket, but longer than a pistol.

carmen – carriers or drivers of a cart; a man responsible for transportation in the city of London, possibly a member of the Company of Carmen (est. 1601).

chard pie – a pie made of 'chard beet', a leafy green vegetable, rather like a cabbage, with thick, red stalks.

citterne / cittron peeles – candied lemon peel.

[claut] / clawth / clowt – a clutch or a handle.

codling / codlyn – an apple, often from Kent, with a tapering end towards the stalk, rather than a spherical shape.

[corslet] / costlet – a piece of defensive armour covering the body.

crabbs – crab apples.

currycomb – a comb or instrument of metal used for grooming horses.

deal / deale – a plank of wood sawn from a timber log.

diapp / [Dieppe] – a type of linen produced in Dieppe, France, often used to make napkins and tablecloths.

[dorser] / dosser – a basket carried on the back, or a pair of baskets attached to a horse.

draymen – men responsible for driving a 'dray', i.e. a cart without sides used for pulling heavy goods, usually barrels or logs.

ell – a measure of length, often relating to fabric or yarn. An English ell† measured approx. 45 inches.

Epsom water – the water of a mineral spring at Epsom, usually taken for medicinal or restorative purposes.

eringoe roots – roots of the seaholm, which was candied or kept in syrup.

ewer – a pitcher or jug with a broad spout, usually kept in a bedroom.

ewry man – within an elite household, the person responsible for maintaining the 'ewer room' or 'ewery', where ewers of water, towels and table linen were kept. Could also be used to describe someone who was not employed directly by the household, but by whom such goods were provided.

fare – a load of goods carried from one place to another.

[filberts] / fillbirds – the fruit of the cultivated hazelnut tree.

firkin – a small cask for liquids, fish, butter, etc., originally containing a quarter of a barrel or half a [kilderkin] / kinderkin.

flasket / flaskett – either a long shallow basket or a small flask or drinking vessel.

fosset – a peg or stopper to stop the vent hole in a cask or vessel.

freesh / [frieze] / frize – a type of coarse woollen cloth.

furrier – someone who deals in or dresses furs.

[gabardine] / gabbedine / gabberdine / gabledine – a loose upper garment of coarse material; a smock frock.

galoses / galoshers / galoshes – an overshoe worn to protect shoes from water or dirt.

gamashin – a type of stocking or hose.

[gimlet] / gymlett – a large shallow basin used for salting bacon and other foodstuffs.

[girth] / gyrth – a broad band of leather or cloth, placed round the body of a horse, to secure a saddle or pack for carrying a load.

glister – a very bright light or lamp.

granado – a grenade or other shot fired from a cannon.

grogram – a coarse fabric of silk, of mohair and wool, or either of these mixed with silk.

grub – to dig superficially, often to clear ground of roots and stumps.

gynny hen – the female of the guinea fowl.

hassock – a thick, firm cushion, often stuffed with rushes or straw, used to rest feet upon or, in places of worship to kneel upon during prayer.

hearnshawe / [heronshaw] – a young heron.

hogsh[ead] – a large cask or barrel used to store liquid, usually beer or wine, in varying quantities.

Holland – a linen fabric from the province of Holland in the Netherlands.

kennel nail / nayle – a condition in which a nail in a horse's hoof has become embedded in the soft tissue and, possibly, infected.

[kilderkin] / kinderkin – a cask containing liquids or fish, of a fixed capacity of half a gallon.

lamprey – an eel-like fish with no scales.

lockeram / [lockram] – a course linen, used for shirts and smocks.

lynge – a rope, cord or string.

lynstock – a staff about three feet long, with a pointed foot to stick in the ground and a forked head to hold a lighted match.

lyter – a small boat or vessel, usually a flat-bottomed barge, used to lighten or unload ships that cannot be discharged (or loaded) at a wharf, etc., and for transporting goods, usually in a harbour.

lyterman – someone employed on or who owns a 'lyter'.

maligo – a type of wine used for medicinal purposes.

[marten] / martyn skins – the fur and skin of the pine marten, a rich dark colour, which was used for clothing in winter.

[Martinmas] / martlemas beefe – the meat of an ox or cow slaughtered at Martinmas (the feast of St Martin on 11 November) to be salted or smoked for the winter.

mattock – a tool similar to a pick, with a chisel type head at one end, used for breaking up hard ground.

muskmelons – the edible fruit of the melon, which have netted rinds and aromatic, usually orange, flesh. Also called nutmeg melon.

[nag] / nagg – a small riding-horse, or pony.

osler / [ostler] – a stableman or groom.

packthread / packthreade / packthred – strong cord or twine used for typing up packs or bundles.

pantler – the head of the pantry.

[pearmain] / pearmayne – a variety of pear or a conical shaped apple.

peck / [pecke] – a unit of capacity of dry goods, equal to a quarter of a bushel.

piggin – a small pail or similar vessel, esp. made of wood, with a long handle. Could be used as a drinking vessel, rather like a ladle, or for milking.

pipkin – a small (usually earthenware) pot or pan. Also, a drinking vessel.

pippin – a kind of sweet apple, typically late-ripening, fine-flavoured and having good keeping qualities.

[pomander] / pomandre – either a small container for holding aromatic substances, or the substances themselves, usually scented with fruit or flowers, to stave off infection and improve the aroma around a room.

pottle – a unit of capacity, mainly used for liquids, equal to half a gallon.

powdering tub / [tubb] – a shallow tub used for salting meat or fish.

[provender] / provinder – dried food used to feed livestock.

rowelling – to 'rowel' an animal, typically a horse, by inserting a thin piece of leather or other material under the skin, to release pus or discharge from a wound.

sconce – a lantern or candlestick with a screen to protect the light from the wind, and a handle to carry it by.

[scythe] / sieth – an agricultural implement for cutting and mowing grass and crops.

skeane / skeene – a small cluster or bundle, often used for sticks, yarn or thread.

spickett / [spigot] – a small peg or plug, usually for insertion into the opening of a cask.

stoned horse – a male horse, not castrated.

[stoup]/ stope – a drinking vessel, such as a flagon or tankard, or a large jar for holding liquids, often wine or other alcoholic beverages.

stronge water – a strong alcoholic drink, an intoxicating spirit.

sursing [surcingle] – a girth or strap to go around an animal, usually a horse, to keep a sheet or cover in place.

tare / [thare] – a very small, bean-like seed of the vetch plant, used for animal fodder.

tearse – a unit of capacity, roughly equating to one third of a pipe (usually 42 gallons of old measure, although this varied according to the contents) and generally relating to liquids, such as wine or beer.

truch / [trush] – a round cushion made of matted flags, for kneeling on in church.

trammell – a device used to prevent a horse from straying or kicking, by means of straps tied to both legs on each side, with a band over the animal's back.

trencher – a flat piece of wood, metal or earthenware, square or circular, on which meat was served and cut up. Sometimes also used to describe a similarly shaped piece of bread which was used as a 'plate' and then eaten when the meal was finished.

vargis – a type of wine.

Westfalia tongs / [tongues] – pigs' tongues from livestock bred in Westphalia.

[wether] / weather – a ram (male sheep), usually castrated.

wharfinger – the owner or keeper of a wharf.

[wimble] / winble – a tool for boring holes into wood or soft soil.

Index

Where names occur in the index, the standard spelling of the name has been adopted, as defined in Appendix 1: Glossary of names, p. 207 above

'The object of the Society shall be to advance knowledge of the history of the Church in England, and in particular of the Church of England, from the sixteenth century onwards, by the publication of editions or calendars of primary sources of information.'

PUBLICATIONS

1. Visitation Articles and Injunctions of the Early Stuart Church. Volume I. Ed. Kenneth Fincham (1994)

2. The Speculum of Archbishop Thomas Secker: The Diocese of Canterbury 1758–1768. Ed. Jeremy Gregory (1995)

3. The Early Letters of Bishop Richard Hurd, 1739–1762. Ed. Sarah Brewer (1995)

4. Brethren in Adversity: Bishop George Bell, The Church of England and the Crisis of German Protestantism, 1933–1939. Ed. Andrew Chandler (1997)

5. Visitation Articles and Injunctions of the Early Stuart Church. Volume II. Ed. Kenneth Fincham (1998)

6. The Anglican Canons, 1529–1947. Ed. Gerald Bray (1998)

7. From Cranmer to Davidson. A Church of England Miscellany. Ed. Stephen Taylor (1999)

8. Tudor Church Reform. The Henrician Canons of 1534 and the *Reformatio Legum Ecclesiasticarum*. Ed. Gerald Bray (2000)

9. All Saints Sisters of the Poor. An Anglican Sisterhood in the Nineteenth Century. Ed. Susan Mumm (2001)

10. Conferences and Combination Lectures in the Elizabethan Church: Dedham and Bury St Edmunds, 1582–1590. Ed. Patrick Collinson, John Craig and Brett Usher (2003)

11. The Diary of Samuel Rogers, 1634–1638. Ed. Tom Webster and Kenneth Shipps (2004)

12. Evangelicalism in the Church of England c.1790–c.1890. Ed. Mark Smith and Stephen Taylor (2004)

13. The British Delegation and the Synod of Dort (1618–1619). Ed. Anthony Milton (2005)

14. The Beginnings of Women's Ministry. The Revival of the Deaconess in the Nineteenth-Century Church of England. Ed. Henrietta Blackmore (2007)

15. The Letters of Theophilus Lindsey. Volume I. Ed. G. M. Ditchfield (2007)

16. The Back Parts of War: The YMCA Memoirs and Letters of Barclay Baron, 1915–1919. Ed. Michael Snape (2009)

17. The Diary of Thomas Larkham, 1647–1669. Ed. Susan Hardman Moore (2011)

18. From the Reformation to the Permissive Society. A Miscellany in Celebration of the 400th Anniversary of Lambeth Palace Library. Ed. Melanie Barber and Stephen Taylor with Gabriel Sewell (2010)

19. The Letters of Theophilus Lindsey. Volume II. Ed. G. M. Ditchfield (2012)

20. National Prayers: Special Worship since the Reformation. Volume I: Special Prayers, Fasts and Thanksgivings in the British Isles, 1533–1688. Ed. Natalie Mears, Alasdair Raffe, Stephen Taylor, Philip Williamson and Lucy Bates (2013)

21. The Journal of Bishop Daniel Wilson of Calcutta, 1845–1857. Ed. Andrew Atherstone (2015)

22. National Prayers: Special Worship since the Reformation. Volume II: General Fasts, Thanksgivings and Special Prayers in the British Isles, 1689–1870. Ed. Philip Williamson, Alasdair Raffe, Stephen Taylor and Natalie Mears (2017)

23. The Further Correspondence of William Laud. Ed. Kenneth Fincham (2018)

24. The Household Accounts of William Laud, Archbishop of Canterbury, 1635–1642. Ed. Leonie James (2019)

Forthcoming Publications

The First World War Diaries of the Rt. Rev. Llewellyn Gwynne, July 1915 – July 1916. Ed Peter Howson

The Papers of the Elland Society 1769–1818. Ed. John Walsh and Stephen Taylor

National Prayers: Special Worship since the Reformation. Volume 3. Ed. Philip Williamson, Stephen Taylor, Alasdair Raffe and Natalie Mears

The Correspondence of William Sancroft. Ed. Grant Tapsell

The Sermons of John Sharp. Ed. Françoise Deconinck-Brossard

The Restoration of the Church of England: Canterbury Diocese, 1663. Ed. Tom Reid

The Correspondence and Papers of Archbishop Richard Neile, 1598–1640. Ed. Andrew Foster

Birkenhead, All Souls, and the Making of Herbert Hensley Henson: The Early Journals, 1885–1887. Ed. Frank Field and Julia Stapleton

Proceedings Against the 'Scandalous Ministers' of Essex, 1644–5. Ed. Graham Hart.

The 1669 Return of Nonconformist Conventicles. Ed. David Wykes

The Correspondence of Francis Blackburne (1705–1787). Ed. G. M. Ditchfield

The Letters and Papers of William Paley. Ed. Neil Hichin

The Correspondence, Diaries and Personal Memoranda of Charles Simeon. Ed. Andrew Atherstone

The Diary of an Oxford Parson: The Reverend John Hill, Vice-Principal of St Edmund Hall, Oxford, 1805–1808, 1820–1855. Ed. Grayson Carter

The Correspondence of Archbishop Lang with Bishop Wilfrid Parker. Ed. Garth Turner

Suggestions for publications should be addressed to Dr Grant Tapsell, General Editor, Church of England Record Society, Lady Margaret Hall, Norham Gardens, Oxford OX2 6QA, or at grant.tapsell@lmh.ox.ac.uk.

Membership of the Church of England Record Society is open to all who are interested in the history of the Church of England. Enquiries should be addressed to the Membership Secretary, Dr Susan Royal, Department of Theology and Religion, Durham University, Abbey House, Palace Green, Durham DH1 3RS.